DAVID DELLINGER

ANDREW E. HUNT

DAVID DELLINGER

The Life and Times of a Nonviolent Revolutionary

New York University Press • *New York and London*

NEW YORK UNIVERSITY PRESS
New York and London

www.nyupress.org
© 2006 by New York University
All rights reserved

Library of Congress Cataloging-in-Publication Data
Hunt, Andrew E., 1968–
David Dellinger : the life and times of a nonviolent revolutionary / Andrew E. Hunt.
p. cm.
Includes bibliographical references and index.
ISBN–13: 978–0–8147–3638–8 (cloth : alk. paper)
ISBN–10: 0–8147–3638–6 (cloth : alk. paper)
1. Dellinger, David T., 1915–   . 2. Radicals—United States—Biography.
3. Political activists—United States—Biography.   4. Vietnamese Conflict,
1961–1975—Protest movements.   I. Title.
HN90.R3H86   2006
959.704'31092—dc22   2005035202
[B]

For Madeline and Aidan

Contents

All illustrations appear as a group following p. 202.

Acknowledgments

THIS BOOK would not have been possible without the help of kind and generous people who not only graciously shared memories but also furnished addresses and telephone numbers, videotapes, newspaper articles, unpublished manuscripts, and, most important, their time.

Three people in particular helped me launch this project. Doug Dowd, a longtime antiwar activist and a friend of my father, offered guidance and inspiration. He also strongly recommended this project to the Social Sciences and Humanities Research Council of Canada (SSHRC). I'm certain his endorsement resulted in the spectacular grant I received from SSHRC to write this book. Without that grant, and his help, this book would not have been possible. Marty Jezer, who, sadly, passed away in June 2005, offered me research suggestions, the names of people to interview, and his own reminiscences of his colorful experiences as a young activist in the 1960s. Marv Davidov, a legend in Minneapolis/St. Paul grassroots struggles for justice and a hero far beyond his community, contacted me as a result of an author's query I placed in *The Progressive* magazine. Marv arranged my first meeting with David Dellinger and Elizabeth Peterson in October 1999, and he gave me all sorts of help, materials, and encouragement along the way. Doug, Marty, and Marv deserve great thanks for all their efforts.

I spent time in several archives and had the good fortune to encounter helpful staff people wherever I went. My enthusiastic praise goes to the archivists at the Tamiment Collection at New York University, where David Dellinger's papers are housed. The Tamiment staff put up with my numerous requests for boxes of materials and diligently replied to repeated e-mail queries. Their generosity will not be forgotten. Equally deserving of thanks was the staff at the Swarthmore College Peace Collection in Swarthmore, Pennsylvania. What a joy it was to work with Wendy Chmielewski, Barbara Addison, Wilma Mosholder, and Anne Yoder, who always were friendly and willing to go the extra distance for me. And thank you to the archivists at the State Historical Society of Wisconsin in Madison; the Lyndon Baines Johnson Presidential Library in Austin, Texas; and the Special Collections Department at Temple University in Philadelphia, home of the papers for *Seven Days* magazine. I hope that my future projects take me back to these wonderful places.

This account relies heavily on oral histories, and I thank the men and women who allowed me to interview them about David Dellinger.

Other individuals offered crucial information, suggestions, insights, and constructive feedback. A heartfelt thank-you to the following people: Norma Becker, Scott Bennett, Bob Birt, Paul Buhle, Jay Craven, Patch Dellinger, Randy Dellinger, Ralph DiGia, Mike Foley, Larry Gara, Paul Krassner, Bob Lamb, Dean McKay, Maggie Palmer Lauterer, Brad Lyttle, William Lovell, Walter Neagle, Gerald Nicosia, Sid Peck, and the folks at Toward Freedom and the War Resisters League. David J. Langum and Maurice Issserman read a rough draft of the entire manuscript for New York University Press, and they each gave me incredibly detailed and thorough critiques. The Department of History here at the University of Waterloo has been an exciting place to work while I've written this book, thanks to my wonderful students and colleagues. In particular, I'd like to single out Keith Eagles, Patrick Harrigan, Stan Johannesen, and Lynne Taylor. I also owe an enormous intellectual debt to Robert Alan Goldberg, which I'll never be able to pay back in full, but I aim to keep thanking him for it.

At New York University Press, my warmest thanks go to Niko Pfund (who has since moved to Oxford University Press), Eric Zinner, Emily Park, Despina Papazoglou Gimbel, Margaret Barrows Yamashita, and the wonderful staff. It has been such a pleasure working with NYU Press, just as it was with my first book, *The Turning: A History of Vietnam Veterans against the War*. In particular, Eric deserves kudos for his support, patience, and kindness. When I almost gave up writing this biography after encountering a few obstacles, he offered me the encouragement I needed to continue.

Finally, I want to thank my family. While I was researching this book, my brother Jeff and his wife Stephanie lost their dear son, Adam.

He died in 2002 at the age of seventeen. Everybody loved Adam. He was gentle and witty and cared deeply about people and the world. Despite this devastating loss, my brother and his family have inspired me with their courage, indomitable spirits, and simple kindness. Thank you to my mom, Linda Hunt, for her ongoing friendship, love, and support. She read each draft of the book more than once and offered great feedback. Thank you to my dad, E. K. Hunt, and his wife, Jodie Hunt, for their warmth and love. My dad also read drafts and provided constructive advice that I always followed. In very different ways, both my parents nourished the insurgent spirit in me. Thank you, Minerva Colemere (Grandma Minnie), for your courageous example and faith in humanity. To my companion, Luisa D'Amato: Thank you for all the love, laughter, and companionship you have given me. Luisa put up with a lot. She read rough drafts, didn't hesitate to let me know when she thought Dellinger was being asinine, and always lifted my spirits. Luisa and her children—Ruth and Tony—have enriched my life beyond words.

And now, for the most special thank-you of all. Thank you, Madeline and Aidan. You have made me the proudest, happiest father in the world. Words cannot express how much I love you. The three of us have been through a lot together. Most of it has been wonderful, but we have also faced our fair share of challenges. I'll never forget something that my own father once said. "I made mistakes," he admitted, "but there was always a lot of love in our home." I couldn't have said it better. Madeline and Aidan, you're the reason I wrote this book. It is dedicated to you, with all my love.

Introduction

WHEN HE DIED on May 25, 2004, at age eighty-eight, David Dellinger was remembered chiefly for his role as the oldest defendant in the Chicago Eight trial, a legal battle that, according to the lawyer and scholar Alan Dershowitz, transformed America. "We have certainly not seen its like in recent years," Dershowitz wrote in 2004. "Perhaps we never will."[1] The trial was of eight anti–Vietnam War activists—each representing a distinct political segment of the movement—charged with conspiring to disrupt the 1968 Democratic National Convention in Chicago. Shortly after the trial began in the fall of 1969, Black Panther leader Bobby Seale was removed from the case, thereby reducing the Chicago Eight to the Chicago Seven. The defendants, pitted against the antagonistic and arrogant judge, Julius Hoffman, transformed the courtroom into a battleground full of emotional outbursts and dramatic confrontations, and the trial seemed to reflect the polarized state of America at that time. Because the intense courtroom drama attracted widespread media scrutiny in 1969 and 1970, it elevated Dellinger and his codefendants to the status of "movement celebrities." Indeed, it became difficult for Dellinger to go anywhere in public without being recognized by other people. He was in his mid-fifties during the trial, and his newfound fame shaped and defined him for the rest of his life. Not surprisingly, newspaper announcements of his death in 2004 concentrated on his ordeal in Chicago but downplayed his lifetime of nonviolent activism.[2]

Despite his remarkable life, Dellinger was not a famous man when he died, not even as an icon of the 1960s. He lacked the enormous following of Martin Luther King Jr., the legendary status of Abbie Hoffman, or the literary talents of Allen Ginsberg. Nevertheless, in certain circles, his very name continued to provoke debate long after his celebrity status as a Chicago Eight defendant faded. "Dellinger, himself," wrote social critic and author Paul Berman, "became the single most important leader of the national antiwar movement, at its height, from 1967 through the early 1970s. You could quarrel with some of his political judgments, but he was always sober, always resolute, always selfless and always brave."[3]

A less charitable assessment of Dellinger came from Thomas Foran, the U.S. attorney and chief prosecutor in the Chicago conspiracy trial. Foran's rage was still evident in 1996 when a newspaper reporter asked him what he thought of Dellinger. "He was the most belligerent, combative, nasty peace-lover I ever met," he said. "Dellinger has always been a fool, he always will be a fool, and he never has anything worthwhile to say about anything. The world would be better off if some people were completely ignored."[4] Conservatives, too, continued to revile Dellinger decades after the Chicago trial. In the 1990s, Peter Collier, an ex–New Left journalist who eventually shifted to the right side of the political spectrum with his close friend David Horowitz, dismissed Dellinger's accomplishments. Said Collier: "Dellinger's youthful followers have gone on to Yuppiedom, but he is still marching in place, stuck on his commitments. . . . If Dellinger has been everywhere, he has learned nothing."[5] After Dellinger died in 2004, conservative Denver talk radio host and columnist Mike Rosen wrote: "Dellinger was no hero to me, nor were his Chicago Seven comrades. I saw no nobility in his various causes. I regarded him as a self-indulgent, anti-establishment renegade; an oxymoronic militant pacifist; a hopelessly idealistic, impractical, coercive utopian; and a recidivist criminal. . . . In his lifetime, Dellinger accomplished nothing positive."[6]

By contrast, leftists celebrated Dellinger's legacy, lionized him as an antiwar leader, and marveled at the longevity of his commitment. "Dave has been an inspiration to a lot of young people because of his steadfastness all these years," remembered historian and activist Howard Zinn. "He was a rock-like figure in the movement."[7] Noam Chomsky added: "He's been at the forefront of everything that's happened since the Second World War. . . . He was always there, in good times and bad, like a beacon."[8] Author, activist, and Chicago conspiracy trial defendant Tom Hayden, who was not always on the friendliest terms with Dellinger in the 1960s, mourned Dellinger's death in 2004 and found ample reasons to appreciate his accomplishments. "Dave was a kind of politician," explained Hayden, "a listener, a fixer of things, a coalition-builder in a movement filled with fanatics and factions and ego-trippers of all sorts. Dave could sit down and make agreements that would allow things to happen, like marches of hundreds of thousands."[9]

Vilified by critics, glorified by supporters, and forgotten by much of the general public, Dellinger remained an enigmatic figure at the time of his death, and the truth about him rests in the contradictions of his life. All at the same time he could be warm to certain people and petty to others; a rigid Gandhian and an "ideologically flexible" supporter of violent revolutionary movements overseas; a methodical coalition organizer and a stubborn sectarian; a tremendously gifted writer and a wordy political hack. More than any other leading figure in the 1960s, he bridged the gap between the Old Left and the New Left. Born into an affluent Massachusetts family, he came of age politically in the Great Depression, embracing pacifism while a student at Yale in the mid-1930s during the heyday of American isolationism. By the time he assumed a leading role in the anti–Vietnam War coalition in 1965, he had been a career activist for nearly thirty years and had gone to jail numerous times, including two lengthy prison sentences as a conscientious objector during World War II.

Before the 1960s, David Dellinger seemed destined to live in obscurity. While a prisoner in the early 1940s, he developed his own distinct anarchistic pacifist ideology and later edited such obscure Gandhian periodicals as *Direct Action* and *Alternative*. He and his wife, Betty, and a group of their pacifist friends created a commune in rural northern New Jersey in the late 1940s, long before such living arrangements became fashionable in the 1960s. Until his early forties, Dellinger remained a marginal figure in a peripheral political movement, struggling to spread his pacifist message to a nation too deep in the throes of the cold war to listen. He was almost always broke and often received financial assistance from his father, a wealthy conservative attorney and head of a respected Boston law firm. David Dellinger continued to suffer physically from beatings he endured at the hands of belligerent counterdemonstrators and angry prison guards. He had a wife and five children—three sons and two daughters—to look after, as well as a foster child who lived with the Dellingers for a few years. Supporting such a large family on the paltry income of an activist proved to be a constant challenge. Political commitments took him away from his family for extended periods of time, leaving Betty alone to raise the children and oversee their vast property in New Jersey.

Were it not for the Vietnam War, Dellinger might have continued living on the fringes of American society. For years he labored tirelessly in obscurity and allowed others to take center stage in post–World War II peace movements. In the antinuclear campaigns of the 1950s, he lacked the high profile of A. J. Muste, and in the incipient civil rights movement, his contributions did not match those of radical pacifists Bayard Rustin and George Houser. His instrumental role in the creation of *Liberation* magazine in 1956, however, greatly enhanced his prestige. Dellinger wrote regularly for the influential radical monthly, and his essays on the arms race, the civil rights movement, and the Cuban revolution earned him a receptive audience among younger generations of New Left radicals. Then the Vietnam War changed everything. At first, A. J. Muste assumed the role of national leader in the newly formed antiwar coalition in 1965. But his death in February 1967 left a void that Dellinger reluctantly filled, although his libertarian sensibilities always were at odds with the demands of leadership. "Don't follow any leaders," Dellinger repeatedly counseled younger activists. "That's the curse of our society."[10]

Throughout the late 1960s and early 1970s, Dellinger proved to be an adept and respected organizer, and his coalition-building techniques were careful and diplomatic. He believed in leading by example, and his frequent championing of civil disobedience earned him the scorn of cautious Old Left veterans and peace movement moderates alike. For his part, Dellinger was often suspicious or dismissive of factions that opposed his militancy. Personality clashes with antiwar leaders such as Fred Halstead, of the Trotskyist Socialist Workers Party, and Sid Peck, a respected coordinator of the National Mobilization to End the War in Vietnam (or the Mobe), led to mutual antagonisms that outlasted even the Vietnam War itself.

Although the Chicago conspiracy trial transformed Dellinger into a national figure, it also did irreparable harm to his personal life. The legal battle cut him off from his antiwar constituency, aggravated long-standing health problems, and contributed to the unraveling of his marriage. The end of the Vietnam War and the winding down of mass protest movements offered a new set of challenges and left Dellinger uncertain about future prospects. "What Dave needs is an immoral war to struggle against," one of his Chicago codefendants remarked in 1973.[11]

For years, Dellinger openly referred to himself as a "revolutionary," a title he adopted at some point while he was in prison during World War II. For much of his life, he grappled with what it meant to be a revolutionary in a nonrevolutionary society. Even though the United States was created from revolution, most Americans have not traditionally been hospitable to revolutionaries living in their midst. At best, they dismiss radicals as cranks and extremists, who, at worst, endure prison sentences, exile, and, in extreme cases, martyrdom. Incentives in American society are usually weighted toward abandoning youthful revolutionary fervor and adopting mainstream sensibilities. Dellinger faced these same pressures throughout his life, and his experiences highlight the many dilemmas of modern American democracy. Compromises always are necessary in America, even for a purist like Dellinger. He could not stay in prison all his life or feed his family or himself on minuscule salaries from small peace groups. Therefore, to survive, he often had to back away from making revolution and work at something else, whether it was at a bakery or his printing press or as a clerk at the War Resisters League offices. In the 1960s and early 1970s, Dellinger's writing and speaking talents turned into hot commodities, largely because of his colorful history. But by the 1980s, 1990s and early 2000s, his life as an activist and writer once again yielded only a modest, sometimes inadequate, source of income. Even though being a successful lifelong revolutionary in America proved to be an almost impossible prospect, Dellinger did his best to adhere to such a life. Even his harshest detractors have grudgingly admired his almost herculean strength and quixotic spirit during trying times.

One week after Dellinger's death in 2004, the fortieth president of the United States, Ronald Reagan, also died. Like Dellinger, Reagan suffered from the debilitating effects of Alzheimer's disease. Reagan had been a contemporary of Dellinger's, born only four years earlier. At various times in their lives, both men enjoyed a political following; both could be evasive and difficult to know; and both regarded themselves as revolutionaries, though of very different types. Obviously, Reagan's influence was far greater and more widely felt. His death was followed by a period of national mourning in the United States, but it also triggered debates about his presidency and political legacy. At the center of the debates were questions about the nature of America and what sort of nation it ought to be in the future. Dellinger occupied a place on the opposite side of the political spectrum from Reagan. He articulated a vision of an America without wars, racism, or poverty, and late in his life he added sexism to his list of grievances. In the short run, it may appear that Reagan's agenda was much closer to triumph, yet Dellinger's vision persists and is deeply rooted in American traditions of social justice. His story, with all its blemishes and errors of judgment, offers critical lessons about the paradoxes of dissent and democracy in America. Dellinger regarded himself as the embodiment of America's finest values. When the House Committee on Un-American Activities subpoenaed Dellinger in 1968 to discuss the "communist presence in the peace movement," the pacifist politely declared his independence. He proclaimed, "There are two Americas, you know. I think I speak for the best interests of the best America."[12]

Dellinger's story is now more relevant than ever. The Iraq War, the second election of George W. Bush, and the reemergence of antiwar activism in the United States all have added a new sense of urgency to this book. All biographies are the products of their times, and this one is as well. But it also contains timeless themes of political and personal commitment, camaraderie, betrayal, endurance, redemption, and love. From the time he experienced a spiritual transformation inside his dark, solitary-confinement cell at the Danbury Correctional Institution in 1940 and saw an image of himself as dead, Dellinger spoke what he regarded as truth to power. He continued speaking—and resisting—until the day he died.

I

Wakefield

I believe that there are mysterious spiritual factors that influence who we are and what we do. For me, beginning in my early childhood, these were the solitary experiences of the ecstasies of Nature and having to deal with the racism and classism of many of the well-to-do adults in the suburb of Boston where I grew up.

David Dellinger

THE APPALACHIAN MOUNTAIN CHAIN reaches its highest elevation in western North Carolina, where it opens up into broad, fertile valleys with numerous streams and rivers. The region is rugged and breathtaking, far away from the din and pollution of the big cities. To the east is the majestic Blue Ridge range; to the west and south rise the Great Smokies; and among the smaller chains in the area are the Unakas, Black Mountains, and Balsams. For millennia, various indigenous peoples—most recently the Cherokee—regarded this area as their homeland. In the early eighteenth century, the earliest white settlers began trickling into the pastures and hollows of western North Carolina, and by the eve of the American Revolution, the flow had grown considerably. "These mountains begin to be populated rapidly," observed the French botanist François Michaux, who noted in 1802 that the purity of the air and water and the richness of the land "induce new inhabitants to settle there."[1]

During the nineteenth century, small towns sprouted up among the pastures and waterways, with farmers' markets, dry goods stores, barbershops, hotels, and saloons luring rural dwellers from nearby farms. Typical of these western North Carolina towns was Altamont, near the foothills of the Blue Ridge Mountains, approximately twenty miles east of the Tennessee–North Carolina border. It was here that David Dellinger's father, Raymond Pennington Dellinger, was born on October 22, 1887, the third of William and Selena Dellinger's nine children. The Dellingers lived in a spacious two-story, ten-bedroom white frame farmhouse near the banks of the Linville River. It was, by Mitchell County's rustic standards, a modern and comfortable house—and one of the earliest dwellings in the area not built of logs—with ample space for the large family. "The upstairs rooms were separated into two spaces with separate stairways," noted one description. "The boys slept on one side and the girls slept on the other."[2] The Dellingers enjoyed a relatively prosperous standard of living, even though Selena Dellinger, like most mothers in the county, knitted socks for her children and churned butter while William worked long days on the farm. Each day the children walked to a one-room schoolhouse about a mile from their home, and on Sundays they attended the nearby Altamont Methodist Church.[3]

The Dellingers had deep roots in western North Carolina, extending back to the mid-eighteenth century. The earliest Dellinger in the region was Johannes Phillip, an enterprising farmer from Wurttenburg, Germany. He arrived in 1757 in a wave of German immigrants that settled on the lands west of the Catawba River. Johannes bought 185 acres of prime farmland adjacent to Leepers Creek in Anson County, and his family joined him there several months later.[4] The Dellingers of western North Carolina gradually established themselves as prosperous farmers, laying the groundwork for future generations. The Civil War, of course, changed the western counties, as the Confederacy actively recruited in the area and established a strong presence in the city of Asheville. At first, the Confederacy was strongly supported in western North Carolina, and during the first six months of the Civil War the region provided more recruits than did any other part of the state. But in a remarkably short time the secessionist movement waned, revealing widespread antiwar and pro-Union sentiments in the mountain communities. The Dellinger family also developed misgivings about the Confederacy early in the war, which only grew when Reuben Dellinger, who had joined Company B, Fifth Battalion, in Mitchell County in June 1862, eventually abandoned his unit to help his father on the family farm and was "hanged or shot" by the Confederates for desertion.[5]

These events increased Raymond Dellinger's ambivalence about his surroundings and the legacy of the Confederacy. He came to believe that the real opportunities for success and happiness were to be found in the thriving big cities, and by his teens, he had dreams of moving to a large city and becoming a "self-made" man. Sometime toward the end of 1904 or beginning of 1905, Raymond had "a painful argument with his father and gained permission to go away to school if he paid his own way and returned in the spring early enough to help on the farm."[6] He agreed to his father's terms and enrolled at Grant University in Athens, Tennessee, where he became an honor student. After graduating from Grant, he enrolled in law school in Chattanooga. But his most significant, life-altering decision came in 1910 when he decided to transfer to Yale University, where he planned to finish law school and enter the legal profession in Boston. Raymond was the first Dellinger to receive a university education, and in New Haven, he finally found the challenges and stimulation he sought in North Carolina. While in law school, he "met and fell in love with" Marie Fiske, a young socialite from the seaside town of Natick. A reserved woman, always aware of her privileged social standing, Marie wanted to marry someone who could provide her with a family and a comfortable life. She admired Raymond's ambition and optimism and believed she could keep his gregarious side in check and perhaps even help him shed his lingering southern ways. Marie's mother, Alice, a lifelong member of Daughters of the American Revolution, volunteered for local charities, and her father Homer was a prominent insurance executive in Boston.[7]

Raymond and Marie married in 1912, in a ceremony conducted in Natick by the Reverend Alfred W. Birks. The couple wished to remain near Boston because Marie's family lived nearby, and the city offered several opportunities for an ambitious young attorney like Raymond. Fresh out of law school, he found a job at a corporate law firm in downtown Boston.

In the fall of 1912, Raymond and Marie Dellinger moved into a two-story, seven-bedroom, three-bathroom house at 7 Shumway Circle in Wakefield, ten miles north of Boston. The town of Wakefield seemed to be an ideal choice for a new family in 1912. It was still a densely wooded, rural community, and it was also a haven of conservative Republican Party politics in an otherwise Democratic Party–dominated state. This appealed to Raymond Dellinger, who had become an outspoken proponent of individual rights and laissez-faire economic policies. Around Wakefield, he developed a reputation for being a gentle and gregarious man, and his skills as an attorney won wide respect, cementing his reputation in Boston's legal circles. An even greater source of pride for Raymond was his volunteer work and charity fund-raising.

He especially cherished a tribute he received during World War II for his years of leadership in the local Red Cross: "You whose sincerity is unquestioned, whose enthusiasm is unbounded, and whose energy is a constant source of inspiration, an outstanding Wakefieldian, a true friend and community leader."[8]

Once they settled in their spacious house on Shumway Circle, Raymond and Marie Dellinger began having children. The first to arrive was Elizabeth "Libby" Dellinger, born in 1914. David came next, on August 22, 1915. Four years later, in 1919, his younger sister Nancy was born, and Fiske, the last of the Dellinger siblings, was born in 1923. Nursemaids took care of the Dellinger children, feeding them, changing their diapers, and following them around the yard.

For a time, Helen Vance, a cousin from Raymond's side of the family, came from Tennessee to live at the Shumway Circle house.[9] The Dellinger children adored Helen, whom they nicknamed "Aunt Neva." She read to them, took them to the movies, and bought them ice cream cones when they visited Boston. Aunt Neva never married, and by her early thirties she became the sort of woman that proper Bostonians referred to as a "spinster." Unlike Aunt Neva, Marie Dellinger had little patience for eccentricities and nonconformity. To her, appearance and propriety were crucial, and she taught her children the ways of the Boston Brahmins. "Be nice to everyone," Marie counseled, "but choose your friends from among the very best."[10] Marie prized the behavioral traits of restraint and civility and sometimes was irritated by Raymond's sudden outbursts of affection, which she regarded as a remnant of his southern upbringing. Much later in his life, David evaluated Marie's mothering methods in a page of unpublished notes he jotted down in preparation for his memoirs. "My Mother, you may have noticed that so far I have written a great deal about my father's heart full of love, but have seldom referred to you in similar terms. The contest is not accidental. For all the time I lived at home, you seemed relatively cold."[11] David never formed a strong bond with Marie, although he found much to admire about her. She organized family trips to the symphony and museums, and every evening she demanded that each member of the family devote a certain amount of time to reading.

David had a strikingly different, though no less ambivalent, relationship with his father. The two were always affectionate and loving toward each other, yet tensions developed, rooted in what eventually became the divergent ideologies of father and son. Raymond Dellinger stressed achievement, and early on David became his clear favorite. Though always modest, Raymond acknowledged that a combination of persistence, hard work, and a firm belief in his own abilities had enabled him to rise from the status of a poor North Carolina farm boy to that of a prosperous Boston lawyer. He also believed that prosperous citizens owed a debt to their community that should be repaid through either philanthropy or good deeds. In accordance with this belief, Raymond became chairman of the Wakefield Republican Committee and eventually the leader of the Middlesex County Republican Committee. He raised funds for the Young Men's Christian Association and various local hospitals and for years taught a popular Sunday school class at Wakefield's First Congregational Church, where he was a member. His activism proved to be a crucial inspiration for David. In a candid letter to a relative, David characterized Raymond as "a warm, generous, loving man whose example in those respects I have always tried to follow and had a lot to do with the kind of politics I came to espouse."[12]

At the Massachusetts Constitutional Convention of 1916, Raymond met and befriended the then state lieutenant governor Calvin Coolidge, who later became the governor of Massachusetts and, eventually, president of the United States. As David Dellinger later recalled, Coolidge occasionally was a dinner guest at the Dellinger house.[13] By his thirties, Raymond had become a staunch conservative, but he retained certain populist sensibilities from his backcountry youth. For example, he encouraged his children to accept other people, including African Americans, foreigners, and especially Catholics, who were often subjected to prejudice and ridicule in his affluent Wakefield neighborhood. Raymond also instinctively felt protective of the vulnerable. On one occasion when the Dellinger family were having dinner at an elegant restaurant, a waitress accidentally spilled some sauce on Marie's new dress. "Everybody was yelling at the waitress," David remembered, but Raymond stood and loudly insisted, "It was my fault, I bumped her arm!" David knew that Raymond had not bumped the waitress's arm. After the incident, Raymond glanced knowingly at David and smiled. The look the father gave his son "brought us closer together," David explained. "We had many disagreements, but we always had that bond."[14] But the son's eventual rejection of his father's conservatism caused friction between them. "He never asked why people were poor," David later wrote, "not if it meant criticizing the economic system that had been so good to him. And he got upset if anyone else did. Especially me when I got older."[15]

Raymond placed an especially high priority on loyalty to family and friends. Thus, when Calvin Coolidge faced his first major crisis as governor of Massachusetts, Raymond immediately came to the governor's assistance. On September 9, 1919, more than eleven hundred Boston police officers—three-fourths of the city's police force—went on strike. The strike was the culmination of a month of bitter labor disputes between the police and city officials. For years, Boston's police force had suffered from poor working conditions, deteriorating precincts, declining wages, longer workdays, and low morale.

The night the police walked out, small, scattered mobs of looters began roaming Boston's deserted streets. They made their way up Washington and Hanover Streets, broke into shops, shattered storefront windows, trashed local businesses, and set small fires in places. Riots also erupted in South Boston, resisted only by small gatherings of non-striking Boston police and private citizens. Although no evidence linked the mobs to radical ideas or movements, many citizens made such connections on their own. On the second day of the strike, Governor Coolidge and Boston mayor Andrew J. Peters mobilized the Massachusetts State Guard. That same morning, Raymond Dellinger awoke to read the following headline in the *Boston Herald*: "RIOTS AND BLOODSHED IN CITY AS STATE GUARD QUELLS MOB."[16]

Fearing the spread of chaos and disorder, Raymond rushed to Boston to report for volunteer law enforcement duty. He and the hundreds of other volunteer police joined the state guard in patrolling the neighborhoods. Governor Coolidge never wavered in his opposition to the strike, and he and the other authorities eventually gained the upper hand over the striking police. By December, the Boston police force was back to full capacity, and the governor sent the state guard home.

Coolidge enjoyed a widespread and enthusiastic outpouring of public support for his tough stance. The national exposure from the police strike elevated Coolidge to the vice presidency in 1920 and, with the death of Warren G. Harding in 1923, the presidency itself. For Raymond, the police strike strengthened his conservatism by reinforcing his belief that radicals threatened the very fabric of American society and that the sanctity of private property had to be upheld at all costs. David was too young to grasp what was happening, and Wakefield was sufficiently distant from the mayhem in Boston. Nevertheless, years later, as David was becoming increasingly politicized, he once asked Raymond, "Why didn't you support the police?" He even suggested that his father had been a "scab." After all, it was the efforts of volunteers like Raymond Dellinger that had given Coolidge the advantage over the striking police. David's comments left Raymond "devastated, defensive and ashamed" of his participation in the volunteer police.[17] "I never brought up the subject again," David later wrote, "not even when I was in college and we had lots of arguments. . . . I didn't want to hurt him again about something in the past that he had always been proud of."[18]

David Dellinger's earliest childhood memories were of the end of World War I. His very first argument with his mother, he later insisted, was in November 1918, almost three months after his third birthday, when he marched inside the house to announce that the war was over. His proclamation was prompted by the enthusiastic rant of a neighbor, Mrs. Fuller, who ran up and down the street shouting the good news at the top of her lungs. But Marie expressed skepticism, and an argument ensued.[19] Two days later, President Woodrow Wilson announced the armistice. David had won his first argument. Few Wakefielders dissented or raised questions about the war, including Raymond and Marie Dellinger, both strong supporters of President Wilson's decision, despite their allegiance to the Republican Party. On October 13, 1919, the Dellinger family attended a victory parade in the center of town. Amid the cheers and a band playing patriotic music, young David sadly watched a wheelchair-bound, legless veteran pass by in the march.[20] After that moment, David never lost his rapport with veterans from all nations who had made enormous sacrifices in wars. In March 1929 while still a junior high student, David accompanied his father to a lecture at the Wakefield town hall given by a German pilot named Count Felix Von Luckner, who recounted his wartime ordeals in the skies over Europe. Town officials in Wakefield had invited Luckner to speak as part of the yearly Sweester Lecture Series, which brought eminent and intriguing figures to town to deliver public talks. After describing some spectacular aerial feats, Count Luckner pleaded for an end to all warfare and encouraged listeners to find ways to unite all humanity. The speech resonated deeply with the impressionable young Dellinger.[21]

David attended Wakefield's public West Ward School on Prospect Street. Always a good student, he seldom missed class, behaved well, and consistently earned high grades. His favorite subjects were reading and physical education. Poetry, in particular, touched him deeply, especially the works of "Shelley, Wordsworth, and the various romantics, as well as the poet Thomas Hood," an Englishman whose verses often focused on the plight of the poor.[22] One of David's most prized possessions was a copy of Pancoast's *Standard English Poems* that had once belonged to Marie Dellinger. In subtle but important ways, Marie nourished an inner curiosity she saw developing in David. For example, she encouraged him to consult the dictionary when he did not understand words and introduced him to the family's fifty-volume collection of the Harvard Classics. "I have a poignant memory of occasionally reading one of my new discoveries to her and seeing the signs of pleasure and sadness on her face," David later wrote, "sadness because reading such things had been crowded out of her life."[23]

A love of athletics rivaled David's zest for reading. Rarely did a day pass when David did not get some sort of exercise. Marv Davidov, who later became one of David's closest friends, explained, "Athletics really meant a lot to Dave. He could really move. He had been an All-American track runner. . . . He became Athlete of the Half Century in Wakefield in 1950. . . . He never lost a race in high school."[24] For David, "it was as natural . . . to catch a ball or tackle a friend as it was for a brook to run downhill or the sun to shine."[25] In addition to playing sports, David closely followed professional sports, routinely monitoring scores in the *Boston Herald*. But it was baseball, more than any other sport, that stirred David's imagination and excited him most. He played the game regularly with his friends at a local diamond near Lake Quannapowitt and followed the Boston Red Sox with great enthusiasm, sometimes making the ten-mile journey to Fenway Park to see a game. According to his close friend Ralph DiGia, David retained his love of baseball as an adult and continued going to baseball games as often as possible.[26] David's oldest son, Patch, recalled, "As I was growing up he was an avid baseball fan and we attended major league games together in New York City."[27]

David's love of sports grew partially out of the bonds he formed with his fellow athletes as a youth. Disillusionment with athletics set in, however, when David reached high school and realized that the goal of winning overshadowed cooperation. He recalled: "There were competitions in which you were supposed to try to be a hero. And if you were a hero then girls wanted to go out with you and guys said 'Hi Dave' when I came out of the locker room."[28] Being an athlete made David extremely popular at Wakefield High School.[29] The effect of this, coupled with his parents' repeated emphasis on the necessity of being "well liked" by his peers, made him feel uneasy. Some of Dellinger's most distinct behavioral traits—his extreme libertarianism, discomfort with leadership positions, and penchant for self-criticism—can be traced to his dissatisfaction with his youthful popularity and his parents' aggressive push for success.

It would be impossible to overstate the importance of Christianity in shaping young David Dellinger. During his entire life, he considered himself to be deeply spiritual, though he lost interest in organized religion at a young age. Each Sunday, the Dellingers attended the First Parish Congregational Church on Main Street.[30] David participated as a baptized and full member of the Congregational Church, but he found the services "grim, negative and life-denying."[31] He eventually concluded that the Sunday services at the Congregational Church had been stripped of "everything that seemed to be fun and lively" and therefore had become little more than a series of fantastic stories, each disconnected from the other, with little relevance to the day-to-day lives of followers.[32]

A significant turning point in David Dellinger's spiritual journey came in junior high school around 1927, when he began reading the New Testament on his own. Before that, he had read parts of it and heard portions quoted in sermons. But he had never read it in its entirety until his early teens. "To my utter amazement, I was thrilled by the Sermon on the Mount. . . . The words came alive completely differently than the way they had been used . . . in the church."[33] Dellinger found a kindred spirit in his schoolmate Paul Lazzaro, a Catholic, Italian American student from a working-class Wakefield neighborhood. The classmates often met to discuss the New Testament and share the sense of awe they felt in discovering a side to Jesus Christ they never knew existed. Reading the New Testament at such an impressionable age confirmed in David's mind that he was no longer a sinner for entertaining notions of leaving the Congregational Church. "I was as selective in my reading as the minister was, because he chose all the passages about Hell and damnation and I chose the ones about people loving each other and forgiving the sinner."[34] By the late 1920s, Paul Lazzaro and David Dellinger had become virtually inseparable. They ran on the high school track team together, went to movies, and had sleepovers during which they stayed up much of the night talking about life and religion.[35] In the mid-1920s, Raymond and Marie began pressuring David to go to private school, but he refused. Ever doubtful of his parents' motives, David assumed the worst, believing that Raymond and Marie were trying to separate him from the "less desirable" elements of the community.[36]

While David's friendship with Paul and commitment to sports absorbed much of his time, he also began discovering his own nascent sexuality and unexpectedly fell in love in junior high. Her name was Rena, a poor Irish girl from the opposite side of Wakefield. David and Rena's relationship seems to have been short-lived, although it is impossible to determine its duration because Dellinger always was vague about exact dates in his accounts and reminiscences. Still intensely religious, David felt that the momentum of their relationship was moving toward sexual intercourse, and he firmly believed that premarital sex, especially between two teenagers, was an unforgivable sin in the eyes of God. Matters worsened considerably when two of David's female classmates reported to Marie Dellinger that they had seen David and Rena together on various occasions after school. The rumor also circulated at Marie's afternoon bridge club, which humiliated and outraged her. One day, Marie summoned David into the living room and sternly reprimanded him, leaving him emotionally devastated. She reminded her tearful son of the sacrifices his father had made and insisted that dating Rena would amount to betraying his father. "He has worked hard all his life in order to make it possible for you to accomplish even bigger things than he has. I'm sure that you don't want to disappoint him by throwing it all away over a girl who isn't worthy of you."[37]

Under intense pressure from his mother and confused by the tension between his religion and his sexual feelings, David ended his first romantic relationship. It had lasted no more than a few months, maybe even a few weeks, but in David's view its significance went beyond its duration and intensity. The confrontation over Rena underscored for the first time what he came to regard as a reactionary and deeply ingrained elitism on the part of his parents.

These troubling questions about class and social hierarchy eventually led to David's radicalism. Now, however, his parents were more worried about his sister Libby, who was dressing "like a flapper" and "running around and smoking cigarettes."[38] Although Raymond became increasingly upset by the changes in his daughter and focused his concern on her, he continued to hold up David as a role model. David maintained loving relationships with Libby and his other sister, Nancy, but he was closest to his younger brother, Fiske, almost eight years his junior. Fiske was "vulnerable" and "loved spending time" with his older brother.[39] But Fiske lived in David's shadow, having to listen to his father's stories about David, particularly about his visit to the White House, when President Coolidge rubbed David on the head and fondly remarked, "He's a smart one. He'll go places."[40] Fiske felt that in Raymond's eyes, he could never measure up to David.

In the late 1920s and early 1930s, David also became acquainted with his many cousins on his father's side of the family. In the summer, the family either drove or took the train to North Carolina. The arrival of the Massachusetts Dellingers to Altamont always caused excitement. The brothers embraced, briefed one another on family developments, and joked about the old days while the cousins ran around the farm and played together. Melba Stroupe, a young girl who lived near Raymond's parents and visited them often in those days, recalled, "When Raymond came in and brought his family from Boston, we'd watch Aunt Lene (Raymond's mother Selena) work for days and days preparing for a big gathering in their honor. It was quite an occasion."[41]

The family trips to North Carolina heightened David's awareness of race because of the state's visible black population. Although David never detected any evidence of racism in his father's family, his trips south forced him to confront segregation, a condition of which he was not aware growing up in a town with only a few blacks. In 1920, only twenty-one African Americans lived in Wakefield, out of a total population of 13,000.[42] Nonetheless, elements of racism were evident in Wakefield as well. David saw the word *nigger* for the first time in the mid-1920s when the *Boston Herald* published a photograph of a sign in a southern community that said, "Nigger, don't let the sun go down on you in this town." Such racism deeply offended him and raised questions in his mind. He wondered, for instance, why Nellie, the Dellingers' African American maid, ate by herself in the kitchen instead of with the family in the dining room. On a trip in the late 1920s when the family stopped at a roadside restaurant in North Carolina, David refused to eat after the restaurant owner ordered two young African American boys to stand near the Dellingers' table and shoo away flies. An embarrassed Raymond apologized to the restaurant owner for David's behavior. David's exposure to segregation and racism in the late 1920s and early 1930s moved him deeply. Although it was not the only thing that radicalized him, such revelations—like his exposure to class tensions when he befriended working-class youths—broadened his worldview.

The arrival of the Great Depression in the fall of 1929 did not worsen the quality of life for the Dellingers. Raymond's law firm weathered the hard times, and the family continued to live on Shumway Circle. But signs of the souring economy were evident nonetheless. A Dellinger family trip to New York at the end of 1929 exposed David to long lines of men waiting for soup. Even the conservative *Boston Herald* ran stories about the spreading agony and acts of desperation. Although they deepened David's empathy for the poor and dispossessed, he seldom discussed such feelings with his parents. Instead, at the dinner table, he discussed his schoolwork and preparations for college. Beginning in the late 1920s, David earned extra money each summer by performing clerical duties in his father's law office, which allowed him to witness at first hand the worsening conditions in Boston. Meantime, his older sister Libby met and eventually married Kenneth Cushman, an affluent businessman from Portland, Maine.

By 1931, David began spending his summers with Libby and Kenneth while working at various jobs in Portland. One summer he was a teller in a bank owned by the Cushman family, and the following year he found a job as a factory laborer and truck driver. "From midnight to three A.M. I worked in the factory. Then I loaded some of the factory's products onto a truck and drove a lonely run of seven to ten hours, making deliveries to a series of outlets scattered through the Maine countryside."[43] Raymond and Marie Dellinger allowed David to spend the summers in Portland because they hoped that working long days as a laborer and bank teller would convince him to aim for higher endeavors in the future, such as law, academia, or politics.

David graduated from high school with the highest honors—earning straight A's on his report card—just before his sixteenth birthday in the spring of 1931. Predicting a bright future for him, his Wakefield High School senior class yearbook exulted:

> Dave has been an ardent and successful athlete, but he excels in track. His specialty is the mile, but he proved his ability as a long distance runner by winning first place at the Harvard Interscholastic Cross-

country Meet last Fall over a field of one-hundred-eighty. Dave is, above all, a good sportsman and will be most valuable to Yale. He displayed his dramatic ability when he played the masculine lead in the Senior Play, and when he won a prize in the Senior Prize Speaking Contest.[44]

In the summer of 1932, seventeen-year-old David Dellinger packed his belongings in preparation for moving into the student dormitories at Yale, his father's alma mater. The time had come to put Wakefield behind him. Away from the scrutiny of his parents and familiarity of his hometown, a world of knowledge and discovery awaited him.

2

The Education of a Pacifist

He had begun to suspect that his worthy father and his other teachers,
the wise Brahmins, had already passed on to him the bulk and best of
their wisdom, that they had already poured the sum total of their
knowledge into his waiting vessel; and the vessel was not full, his in-
tellect was not satisfied, his soul was not at peace, his heart was not still.

Hermann Hesse

DAVID DELLINGER'S SHELTERED UPBRINGING did not prevent
him from being troubled by the paradoxes of American society. He considered the implications of racial discrimination and class tensions at an
unusually young age, preparation perhaps for his later shift to radical
pacifism. When he went to Yale in 1932, he knew little about the ways
of the world, but he was receptive to new ideas. Initially, his main focus
was on his scholarly pursuits, new friendships, and obsession with athletics, but the politics of the Great Depression left a deep imprint on
Dellinger. Poverty, the pacifist movements of the mid-1930s, and the
growing antifascist activism in the second half of the decade moved
millions of young men and women to action, including Dellinger. Traveling through Europe and seeing the spread of fascism further accelerated his transformation. These tumultuous and uncertain years led to
his lifelong commitment to revolutionary nonviolence.

Although the Great Depression left almost no part of the United States
untouched, some sectors of society were less affected than others.
Through the Great Depression, Yale remained a training ground for
America's finest doctors, lawyers, scholars, and government officials. In
keeping with that tradition, David Dellinger majored in economics at
Yale, with his high grades winning him a spot in the newly created honors program. Two professors whom he found most inspiring were R. R.

R. (or "Triple R") Brooks, a labor economist, and Irston R. Barnes, a key figure in the American branch of institutional economics. Professor Brooks "took special delight in shocking his students with carefully documented exposés of the hypocrisies and injustices of the U.S. economic system," while Professor Barnes's courses "provided an ideal context for searching, exploration and discovery."[1]

David also made new friends at Yale. One of his classmates was William Lovell, who shared David's humanistic Christian impulses. William and David met at Dwight Hall, which housed the Yale Christian Association, and students referred to the association by the name of the building. The Yale Christian Association, or "Dwight Hall," was founded in 1886 as a nonprofit organization where Christians could engage in worship, social justice organizing, and public service work in New Haven and other communities. William Lovell remembered meeting Dellinger there: "We got to know each other actually in our first year, at Dwight Hall. I was active in Dwight Hall, and so was he. I don't remember exactly when we first met, but it was early, when we were still freshmen, probably in early 1933."[2]

Both of Lovell's parents enthusiastically supported his Christian social justice activism. Born in China in 1914 to Presbyterian missionaries, he grew up with three siblings and attended a missionary school with Chinese children until he was five. His parents returned to the United States in 1919, to Oberlin, Ohio, where they lived for eight years before settling in Poughkeepsie, New York, where his mother became a professor of religion at Vassar College and his father continued the ministry. Activism was important in William Lovell's family. His parents encouraged peaceful protest against injustice, and an aunt on his father's side was an early member of the pacifist Fellowship of Reconciliation (FOR). As a freshman at Yale, Lovell immersed himself in Dwight Hall activities, organizing educational seminars on peace issues and eliciting support for New Haven's poor. Lovell explained: "From the very first year, the secretary of the Christian Association was a close friend of mine, was a mentor, really. Reverend Fay Campbell was his name. And Sid Lovett was the chaplain. I spent two summers with Sid and his family in New Hampshire as a third adult helping take care of his children. They had two kids. So I felt very close to Lovett and Campbell."[3]

The Reverend Sidney Lovett arrived at Yale in 1932 as the university chaplain. Besides championing ecumenical practices, Lovett was a pioneering advocate of a Jewish presence on campus at a time when few dared to oppose the widespread anti-Semitism at Yale. With the support of Chaplain Lovett, Lovell became the president of Dwight Hall.

David Dellinger's work with William Lovell at Dwight Hall strengthened his humanitarian Christian convictions, and he became more politicized after forming a friendship with Walt Rostow, who later became an adviser to Presidents John F. Kennedy and Lyndon B. Johnson during the Vietnam War and a supporter of U.S. intervention in Southeast Asia. Rostow grew up in New Haven and was one of eight local high school students to receive a scholarship to study at Yale in 1932. Toward the end of his life (he died in February 2003), he seldom discussed his early years and refused to write his memoirs, but he admitted being drawn "to democratic socialist ideas at Yale."[4] Rostow was not alone. Radical politics attracted many Yale students in the 1930s, who gathered at various spots on campus to debate the merits of communism and the failures of capitalism. Rostow never joined the Communist Party, although he sympathized with some of its positions at the time.[5]

Rostow decided that Dellinger was "sheltered" and "naive,"[6] and Dellinger agreed: "When I first arrived at Yale—and for a long time afterwards—I felt like a young, inexperienced, small-town boy . . . who had suddenly stepped into a new and exciting world."[7] The two young men assumed a sort of student-teacher relationship, with Dellinger acting as the pupil and Rostow the instructor. Rostow routinely lent Dellinger books and articles presenting the orthodox Marxist position on some of the most important political subjects of the day, from the New Deal to the rise of fascism in Europe. The two young men talked politics for hours in their dorms and over meals, but David soon found that Walt frequently dominated the conversations and seldom listened carefully to what others said. Although Dellinger initially found Rostow's interpretation of recent events fresh and compelling, he gradually lost interest in listening to Rostow talk and stopped reading the books that he recommended. Eventually, David came to regard Walt as an ideologue who saw the world as a gigantic "geopolitical chess game," with the leaders of various powers assuming the role of players and ordinary people as the pawns.[8] Despite their disagreements, Rostow's influence on Dellinger's thinking was undeniable. "I think he helped radicalize me," Dellinger reflected, "though he also helped prevent me from turning into an orthodox Marxist communist, because it [Rostow's brand of Marxism] was so abstract and mechanical and lacking human-relatedness."[9]

The two remained friends throughout their undergraduate years at Yale and traveled together to England to study at Oxford. Then in 1937 they drifted apart. Later each insisted that the other was a communist. Rostow labeled Dellinger a "working communist," and Dellinger maintained that Rostow "was a communist at that time, and he kept trying to convert me."[10] This odd war of words continued well into the 1990s. In his 1994 account of the anti–Vietnam War movement, *The War Within*, sociologist Tom Wells found Rostow to be "particularly fixated on Dellinger's links to foreign communists. Both times the issue of communist subversion came up, he immediately mentioned Dellinger."[11] In a draft of his 1993 memoirs, Dellinger fanned the flames by referring to Rostow as a "communist." "I mentioned [in an early draft of *From Yale to Jail*] that . . . Rostow tried to get me to join the Communist Party at Yale," he told an interviewer. Dellinger's allegation prompted a reply from the uneasy editors at Random House, whose subsidiary Pantheon was publishing *From Yale to Jail*, indicating their discomfort with the claim. David "fought over that for months" with his editors. "They would say, 'Get a statement from Rostow that he was a communist.'"[12] Beyond Dellinger's charges, however, there is no evidence that Rostow was actually a member of the Communist Party, which was the Random House editors' criterion in determining whether he was a "communist." The editors prevailed. In his memoirs, Dellinger omitted the "communist" references but still portrayed Rostow as a zealot who "didn't seem to have strong emotions about any human beings, not love and not hatred."[13]

Athletics assumed a central place in David Dellinger's undergraduate years at Yale. His acceptance on the varsity track team in 1932 was particularly important, as his obsession at the time was to qualify for the 1936 U.S. Olympic Team. The demanding regimen of running still left David sufficient time to develop his friendships, and he became good friends with his roommate at Yale. In David's various accounts of his Yale years, he never revealed the name of his roommate, likely out of a respect for his privacy. The roommate grew up on a ranch in Colorado managed by his father, and attended a small private school near his home before receiving a scholarship to study at Yale. Almost everything about their "background and temperament was different," yet the two shared a strong connection and mutual affection that lasted for much of their time at Yale. At the start of the fall semester 1933, David and his roommate traveled north to Wakefield and spent a weekend at the Dellinger family's home. Raymond and Marie warmly welcomed David's friend as they would "a member of the family."[14]

In the presence of his roommate, David experienced certain emotions he had never before felt, which both excited and worried him. The joy of forming such a solid bond was diminished somewhat by David's fear of a potential homosexual encounter. Growing up in conservative Wakefield, he had been exposed to years of "strong conditioning against homoeroticism," and at this point in his life "it was inconceivable" to him that he would "ever . . . feel sexually attracted to a male."[15] David therefore simply accepted the friendship as an unusually close one and went on dismissing "homosexuality as a disease that had nothing to do with love."[16] At one point, though, David discussed his feelings with his roommate.

> My friend was . . . shocked and begged me, for my own sake, never to tell anyone else about it. People wouldn't understand, he said. He was too good a friend, within his own understanding of friendship, to 'insult' me by coming right out and saying that only a queer could fall in love with his roommate.[17]

Outside pressures also ensured that Dellinger would remain too busy to engage in much self-exploration. His continuation on the track team meant long days of practice and several bus trips to meets at other campuses. In a relatively short time, Dellinger became one of the stars of Yale's track team, but this did not last. His promising athletic career began to unravel during his junior year, in the spring of 1935, when he went to a meet at Harvard as a member of Yale's cross-country team. At the Harvard race, David's right leg took a terrible beating, and he came in fifth.

The following week, his leg injury kept him out of the highly touted Intercollegiate Amateur Athletic Association championships, at which Harvard took first place. The sting of the Harvard victory drove David to incredible acts of endurance in the following weeks. On the advice of his coach, he tightly wrapped his right leg with a special runner's tape, which served as a splint during races. The practice was a gamble. As long as the tape held together, David performed well, often winning. But when the tape broke, which happened a few times, he collapsed and had to be carried off the track by medical personnel. But Dellinger persisted, and one of his greatest accolades at Yale came in May 1935 when his coach and teammates selected him as team captain for the 1935/1936 school year. In the meantime, his running skills kept improving, although he remained silent about the recurring bouts of pain in his right leg. At the Connecticut Championships in the spring of 1935, David came in first in the half-mile, mile, and two-mile races. Following this string of victories, the coach began encouraging David to try out for the 1936 U.S. Olympic team. By the late spring and early summer of 1935, David was pushing himself harder than ever, putting up with terrible leg pains because he believed that the Olympic team was within reach. But he could not completely conceal his physical problems from his teammates and his coach.

At the next-to-last track meet of the season, between Yale and Princeton, David could not walk from the inn where the team stayed to the stadium across the street. The coach confronted David privately, suggesting that he not run and give his damaged leg a much-needed rest, but David pleaded with the coach to let him run. The coach obtained some "extra-strength" tape from the Yale team trainer and ordered David to wrap it tightly around his leg. When the race began, he took off at an impressive pace, quickly assuming the first-place position. Surging ahead, he felt a sudden snap and recalled what happened next: "The tape broke again, and I literally crawled across the finish line, losing my lead as two or three other runners swept past me."[18] The Princeton meet was David's last race.

In the summer of 1935, David went to Colorado, where he spent weeks in the woods helping his roommate's family build a log cabin in the Rocky Mountains to be used as a summer vacation home. The strain of building the cabin took a toll on David's leg, particularly the time he spent performing "pick-and-shovel work excavating for the foundations, followed by a couple of days mixing and hauling cement."[19] Once again, David's right leg ceased functioning, and he had to return to Massachusetts for emergency medical attention. But he stubbornly refused to give up running and spent the first two weeks of fall semester training rigorously with his sights still set on the Olympics. During the second week of training, David participated in the intrasquad time trial, and as he rounded a corner, his right calf muscles completely ruptured.

He was taken to a nearby hospital, where a physician operated on his severely damaged calf muscles. During the surgery, the doctor discovered that two major muscles had completely separated, making it impossible for David to walk. So the surgeon sewed the muscles together, essentially creating one where there had once been four, and he later told Dellinger that any hopes of running again were out of the question. The doctor also speculated that David would walk with a pronounced limp for the rest of his life. Dellinger was despondent as his "dreams of being an Olympic champion came crashing down."[20]

He had time to reflect during his convalescence. Although he was only twenty years old, his relentless drive to succeed had already destroyed his ambitions and caused bodily harm. The acute pain from his injury contributed to his deepening depression. He began to reevaluate his definition of success and for the first time wondered why he was even attending Yale and what would await him when he received his bachelor's degree. His parents' obsession with success had been unhealthy, he concluded, because instead of bringing them joy, it had heightened their anxieties, and their unrealistically high expectations of David had aggravated his own inner turmoil. But then depression gave way to exhilaration in the hospital as David's mood brightened. He explained:

> I no longer cared whether I would make the Olympic team or even win another race at Yale. I felt as if I had been in a kind of prison of my own making, and that I was a prisoner of my own myopic ambitions. Suddenly and unexpectedly I was free and the simplest things in life became enchanting again.[21]

A week after his surgery, David Dellinger hobbled on crutches out of the New Haven hospital to begin his senior year at Yale. He emerged from the hospital a changed man.

The highly charged political atmosphere of the 1930s shaped David Dellinger's ideas. Antiwar sentiments were flourishing alongside political isolationism, as the economic hard times fostered a spreading sense of disillusionment. In particular, a broad segment of the American public in the 1930s condemned their nation's entry into World War I. They did not understand the rationale that led the United States into the war, and they questioned why so many young Americans—approximately

49,000—had died in a conflict that by the early 1930s made little sense. One common explanation placed the blame on the nation's banks and arms manufacturers and their supporters in Congress. Depression-era critics of the war coined the term *merchants of death* to describe the bankers and munitions makers that they believed had turned the United States in 1914 into a silent partner in the Allied war effort and, by 1917, a full participant. Even President Franklin D. Roosevelt, sensing the prevailing mood of the nation, inveighed against the wrongdoings of the munitions makers when he proclaimed: "The time has come to take profit out of war."[22]

Americans in the 1930s vowed to avoid a repeat of 1917. Across the country, scores of newly created religious and leftist antiwar organizations agitated against militarism and warfare. Conservatives, too, established isolationist leagues, and in 1940 a group of right-wing politicians and businessmen founded the America First Committee for the purpose of keeping the United States out of the war in Europe. Many of the so-called America Firsters praised Adolf Hitler for assuming a central role in the global crusade against communism. Overnight, internationalists became pariahs in Washington, D.C., and any proposals of overseas intervention, no matter how modest, drew criticism. The nation's churches led the way in promoting the antiwar sentiments, with clergy from virtually every denomination opposing all forms of armed conflict. In 1935, Reinhold Niebuhr, the nation's leading theologian, echoed the attitudes of clergy across the nation: "I do not intend to participate in any war now in prospect." Although he rejected absolute pacifism, he could see "no good coming out of any wars confronting us."[23] Opinion polls conducted in the 1930s by major churches in the United States indicated widespread antiwar beliefs among clergy and lay people alike. In addition to the Christian churches, much of America's Jewish population embraced the dominant antiwar sentiments. In World War I, the nation's most eminent Jewish leader, Rabbi Stephen Wise, had taken a job in a naval shipyard to help the war effort. But in 1931, he declared that the nation's clergy "committed a sin when they blessed war banners," adding, "I for one will never again commit that sin. . . . War never ends war. War ends nothing but peace."[24]

The growing religious commitment to nonviolence mirrored secular trends. A February 1937 poll asked Americans, "If another war like the World War develops in Europe, should America take part again?" Ninety-five percent responded "no."[25] Such sentiments fueled activism, particularly on the nation's college campuses. University students in the 1930s organized numerous antiwar events, even though at that time the prospect of America's entering a war was uncertain and had little support from either political party.

At Yale, the Dwight Hall volunteers planned a series of antiwar activities for April 12, 1935. William Lovell, by then president of Dwight Hall, remembered "convening the cabinet . . . and [we] passed some very vigorous resolutions" preemptively condemning any potential "military actions on the part of the United States."[26] David Dellinger participated in the spring Dwight Hall actions and coincidentally began reading a recently acquired book, Richard Gregg's *The Power of Nonviolence*. Gregg's writings introduced Dellinger to the teachings of Mohandas Gandhi, the leader of the nonviolent independence movement in India. Equally impressive to David was the example of the book's author, Richard Gregg, who, like Raymond Dellinger, had been a high-paid Boston lawyer. Driven by a desire to learn about peaceful conflict resolution, Gregg went to India in 1925 to study Gandhi's teachings. He lived on Gandhi's ashram for seven months and remained in India for four years, becoming a committed supporter of the nonviolent independence struggle. When Gregg returned to the United States, he began writing a synthesis of Gandhi's ideas for a Western audience, resulting in the 1934 publication of *The Power of Nonviolence*. Gandhi's teachings on nonviolent struggle represented, in Gregg's view, a much-needed alternative to the traditional American pacifist emphasis on avoiding all conflict. Pacifism did not mean being passive, Gregg insisted, and Gandhi's example showed that nonviolent actions could be used to combat a variety of social ills. Dellinger also read the sermons of Rev. John Haynes Holmes, a Unitarian minister and social activist from Massachusetts who, like Gregg, became a follower of Gandhi after World War I. A pacifist and spokesman for the War Resisters League, Holmes opposed World War I and encouraged nonviolent resistance against all armed conflict. Although Holmes did not meet Gandhi until 1931, beginning in 1918 he was inspired by Gandhi's writings and activism. Both Richard Gregg and John Haynes Holmes popularized Gandhi's teachings in the United States, resulting in the dissemination of his nonviolent principles across the country. The notion of using nonviolent methods to resist injustice strongly appealed to Dellinger, and he began seeking kindred spirits who shared Gandhi's philosophy.

But the options facing a young advocate of nonviolent protest were not promising in the 1930s, despite the pervasiveness of pacifist attitudes. The American Left was deeply divided on the issue. The Communist Party, the dominant force in American radical politics during the Great Depression, often fluctuated on the question of tactics and means of resistance, largely because of its subservience to the ever-changing dictates of the Soviet government. When Dellinger began his senior year at Yale in 1935, the party was in a state of transition, gradually shedding its anticapitalist militancy in favor of a more pragmatic Popular Front policy that its leaders hoped would unite radicals and liberals in opposition to the expanding fascist threat overseas. Although the Connecticut branch of the American Communist Party attempted to recruit David Dellinger in the 1930s, he did not join. Throughout his adult life, Dellinger had strongly mixed feelings about the Communist Party. The communists, he wrote, "were by far the most energetic organizers of many of the struggles I supported, for racial and economic justice, industrial unionism, and even civil liberties."[27] Communists stood at the forefront of many of the era's most important struggles for social justice. "A lot of wonderful people joined the Communist party," David conceded.[28] For instance, without the aid of the Communists, the so-called Scottsboro Boys, nine African-American youths accused with flimsy evidence of raping two white women in Alabama in 1931, would have gone straight to the electric chair. By 1935, the Communists were drawing attention to the threat of European fascism at a time when isolationism drove most Americans to look inward. Dellinger admired them for taking these principled stands, and he formed enduring friendships with party members. He even admitted that for a brief time during his senior year at Yale, he thought he "was going to end up joining the party."[29]

But Dellinger was far too anarchical, in both personal temperament and politics, ever to join the Communist Party. His respect for certain members notwithstanding, he did not admire the party's leadership, which uncritically backed the Soviet Union and directed its members to do likewise. Thanks to Walt Rostow, Dellinger read books and articles discussing the party's line on capitalism and fascism, yet he found most of them mechanical and lacking humanity. But he faced a difficult dilemma. Dellinger knew that communists in the United States were harassed by federal, state, and local authorities. In fact, in order to minimize dissent, opponents of radicalism vilified certain social critics by labeling them *communists*, regardless of whether they were actually party members. The last thing Dellinger wanted to do was play into the hands of such attacks on free speech. He therefore sought a flexible position on the Communist Party, one that enabled him to voice doubts about its leadership but defend the right of Communists to speak freely without being impugned for their membership in the party. Eventually, the Communist Party vacillated again on the question of war. In late August 1939, Nazi Germany and the Soviet Union signed a nonaggression pact, prompting the American Communist Party to abandon its Popular Front preparedness campaign in favor of a nonintervention, antiwar platform more in line with Dellinger's position. But even that position was abruptly abandoned when the Germans invaded Russia in June 1941. It troubled Dellinger that so many communists "placed their hopes so long on some foreign power outside of our own country and remote from their own lives."[30]

The American Socialist Party came much closer politically and philosophically to Dellinger's own beliefs. At Yale, he attended speeches given by the party leader Norman Thomas, who "very much influenced" his views.[31] Dellinger even briefly joined the Socialist Party in the late 1930s and served on its executive committee in 1939/1940. But by the 1930s the party's glory days had passed. Even in the depths of the Great Depression, when millions of Americans became more open to radical ideas, the Socialist Party languished. Years of sectarian conflicts, government repression, losses of members, and the death in 1926 of its charismatic leader, Eugene V. Debs, had taken a toll on the organization. Under Norman Thomas's capable leadership, the Socialist Party briefly revived in the late 1920s and early 1930s. But by the middle of the decade, the New Deal had codified into law many of the reforms that Debs had championed earlier in the century. In the 1936 presidential race, Thomas received only 187,000 votes, a poor showing even by the party's standards. A year later, the party rosters plummeted to a mere 6,500 members, and the organization never rebounded. "Socialism which we had hoped would triumph 'in our time' is everywhere on the defensive," a discouraged Norman Thomas admitted.[32]

Ultimately, Dellinger's Christian radicalism was more closely aligned with anarchism than socialism, and most of his life he refrained from joining any organizations. He later admitted to a reporter from the *New York Times* that while he briefly belonged to the Socialist Party in the late 1930s, his anarchistic impulses drove him to leave it. "I've grown more militant since then," he declared.[33]

In June 1936, David Dellinger graduated magna cum laude in the economics honors program and was elected to the honors society Phi Beta Kappa. Upon graduation, David planned to continue following in his father's footsteps by becoming a lawyer, representing "the newly emerged industrial unions, and the poor, oppressed and needy."[34] He also had received the Henry Fellowship, one of the top awards given to Harvard and Yale graduates to attend New College at Oxford in England.[35] Oxford also chose Walt Rostow to be a Rhodes Scholar, and the two friends made plans for their year abroad. During his four years at Yale, Dellinger had evolved from a sheltered Wakefield teenager to a young man who had formulated a "nonviolent philosophy . . . at Yale under the combined influence of Mahatma Gandhi and Dwight Hall's brand of Christianity."[36] Yet his decision to attend Oxford and eventually become a lawyer—even a poor people's lawyer—left him conflicted. He confided in an unpublished account of his life that he "had applied only because my roommate and several of my other friends were applying and I had gone along with it, doing what everyone else was doing and not seriously expecting to be chosen."[37]

A few weeks after commencement, standing on the deck of the ship headed to England, Dellinger came to a crucial realization:

> Something happened inside me that recreated and intensified feelings such as those I had felt listening to a lonely train whistle, or the chug-chug of the lobster boats; or running home, uphill, in the cool of an early evening after baseball by the lake. Immediately, I knew that I would never be a lawyer. . . . Law seemed too limited, important though it might be, too elitist and separatist.[38]

Dellinger told no one about his decision, and he remained bound to his agreement to attend Oxford for at least a year. But in England, he parted ways with the other Oxford-bound students so he could travel to Spain along with a student delegation organized by Bob Rosenbaum, a fellow Yale student. It was a perilous time to visit Spain. Following a nationwide election in February 1936 that had brought to power a democratically elected left-wing Republican government, a revolt by fascist and conservative militarists erupted in Morocco on July 17 and spread to the mainland the following day. Under the leadership of General Francisco Franco, the fascists—calling themselves Nationalists—enjoyed ample support from Germany and Italy in the form of military advisers, weapons, and matériel. Dellinger arrived shortly after the fascist revolt, having first heard about it on the ship's radio during his trans-Atlantic voyage.[39]

In a brief biographical sketch of Dellinger that appears in the 1994 memoirs of the radical lawyer William Kunstler, attorney for the Chicago Seven, he claims that Dellinger worked as volunteer ambulance driver for the left-wing Loyalist armies.[40] But the real story was decidedly less dramatic. David and his roommate stopped in Paris on their way to Spain in late July 1936 and stayed at a small, inexpensive Quaker-owned hotel. They arrived at the hotel late one night, and "at breakfast the next morning, there was an elderly, sweet old Quaker lady speaking very loudly about the fact that they couldn't get anybody to go to Spain as an ambulance driver."[41] David introduced himself, and the woman told him that earlier volunteers had already driven ambulances to Spain but had allowed the vehicles to be used by Republican soldiers to ship weapons to antifascist forces across the country. Therefore, she said, the Quakers sought a "true pacifist" to deliver one of the ambulances, a driver with no interest in participating in the armed conflict. Dellinger volunteered and took a taxi to the address given to him by the elderly woman. He arrived only to discover that "they had no ambulances."[42]

Within days David and his roommate arrived in Madrid. Dellinger sympathized with the reforms of the left-wing Republican government. The literacy programs, collectivized farming experiments, and workers' councils and programs to feed the poor all seemed to be in harmony with his evolving radical Christian ideas. He also had the highest regard for the international brigades that traveled to Spain from countries around the world to resist the fascists, particularly the three thousand or so members of the Abraham Lincoln Battalion from the United States. Indeed, watching the truckloads of Republican soldiers driving toward the frontlines forced David to reevaluate his pacifist commitment.

> For an agonizing 24 hours, I wrestled with the urge to pick up the gun in the anti-fascist cause. In the background, as I paced the streets of

Madrid were the sounds of the battle, a few miles away. Spanish friends I had come to love and admire were on their way to the front, some of them unarmed but expecting to pick up the guns of their dead comrades and continue the battle.[43]

But he was alarmed by the growing sectarian violence that divided the antifascist forces. "Communists were shooting at the Trotskyites and the Trotskyites were shooting at the Communists. When our car made a wrong turn [in Barcelona] and went into the Anarchist sector, we met another blast of gunfire and the car backed up."[44] Traveling across Republican-controlled Spain strengthened David's antifascist sentiments. It was the only time in his life that he considered renouncing his pacifism and participating in armed struggle, and his verdict not to stay and fight troubled him for the rest of his life. He acknowledged that "it was probably the hardest and most critical decision of my life."[45]

Dellinger left war-torn Spain to travel briefly through Italy on a "pilgrimage . . . tracing the steps" of his personal hero, "Francis of Assisi."[46] After roaming around Assisi for a few days, Dellinger boarded a train bound for Germany, where he planned to link up with his roommate from Yale and tour the country before returning to Oxford to begin his fall courses.[47] During the Olympic games being held in Berlin, David Dellinger visited Jewish bookstores searching "for the works of Heinrich Heine, one of my favorite poets, whose works were banned because he was Jewish."[48] One Jewish bookstore manager sent David to a bed-and-breakfast in the ghetto, and during his visit to Germany he "often stayed in similar places in other cities."[49] The status of Jews was still in transition when David arrived in Germany in the summer of 1936. Since April 7, 1933, Jews had been excluded from government employment, including teaching jobs at all levels. Two years later, on September 15, 1935, the Third Reich issued anti-Jewish racial and citizenship laws, and by the time Dellinger arrived, Jews already were suffering physical assaults, economic boycotts, and expulsion from the civil service and professions.

The anti-Semitism of the Third Reich came as a shock to Dellinger. He had not known any Jews before going to Yale in 1932, where Walt Rostow was one of his first Jewish friends. At Yale, David worked primarily with ecumenical Christians such as Rev. Fay Campbell and Rev. Sid Lovett, both uncompromising opponents of anti-Semitism. Yet it was difficult to ignore the anti-Semitism at Yale in the highly polarized

1930s, where, as one account noted, "Nazi flags festooned numerous student rooms, and Jews were excluded from many clubs and societies."[50] David also remembered seeing clubs and swimming pools in New Haven that banned Jewish patrons. Such examples of discrimination paled, however, compared with the gathering storm in Germany. Traveling through Nazi Germany, David met Jews who asked him why U.S. immigration quotas for Jews were so low and encouraged him to return to the United States to resist anti-Semitism and teach Americans about "the horrors of fascism."[51]

The events in Spain and Germany in the summer of 1936 left a permanent impression on Dellinger. When he arrived at Oxford University to begin his fall courses, he brought with him a more sensitive antifascist conscience and spent much of his first year at Oxford eager to return to the United States to participate in social justice activism. Dellinger missed his undergraduate days and volunteering at Dwight Hall, as Oxford offered him little spiritual or intellectual sustenance. His peers were driven and highly successful young men who were already charting their futures as academics, medical doctors, government officials, diplomats, and attorneys. Many lacked the contemplative qualities of his old activist cohort at the Yale Christian Association, and much to his dismay, the original Oxford Pledge group was disbanded before 1936. Dellinger did, however, join the Oxford Pacifist Society and met Bertrand Russell when the philosopher came to speak at the university.[52]

In the spring of 1937, David informed Oxford that he did not intend to stay for another year. He wanted to return to the United States and resume his activism. "Giving up Oxford was not . . . [a] problem," he later wrote.[53] At the end of his year at Oxford, Dellinger decided to return to Germany, this time with his parents, before going back to the United States. During his year at Oxford, David had met a German Rhodes scholar named Jobst von der Gröben, who "came from a leading family and had a brilliant record."[54] They became friends, and von der Gröben—who feared returning to Nazi Germany—gave David the names of various anti-Nazi figures to talk to in Germany. Traveling to Nazi Germany a second time strengthened Dellinger's anti-fascist position. Early in the trip, David separated from his parents so they could tour the cities and the countryside while he visited some of the people suggested to him by von der Gröben. Dellinger noted that on this trip, he "stayed longer with Jews and had some contacts with the anti-Nazi underground."[55] But such contacts, he admitted, were "superficial" and involved relaying messages from one anti-Nazi figure to another or quietly conversing with activists about their methods of opposition.[56]

Dellinger returned to the United States in September 1937 even more deeply politicized than he had been when he graduated the previous year. His exposure to fascism underscored, in his mind, the need to redouble his commitment to nonviolent activism in order to improve conditions at home. He moved to New Haven, rented an apartment, and accepted a full-time job at Dwight Hall counseling freshman students and planning various events for the Christian Association. He plunged resolutely into leftist Christian social activism. The years between 1937 and 1940 were a critical period in his radicalization, when his nonviolent pacifism crystallized and matured. In addition to his job at Dwight Hall, Dellinger spent a great deal of time experimenting with various types of activism and expression. He picketed against discrimination and immigration quotas, assisted the Steelworkers Organizing Committee in a New Jersey company town, and lived in impoverished neighborhoods in New Haven and New York City.

Experiencing the hardships of the poor "in a more comprehensive way" than he ever had before became a high priority for Dellinger. "I wanted to test my beliefs," he wrote.[57] Accordingly, when the crisis in the United States worsened as a result of a dramatic economic downturn in late 1937, Dellinger put on an old suit and left his New Haven dwelling to live among the poorest of the poor. For weeks, he endured cold weather, police harassment, and a painful existence in a hobo camp located near a marsh in New Jersey. The fireflies hovered in the night sky as David shared stew and coffee with hoboes and sometimes slept under corrugated tin and wallboard to protect him from the elements. He rode inside boxcars and, with other vagrants, rummaged through dumpsters behind diners for food.[58]

Dellinger's travels through the Depression-ravaged landscape of New York and New Jersey in late 1937 also amounted to both a rebellion against Raymond and Marie Dellinger's lifestyle and values and an effort to chart his own destiny. He had gone to Yale to satisfy their expectations of him and had spent an unfulfilling year at Oxford because he wanted to please his Yale classmates. "Clearly my life at Yale was challenging, engrossing and rewarding, on a variety of fronts," Dellinger explained. But at Yale and Oxford, he began to recognize "extensive . . . contradictions . . . between the way I wanted to live and behave and a lot of the ways I was living, thinking and acting."[59] The lessons he learned in shantytowns and hobo camps also taught him the limitations of pacifism. Pacifists devoted so much attention to wars and armed conflict, Dellinger reasoned, that they ignored the violence caused by indigence and a lack of meaningful opportunities. Pacifism, he concluded, "does not make economic violence a major concern."[60]

Dellinger now began living a life that reflected his principles. Living among the poor, experiencing the violence of poverty, and discovering the humanity of homeless people offered him a spiritual nourishment that had often eluded him at Yale and Oxford. Dellinger now sought a platform to resist injustices in American society, an opportunity that arrived in the fall of 1940. By then a student at Union Theological Seminary in New York City, he made one of the most fateful decisions of his life.[61]

3

The Hole

Our consciences are more moving than any man-made penalty. War,
which is systematic mass murder of our human brothers, is completely
contrary to our best intelligence as well as to the teachings of Jesus.

David Dellinger

IN MAY 1939, David Dellinger traveled from the church in New
Hampshire where he was doing volunteer work to visit the campus of
Union Theological Seminary in New York City.[1] Since his return from
Europe in 1937 following a disappointing year at Oxford, Dellinger had
been pondering what he should do next. Working as graduate secretary
at Dwight Hall, living near the Yale campus, and auditing courses at
Yale Divinity School kept him tied to his alma mater. Finally, in 1939, he
enrolled at Union Theological Seminary in New York City, to "explore,
study and understand" the history of Christianity. Arriving at the campus in Morningside Heights shortly after his twenty-fourth birthday,
the new divinity student believed that Union "had a reputation for activism and radicalism."[2]

In September, Dellinger moved into the student dormitories at
Union and discovered that several of his classmates shared his commitment to socialism and pacifism. Many had come to Union to study
under America's leading theologian, Reinhold Niebuhr, professor of
Christian social ethics. In his early career, Niebuhr had developed a radical democratic socialist approach to solving social problems and had
become involved in matters of racial and economic justice.[3] In 1928,
Union offered Niebuhr an associate professor position, and he moved
with his family to New York City, where he gravitated to the center of a
group of leftist Protestant intellectuals that included such noted pacifists as Norman Thomas, Devere Allen, and Kirby Page. But Niebuhr
parted ways with the pacifists during the Great Depression, first with

his influential 1932 book *Moral Man and Immoral Society*, in which he justified certain acts of violent resistance as a means of achieving social justice. His disgust with the rise of fascism and Japanese militarism in the 1930s led him to renounce pacifism, embrace liberal internationalism, and support President Franklin D. Roosevelt. The war in Europe solidified his stance, and Niebuhr left the Socialist Party to protest its pacifist policies. As he argued in *The Nation*, the pacifist socialists enjoyed "the luxury of utopianism" and made the mistake of "measuring all significant historical distinctions against purely ideal perspectives and blinding the eye to differences which may be matters of life and death in a specific instance."[4]

Niebuhr's impassioned critique of Christian nonviolence presented a formidable challenge to the Union students' idealistic assumptions, though even the most ardent pacifist students recognized his brilliance. Union student Howard Spragg, one of Niebuhr's students in 1939, explained, "Niebuhr was probably the main reason why I went to Union Seminary. Niebuhr, in the midst of my coming into an interest in socialism and . . . pacifism, was raising the kinds of questions that made me critical. Even while I continued to be a socialist and a pacifist."[5]

Although classes and fieldwork demanded much of David Dellinger's attention, he had enough time to form friendships with two other Union students, Meredith Dallas and Don Benedict. Benedict and Dallas had much in common: Both were born in Detroit around the same time; both were Methodists; both had gone to Albion College in Michigan; and they became roommates at Union. The two young men also had become pacifists before arriving at Union. Owing to his superb talents at baseball, Benedict never had a problem making new friends. At Albion, he had played on the baseball team and met Dallas, who organized peace rallies and occasionally gave antiwar speeches. Like Benedict, Dallas knew at a young age that he was "headed for the ministry," and he began his first year of studies at Union in the fall of 1939.[6] Although he "didn't really enjoy the seminary," he "loved to get away and go over to" his first-semester fieldwork at a settlement house in East Harlem, where he supervised a group of children ranging in age from seven to ten.[7] During the fall semester, Dallas and Benedict developed warm friendships with Dellinger. The three took courses together and often met in the dorm at night to discuss Christianity, pacifism, and world politics. In the early weeks, Benedict noticed that "Spain weighed heavily in David's mind," and Dellinger spoke often about the need for pacifists to somehow confront the fascist threat abroad.[8]

The three stayed close, enduring Niebuhr's repeated attacks against pacifism during the day and sitting together at dinner in the evening. Dellinger even came to regard Dallas and Benedict as a surrogate family, providing the moral support and encouragement that his parents, siblings, and earlier friends had once supplied. Early in 1940, Benedict went with Dellinger to a railroad yard where the two got on a boxcar and, along with hobo traveling companions, went to Washington, D.C. First Lady Eleanor Roosevelt had heard about Dellinger's antiwar work and invited him to meet with her and other student peace activists for tea at the White House. After a short visit that left Dellinger greatly impressed with Roosevelt, the two seminarians jumped on a railroad flatcar for New York. Back at Union, pacifism had become "negative pretty totally in the seminary," remembered Dallas, and nonviolent ideas actually lost adherents amid the growing interventionist sentiment in late 1939 and early 1940. "We were all there together," Dallas explained, "and I think we were of similar minds and talked about it."[9] By that time, Dellinger had evolved into a seasoned activist, "radicalized by the Depression plus by the New Testament and the Acts of the Apostles where they sold all their worldly goods."[10]

Dellinger soon grew disillusioned with his courses at Union. In particular, he found Reinhold Niebuhr a "grievous disappointment."[11] Energetic and impatient, Dellinger wanted more action and less theory and found an ideal outlet for his activism in Union's rewarding field-work program. His assignment at Jube Memorial Congregational Church in Newark, New Jersey, thrilled him, especially the opportunity to work with poor African American youths. Late in the fall semester of 1939, he considered creating an egalitarian Christian communal experiment in one of Harlem's impoverished neighborhoods. He secretly discussed his plans with Dallas and Benedict and found an enthusiastic response. "The poorer neighborhoods of New York drew us," recounted Benedict, "and those of us who were socialists and pacifists began to criticize the cloistered atmosphere in which we found ourselves."[12]

Early in 1940, Dellinger, Dallas, and Benedict searched for an apartment in a poor, predominantly African American neighborhood in Harlem, but suspicious landlords worried that they might be pimps, Jehovah's Witnesses, or federal agents. Eventually the three found a spacious "six-room walk-up" in a dilapidated apartment building on 128th Street and Eighth Avenue. Although the apartment required much refurbishing to make it habitable, a more difficult task was persuading the president of Union Theological Seminary, Henry Sloane Coffin—Uncle Henry, as students called him—to allow them to move into a squalid Harlem tenement. Uncle Henry threatened to withdraw their scholarships and raised the possibility of expulsion if they insisted on pursuing such a course of action. But the three young men disregarded his threats and moved out of the Union dormitories in February, correctly predicting that Coffin would not expel them. Living in an African American neighborhood in Harlem presented a host of unanticipated challenges. Even though Harlem had been the epicenter of an African American cultural and artistic renaissance from the end of World War I until the mid-1930s, much of it remained desperately poor in 1939. Not surprisingly, some Harlem residents regarded Benedict, Dallas, and Dellinger as interlopers who could not be trusted. "It turned out to be a complicated experience in which we were initially treated with . . . suspicion," Dellinger remembered.[13]

The three men divided their time between courses at Union, community service in Harlem, and volunteering in the predominantly African American neighborhood in Newark where Dellinger performed his Union fieldwork. They collected canned fruits, vegetables, and soup for food banks; helped residents in neighborhood cleanup efforts; served hot meals at the church; and gathered coats, blankets, and donations for the cold winter months. They became acquainted with prostitutes, derelicts, train porters, industrial workers, and single mothers who struggled against enormous odds to feed, clothe, and shelter their children. On one particularly cold night, Donald Benedict carried home an unconscious homeless man, a "hulking fellow, revoltingly dirty and frowzy, altogether a disgusting sight, steeped in the sour smell of vomit and the stench of alcohol," and laid him down on one of the beds in the apartment. The following day, the homeless man regained consciousness, introduced himself as George, and made lamb stew for everybody in the apartment.[14]

Some encounters did not turn out so well. Meredith Dallas once brought home two unemployed men he had found in a bar who wanted to start a traveling tap-dancing troupe. After a few days in the apartment, the guests left in the middle of the night, stealing the seminarians' typewriters and most of their clothes. "We had taken them in, shared what we had, and offered to hold them over until they could find work," Benedict remarked, "where had we failed?"[15] At Union Theological Seminary, the administration kept tabs on their activities, and some students responded to the experiment with scorn and ridicule. But a handful quietly expressed admiration and hope that the Union administration would eventually support such efforts. When the seminarians held an open house in Harlem in the early spring, they were amazed to see half the Union faculty and numerous students show up for sandwiches, cake, and tea. Several professors expressed their support and offered to help. Gradually, other Union classmates began volunteering at the Harlem apartment on the weekends and in the evenings. Thus the experiment proved enormously rewarding for Dellinger, Dallas, and Benedict, even though some of the Harlem residents never got over their initial suspicion and distrust. Dellinger later reflected:

> During the time I lived in Harlem, I had fun getting acquainted with some of our neighbors by playing stickball, shooting pool, having a beer and listening to the ball game at the corner bar, hanging out on the stoop at night. . . . It took a while to break down the barriers, and we never did break all of them down, but it helped that we were on the Black people's turf.[16]

In the spring of 1940, the three moved their experiment to Newark, near the church where Dellinger was doing his Union fieldwork. He convinced Benedict and Dallas that they should shift their attention to the desperately poor neighborhoods of Newark, where they would receive some institutional support from Jube Memorial Congregational Church. At Jube, Dellinger planned a summer community service program and went door to door in an effort to attract local residents to church services. He explained the process: "What we did is . . . worked out a budget where they paid me to be the director and I could hire either one or two staff people. . . . I hired blacks from the neighborhood but we figured out that my friends and I could all live on my salary."[17] Meredith Dallas remembered that the communal dwelling in Newark "became known as the Newark Ashram, after Gandhi's Ashram."[18]

The Newark Ashram—christened "the Newark Christian Colony" by Dellinger—thrived, as did the Harlem experiment, becoming a center of community service and inner-city activism. At any given time, five to seven additional volunteers lived and worked at the ashram with the three friends. Benedict, Dallas, and Dellinger ran a Bible school five days a week, organized after-school programs for children, and, over the summer, worked alongside a church staff of twenty people at Jube to plan various neighborhood support activities, such as painting houses and distributing food. They even rented a farm in northern New Jersey and transported families and children there aboard buses to escape the city for a while to work and play outdoors. The activities at the ashram went more smoothly than expected, but to the chagrin of its participants, a lack of money occasionally hindered the experiment. To finance the ashram, Benedict, Dallas, and Dellinger had to find part-time employment.

Living at the Newark Ashram was simultaneously painful and exhilarating. The constant pressure of simply running the experiment, coupled with commuting to New York City, taking courses at Union, and working part-time jobs left the three seminarians exhausted. There was nothing romantic about the poverty that pervaded Newark's neighborhoods, and such conditions challenged the faith of even the most idealistic Christian activists. Still, living and working in Harlem and Newark strengthened the three men's commitment to working with the poor, and it gave Dellinger a "better education than I got at Yale, Oxford, or Union."[19] As rewarding as it was, however, the Newark experiment could not last. The seminarians did not have the foresight in the spring and summer of 1940 to anticipate that the Newark Ashram would eventually become another casualty of the war.

"The fact which dominates our world is the fact of armed aggression, aimed at the form of government, the kind of society that we in the United States have chosen and established for ourselves," President Franklin D. Roosevelt told the American people on July 19, 1940.[20] Roosevelt was, of course, referring to the rise of Adolf Hitler in Germany and the increasing militarism in Japan. Anticipating war, heated debates about initiating a peacetime draft pitted isolationists against liberal, antifascist interventionists. The passage of the Burke-Wadsworth Bill in Congress in June 1940 introduced the first peacetime draft in American history. Unlike the Conscription Law of 1917, the Burke-Wadsworth Bill—also known as the Selective Service Act of 1940—recognized religious objection as a legitimate reason for legal conscientious objection status. With the passage of the bill in both chambers of Congress, the tide began to turn against isolationism.

The absence of widespread public protest against conscription underscored the dismal state of the once-thriving peace movement in America. The movement declined as a result of internal conflicts, a lack of overarching goals, a diminishing stream of volunteers, and a divided and vacillating leadership. More than any other issue, the struggle against fascism in Spain had caused pacifists to reevaluate their commitment to nonviolence. Despite the ebb in antiwar activities, advocates of overseas intervention approached conscription cautiously. Until the Burke-Wadsworth Bill was introduced in Congress in June 1940, opinion polls repeatedly indicated strong public misgivings about conscription.[21]

Some pacifists stayed the course. A small group of students at Union Theological Seminary took turns writing and editing an antiregistration statement to be signed by students. These students stood to lose a great deal by their actions. As long as they registered for the draft, the liberal terms of the Selective Service Act of 1940 allowed clergy and seminarians to accept deferments excusing them from military service. The authors of the antiregistration statement at Union were aware of the terms of the conscription law and understood that if they registered, they would be exempted from being drafted into the armed services. But instead they refused to register, declaring it to be an illegitimate exercise of authority. The leaders of the antiregistration effort were Howard Spragg, president of the senior class at Union, and students George Houser, Don Benedict, and David Dellinger.

Howard Spragg, born and raised in Massachusetts, moved to New York City and began his studies at Union Theological Seminary in the fall of 1938. He planned to pursue a career in the Christian ministry and stayed active in the Congregational Church. Like his pacifist classmates, Spragg's radicalization owed much to conditions in the Great Depression. While volunteering in the cotton mills of Alabama and the mining towns of Harlan County, Kentucky, he encountered some of the worst living conditions in the United States.[22] "My sympathies were socialist," he explained, "Norman Thomas socialist." He found a network of "kindred souls" at Union Theological Seminary, and when he was not doing his fieldwork at a Hungarian settlement house in Yonkers, he organized a local branch of the radical Workers Defense League and picketed against the anti-Semitic speeches of the Brooklyn-based Irish American fascist Joe McWilliams.[23]

Spragg, Dellinger, and Benedict together wrote the initial statement against draft registration and then circulated it among the other students. George Houser, a senior at Union, took a keen interest in the effort. Born in 1916, Houser moved from place to place with his Methodist missionary family, living in Ohio, New York, California, and overseas in China and the Philippines. He finally settled in Colorado with his parents to attend the University of Denver, where he assembled a mix of Gandhian, antifascist, and left-wing Christian views. He began his studies at Union in 1938, and in June 1940 he read about the draft in the *New York Times* and concluded, "We were going to have to face it. So, I remember doing some thinking in isolation."[24] Houser concluded that a bold act of resistance against conscription was necessary. "We met constantly," he recalled, "but it all happened in a fairly short period of time. We got back to seminary in mid-September and the first registration day was coming up on October 16."[25]

Houser edited and added to the original statement. Meredith Dallas also proposed various suggestions and changes. A welcome addition to the group of pacifist resisters was William Lovell, David's former Yale classmate and fellow Dwight Hall volunteer. Since graduating from Yale with Dellinger in the class of 1936, Lovell had moved to Cleveland, befriended Victor and Walter Reuther, and spent a few years as an organizer for the United Automobile Workers. He began his first year at Union in the fall of 1938, and two years later he joined his fellow pacifists in drafting the anticonscription statement. "There was a small group of us who were socialist pacifists," he explained, "and . . . our pacifist position was as much out of a socialist orientation as it was out of a pure Christian pacifist orientation."[26]

The Union pacifists finished their statement and began soliciting support from other students. Many expressed sympathy but refused to endorse the statement publicly. Most students simply ignored the effort or reasoned that they had nothing to worry about because they could receive a deferment. In the end, twenty Union Theological Seminary students signed the statement. They then submitted the statement, with the twenty signatures attached to it, to *The Christian Century*, a highly respected, nondenominational magazine of Christian theological thought. Established in 1884, *The Christian Century* seemed like an ideal choice to print the declaration. Theologians and Christian intellectuals across the country subscribed to it, and thus they would know the students' reasons for not registering. The editors agreed to print the statement. In the few weeks of quiet that followed the submission, the pacifist seminarians discussed the controversy their action was bound to generate. According to Don Benedict, "We talked in Newark about the draft, and . . . decided to go on living there, continuing to work with children and identifying ourselves with workers and lay people."[27]

The statement appeared in *The Christian Century* in October and touched off a debate and reaction even more intense than the pacifists had predicted. At the same time, the pacifists released the statement to the press on October 12. It opened with a simple preface: "We are a group of students at Union Theological Seminary. After much consideration and prayer, we have come to the conclusion that as Christians we should not cooperate with the government in any way in regard to the Selective Training and Service Act of 1940." The statement then outlined their position with regard to conscription and war. War, they reasoned, "is an evil part of our social order, and we declare that we cannot cooperate with it in any way." In all instances, the seminarians insisted, war violates the teachings of Jesus Christ, results in horrific death and destruction, and contributes to the rise of other, unforeseen evil forces in the future. The document treated conscription as a "totalitarian" practice that eliminated the individual's option of obeying higher moral laws. The signers acknowledged that by simply registering for the draft and remaining silent, they would receive deferments. Yet such silence would amount to a betrayal of their deepest Christian convictions, for it necessitated complicity with the "war machine" at a time when other young men were being sent overseas to fight. By contrast, building a nonviolent movement for social justice that could oppose the "encroachments of militarism and fascism" would, in the long run, "show an increasing group of war-disillusioned Americans how to resist foreign Hitlers."[28]

At Union Theological Seminary, the administration responded swiftly and decisively to the statement. Union President Henry Sloane Coffin, seminary officials, and faculty members tried to persuade the signers to disassociate themselves from the effort. Reinhold Niebuhr met with each one individually behind closed doors and declared their effort to be foolhardy, even though he admired the spirit in which it was undertaken. The Union administration brought in influential public figures, including the civil libertarian Roger Baldwin, the eminent theologian Harry Emerson Fosdick, and the nationally syndicated radio pacifist Ralph Sockman, to try to convince the seminarians not to resist the draft. Dellinger remembered that "at least a dozen horrified peace leaders rushed to Union to get us to change our mind."[29] In the meantime, the telephones rang constantly with calls from newspapers and newsreel makers. George Houser noted: "Our intended action became a major news story: headlines in the press, top billing in the movie house newsreels, massive radio coverage. One of my aunts was shocked to learn of our action when the news came on at a theater in Florida."[30]

Determined to derail the protest, Coffin intensified the pressure by sending telegrams to the parents of the protesting seminarians spelling out the possible perils their children faced. A typical telegram read: "Your son . . . has signed a statement that he will not register next Wednesday under the Selective Service Act. The penalty for such an offense may be five years in prison. I have been unable to deter him. Can you prevent this tragedy?"[31] Coffin also threatened to reveal the names of protesters to their hometown newspapers as a way of publicly humiliating their families. "I never forgave Henry for that," Howard Spragg admitted almost a half century later.[32] Intense pressure from the Union administration began having an effect. A dozen signers rethought their decision and removed their names from the statement. Only eight refused to succumb to the pressure.

The Union Eight, as they came to be known, were Don Benedict, Joe Bevilacqua, Meredith Dallas, David Dellinger, George Houser, William Lovell, Howard Spragg, and Richard Wichlei. Their parents' reactions to the news varied. "I remember somebody asking my mother what she thought about it," said Lovell, "and she said, 'Well that's what he's been taught all his life.' She and my father were both supportive."[33] George Houser explained, "My mother was emotionally disturbed and saddened. My father stood up and took a courageous position as minister of the Trinity Methodist Church at the time preaching in support of us."[34] When Howard Spragg's father received the telegram from Henry Sloane Coffin, he wrote a short note to his son: "I have this telegram from Dr. Coffin. Do what you think is right."[35] Don Benedict's parents had mixed feelings about their son's actions but continued to offer him love and emotional support. "My mother had some understanding from a Christian background and could understand it. . . . I think my dad didn't really understand it, but [his attitude was] it's your life and you . . . make your own decisions."[36]

Of the eight seminarians, David Dellinger faced the most resistance from his parents. When Raymond Dellinger heard about David's actions, he panicked. He telephoned his son and threatened to kill himself if David persisted with the protest. Raymond frantically asked, "What would people in Wakefield think? How will my friends and family and associates take this?"[37] "Dave's father I remember particularly," Houser said. "And I remember Dave discussing it. His mother talked about having a heart attack over it; his father talked about committing suicide. He was subjected to that kind of pressure."[38] Don Benedict recalled "Dave's father threatening to kill himself over this. And Dave didn't take those threats lightly."[39] Bill Lovell was with Dellinger during his painful telephone conversation with his parents. "Dave's father said he'd commit suicide. He never did, of course."[40] David spent a few hours on the telephone trying to convince his father not to commit suicide. "I did my best to comfort and reassure him, but he said that he would not hang up until I promised to register; if I hung up, he would kill himself immediately. We talked for what must have been an hour or more before the crisis finally passed."[41] Shaken by the confrontation with his father and with no support from his family, Dellinger persisted with his protest.

At Union Theological Seminary, the local draft board set up tables at all the entrances to give the students a convenient place to register for the draft. The eight draft resisters passed by the tables each day. Simply signing on the dotted line would enable them to avoid imprisonment. "As a divinity student I was exempt from everything except registering," Dellinger explained. But he could not bring himself to do it. He regarded signing the Selective Service registration form as "acquiescence in a policy I abhorred. I did not want to accept a privileged exemption while others from a different class background or lacking a religious orientation would have to bear the burdens of conscription then and war later."[42] But he had misgivings about his actions. "You know I have always felt close to the men and boys who have gone off to war during my lifetime," he confided years later in a letter to a friend. "World War II was the hardest one for me not to fight in." In any case, he expressed "support and solidarity" with the GIs that fought in the war, "despite the different paths we took."[43]

The eight students of Union Theological Seminary who refused to register for the draft by the deadline of Wednesday, October 16, 1940, appeared in the U.S. District Court in Manhattan on October 21 to face indictment. A few days before their arraignment, they met with their attorney, Kenneth Walser, a Wall Street lawyer with pacifist sympathies. The news was not good, Walser told the eight seminarians. They could expect to do time in a federal penitentiary, perhaps many years. As Don Benedict explained, "He pointed out something that had not occurred to any of us. Our joint signing of the letter indicating our intentions opened us to a possible conspiracy charge that carried a maximum sentence of forty-three years rather than the five years maximum for draft violation."[44] In the days between the October 16 registration deadline and the October 21 indictment, the eight were warned by the U.S. Attorney's Office and the grand jury to lawfully register or else face the consequences.[45] They refused, remaining unshakable in their resolve, and appeared in front of the New York County grand jury for their arraignment on October 21 in ebullient spirits, eating sandwiches and talking. The indictments stated that each defendant "unlawfully, willfully and knowingly failed and neglected to present himself for and submit to registration as required by provisions of" the Selective Service Act of 1940. All eight men pleaded guilty to the charges, which carried a maximum sentence of $10,000 and five years in prison.[46] The media blitz that followed the arraignment jolted the seminarians. As George Houser recounted, "It hit the headlines. I was not used to this sort of thing. The press was all over it. Our pictures were everywhere."[47] Newspapers and newsreels regularly updated the story. Some family members and notable figures continued to pressure the seminarians to relent, but to no avail. Even though Union Theological Seminary publicly declared that the eight would not be expelled, Coffin privately made veiled threats. "When we did take the stand we did, we were kind of outlaws," Meredith Dallas recalled.[48]

Despite the thorough media coverage, the actions of the eight seminarians failed to immediately touch off a widespread antidraft movement in the United States. In New York State, five other objectors who refused to register by the October 16 deadline—all leftist pacifists like the Union Eight—received prison sentences ranging from eighteen months to two years.[49] From across the country came reports of several isolated, individual, acts of draft resistance. Even though the Union Eight's actions had little effect, a small but committed number of objectors did resist conscription before and during World War II.

The Union Eight seminarians tried their best to retain a semblance of normality before going to prison. In Newark, the ashram had a rare happy moment in late October when Meredith Dallas married his college sweetheart, Willa, in a small ceremony attended by friends and a few family members, including Dave Dellinger and Don Benedict. Meredith and Willa had met at Albion College, and during the fall of 1940 he proposed to her and she accepted. "It was a couple of weeks before I went . . . into prison. . . . We knew we were going to be married," Dallas recalled, so they hurriedly wed after the arraignment.[50]

On the morning of November 14, 1940, the eight defendants arrived at the courthouse in New York City wearing their finest suits, surrounded by journalists, newsreel cameras, and photographers. "The courtroom was crowded," observed a *New York Herald* reporter, filled with a "sad-faced and hushed" audience.[51] Among the observers that morning were Dellinger's despondent parents. The seminarians appeared before Judge Samuel Mandelbaum, and each read a short statement explaining his reasons for not registering. Defendant Joe Bevilacqua, from Buffalo, New York, summed up their legal position in his statement:

> We want to identify ourselves not with a selected group of men or class of people, but with the vast majority . . . who have come to feel that war is a definite evil and that any step taken towards war . . . should be met at the very beginning with firm opposition. Knowing that in the eyes of the law I have violated a man-made act, I expect to receive the penalties which it entails and ask for no leniency whatsoever.[52]

Mandelbaum listened attentively, not wanting to send the eight men to prison but legally having no other choice. "They all knew that Judge Mandelbaum wanted to set them free, if only they would at last comply with the law," noted a *New York Times* reporter.[53]

Judge Mandelbaum could have convicted the eight men under the harsh conspiracy charges about which Walser warned them at their pretrial legal meeting, but he opted instead for leniency. U.S. attorney Thomas Cahill reminded Mandelbaum that the defendants were exempt from military service under the draft and that all they had to do was register. The Selective Service Act of 1940 included special provisions for conscientious objectors, a status for which the eight divinity students could have applied. Draft officials pressed the young men right up until their sentencing date to comply with the law and informed them that not doing so would have grave consequences. "They have, however, persisted," Cahill said, "and they continue to persist in their refusal to register."[54]

Defense attorney Kenneth Walser emphasized the sincerity and character of each defendant. They were among the brightest students at the finest seminary in the nation, he pointed out, and serving time in prison for a felony crime could "ruin their careers in the church." Stopping to survey the eight young men sitting silently in the courtroom, Walser turned to Judge Mandelbaum and launched into an impassioned plea. "The trouble with them is that some time ago each one of them heard the call to promote the teachings of Jesus Christ. . . . They believe those teachings to mean what they say, and they find in them instructions to have nothing to do with that mass killing which is called war."[55] After the arguments, Judge Mandelbaum praised the eight defendants as "fine young men" but warned that the United States was in a "state of national emergency" and that resisting the draft would only make matters worse. He imposed sentences of a year and a day in federal prison for each defendant, the minimum length of a felony sentence, to be carried out at the new federal correctional institution in Danbury, Connecticut. "Some of the girls and older women in the courtroom wept," the *New York Times* reported, "and one elderly man, who carried a book stuffed with tracts, was heard to say: 'Another triumph for Hitler.'"[56]

Newspapers across the country carried wire service reports of the trial. Often accompanying the print coverage was a widely circulated photograph of the eight seminarians, all plainly visible in their suits and overcoats seated in the back of a police paddy wagon. An Associated Press photographer snapped the picture just as the men were about to be transported to the federal detention center in Manhattan. Reactions to the fate of the protesting seminarians were mixed. Predictably, Henry Sloane Coffin expressed frustration and regret over their decision.

> On behalf of the seminary let me say that we are sad at heart that these young men, whose Christian characters and devotion we admire, have persisted in their defiance of the law. . . . One hopes that having made their positions clear, they will see that no further purpose can be served by persisting in this course.[57]

Their harshest critic, Reinhold Niebuhr, lambasted their decision in his correspondence with various pacifist friends. "I have every appreciation for the integrity of our eight young men," he wrote to one associate, "but I do not see how they can be helped when in effect they courted martyrdom in the hope that their situation would start a general movement in the country."[58] Newspaper editorials typically inveighed against the actions of the seminarians, dismissing them as unlawful and rash. The *Chicago Daily News* blamed the "ignorant teachers" at Union for failing to properly teach the young seminarians about world events and concluded, "Pacifism is simply out with the American people."[59] The *New York Herald Tribune* emphasized the threat of civil disobedience to the survival of the republic while a perilous war raged overseas. The "logical upshot" of the eight men's actions "is anarchy," the *Herald Tribune* proclaimed. "The state has no recourse . . . but to exercise its police powers."[60] The religious press was somewhat more inclined to be sympathetic, as evidenced by a headline in the *Rocky Mountain Churchman* of Colorado: "Students Reproduce New Acts of Apostles."[61]

The Union Eight languished for a week in New York City's West Street Federal Detention Headquarters, nicknamed "West Street," located on Eleventh Street near the Hudson River. Numerous conscientious objectors were processed through West Street before being transferred to a federal prison, usually Danbury in Connecticut, Lewisburg in Pennsylvania, or Ashland in Kentucky. The eight new prisoners shared cells with felons from New York's notorious Murder, Inc., an organized crime outfit whose key members had recently been netted in a citywide police crackdown. Among the prisoners at West Street was the notorious boss of Murder, Inc., Louis Lepke, at the time awaiting execution. At first, the mobsters did not know what to make of the pacifists, but in time they developed a grudging respect for the unwavering nonviolence of their new cellmates. "I'm in jail for killing people but you are here for refusing to kill anyone. It doesn't make any sense," one of the hit men told David Dellinger.[62]

In the meantime, the eight resisters benefited from the aid of a small network of religious and pacifist organizations, most based in New York City. The Fellowship of Reconciliation (FOR), a Christian pacifist organization whose American offices first opened in 1915 in opposition to World War I, constantly offered assistance and encouragement. A. J. Muste, recently appointed as the executive director of FOR, had acquired a reputation by this time as the dean of American pacifism. Born in the Netherlands in 1885, Muste came to America at age six and had a long history of involvement in a variety of progressive Christian and labor causes. After being ordained a minister in the Dutch Reformed Church in 1909, Muste attended Union Theological Seminary and graduated in 1913. He protested America's entry into World War I, served as the director of Brookwood Labor College in Massachusetts throughout the 1920s, and briefly embraced revolutionary Trotskyism in the 1930s. He returned to radical Christian pacifism in 1936 after a solitary, deeply moving spiritual experience inside a European cathedral. A lanky figure usually seen at peace marches wearing an overcoat and fedora, Muste radiated warmth and listened carefully to the ideas and suggestions of other people, particularly those with whom he disagreed. He fully understood the extent of Hitler's ferocity and determination to conquer the world yet insisted that pacifists must maintain a nonviolent approach to solving violent conflicts. The challenge of pacifism, he said, was to offer an alternative to the warfare and barbarism that in 1940 seemed to be engulfing the world. The advocate of nonviolence must be prepared to resist "the divine foolishness, to break the evil spell that is on mankind" and to "lay down . . . [his] arms." At a Sunday Quaker worship meeting in 1940, Muste proclaimed, "If I can't love Hitler, I can't love at all."[63]

Muste and pacifist Evan Thomas drafted a statement on behalf of FOR supporting the eight jailed men. In addition, in his capacity as the executive secretary of FOR, Muste wrote a letter to David Dellinger on October 17 encouraging him to continue his draft resistance. Not registering for the draft, Muste told Dellinger, was "the patriotic and Christian" thing to do, even though critics of the Union Eight, including several pacifists, insisted that their actions were "injurious" to the peace movement. "Even if that were to be the case, and I don't think it will, you will still learn that in a moral universe great good always results when men stand unflinchingly by their convictions and act on them."[64]

The War Resisters League (WRL), a secular pacifist organization founded in 1923 to support conscientious objectors as well as nonviolent struggles for social justice, also backed the Union Eight. Frank Olmstead, the WRL's national chairman, called the eight men "the true heroes of this period" and declared that it would be "wise and just" for President Roosevelt to commute their prison sentences without delay.[65] Ernest Angell of the Committee on Conscientious Objectors, a group affiliated with the American Civil Liberties Union, called for leniency by pointing out that in Great Britain, "the maximum sentence for the non-registration of conscientious objectors is a fine of only five pounds."[66]

Such efforts made little difference. After one week of incarceration at West Street, the Union Eight were transferred to Danbury. Arriving to meet the eight prisoners in person was Edgar Gerlach, the new warden of Danbury and a former criminologist from the University of Michigan. Gerlach projected a "combination of solemn self-importance and fussy mannerisms," according to Don Benedict.[67] Late at night, the eight prisoners were loaded into the waiting cars without handcuffs or any sort of restraining device. Meredith Dallas sat next to Gerlach during the long drive and remembered: "I think he thought we were going to be his assistants in prison. We really turned out to be a big pain in the neck."[68]

Construction crews had recently completed work on FCI (Federal Correctional Institution) Danbury when the Union Eight arrived there shortly after 3 A.M. on November 21, 1940. Warden Gerlach, a devout liberal, boasted that Danbury epitomized the most advanced reform accommodations in the U.S. Bureau of Prisons. He preferred to call Danbury a "correctional institution" rather than a prison. The prison grounds had no walls. Instead, the architects had designed the facility to be built as a quadrangle, with its four massive wings enclosing the prison grounds, making escape impossible. Warden Gerlach relished telling the prisoners, "It's a privilege to be at an institution like Danbury."[69]

David Dellinger lay awake on his cot for hours on his first night at Danbury, unable to sleep. He had come a long way since his privileged upbringing in Wakefield and his years at Yale and Oxford. Just a few years earlier, he could have chosen a career with a level of prestige, wealth. and power far beyond the imaginings of his father. Now, at the age of twenty-five, Dellinger had fashioned for himself a life free of the material trappings, conspicuous displays of wealth, and overriding ambitions of his parents. "In prison," he noted, "the gloves were off, the comforting rhetoric and rationalizations were absent." From then on, David deliberately opted for a "life among the poor, without conventional financial security and as a nonviolent 'activist' for peace and justice—as I understand them and in accord with my chosen way of working."[70]

Dellinger and his fellow inmates adapted quickly to the rigors and routines of life in prison. The Union Eight performed a variety of jobs at Danbury. William Lovell tutored Warden Gerlach's son in Latin and other subjects. George Houser divided his time between acting as the chaplain's assistant and working in a shop that manufactured parachutes. Meredith Dallas served as a medic in the prison hospital. Donald Benedict and Dave Dellinger performed menial outdoor labor on a part of the prison grounds called "the farm." Within a few months, other war resisters arrived at Danbury, more than doubling the prison's population of conscientious objectors. Although the pacifists naturally gravitated toward one another, their radical socialist politics led them also to become acquainted with Danbury's broader prison population. "One of the impressions that I remember," explained William Lovell, "is that most us, perhaps all of us, had from our background a sense of being one with these other guys that were there."[71]

Warden Gerlach baffled the inmates. One moment he could be soft-spoken and sanctimonious, the next a rigid disciplinarian. "Gerlach was a pathetic kind of person," recalled Lovell, a "mildly schizophrenic . . . and deeply insecure" man.[72] The warden unhesitatingly administered harsh punishments, frequently sending prisoners to solitary confinement for even the slightest infraction. Dellinger discovered this the hard way on his first Saturday night at Danbury. Each Saturday evening, prisoners set up folding chairs in the gymnasium, and by seven o'clock the enormous room had filled with cheering inmates as guards wheeled a projector into the back of the room for a movie. Taking his seat for his first ever Saturday night at the movies, Dellinger made the mistake of sitting among the African American inmates on the right side of the gymnasium. "I was new and it wasn't part of an organized protest," he explained, "just sitting next to someone I had been talking with when we walked in." A guard approached him and informed him that "this section is for 'colored' prisoners. You'll have to move." Dellinger refused, stating that he preferred to remain in his seat. The guard ordered him a second time to move, and Dellinger again refused.[73]

For his obstinacy, the guards placed Dellinger inside solitary confinement, which was nicknamed the "Hole" by prison staff and inmates. The maximum stay in solitary confinement at Danbury was ten days. Located on the top floor of the maximum-security wing, each cell in the Hole measured five by eight feet, with nothing inside except a porcelain toilet bowl. When the door closed on Dellinger, complete blackness enveloped him. "It was entirely black," he recounted, "and you lost your sense of time."[74] At night, guards stuffed a single wool blanket through sliding slot at the bottom of the door, and returned to collect it early the next morning. Dellinger did what he could to keep from becoming too stiff. In the darkness, he performed a daily regimen of push-ups, sit-ups, jogging in place, pacing the short length of the cell, and stretching his muscles. A few times a day, a prisoner named Hudson entered the cell, accompanied by a guard, to bring David his meals, which often consisted of porridge or sandwiches made with stale bread and served with cold coffee. Inside the Hole, Dellinger lost all sense of time. Minutes felt like hours, and vice versa. Sometimes a single day seemed to last forever, and other times a week passed astonishingly fast. Dellinger sat on the toilet for hours, his elbows resting on his knees, his back hurting due to the lack of support, and his thoughts drifting all over the place. Occasionally he swayed in and out of consciousness while sitting in the darkness or lying on the cold, hard ground.

One morning, the heavy iron door of Dellinger's solitary confinement cell clanked open. In the blinding light of the doorway stood the silhouette of a prison guard, who informed David it was time to return to his cellblock. Dazed, bewhiskered, and reeking of body odor, Dellinger hobbled out of the Hole, showered and shaved, and returned to his daily routine. He revisited the Hole several more times. A few weeks after his first stay in solitary, a prison guard performing a routine inspection of the cells protested that David had made his bed incorrectly. The guard angrily stripped off the bedclothes, tossed them into a pile on the cell floor, and ordered David to remake it "like a soldier." David calmly refused and ended up in solitary confinement again for his resistance. For hours, he sat in the darkness, cross-legged on the floor, leaning back against the wall, or sometimes on the toilet. He had seen men crack under the pressure from spending too much time in the Hole. He would never forget hearing one prisoner, nicknamed "Tough Tony," who "was supposed to be a hit man for the Mafia," suffering a nervous breakdown as a result of staying in solitary too long. The guards escorted the screaming, sobbing inmate out of the Hole in the middle of the night and delivered him to the mental ward. But most of the prisoners returning from solitary confinement appeared morose and defeated. "From then on they had a haunted, hunted look that I'll never forget," Dellinger later wrote. "It wasn't just that they couldn't look the guard in the eye, they couldn't look anyone in the eye, not even themselves—like dogs that have been beaten until they are broken."[75]

Prison officials at Danbury did what they could to break Dellinger's spirit. At one point, Warden Gerlach sent a telegram to his parents indicating that their son was ill and on the verge of a nervous breakdown. It was a lie, yet it brought them down from Wakefield to see their son, who spent hours convincing them that he was all right. On other occasions, the guards threatened that if he did not "straighten up," he would not "get out of prison alive."[76] Like Dellinger, Donald Benedict went to the Hole several times for various acts of resistance and grew despondent as a result of the blackness and the absence of sounds, fresh air, and human contact. "It is not true that one can think in solitary," he remembered. "Or, rather, one cannot trust one's thinking here, which is far worse. There is nothing to hear or look at, the emptiness seems to swallow up deliberate thought."[77]

As a result of the weeks he spent in the Hole, David Dellinger developed a fearlessness that in later years helped him maintain a calm demeanor in the face of unrelenting adversity. He took solace in his ability to endure one of the most severe punishments imposed on Danbury prisoners. He even once experienced an inexplicable wave of euphoria in the Hole, accompanied by a critical awakening. He claimed that one day he suddenly "died" in the Hole. As Dellinger put it, "There is no way to describe it except to say that I died. I faced my own death and embraced it. . . . I had faced the worst, had decided to continue in the direction that life was taking me and suddenly, unaccountably, I was free."[78]

Following each visit to the Hole, Dellinger returned to the general prison population and resumed his regular work schedule. Regimented routines and long periods of boredom characterized much of his stay at Danbury. When not working, David had plenty of time to read and meditate in his cell. During his outdoor recreation periods, he walked briskly around the yard or played sports with the other inmates. He always carefully considered his next act of protest, and over meals in the crowded dining hall he counseled his fellow war resisters to remain hopeful. The pacifists "did things together as a group, we were in touch with each other," remembered George Houser. "We wrote statements of protest to the prison bureau, to the warden, and we would co-sign these things. I often wrote them because . . . I was the chaplain's assistant, and I had use of the office. He was there only three days a week."[79] Eventually Dellinger and the other radical pacifists tried, with limited success, to organize prisoners' "councils," which would give inmates a small taste of democracy by enabling them to elect leaders who would collectively bargain on their behalf. William Lovell remembered the pacifists drawing up designs "for an inmate council and got a number of the other inmates to support us in it, and we took it to the warden, tried to get somewhere, and didn't get anywhere with him particularly."[80]

Warden Gerlach ignored all the war resisters' statements, manifestos, petitions, and correspondence. The futility of all their attempts to air their grievances, along with the dehumanization of prisoners at Danbury, left the imprisoned pacifists deeply discouraged. Resisting racial segregation and authoritarian prison policies was their shared aim, yet recruiting new allies to their cause proved to be difficult.

The scores of Jehovah's Witnesses who entered Danbury in late 1940 and early 1941 as draft resisters rejected the radical pacifists' leftist antiwar politics. The few Communist Party members imprisoned in Danbury initially impressed the radical pacifists with their stirring denunciations of war and U.S. "imperialism." But after the German invasion of the Soviet Union on June 22, 1941, they changed their position. Following the invasion, Communists advocated preparedness, proclaimed the need to protect "democracy" overseas, and distanced themselves from the pacifists. As Dellinger was collecting trash one day, a few Communist inmates spat at him and called him a "fascist." Shortly after June 22, the labor organizer and Communist Party member Joe Winogradsky remarked to George Houser, "Well, I'm against you guys now."[81]

Most of the Danbury inmates simply steered clear of all forms of trouble. Danbury is a minimum-security institution, and it has always had a reputation as the "country club" of American prisons. At that time, the overwhelming majority of prisoners served relatively short sentences for minor felonies and cooperated with prison authorities in the hopes of cutting their stay short. Thus persuading the average Danbury prisoner to participate in protest activities was a losing proposition.

Still, the radical pacifists discovered other ways of nurturing camaraderie with their fellow prisoners. Most of the pacifist inmates at Danbury participated in athletics, which the warden encouraged. A sports lover, Gerlach placed an especially high priority on creating a victorious softball team. The prison grounds had a baseball diamond, complete with bleachers, and several of the pacifists, including Spragg, Dellinger, Houser, Dallas, and Benedict, played on the team. Danbury Correctional Institution joined a league that pitted their team against softball teams around the region. Private businesses, municipalities, local colleges and seminaries, fire and police stations, churches, and community organizations sponsored players for the opposing softball teams. A winning softball team served a vital function at Danbury. It boosted the morale of the prisoners and staff, created a sense of community within the prison, and provided an opportunity for the inmates to prove their talents on the diamond.

After the Union Eight arrived, Gerlach discovered that Donald Benedict had pitched baseball and softball for years in a variety of leagues. Now Benedict's lifelong dream of playing for the big leagues yielded unanticipated returns. Gerlach allowed Benedict to leave work early each day to practice pitching and ordered the guards to avoid abusing the pacifist. As Howard Schoenfeld explained, "The prison team, built around Benedict's pitching, was tied for first place in its league, and his ability to hold the opposition scoreless had placed it there."[82] Being the star pitcher for Danbury's softball team elevated Benedict to near-mythical status in the prison, and inmates turned out by the hundreds to watch him pitch at games.

Unbeknownst to the prison authorities, the pacifists planned an act of resistance during one of the most important games of the softball season. On April 12 they declared a work stoppage to show their support for the International Student Peace Day. Although the Peace Day had diminished in size and scope since its heyday in 1935, scattered nonviolent activists around the country still celebrated it. The Danbury pacifists announced their plans ahead of time, causing a stir within the prison administration. Warden Gerlach assembled all the prisoners at Danbury in the yard, and he pointed to dust on his trousers and said he had been on his knees praying for them. The pacifists had been treated exceptionally well, he said, and he warned that a strike would jeopardize the efforts of prison officials to modernize and liberalize Danbury. "If they carry out this threat I will be forced to take away all yard privileges for inmates—also Ping-Pong, softball, movies, and library privileges."[83] The pressure intensified when James V. Bennett, superintendent of the U.S. Bureau of Prisons in Washington, D.C., visited Dellinger in Danbury in an effort to persuade him to call off the work stoppage. Bennett targeted Dellinger as the "ringleader" of the pacifists.

"Dellinger, the American prison system is the most authoritarian institution in the world," Bennett warned him, "and if you don't straighten up and obey every order that it gives you, no matter what it is, the full weight of that system will come down on you."[84]

Bennett's talk failed to dissuade Dellinger, so Warden Gerlach took decisive action. In a preemptive move, the prison disciplinary board sentenced the pacifists to one month in solitary confinement before their proposed disruption even began. From time to time, Warden Gerlach allowed Benedict, whose formidable pitching skills were indispensable, to leave the Hole to pitch for the Danbury softball team. Two weeks into his month-long sentence, the captain of the guards arrived to escort Benedict to one of the most important games of the season, which would determine Danbury's standing in the league.[85] But Benedict refused to play unless the warden released all the prisoners from solitary confinement, not just the pacifists, and excused them from serving the rest of their sentences. At first, the irate captain of the guards refused, slamming the door on Benedict. The game began in the late morning, and the captain repeatedly returned to Benedict's cell with counteroffers. Benedict refused each time, sticking to his original demand. Finally, during the bottom of the fourth inning, with all the prisoners in the bleachers chanting "We want Benedict!" the warden relented and agreed to Benedict's demands.[86]

The disheveled prisoners emerged from two weeks in the Hole and fanned out to their places on the baseball field while the audience cheered in the inmate stands. "Benedict . . . summoned the strength after the long weeks of demoralized living," wrote Howard Schoenfeld, "and, in a superhuman and prodigious performance, pitched batter after batter out, enabling the prison team to rally and score, and win the series."[87] Immediately after the game, Warden Gerlach ordered the inmates from the Hole to return to solitary confinement, leaving the perplexed prisoners wondering why he reneged on his deal. Prison guards escorted Benedict, Dellinger, and the other inmates from solitary confinement back to their dark cells. A few hours later, the guards led the men from the Hole to the mess hall for dinner, where hundreds of prisoners awaited, banging their cups on the tables and enthusiastically chanting Benedict's name.

Deafening cheers greeted the unkempt solitary inmates as they entered the mess hall. Guards attempted to restore order, but to no avail. This stirring moment belonged to Donald Benedict, although later

Dellinger jokingly took partial credit for his friend's glory: "I always claim that I saved the no-hitter for him by sliding on my chest and catching a sinking liner that would have scored the winning runs for the other team. Of course it's not true."[88] The frenzied crowd of prisoners applauded Benedict, patted him in the shoulder, shook his hand, embraced him, and one inmate placed a baseball cap on his head. For the young man from a small town in Michigan who entertained dreams of playing in the major leagues, it was a poignant moment. Howard Schoenfeld surveyed the immense crowd and later suggested that the outburst amounted to more than a simple celebration of a softball game victory. "A mass catharsis of human misery was taking place before our eyes," he wrote. "Some of the men were weeping, others were laughing like madmen. It was like nothing I had ever seen before, and nothing I expect to see again."[89]

On September 3, 1941, the Union Eight walked out of the Danbury Federal Correctional Institution as free men. The prison authorities shaved two months off the end of their sentences for good behavior. Before their release, Danbury gave each one a prison-made suit and ten dollars. Warden Gerlach met with the prisoners before their departure and asked each man to sign a card. The card, it turned out, was a draft registration form, and none of the men signed it. Gerlach warned that not signing it subjected them to another term in prison, but the eight men took their chances. There were no journalists or newsreel cameras to greet them at the front gates. Much had changed in the intervening nine and a half months since they arrived at Danbury, and the press now ignored the pacifists.

Months earlier, Henry Sloane Coffin had visited Danbury and brought with him a letter offering the eight young men readmittance to Union Theological Seminary if they promised to avoid "any course of action which would bring similar publicity" to their draft resistance.[90] The former seminarians rejected Union's conditions. Five of them—Joe Bevilacqua, George Houser, William Lovell, Howard Spragg, and Richard Wichlei—went instead to Chicago Theological Seminary, where they received support and encouragement from its president, Albert W. Palmer. The remaining three, Benedict, Dallas, and Dellinger, returned to the Newark Ashram to continue their community work.

The trial and imprisonment of the Union Eight was a watershed in David Dellinger's life. Doing time in Danbury amounted to a baptism by fire that sealed his fate as an activist. The lessons he learned in prison guided him through an often turbulent and challenging life of radical resistance. He formed his first lifelong friendships with his fellow imprisoned seminarians, forging a bond that continued well into his old age. Theirs had been an act of moral witness, a means of speaking truth to power, to borrow one of Dellinger's favorite Quaker expressions. In a world marching headlong into an apocalyptic world war, their act of refusal represented a desperate, existential plea for peace.

After leaving prison, David Dellinger returned to Newark and soon thereafter met and married his lifelong companion, Elizabeth Peterson. Their marriage underwent its first test early—in 1943—when David returned to prison, this time serving a sentence at Lewisburg Federal Penitentiary in Pennsylvania. Longer and more arduous than the Danbury stay, his ordeal at Lewisburg almost destroyed his marriage and, ultimately, his life.

4

"Conchies"

If I am accused of being too ambitious I shall plead guilty. If I am told that my dream can never materialize, I would answer "that is possible" and go my way. I am a seasoned soldier of nonviolence and I have evidence enough to sustain my faith. Whether, therefore, I have one comrade or more or none, I must continue the experiment.

Mohandas K. Gandhi

WORLD WAR II offered both challenges and opportunities to David Dellinger. The Japanese attack on Pearl Harbor on December 7, 1941, destroyed the last vestiges of isolationism and the Depression-era peace movement in America. Only small pockets of absolutist pacifists and scattered followers of the exiled Soviet revolutionary Leon Trotsky resisted the war, and they often were often reviled as "slackers" and "conchies" (a derisive nickname for conscientious objectors). But World War II only reinforced David Dellinger's devotion to nonviolence. In his view, the war's overwhelming popularity merely underscored the need to stay the course. Dellinger's wartime experiences also transformed his pacifist ideology, which gradually moved away from its Christian theological foundations to an increasingly secularized radicalism that dominated his political thinking for the remainder of his life. Although he did not abandon Christianity completely, he did broaden his outlook and find other sources of inspiration. His imprisonment at Lewisburg Federal Penitentiary in Pennsylvania from 1943 to 1945 hastened his metamorphosis into a nonviolent revolutionary. During the war, Dellinger also met, fell in love with, and married Elizabeth Peterson, initiating a lifelong relationship that had the dual effect of nurturing his activism and pressuring him to cut back on his commitments on order to spend time with his family.

■

Earlier, while he was in prison in FCI Danbury, David Dellinger had corresponded with his close friend Roy Finch. Their friendship dated back to when David was the graduate secretary of the Yale Christian Association in Dwight Hall, where the two first met. Three years younger than Dellinger, Finch was the son of a successful Wall Street investor.[1] Roy had felt the pull of pacifism in his youth. Although his brothers had joined the military as World War II drew closer, Roy's grandmother encouraged his intellectual nonconformity, and his deep commitment to Christianity buttressed his nonviolent outlook. As Margaret Finch, later his wife, remembered: "At one point, he almost became a monk. He always took religion with the utmost seriousness. If you were going to be a Christian, you should be a Christian as Christ would've been a Christian, and that involves saying no to war."[2] At Danbury, Dellinger confided his innermost thoughts to Finch, who covered the trial of the Union Eight for the *New York Herald Tribune*, writing stories sympathetic to the defendants.

Prison regulations required that inmates limit each letter to two pages and allowed only two letters per week to all correspondents. Prison, Dellinger wrote Finch, offered inmates security, routines, and "freedom from responsibility," but with those benefits came "a tendency to make us intellectually and spiritually lazy."[3] His correspondence with Finch showed that few matters absorbed more of Dellinger's attention than his upcoming release and plans to return to the Newark Ashram in the fall. He planned to start a volunteer seminary in Newark and wrote letters from inside Danbury to prospective teachers across the country encouraging them to come to the ashram for a free seminary, open to anyone who wished to participate.

Upon his release on September 3, 1941, along with Donald Benedict and Meredith Dallas, Dellinger returned to New Jersey. A handful of volunteers had kept the Newark Ashram alive while the three men served time in Danbury, but the experiment required Dellinger's charismatic personality to revive it. Once again, the ashram's residents offered shelter to transients, gathered food and clothing donations for distribution in the neighborhood, and collected enough money from David's parents and other supporters to buy a small farm in the New Jersey countryside. The Newark Ashram also hosted neighborhood dances, weekly guest lectures, and afternoon Bible study groups. At night, Benedict, Dallas, and Dellinger worked in a bakery to help finance the experiment, and soon residents from miles away began appearing at its events and attending Sunday services at the Jube Memorial Congregational Church. In the meantime, Dellinger established close ties with pacifists in New York City, including the radical Catholic activist Dorothy Day and her supporters in the offices of the leftist *Catholic Worker* magazine. Dellinger also befriended the pacifist Jay Holmes Smith, who oversaw a similar ashram in Harlem.[4] In the fall of 1941, after two months of living and working at the Newark Ashram, Benedict received an invitation from a friend, Bill Perkins, to move to Detroit to help create similar community outreach programs. Benedict accepted the offer and headed to Detroit, where he joined a group of activists who "settled down in a . . . mixed black and white community of working people."[5]

For months the communal experiment thrived. But in December, Dellinger emerged from Sunday services at Jube Memorial with other worshipers to hear the terrible news that Pearl Harbor, on the Hawaiian island of Oahu, had been bombed by the Japanese. Details were sketchy at first, suggesting death tolls in the thousands. The unprovoked attack struck battleship row at the naval base, various military targets, and two key airfields. Japanese planes bombed and strafed eight battleships, three destroyers, and three cruisers, killing 2,323 servicemen. Later, in 1943, Dellinger wrote down his thoughts about the Japanese attack in an unpublished essay. For years the Roosevelt administration had tacitly supported Japan's conquests, even assuming the role of silent partner in the Japanese invasion of China during the 1930s. Dellinger believed that the stringent embargoes that cut off the flow of oil, rubber, and steel to Japan, passed by Congress and supported by the president in the summer and fall of 1941, were intended to provoke Japan to strike against America, its chief competitor for hegemony in the Pacific.[6] He even supported the highly dubious claim that "the United States had broken the Japanese code," and "knew in advance when and where the Japanese attack would take place."[7]

Such views placed David Dellinger far outside the American mainstream, and even he was cautious about voicing them. The millions of Americans who claimed to be pacifists only six years earlier had dwindled to a dedicated few on the fringes of society. Indeed, even before the Japanese attack, the largest antiwar organization of the 1930s, the Keep America Out of War Congress, had declared bankruptcy and abandoned its offices.[8]

By abstaining from the war effort, Dellinger and other pacifists withdrew from the central event of their generation and thus forfeited any claim to be a part of America's struggle against Nazism, fascism, and Japanese military aggression. It was an agonizing decision, but Dellinger arrived at it long before the Japanese attacked Pearl Harbor. Engaging in the war effort, he believed, would be a renunciation of Christian nonviolence, which he regarded as sacrosanct. He conceded that Nazism was "a catastrophic evil that had to be resisted." But, he added, "it was also catastrophic for people who believed in human dignity to think that they could resist fascism under the leadership and by the methods of big business, big government and the military."[9]

Although American pacifists were horrified at the attack on Pearl Harbor, they still urged restraint. Organizations such as the War Resisters League (WRL) and the Fellowship of Reconciliation (FOR) issued statements opposing the war. But most pacifists understood that any prospects of preventing a war vanished after the Japanese attack on Pearl Harbor, and they had neither the public support nor the resources to mount an effective challenge against the war.

After the bombing of Pearl Harbor, Dellinger stepped up his efforts at the commune, working long, tiring days. News of friends and acquaintances being inducted into the armed services and shipped overseas discouraged him even more. As the Christmas season neared, David returned to Wakefield for an uneasy reunion with his family. His sisters Libby and Nancy had married successful businessmen, and Libby now had two sons. David's younger brother Fiske was a student at Swarthmore College near Philadelphia and planned to volunteer as an ambulance driver overseas for the American Field Service. It was an awkward gathering. The family carefully avoided all talk about the war and instead focused on their personal lives and gossip about relatives, particularly the North Carolina Dellingers.[10] The day after Christmas, Dellinger left Wakefield and traveled to the Student Christian Movement National Conference in Miami, Ohio, where he planned to deliver a speech on nonviolence and the war. It was a risky trip. His continued antiwar activism carried with it the threat of a second prison term, and Dellinger knew he "would be rearrested as soon as I made a speech at a major forum in favor of nonviolent resistance to U.S. militarism."[11]

At the Ohio conference, held during the last week of 1941 and first few days of 1942, Dellinger met Elizabeth Peterson and felt an instant rapport with her. Peterson, a vivacious and energetic twenty-one-year-old activist, had traveled from Oregon to take part in the event. A student at Pacific College in Newburgh, Oregon, she already was a self-proclaimed pacifist and a veteran of civil rights struggles. "David was my ideal. He believed in voluntary poverty, which was something I was coming to after working in a migrant camp one summer. And he believed in communal living, which I felt was closer to the original idea of Christian living." After Dellinger's speech, she introduced herself and requested an interview.[12]

Elizabeth Peterson was born in Fort Worth, Texas, on July 23, 1920, the second of Walter and Elizabeth Peterson's three children. "Since my mother's name was Elizabeth, everybody in my family called me Betty," she explained.[13] Her mother came from Texas, her father from a Swedish immigrant community in Minnesota. He had worked as a homesteader for a few years on his own land in Montana before moving to Chicago before World War I. Both he and his future wife, Elizabeth Hudson, were students at George Williams College in Chicago, but they dropped out, moved to Texas, married, and began having children. Their restlessness presaged a lifetime of frequent moves around the country. In Fort Worth, Walter worked at the local YMCA and Elizabeth at the YWCA, but they returned to Chicago in 1926 so they could finish their degrees at George Williams College in physical education. They left six-year-old Betty in Fort Worth for one year, where she lived with her grandmother and aunt during the first grade. "They left me with my grandmother because they thought that I wouldn't be safe after school, or being left alone a little bit in the apartment."[14] Betty finally joined them in the summer of 1927. My father "found a place for us in a very low-income area," Betty recounted, "near the north side of Chicago, which was Italian and German being replaced by blacks."[15] Upon graduation, her father received a call to serve at the Presbyterian Church in Bessamer, a small town in northern Michigan, near Wisconsin.

Because Betty's family moved so often, she did not establish deep roots in any particular community and therefore developed an instinctive sympathy for outcasts and people living on the periphery. "We moved a lot. I never was able to make good friends that I kept for the rest of my life. I always felt alone."[16] The frequent moves meant Betty went to three different universities: the University of Michigan in Ann Arbor, the University of Washington in Seattle, and Pacific College in

Oregon. Betty discovered pacifism in 1939 in Ann Arbor, when she met young men at the campus YMCA who vowed they would resist another war if it came. In Ann Arbor, she immersed herself in a local civil rights campaign, joining students and community activists who resisted segregation and inequality on campus and in the local Presbyterian church.

When the war began, Betty's older brother was already in the Navy and her younger brother joined the Army. Betty, by contrast, had evolved into a committed pacifist. She went to Miami, Ohio, after the Christmas holidays to find ways of increasing her involvement in antiwar work. At age twenty-one, Betty was still relatively inexperienced in both activism and men. "I really didn't have a boyfriend because I wasn't one of the fast girls. I was the minister's child, so therefore nobody asked me out for dates."[17]

Despite his athletic prowess and strikingly handsome features, David Dellinger did not have a long list of prior love interests either. Over the years he had dated but had avoided commitments, chiefly because he could not find the right companion. He had had no girlfriends at Yale or Oxford or during his travels through Europe. His community activism in the late 1930s and early 1940s had exposed him to few women who shared his radical convictions. His first encounter with Betty was thus a revelation. "Something in that first brief meeting made my whole being want to get to know her whole being."[18]

After the conference, Betty returned to Oregon, and David went back to Newark. He began telephoning her from Jube Memorial Church, and within a few weeks he hitchhiked west to Oregon, where he picked up Betty to escort her to her parents' home in Seattle. It was late January 1942 when a motorist dropped them off in front of the Petersons' house near Puget Sound. Although Betty's mother was troubled by David's activism, Walter Peterson wholeheartedly supported and trusted his daughter. Walter had served as a chaplain in the U.S. Army during World War I and had pacifist sympathies. He instantly liked Dellinger. Although David asked Betty to return to Newark with him, she insisted they get married first. Rather than plan an elaborate wedding that both families could attend, the impatient couple decided to get married right away so that she could return to Newark with him. She recalled:

> My mother and father were surprised. . . . His mother and father were surprised too. And they were hurt because we didn't invite them to the

wedding. I had no idea anybody in that world could get on an airplane and fly across the country, that anybody would have the money to do that. He hid a lot from me before we got married. I didn't know he'd gone to Yale. I didn't know his family was very well off. I was mending his pants the day before we got married because there was a hole in the knee.[19]

On February 4, 1942, David Dellinger married Elizabeth Peterson at a modest gathering in Seattle, their ceremony performed by Walter Peterson. Betty's parents and a few friends attended, but commitments in the armed forces kept her brothers away. David and Betty spent their honeymoon in a cottage near the shore of Puget Sound. On February 7, David wrote to his friend Roy Finch:

> We will live, of course, at Newark in the project. I am very anxious for you and Betty to get acquainted. You will be very pleased. We expect an interesting trip back. We will take the bus a little ways over the mountains, then hitchhike. We shall keep moving but will not rush.[20]

David and Betty returned to Seattle to say good-bye to Betty's parents and boarded a bus bound for Utah. In Salt Lake City, they began hitchhiking, steadily making their way across wintry, wartime America. On the way they stopped in Chicago for a few days and stayed with some of David's Union Eight comrades. Rested and refreshed, they pressed eastward. Betty reached Newark, having never set foot anywhere east of Detroit. She could see Manhattan in the distance when a motorist dropped them off in neighboring New Jersey. "We walked the last few miles," David recalled, "bags and all, from where the last ride had let us off. By then we were physically exhausted."[21]

Living at the Newark Ashram demanded a drastic change of lifestyle for Betty. Her past involvement in community activism did not prepare her for the rigors of communal life. Even though David and Betty had their own room, they seldom were alone. Each person at the ashram helped with the cooking, cleaning, gardening, and home repairs. They ran a cooperative store, taught classes during the day, and took neighborhood children out to the ashram's farm in the countryside.

The Newark Ashram became a hotbed of radical pacifist organizing and a temporary residence for conscientious objectors on their way to prison. Dorothy Day visited occasionally; members of the War Resisters League met in the living room to discuss strategies; and draft evaders slept on couches and the floor. Agents from the Federal Bureau of Investigation also developed a keen interest in their activities. "The FBI was always floating around," remembered Meredith Dallas. "It got so we could spot them anywhere. The gabardine suits."[22] Occasionally the agents tipped off law enforcement officials, who arrested visitors and residents of the community. In July 1942 police picked up twenty-three-year-old William H. Sutherland Jr., an African American conscientious objector, while he was working at the ashram. Sutherland had grown up in a suburb of Newark. "My father was a dentist and so I had a fairly comfortable upbringing," he recounted.[23] He was first exposed to pacifist ideas during the Great Depression, while he was still in high school. The minister of his church, a white southerner, delivered impassioned sermons that moved Bill to embrace nonviolent activism. When he met David Dellinger at Christian youth conferences, Sutherland was a university student at Bates College in Maine in the late 1930s. "By that time he'd become a big shot in the movement and I was still something of a minor player," he explained.[24]

Unlike Dellinger, Sutherland cooperated with the draft, signing his Selective Service forms and submitting a request for conscientious objector status. But when the time came for him to report to one of the newly opened Civilian Public Service (CPS) camps where COs were expected to live in barracks and perform various types of war-related labor, he refused. Instead, he volunteered at the Newark Ashram, insisting that it more closely reflected his principles than the CPS camps did. Authorities arrested him in July after he had been there for about eight months. On July 20, Judge William J. Barker sentenced Sutherland to four years at Lewisburg Penitentiary in Pennsylvania.[25]

"I knew it was just a matter of time before they came for me," Dellinger remembered. "It was not a matter of *if*, but *when*."[26] The FBI and local police departments across America cooperated in the hunt for draft evaders, ultimately arresting thousands. In early 1943, authorities arrested Don Benedict, who was traveling back and forth between Newark and Detroit organizing community service activities in both cities.[27] At the same time Roy Finch received orders to report to a CPS camp in Coleville, California. Throughout the war FBI agents visited the offices of the War Resisters League in New York City more than 160 times, mainly searching for information about conscientious objectors.[28] At the Newark Ashram there was a "constant turnover" of volunteers "as the FBI came in and took us away," Bill Sutherland remembered.[29]

Dellinger could have assumed a lower profile. Remaining quiet and spending the war years in obscurity might have spared him a second prison sentence. Yet the appeal of political action was too strong. In the spring of 1942 he joined the War Resisters League and launched his own antiwar organization called the People's Peace Now Committee (PPNC). The PPNC encouraged U.S. government officials to look for alternative ways of achieving peace other than the unconditional surrender of America's enemies. The organization also called for a democratic socialist transformation of the postwar world and an end to "Jim Crowism and Anti-Semitism." A PPNC leaflet printed in 1943 stated: "Month after month the peoples of Europe and Asia are being shattered by mass bombing raids, deliberate starvation and total war. Peaceful Americans have been conscripted to help commit these acts of destruction."[30]

In addition to his antiwar work, Dellinger had an ongoing conflict with the local draft board in Newark. The board had notified him in October 1941 that he had been drafted into the military. Although he ignored the letter, the mail carrier continued to deliver follow-up notices for the next few months. As Dellinger later learned, the local draft board had acted on a registration form sent to them by Warden Edgar Gerlach of Danbury with Dellinger's forged signature on it. The board eventually received a letter from Dellinger explaining his reasons for refusing to serve: "My religious opposition to the whole war system, of which conscription is an obvious part, made it impossible for me to register or cooperate with the Selective Service Act. I have already served a sentence of one year and one day for this."[31] The board responded to Dellinger's letter by recommending that the federal government strip him of his citizenship. The board issued a statement proclaiming, "Cowards, slackers, and hypocrites, who hide behind so-called conscientious scruples, must be denied membership in a free society. We owe it to our fighting men and to those who are patriotically working for our preservation, to make an example of those who refuse."[32]

Another difficulty for Dellinger was his damaged relationship with his parents. At Betty's urging, the newlyweds went to Wakefield in the spring of 1942 to meet them. Betty was taken aback by the splendor of Dellinger's childhood home. Raymond Dellinger, by now the head of a large and profitable Boston law firm and chairman of the Greater

Boston United War Fund, warmly greeted Betty with hugs and good cheer, while Marie Dellinger was cordial yet somber.[33] A few days later they hitchhiked back to Newark. The Wakefield trip temporarily relieved the strained relationship, but afterward Betty inadvertently intensified the rift in the Dellinger clan. "I tried very hard to please them, but I upset his mother so much after my first visit. I wrote her a thank-you note on my stationery that had 'Betty Peterson' printed on it and she got so upset." Marie threw a fit and shouted, "Isn't Dellinger a good enough name for her?" Her angry reaction prompted Betty to change her last name to Dellinger. "I was going to keep my own name at the beginning of the marriage, but I . . . wanted her to like me."[34] Perhaps as a sign of reconciliation, Raymond and Marie visited the Newark Ashram on Easter Weekend in early April 1943. They were on their way back to Wakefield from a trip to Ohio, and they stayed a few days at both the ashram and the farm, joining in the Easter sunrise service with David and Betty.[35]

The authorities closely monitored the Newark Ashram. Residents of the commune drew attention to themselves by engaging in local civil rights and antiwar agitation, leafleting and picketing at segregated eating establishments, stores, movie theaters, and other public facilities. David "would go places to speak," remembered Betty, "and he would have to hitchhike. He would ride the freight trains and things like that that I wasn't ready to do."[36] On April 6, 1943, Dellinger attended a small PPNC rally outside the Capitol in Washington, D.C., and afterward participated in antiwar gatherings in Newark and New York City. In May, he received a letter from his local draft board ordering him to report for a physical examination, which he disregarded. Each day Betty feared federal agents would burst into the Newark Ashram to arrest David. On July 7, 1943, Meredith Dallas sent a telegram to George B. Reeves of the War Resisters League informing him that police had arrested David Dellinger for failing "to appear at a physical."[37]

Dellinger spent about a week in the Hudson County jail in New Jersey before being released on his own recognizance, but he knew that a longer prison sentence awaited him. On July 18, 1943, he sat down at a typewriter in the Newark Ashram and wrote a statement expressing his reasons for opposing the war. It began: "I believe that all war is evil and useless." Even wars of self-defense, he insisted, degenerate into horrific bloodbaths, in which the drive for vengeance leads to the wholesale destruction of cities, wanton massacres of civilians, and the creation of legions of orphans. War also "violates the life and teachings of Jesus," Dellinger reasoned, by ruining goodwill and mercy. On a purely practical level, World War I had failed to solve the world's problems. "Remember, the 'democracies' fought and won a violent war, from 1914 to 1918. But it achieved nothing—at tremendous cost." Dellinger encouraged the use of nonviolent methods such as strikes, civil disobedience, and passive resistance as a means of destabilizing tyranny. Although the current war might rid the world of Nazis and Japanese aggressors, the global conditions that had led to the rise of repression would remain unaltered, he cautioned. Unquestionably the most troubling element of Dellinger's statement was his emphasis on the Allies' responsibility for the hostilities. He blamed Nazi Germany and fascist Italy for the war by labeling them "dangerous Frankensteins," initially subsidized and underwritten by "British and American politicians and industrialists" who sought a European bulwark against Bolshevism. The United States, with its aggressive naval maneuvers against the Japanese navy, he maintained, had provoked Japan into attacking. Dellinger also insisted the Soviet Union had "poisoned" the "left-wing movement" around the world "with dishonesty, opportunism, and violence. This has aided fascism and violence everywhere." He concluded with a plea: "Each in his own way, let us search our hearts and purify our lives."[38]

In late July, Dellinger was sentenced to two years in prison at the Lewisburg Federal Penitentiary in Pennsylvania for violating the Selective Service Act of 1940. A few weeks later, a judge sentenced Meredith Dallas to four years at the Ashland Correctional Institution in Kentucky. Without Meredith Dallas and especially without Dellinger, the Newark Ashram quickly fell apart. According to Dallas, "David was our leader, really, even though he would've denied that he was."[39] Even before the arrests, the community had been beset by internal tensions. "Every man there was either on his way from prison or on his way to prison," Betty explained. "Every woman there was related to one of these men and had that sense of never knowing when it was going to happen."[40] At the end of 1943, the Newark Ashram closed. Privately, Betty Dellinger was distraught that her husband faced another prison sentence, but she managed to conceal her anxieties and offer David unconditional support. A few months before David's sentencing, Betty discovered she was pregnant with their first child.

■

The conscientious objectors of World War II included members of the three "peace churches" (Quakers, Church of Brethren, and Mennonites), black Muslims (including Nation of Islam leader Elijah Muhammad), and small numbers of Catholics and Jews. No single religion produced as many COs in World War II as did the Jehovah's Witnesses, who unsuccessfully sought ministerial exemptions from the draft and therefore refused to cooperate with the draft boards. During the war 4,441 Jehovah's Witnesses were convicted of violating the Selective Service Act,[41] but only a small percentage of conscientious objectors served time in prison. Approximately 25,000 COs entered the armed forces and were classified as 1-A-O, or "willing to take noncombatant military assignments."[42] Another 11,996 were sent to Civilian Public Service (CPS) camps across the country.[43] A joint creation of the Selective Service System and the historic peace churches, the CPS camps provided facilities where COs lived and performed menial labor for little or no remuneration. In 1940 the peace churches founded the National Service Board for Religious Objectors (NSBRO) as a liaison between the pacifists and the Selective Service System. The NSBRO oversaw a network of 151 CPS camps funded by a combination of philanthropic and government support. Conditions in CPS camps varied. Whereas some camps were rebellious, others housed COs who enthusiastically backed the war effort and allowed themselves to be used as human "guinea pigs" in medical tests to help the Allied cause.[44]

Acting on the basis of a complex mixture of religious, philosophical, and political motives, more than six thousand objectors refused to cooperate in any way with the Selective Service Act. They were sent to penitentiaries, correctional institutions, reformatories, and prison camps. Among them were Hopi Indians, whose spiritual traditions forbade violence, Japanese Americans who were outraged by the internment of their loved ones and friends, African Americans who were resisting Jim Crow segregation in the armed forces, and small numbers of disaffected Puerto Ricans who felt no loyalty to the war effort. Actual war resisters, like David Dellinger, were only a minority. The leftist objectors were either followers of Leon Trotsky, many of whom belonged to the Socialist Workers Party (SWP), or so-called radical pacifists. The leftists had gotten their start in the local, grassroots political struggles of the 1930s. They marched in antiwar rallies, organized workers in factories and mills, and performed church work in inner cities and impoverished rural areas. The radical pacifists believed that some sort of system of decentralized democratic socialism was preferable to the inequalities of capitalism or totalitarianism of Soviet communism. Unlike the communists, the radical pacifists found more inspiration in the Bible and Henry David Thoreau than in the writings of Karl Marx or Vladimir Lenin. Although the war resisters of World War II could be faulted for underestimating the evil of the Third Reich or the relentlessness brutality of Japanese militarism, their actions arose from humanitarian, Gandhian convictions. As CO Howard Schoenfeld observed: "They were the finest people I had ever known. Gathered up from everywhere they seemed to me to embody the conscience of America."[45]

The prison authorities, however, had a less celebratory view of the radical pacifists. James V. Bennett, director of the U.S. Federal Bureau of Prisons during World War II, had in mind the militant war resisters when he described the typical conscientious objector as a "problem child—whether at home, at school or in prison. . . . Many members of this group come from respectable families and communities unaccustomed to prison life." To coddle COs or otherwise treat them differently than other prisoners, Bennett insisted, would invite additional trouble in America's prisons. He dismissed the COs as products of "over-protective homes" suffering from "mother fixations."[46] Nevertheless Bennett, a liberal and a supporter of Roosevelt, assured A. J. Muste that the Bureau of Prisons had "ameliorated all of the traditional methods of prison discipline in federal institutions and use only those which are reasonable, humane and effective."[47]

The public had grown more tolerant of conscientious objectors since World War I. Gone were the days when mobs of frenzied war supporters, quietly goaded by federal and local authorities, terrorized and beat COs. The religious exemptions in the Selective Service Act and the establishment of CPS camps represented a tremendous leap forward in the treatment of war objectors. Even the imprisoned COs fared better in World War II than they had in World War I. Yet widespread antipathy persisted. In isolated cases, "conchies" or "slackers" were beaten up or denied service in restaurants when they could not produce their draft cards. Signs hanging in businesses grouped them together with Nazis and Japanese as threats to the United States. A January 1940 Gallup Poll asked respondents what should be done with war objectors if America went to war. A mere 13.2 percent supported their exemption from military service; 24 percent advocated forcing them to serve; and 9 percent wanted them executed or put in jail. Only 34 percent approved of allowing the COs to perform noncombatant military service.[48]

Dellinger was initially sentenced to the Lewisburg Farm Camp, located outside the prison walls and housing inmates who required only minimal supervision. Camp inmates worked on a farm owned by the prison, supervising dairy and crop operations and running a slaughterhouse that processed beef cattle from nearby Allenwood. But the only COs at the farm camp were Jehovah's Witnesses, and Dellinger had grown weary of their proselytizing and apocalyptic prophecies. He wanted to be inside the main prison with the radical pacifists. Adding to his sense of urgency was a rumor that about a dozen war resisters were on strike against racial segregation in the penitentiary. So he promptly engaged in a one-man work stoppage, which immediately earned him a trip into the maximum-security penitentiary.[49]

By the end of August Dellinger had appraised the situation inside Lewisburg and had connected with the war objectors. Since late May, his friend Bill Sutherland from the Newark Ashram and a group of COs had been participating in a strike against racial segregation in the prison mess hall. The protesters were resisting a prison policy forcing whites and African Americans to sit at separate tables. The strike began when eight COs refused to eat in the segregated Jim Crow hall in the spring, and over the next few weeks other inmates joined the action. The Lewisburg strike coincided with an equally dramatic work stoppage by eighteen COs at Danbury that began in August. The charismatic radical pacifist Jim Peck led the resistance against segregation in Danbury, which lasted for 135 days. The protesting inmates in Lewisburg and Danbury offered each other solidarity and moral support through a network of mutual pacifist contacts on the outside. News of their activities also trickled south to the Ashland Correctional Institution in Kentucky, inspiring COs there to organize similar actions. The protesting COs at Lewisburg expressed their frustration to Dellinger, questioning the effectiveness of their protest after three months. Lewisburg's warden, W. H. Hiatt, remained firm in his resolve to ignore the prisoners' demands. "The position which we have taken," James V. Bennett assured A. J. Muste, "is one approved by many leading sociologists and idealists both white and negro."[50]

Dellinger thought it was time to raise the stakes and proposed launching yet another protest of the censorship of mail by prison authorities and the use of solitary confinement. This latest action, Dellinger told his comrades, should be carried out in support of the current struggle against Jim Crow segregation. The main weapon in David's arsenal, the hunger strike, had never been tried before in Lewisburg. But he had seen hunger strikes produce dramatic results elsewhere. As an active member of the War Resisters League in Newark, Dellinger had carefully followed the dramatic hunger strike waged by Danbury prisoners Stanley Murphy and Louis Taylor. In October 1942 Murphy and Taylor gained fame in when they walked out of the CPS camp 46 in Big Flats, New York, to protest conscription. In January 1943 they were tried, convicted, and sentenced to two years at Danbury. When they refused to work, the authorities placed them in solitary confinement. The two men then began an extraordinary hunger strike that lasted for eighty-two days. Prison officials eventually transferred the two men to the infirmary and ordered them to be fed intravenously. Their bold hunger strike stirred the pacifist community, inspired David Dellinger, and "served to wake up the pacifist movement."[51]

Dellinger called for a repeat of the Murphy-Taylor hunger strike at Lewisburg. Some prison censorship is necessary, he admitted, and he had no quarrel with the policy of prison officials inspecting mail to ascertain whether it contained drugs, explosive materials, escape tools, or any other harmful elements. Instead, Dellinger wanted to end the confiscation of such leftist magazines as *The Call*, *The People's Daily World*, and *The Conscientious Objector*. Prison authorities also regularly seized incoming and outgoing mail because they did not approve of its religious or political content. At other times they arbitrarily held mail for months at a time for no apparent reason, finally giving it to the inmate for whom it was intended long after the postmarked date. Dellinger wrote a letter to his father proclaiming the hunger strike "was the only method we have" of resisting censorship, which he said "places individuals at the mercy of a totalitarian system by denying them appeal to the outside world and encourages prison abuses by guaranteeing secrecy."[52]

Dellinger began his hunger strike on September 28. Five other inmates—Jack Dixon, Bill Kuenning, Bill Lovett, Paton Price, and Tom Woodman—joined him. "I was nervous about it, sure, but I knew it was something I had to do. We were resisting an unjust policy," recalled Bill

Lovett.[53] Lovett was only twenty-one when he entered Lewisburg on January 20, 1943. He had grown up in a Quaker family in Fallsington, Pennsylvania, and was doing volunteer work for a Quaker agency in Mexico when the United States entered the war in December 1941. He remained in Mexico until the fall of 1942 and was apprehended by authorities upon entering the United States. Lovett was given the opportunity to avoid a jail sentence by registering for the draft, but he chose instead to become a conscientious objector and so was sent to Lewisburg. He found a kindred spirit in David Dellinger and in early October 1943 joined the hunger strike. On October 22, he wrote home to his mother: "As for myself, tomorrow will end my second week without food. I feel pretty well, considering, and am able to walk about easily if I do not get up too quickly."[54]

Reaction to the protest in the pacifist community was mixed. Evan Thomas of the War Resisters League never vacillated in his support for the strikers, and the Socialist Party proclaimed solidarity with them at its annual conference in November. By contrast, A. J. Muste of the Fellowship of Reconciliation (FOR) questioned the methods, timing, and purpose of the hunger strike. Muste's position antagonized Dellinger. The two pacifists' relationship, dating back to Dellinger's first prison term in Danbury, was only lukewarm, as Dellinger thought Muste had failed to offer adequate support for the Union Eight during their imprisonment. But Dellinger did not understand the extent of Muste's commitments at the time. The man described by *Time* magazine in World War II as "the Number One U.S. Pacifist" indeed supported the Union Eight but faced a host of other demands. Muste went to several meetings a day and attended events across the country, and he corresponded with scores of people. Muste did not attempt to conceal his misgivings about the hunger strike. Although he supported "intensive activity for the abolition of censorship" and segregation, he felt that the tactic of the hunger strike was too extreme for its targeted injustice. "I am strongly convinced that it is time that the boys in Lewisburg tried another tactic and terminated or suspended their strike," he wrote to Caroline Lovett, Bill Lovett's mother.[55] In late October, at Muste's urging, Roger Baldwin, the director of the American Civil Liberties Union, sent representatives to Lewisburg to meet with the hunger strikers. Baldwin hoped to persuade the prisoners to accept any reasonable settlement offered by the prison bureau. But he feared the worst. "If the issue is not settled," he told the press, "the government faces the inevitable alternative of forcibly feeding and the possible death of one or more of the men."[56]

The hunger strike continued for weeks. On October 17, in a letter to Betty, a dizzy and thinning Dellinger further articulated his reasons for not eating. "Prisoners lose all their rights and are punished by men who have totalitarian control over every second and detail of their life. No modernization of the system, improvement of facilities, or extension of pleasure alters this basic philosophy. I cannot work in such a system."[57] On October 22, Paton Price collapsed while returning to his prison cell. Lying on a stretcher bound for the infirmary Price opened one eye and whispered to his comrades, "I'm fine. Don't give up."[58] Warden Hiatt called in the parents of the hunger strikers and warned them of unpleasant consequences if it continued. Caroline Lovett visited Lewisburg on November 2 to see her son Bill but first met with Warden Hiatt for half an hour. "He talked at length—not particularly pleasantly—about the unreasonableness of the boys' demands. He insisted that a few weeks of the sort of thing they demand would wreck every federal prison, since they would be wide open for plotting, riots, etc."[59] Hiatt also met with Dellinger and told him that Betty was dying of pregnancy-related complications and had asked that David abandon the strike. Until he later discovered that this was a lie, Dellinger panicked.[60]

Transferred to the infirmary and strapped to beds, the strikers endured painful force-feeding. Because Dellinger refused to allow a tube in his mouth, the doctor inserted it into his nose. "We have been moved from the small rooms to one large one on the same floor," wrote Bill Lovett on November 5. "The doctors are all very considerate."[61] The strike had become a stalemate, a battle of wills between the strikers and the prison authorities. By late November Dellinger began hallucinating and experiencing painful heart spasms. When his consciousness returned, he was delighted to see Bill Sutherland, who had requested a nursing assignment. Sutherland had refused to join the hunger strike because he thought it drew attention away from the struggle against Jim Crow segregation. Personal loyalty, however, brought him to his comrades' bedsides. "Dave looked pretty bad," Sutherland conceded. "You could see his bones. He was in bad shape." With a jittery hand, Dellinger scrawled a note, written in the third person, to be delivered to the War Resisters League. "On Nov. 31 word came that his . . . heart condition is now serious. Dec. 1 is his 63rd day of hunger strike. Is in Lewisburg (Pa.) Penitentiary."[62]

In early December 1943, James V. Bennett—who was described by First Lady Eleanor Roosevelt as "a very humane man"—dictated a memorandum that he hoped would finally end the protest.[63] This memorandum became the foundation of a new policy in the U.S. Bureau of Prisons. Bennett emphasized the importance of inspecting inmates' incoming and outgoing mail and books for security purposes but forbade "censorship or control over political, social or religious opinion or belief." Prison officials, he ruled, would continue to inspect incoming and outgoing inmate mail for contraband, escape plans, and plots of violence. But they would no longer confiscate letters or "reading material, books, and magazines" as a means of censoring ideas. Although Bennett did not address the issue of solitary confinement, for the hunger strikers, his statement about censorship was sufficient. On December 2, 1943, the six Lewisburg hunger strikers ceased their protest and even in their weakened state rejoiced at the news that six dedicated people had managed to transform the American prison system.[64]

Betty Dellinger, pregnant and on her own, stayed at the Newark Ashram for several months after David's arrest in July 1943. Most of its male residents had already been arrested or had received orders to go to CPS camps, and the few men and women remaining could not sustain the experiment. Betty's meager savings were running low. Thelma Mielke, a friend of the Dellingers, sent an open letter to pacifists around the country in November 1943 soliciting help for the Newark Ashram. "At the moment the situation at the Newark Christian Colony is serious. Dave is on a hunger strike at Lewisburg and Betty is expecting a baby soon. . . . We urge you to give what you can in money, clothing or food."[65] Supporters dug deep into their pockets, but their donations were not enough. In late 1943 the few remaining stalwarts dropped out of the Newark Ashram. Betty wrote letters to arouse attention and sympathy for the hunger strike. "It is up to you to support the strikers by expressing your opinion to officials. MAKE THEM HEAR," she wrote in an October 25 letter to prospective supporters.[66] She worried about David and occasionally wondered whether she would see him alive again.

A crucial source of encouragement for Betty was Esther Eichel, wife of the war resister Julius Eichel. The Dellingers and Eichels had grown close in the early 1940s, spending time together at the Newark Ashram and the Eichels' home in Brooklyn. Julius came from a family of Jewish socialists who had emigrated from Austria around the turn of the century. He had the distinction of being a war objector in both world wars and had served time in jail during both conflicts for resisting the draft. Julius and Esther married in 1928 and settled in Brooklyn, where they opened a chemical supply store and reared their son Seymour. The couple published their own pacifist newspaper called *The Absolutist*, which regularly featured contributions from Dellinger. Esther offered moral support to Betty during David's stay in Lewisburg, occasionally visiting and collecting baby clothes and other supplies to send to Betty. Esther advised Betty to get in touch with the Quaker Emergency Committee, which could offer financial assistance for the new baby.

On January 2, 1944, Betty gave birth to nine-pound Evan Patchen Dellinger, named after two of David's heroes, Evan Thomas and the poet Kenneth Patchen. In the spring she moved out of the defunct Newark Ashram, settling temporarily in Chester, Pennsylvania. She and Evan lived in a boardinghouse owned by a family of pacifist African Americans. A little financial assistance trickled in from her parents and the Quakers. Activism continued to be an important part of her life, and the pacifist movement also offered much-needed companionship. Betty had a few affairs while David was in prison. They "just happened" because "I was kind of naive . . . and got myself into a situation where I just thought I shouldn't refuse, because they were all good friends and like brothers."[67]

At Lewisburg, elation over the successful hunger strike soon faded. For almost two years, Dellinger was subjected to arduous work schedules, repeated bouts of solitary confinement, and disagreements with other prisoners. The COs at Lewisburg looked to him to provide leadership and direction. Larry Gara, imprisoned at Ashland and Lewisburg, remembered that Dellinger "always had some sort of following" owing to his charismatic personality.[68] He organized pacifist study groups and encouraged his CO comrades to form relationships with other prisoners. In February 1944 Dellinger led fifteen other Lewisburg war resisters in signing a hostile letter of resignation from the Fellowship of Reconciliation (FOR). The signers took FOR to task for its support of the CPS camps, which they believed were part of an authoritarian "military conscription" system. They also characterized FOR as an undemocratic and ineffectual antiwar organization that uncritically backed the camps. The letter contained several caustic passages, including a reference to the FOR as "the Fellowship of Reconciliation-

With-Evil." The COs urged Muste to resign from the FOR and join them in building "a nonviolent revolutionary movement which will be a dynamic factor in the post-war world."[69] So disheartened was Muste that he waited two months to reply to the polemic. In his April 4 response Muste said he "could not understand the mental processes of pacifists and men who profess allegiance to the spirit of Christ" who attacked, so vehemently, the most vital and effective antiwar organization in existence during the war.[70] The resignations deepened the rift between Dellinger and Muste, which grew even worse when Muste arranged the parole of Alfred Hassler, a Lewisburg CO who had had no contact with Dellinger and the radicals. In exchange for parole Hassler agreed to work at FOR's main office and not to speak or write about the war. Although Dellinger had been offered this same arrangement, he rejected it as a "bribe." "Many of the objectors at Lewisburg never forgave" Muste for "this and other actions he took during that period," he explained.[71]

The COs' militancy never abated in Lewisburg. More hunger strikes were staged in the late summer and early fall of 1944, triggered by discriminatory prison parole policies that targeted war resisters. The Lewisburg CO protests, however, were only part of a nationwide struggle inside the nation's prisons. "Jim Crow Must Go" became the rallying cry of imprisoned COs across America.[72] In Danbury, a strike lasting for four months resulted in the institution's becoming the first federal prison to desegregate its mess hall. Protesting COs in Tucson, Arizona, conducted strikes that resulted in better prison food, relaxed letter censorship policies, and prison visits in private areas without constant supervision by guards. War objectors in Milan, Michigan, took part in several strikes beginning in 1942 against Jim Crow policies, which led to desegregated cell blocks and mess halls. Only in Ashland did the authorities respond to protests by paroling COs or transferring them to other prisons. Thus, COs were constantly entering Lewisburg from Ashland, refreshing and emboldening the CO protest movement.[73]

Dellinger participated in the 1944 strikes, lost more weight, and developed health problems, including a severe case of colitis that plagued him for much of his life. Months of imprisonment left him weary and exhausted well beyond his twenty-nine years of age. He also paid an enormous personal price for being imprisoned. He missed his son's first year of life, although he cherished the memory of briefly holding him during one of Betty's visits. In the fall of 1944 Betty brought the baby, nicknamed "Patch," into the visiting room. At a certain point in the conversation she stood and lifted him over the barrier. David held Patch in his arms for a moment and then quickly returned him to Betty. She described what happened next: "Bells rang! They lectured me for a half-hour and David was strong-armed and a lot of other things, but at least he held his baby for one minute."[74] A guard angrily wrestled Dellinger to the floor, and he was escorted back to his cell.[75]

By early 1945, thoughts of freedom overrode his focus on prison activism. He envisioned moving to Trenton, New Jersey, and settling in a small house with Betty and Patch. "My wife and I plan to live much more quietly, for a time at least, in Trenton," he wrote to Roy Finch on February 21.[76] Dellinger nevertheless took pride in helping build a new radical pacifist movement behind bars. The ordeal of imprisonment encouraged the community of war objectors in Lewisburg. Together the idealistic objectors fashioned a revolutionary pacifist ideology rooted in visions of decentralized, mutually cooperative societies free of war and poverty. Galvanizing their opposition to all forms of warfare were the sporadic and sketchy news reports of the final, devastating throes of World War II. Despite their horror at the news of the mass murder of European Jewry by the Nazis, they remained convinced that they had been right to go to prison and not fight. The success of the anti–Jim Crow protests in prisons and CPS camps across America raised their morale and became a model for later civil rights agitation. Not all pacifists stayed the course, however. At Danbury, Don Benedict—one of David's closest friends—joined the U.S. Army midway through his prison sentence. His decision grew largely out of the troubling information he learned about the Nazis' crimes against humanity. Benedict did not abandon his commitment to humanitarian Christian radicalism, but he proudly served in the army in the South Pacific in 1944 and 1945. "I guess I just wasn't as much of an absolutist as Dave," he later explained.[77]

At Lewisburg, David Dellinger gradually embraced a more anarchistic political outlook, which grew out of his rapport with other prisoners, even the nonpacifist inmates. Years later he revealed: "One of the things I found out was that . . . the people who had done the most vicious things weren't that different from you and me. They'd done some of those things, but they still had what I call a spark of divinity, or whatever you want to call it."[78] On April 5, 1945, David Dellinger walked out of Lewisburg Federal Penitentiary. For the second time in his life he savored his newfound freedom. Prison authorities shaved three months off his two-year sentence, officially for "good behavior," but more likely because they recognized Dellinger's unique ability to stir resistance behind bars. Betty Dellinger and their son, fifteen-month-old Patch, greeted Dave with tears and hugs, and for a time the Dellingers lived in Chester until they found a bigger house in New York State to raise their family. A free man, David Dellinger was prepared to move on with the next phase of his life.[79]

5

A Rebel in Cold-War America

Henceforth, no decent citizen owes one scrap of allegiance (if he ever did) to American law, American custom, or American institutions.

David Dellinger (1945)

Today there is no place for rebels to go.

David Dellinger (1952)

AFTER HIS RELEASE from the Lewisburg Penitentiary, Dellinger was able to reflect on the significance of his wartime prison experiences. Among the small enclaves of radical pacifists, wartime protests in prisons and CPS camps sowed the seeds of nonviolent revolutionary struggle. As the radical pacifist Roy Kepler later explained, "Our theoretical testing of Gandhian concepts satisfied a number of us that there was something here at which we could become more effective. . . . The biggest single mistake the government made was introducing us to each other. They helped build the pacifist network."[1] In April 1945 Dellinger took the lessons he had learned in Danbury and Lewisburg to the outside world and eagerly applied them. Yet the cold war posed a new set of challenges. Mounting fears of communism forestalled a renaissance of dissent, and the atomic age heightened anxieties across the nation. When nuclear weapons threatened global annihilation, pacifists found themselves poorly prepared to confront them.

Family became David Dellinger's other priority after World War II, with the demands of activism and the needs of family often pulling him in opposite directions. When activism prevailed, David and Betty's marriage suffered. David tried to mitigate the conflict by blending family and politics. He moved his family to a communal farm in Glen Gardner, New Jersey, and there operated a printing press that turned out radical books and pamphlets. Still, the tug of war between family and activism that began for David during World War II persisted and became the central conflict in his life. It was a problem that even in his old age, he never adequately resolved.

When he was freed in early April 1945, Dellinger went with Betty and Patch to Chester, Pennsylvania. Then in late April, the Dellingers moved to a cottage near the Catskills in upstate New York, northwest of Albany. On May 3, David wrote to Abe Kaufman of the War Resisters League: "We had to move fairly fast, so we decided to come here where we were assured of a home and garden."[2] David found work at a nearby dairy farm, which provided him with steady, forty-hour-per-week employment while Betty took care of the baby. On May 12 David wrote to Julius and Esther Eichel: "Most of our time has been spent moving, fixing up the place, and looking for work."[3] Health problems related to his two years in Lewisburg continued to bother him. In August, he visited Dr. Evan Thomas in New York City, who diagnosed Dellinger's malady as a severe case of colitis—acute inflammation of the colon—a source of much pain and discomfort for David. "He really was suffering still from the results of that strike and he didn't realize it and nor did I. The long-term physical effects were very damaging," Betty recalled.[4]

Dellinger worked long days at the farm, taking care of livestock, working in the fields, and picking apples. The evenings he spent with Betty and Patch, relishing the opportunity to see his son growing. Late at night he typed letters to friends and sketched out his plans for a new nonviolent struggle for peace, justice, and equality. The Truman administration's decision to drop atomic bombs on Hiroshima and Nagasaki in August prompted David to intensify his efforts. Days after the bombings he typed a terse and effectively worded statement of purpose entitled "Declaration of War," in which he articulated his vision of a new, Gandhian revolutionary movement on American soil. Dellinger called for a "war for total brotherhood," a nonviolent struggle that would topple war and exploitation.

> There must be strikes, sabotage, and seizure of public property now being held by private owners. There must be civil disobedience of laws which are contrary to human welfare. But there must also be an uncompromising practice of treating everyone, including the worst of our opponents, with the respect and decency that he merits as a fellow human being.

This statement served as a benchmark of David's changing views. Once a Christian socialist, Dellinger had evolved into a secular anarchist in Lewisburg.[5]

"This is such a period of flux and uncertainty," he admitted in a letter to Roy Finch, yet he pressed forward with his ambitious plans.[6] High on his list was launching a journal of pacifist thought that he hoped would unify a new Gandhian movement. His first step came in the summer when he borrowed money from his father to buy a printing press, which he assembled in an abandoned building in Mount Pleasant, a community in the Catskills. This was the first of many times that Dellinger's politically conservative father began quietly funding the activities of his pacifist son. David planned to start his new magazine, called *Direct Action*, in the fall. "The work of getting out the mag," he anticipated, "would probably involve five persons working an average of four hours a day, for two weeks."[7] Stalwarts such as Bill Kuenning, Albon Man, and George Houser offered their assistance, and Dellinger also was introduced to Roy Kepler, a dynamic and creative young pacifist and war objector who had been assigned to the San Dimas Experimental Forest CPS camp near Glendora, California. Dellinger was pleased as well by the addition of Ralph DiGia to the volunteer *Direct Action* staff. DiGia, a resolute pacifist with a gentle personality, had met David in the Lewisburg Penitentiary.

A native of New York City, DiGia's background was Italian radicalism. "I was very much influenced by my father. . . . He took me to a demonstration against the execution of Sacco and Vanzetti," DiGia remembered. "So I had this background about the economic system and the plight of the poor here."[8] As a student at New York's City College in the 1930s, DiGia took the Oxford Pledge and marched in antiwar demonstrations. In 1940 he registered for the draft, indicating on his form that he was a conscientious objector. His reasons for claiming CO status were rooted in secular rather than religious objections to war, however, and his local draft board denied his claim and, in the spring of 1942, ordered him to report for induction. Upon receiving his induction notice in the mail, he had a long, soul-searching conversation with his mother and father. His father urged him to report for induction, insisting that refusing to obey the law would likely destroy the young man's future job prospects. DiGia respectfully disagreed with his father. "I argued that I had gotten many of my ideals from him," he remembered, "and now that the moment had arrived for me to live up to them, he was asking me to give them up."[9]

DiGia chose to resist induction and established contact with the War Resisters League (WRL) and Julian Cornell, a sympathetic Quaker attorney. Cornell and the WRL offered help, but in March 1943 a judge sentenced DiGia to prison. Like Dellinger, he was initially processed through the West Street jail in New York City. He first went to Danbury, where he was among the most militant of the pacifist prisoners, particularly when organizing anti–Jim Crow protests. In response, the prison authorities transferred him to Lewisburg. Days after DiGia's arrival, a non-CO convict approached him and asked, "Are you a friend of Dave Dellinger?" Although DiGia only knew of Dellinger, he replied yes. The convict replied, "Any friend of Dellinger's is a friend of mine. If anybody bothers you, let me know and I'll take care of it."[10] DiGia later learned that Dellinger had forged close ties with many non-CO convicts by advocating on their behalf when he felt they were being abused. Dellinger and DiGia finally met while walking around the prison grounds, and it marked the beginning of a lifelong friendship. Although DiGia faced numerous ordeals in prison, including repeated sentences of solitary confinement and threats from guards and prisoners, he never faltered in his nonviolent commitment. He walked out of Lewisburg in June 1945, almost two months after David was released. By the fall he had moved to upstate New York to live near the Dellingers and fellow CO inmate Bill Kuenning. "Dave and Bill worked on a farm," DiGia recalled, "and I got a job in a summer hotel. Before long we became active again."[11]

Dellinger, DiGia, and Kuenning put out the first issue of *Direct Action* in October, which called itself "a magazine devoted to an American Revolution by non-violent methods."[12] This issue featured Dellinger's "Declaration of War," as well as an editorial on the growing hunger crisis in war-ravaged Europe, an article advocating amnesty for army prisoners and COs, a personal account by a female pacifist living in a cooperative, a forum discussion of unemployment, and an anonymous letter from an imprisoned CO. Dellinger assembled an impressive mailing list, and the first issue went out to hundreds of potential supporters across the country. But it was the only issue of *Direct Action* ever published. Shortly after it appeared, the building housing Dellinger's printing press burned down in a mysterious blaze. Dellinger and his friends salvaged the printing press, and it was operating again by the spring of 1946. At the end of April, Dellinger wrote: "We rebuilt the old press after the fire, from top to bottom ourselves, with a little expert advice, and tested it yesterday with our breaths held. It prints as well as ever."[13] Although he needed five hundred dollars to print and distribute the next issue of *Direct Action*, his repeated solicitations did not generate enough.

In early 1946 the Dellingers moved again, this time to a house in Newark. David put his printing press into the basement of a nearby building and opened a print shop. DiGia and Kuenning also moved into the neighborhood and helped Dave in its operation. The business flourished, and Dellinger soon upgraded to a larger press. Meantime, the Dellinger family continued to grow. On April 29, Dellinger wrote to Roy Finch: "We now have a Raymond (8 weeks) as well as a Patch. Betty is in the best of health and spirits."[14]

In an effort to fulfill another of his postwar goals—building a viable radical pacifist organization—David went to Chicago on February 6 through 9, 1946, to take part in the founding of the Committee for Nonviolent Revolution (CNVR). About a hundred activists attended the gathering, which reunited David with some of his old prison comrades, such as Bill Sutherland and George Houser, and also introduced him to new faces. The conferees assembled at Chicago's Labor Center on Clifton Street to debate tactics and discuss the future prospects of American radicalism. The topics included "Decentralized Democratic Socialism," "War Resistance," "International Revolution and World Government," and "The Process of Revolutionary Change."[15] Dellinger gave several talks, and the content of his speeches indicated that his conversion to nonviolent anarchism already was well under way. He criticized radicals who placed too much emphasis on charismatic leaders and national organizations, called for more localized protest actions in communities across America, and expressed pessimism about the prospects of a viable United Nations. Instead of pressuring world leaders to participate in the UN, he argued, ordinary people should concentrate on building "up local groups of resisters . . . and to encourage their cooperation regionally and throughout the world."[16]

The CNVR temporarily served as the primary organizational vehicle of radical pacifists in the immediate postwar years. The group sponsored pickets and demonstrations, mainly in the New York City area, and compiled mailing lists of nonviolent militants and prospective supporters. Dellinger used his reconstructed printing press, now attached to his home in Newark, to print CNVR fliers and position papers. A typical CNVR leaflet proclaimed, "This Is the Era of One World and Two Classes: We Must Attack War and Inequality Directly!"[17] On August 8 through 10, 1947, Dellinger attended the second major CNVR gathering at the Catholic Worker farm near Newburgh, New York. The conference theme was "Radicalism in the Next Five Years," which brought together radical pacifists from across America. The three-day meeting produced several position papers, most notably a fierce attack against the Communist Party of the United States (CPUSA), which the radical pacifists dismissed as an essentially Machiavellian and violence-prone organization. The pacifists hoped their alternative, the CNVR, would attract independent, non-Stalinist radicals. Other conference statements urged pacifists to focus on local grassroots campaigns involving peaceful resistance, especially against the arms race. "There is only one conclusion—we must be nonviolent revolutionists," proclaimed a closing statement. "That means that we must engage in an all-out nonviolent struggle against the existing system. Specifically, we must learn to carry on strikes, sit-downs, and campaigns of civil disobedience without resort to any violence against any human being."[18]

The CNVR proved to be a disappointment for Dellinger. It lacked sufficient resources, membership, and direction and so ultimately failed to attract the critical mass needed to spread the group's gospel beyond New York City and Chicago. In addition, the CNVR's inflammatory rhetoric and anarchical politics alienated more moderate pacifists, such as A. J. Muste and Abe Kaufman. The political landscape of cold-war America simply would not accommodate ultraradical sects like the CNVR. One of its founders, Lewis Hill, expressed in his position statement the discouragement shared by many of his colleagues: "When one is looking for the proletariat one looks for chains; but in the industrial class in America what one sees is bathtubs and credit-plan refrigerators, with a heavy sprinkling of life-insurance investments."[19]

Nevertheless, the pacifists persisted, their sense of urgency strengthened by the events of the cold war. Soaring defense budgets and an expanding nuclear arsenal, deteriorating relations between the United States and Soviet Union, and the many postwar global crises convinced American war resisters that their efforts were desperately needed. On February 12, 1947, the New York City–based Break with Conscription Committee sponsored the nation's first draft card burning, held at the Labor Temple on 242 East Fourteenth Street. It was a bold protest that attracted a respectable amount of publicity and a decent turnout. Dellinger addressed the crowd, sharing the stage with A. J. Muste and Dwight MacDonald, a literary critic and editor of the recently created *Politics* magazine. The speakers were introduced by Bayard Rustin, a charismatic African American pacifist who had been imprisoned as a CO in both Ashland and Lewisburg. His friendship with Dellinger dated back to the Newark Ashram, where Rustin had volunteered in the early 1940s. At the Labor Temple event, sixty-three young men, in the presence of police and FBI agents, deposited their draft cards into an outdoor incinerator. Organizers of the event sent mass mailings across the country inviting other draft-age men to participate in individual acts of protest. In total, four hundred to five hundred draft-age men either burned their draft cards at the rally or returned them to government officials as a show of solidarity with the draft card burners.[20]

The following month, David learned that his younger brother, Fiske, had been murdered in New York City. It had happened in the early morning hours of Sunday, March 30, 1947. A woman on her way to the subway discovered Fiske's body around 7:45 A.M. while taking a shortcut through a vacant lot. She immediately called the police, who ruled out robbery when they found twenty-six dollars and several pieces of jewelry in Fiske's pockets. The tragedy left David stunned and bewildered. For years, Fiske, a quiet and sensitive young man, had lived in his brother's shadow. But after David went to prison in the fall of 1940, his parents "transferred their parental ambitions" from David to "their only remaining son," Fiske.[21]

Initially it appeared that Fiske would not disappoint them. In the early 1940s he attended Swarthmore College in Pennsylvania and Kenyon College in Ohio, earning high grades and dabbling in peace activism without throwing himself into it in the way that his older brother had done in the 1930s. He volunteered for the American Field Service and drove ambulances for the Allies in war-torn Italy. But his experiences overseas changed him, and he returned home a morose loner who turned to alcohol for solace. Raymond and Marie Dellinger were ashamed of their son's behavior and expressed their disappointment to him. Then the lonely twenty-four-year-old Fiske took a job with Scandinavian Airlines as a reservation clerk at La Guardia Airport in New York and lived alone in a rooming house on Eighty-eighth Street. On the night of Saturday, March 29, he went to a tavern in Elmhurst for a night of heavy drinking with a new friend, an unemployed twenty-two-year-old army veteran named William Albrecht. They drank until about 3:15 A.M. and then walked down the street to an all-night diner. Returning to the tavern an hour and a half later, they found it had closed, so they started for home. Albrecht claimed that Fiske made "two improper advances" toward him as they walked through a vacant field, and when Albrecht resisted, Fiske got rough. Albrecht then picked up an enormous stone and smashed it against Fiske's head.[22]

David went to Wakefield to be with his grieving parents. A shaken and distraught Marie Dellinger had just heard that Fiske had made a pass at his male friend before he was killed. When she saw David, she cried, "My son wasn't sick, was he?"[23] David helped his parents in planning and carrying out Fiske's funeral. The body was brought to Wakefield in early April, and the family had a small service. More than any other event in David's life, the murder of his younger brother confirmed the depravity and futility of violence. It also brought him closer to his parents, who took comfort in stories about their new grandchildren, three-year-old Patch and one-year-old Ray. For years Raymond and Marie had avoided talking about David. He "had become a nonperson within the family as far as their friends were concerned," David explained.[24] Now they expressed their love for him more openly and, like all doting grandparents, adored their grandchildren. Although they did not agree with David's activism, they respected his principles. Haunted by Fiske's gruesome fate, Raymond and Marie never lost their concern for David. Years later, when David was preparing to leave on his first trip to the South to help in civil rights organizing, his parents told him, "We wish you wouldn't but we understand why you feel you have to. Please don't do anything foolish."[25]

In the summer of 1947, the Dellingers and three other families pooled their funds and purchased a tract of heavily wooded land in Hunterdon County, New Jersey, approximately fifty miles west of New York City. "It was bought as a cooperative," Betty recalled, "and his parents and my parents helped give us our share to buy it." David and Betty agreed that it was time to leave Newark, preferably for a more rural setting. The couple envisioned living in a commune with other like-minded inhabitants and selected a quiet area in western New Jersey where they could escape the hectic pace of city life. The closest town was Glen

Gardner, a few miles up the road, hence David's name for the commune, the Glen Gardner Intentional Community. The word *intentional*
was meant to suggest a purposeful or utopian community. At first,
Betty sought companionship with the other couples at the commune.
All the men—Bill Kuenning, Ralph DiGia, and Bent Andressen—had
been conscientious objectors during World War II and had been friends
since their imprisonment with Dellinger in Lewisburg. The relationships among the women at the Glen Gardner community were not as
cordial, however. Betty and Ralph's wife Adele became good friends,
but the DiGias stayed at the commune only on the weekends. Betty did
not get along so well with the other wives, Taddy Andressen and Char-
lotte Kuenning. "They weren't ready for communal living," Betty admitted.[26]

Betty urged David to find work closer to home, especially after the
they became the foster parents of an orphan in his early teens named
Howie Douglas, who had previously lived in an abusive Newark or-
phanage. In Newark, Howie often visited the Dellingers' print shop,
and David found odd jobs for him to do, such as sweeping and organizing files. In the fall of 1947, Howie moved into the Glen Gardner commune, adding to Betty's responsibilities. In an effort to help Betty, David
decided to relocate the printing press from Newark to Glen Gardner.
Enlisting the aid of fellow pacifists, he constructed a building to house
the press "high on the Polktown Mountain above lower Glen Gardner."[27] Piece by piece, he disassembled the elaborate machine in
Newark and reassembled it near his home. By the spring of 1948, his
new facility, "Libertarian Press—A Workers Cooperative," was fully op-
erational. A combination of loans and donations enabled David and a
handful of his comrades to launch *Alternative*, a slick, four-page
monthly printed at the Libertarian Press. Joining David on the editorial
board were his close friends Ralph DiGia, Roy Finch, and Bill Kuenning,
and a newer acquaintance, Roy Kepler, the former editor of the pacifist
Pacifica News and one of the founders of KPFA, a leftist, countercultural
radio station in Berkeley, California. The first issue of *Alternative* appeared in April 1948. Its "Statement of Purpose" proclaimed, "We will
explore ideas and actions which free and strengthen the individual, and
we will do so without respect for custom, law, or authority."[28]

Contributions to *Alternative* reflected the strengths and limitations
of radical pacifist thought in midcentury America. Its pages contained
anarchist critiques of the cold war different from those of any other left-

ist periodicals at the time. The editors invited "writing and thinking that will lead to action—nonviolent direct action" and attacked American capitalism and Soviet communism with equal fervor.[29] *Resistance* was a word often repeated in *Alternative*. Its authors urged resistance to Jim Crow policies, conscription, atomic weapons, McCarthyism, Stalinism, the H-bomb, violence, the Democratic Party, the Republican Party, the Communist Party, the UN, unemployment, conformity, consumerism, and so on. For a radical periodical, *Alternative* enjoyed a respectable circulation and life span. Dellinger had managed to amass a subscriber base that kept it afloat for three years. It was only after postal authorities banned the monthly from the mails in early 1951 for opposing conscription that it folded. Years later, in 1968, the historian William Appleman Williams, a nonpacifist leftist, could have been describing the whole radical pacifist movement in his evaluation of the publication. "*Alternative*," he wrote, "undoubtedly played an indirect but nevertheless significant role in the long effort to mobilize . . . a movement of protest and resistance. On the other hand, the failure of *Alternative* to offer any significant or creative options beyond protest and resistance also influenced the character of that movement."[30]

In April 1948—the month that *Alternative* made its debut—David went to Chicago to attend the founding conference of the Peacemakers, a new organization that he hoped would succeed the moribund Committee for Nonviolent Revolution. He joined approximately 250 other pacifists at the event, formally called the Conference on a More Disciplined and Revolutionary Pacifism. This time, veterans of the CNVR had learned from past mistakes and deliberately toned down their militant rhetoric to accommodate such moderates as A. J. Muste and Milton Mayer. Poverty, segregation, the arms race, and conscription were high on Peacemakers' list of targets for direct action. The gathering energized Dellinger, who traveled to Chicago with Bill Lovett uncertain about what to expect. "Our message is addressed to the nation and we seek to reach all groups more effectively than ever before," declared the Peacemakers' founding statement.[31] Its executive committee consisted of such diehards as Dellinger, Muste, Dwight MacDonald, George Houser, Bayard Rustin, and Roy Kepler. True to their libertarianism, they organized a nonhierarchical organization that functioned as a network for autonomous, local cells. "We place emphasis on the grass roots activity and upon the affiliations as being of cells . . . rather than individuals on a mailing list of a central organization."[32]

To finance his rural ashram, Dellinger used his entrepreneurial skills at Libertarian Press to win printing contracts from New York businesses. Museums, publishers, Broadway theaters, sightseeing companies, and a variety of other firms hired the press to print their materials. The business also published a handful of radical pacifist books, including Lowell Naeve's highly acclaimed memoir, *Field of Broken Stones*, and itinerant radical Ammon Hennacy's *Autobiography of a Catholic Anarchist*. The outfit relied on a few different presses, including photo offset and linotype machines. In 1948, Bill Lovett moved to Glen Gardner with his wife Janet and went to work full time in the print shop. The staff grew to three with the addition of wartime conscientious objector Igal Roodenko, who commuted to Glen Gardner each day from New York City. Roodenko, the son of a Ukrainian Jewish immigrant, grew up in a Zionist/socialist family in New York City. He earned a degree in horticulture from Cornell University in 1938, after which he worked at private farms and federal agricultural agencies. In his youth he had developed a passion for nonviolence and social justice activism, which remained with him for his entire life. During World War II, he worked in CPS camps in Maryland and Colorado, where he took part in militant protests, including a hunger strike in support of the Lewisburg hunger strikers. Roodenko and Dellinger became friends in 1948 and shared a strikingly similar vision of the Libertarian Press's purpose and goals. "Our idea, aside from making a living," Roodenko told a reporter, "is to publish material intended to help people live more sensibly and beautifully."[33] The three men ran an efficient enterprise that was occasionally undermined by the priorities of the larger community. Lovett recalled: "When visitors would come they would put down their work and they'd all go and bullshit and visit."[34]

In the late 1940s, Dellinger finally stabilized his personal life. The remainder of his life was characterized by cycles of intense political involvement followed by retreats to personal family matters. During the final years of the decade, David maintained only a moderate commitment to activism. He sensed the toll that his imprisonment at Lewisburg had taken on Betty and felt the tension every time he went away to events and gatherings. Some of Dellinger's pacifist comrades, especially the unmarried ones, were not always sensitive to the needs of his family and could not understand why David could not drop everything on short notice and attend conferences and demonstrations. However, the time he spent with his family provided spiritual and emotional sustenance that his writing and activism lacked. The birth of Natasha Dellinger on July 26, 1949, gave the Dellingers their third child and first daughter. The children influenced David in meaningful ways, as Betty recalled: "When we had the children, that helped bring us together. It did help a lot. He didn't stop going away on trips, but he did help take care of us more."[35]

The intensification of the cold war in 1950, however, spurred David back into action. News of the outbreak of hostilities in Korea in June 1950, reports of the government's plans to develop a powerful hydrogen bomb, Senator Joseph McCarthy's meteoric ascendancy, and confirmation of the Soviet Union's first successful A-bomb test the previous year heightened anxieties across the nation. Radical pacifists such as Dellinger, Muste, and Bayard Rustin believed that the times called for dramatic tactics. Accordingly, the Peacemakers convened for an "emergency conference" on the weekend of February 25 and 26, 1950, in response to "the hydrogen bomb crisis." At the conference, Muste proposed that the Peacemakers sponsor a seven-day fast in Washington, D.C., to be held during the week before Easter Sunday in April. He suggested that a group "of about 50" participants stay at the spacious Inspiration House beginning on "April 1, and live together until Easter Sunday, April 9."[36] In addition, the fasters would distribute leaflets, attempt to meet with clergy and government officials, and conduct sit-ins at the offices of the Atomic Energy Commission and the Central Intelligence Agency. Dellinger joined seven other pacifists, including Muste, Rustin, and Dorothy Day, on the planning committee for the event. On March 20, Rustin sent press releases to newspapers across the nation alerting them to the event and requesting that supporters who could not come to Washington organize "parallel actions" in their communities as a show of solidarity.[37]

Planning for the event was thorough, right down to the information sheets printed by the Peacemakers that detailed what physical sensations to expect during a fast. In New York, Rustin organized a carpool that transported numerous pacifists, including Dellinger and his foster son Howie Douglas, to Washington, D.C. The event brought Dellinger and Howie Douglas closer together and reunited Dellinger with old friends, such as George Houser and Jim Peck. From time to time Dellinger and Peck sneaked away to smoke cigars and reminisce about earlier days. For David, a hardened veteran of hunger strikes, a week of fasting seemed effortless. Newcomers, by contrast, were not accustomed to spending such long periods without food. "I've only been a pacifist a month," proclaimed Lucie Lord, a twenty-two-year-old French and philosophy major at New York's Hunter College. "I'd been seeking something for a long time. Then I found it in the idea, 'Do good if possible, but never do evil.'"[38]

News of parallel actions trickled in from across the country and abroad. The Washington, D.C., fasters tried unsuccessfully to meet with the staff at the White House and the Soviet embassy. Letters to President Harry Truman, members of Congress, and the Atomic Energy Committee received no replies. But the outpouring of support from across America and the presence of journalists and newsreel cameras at Inspiration House convinced the organizers that the event had been a success. As a journalist reportedly told the fasters, "People may not agree with your ideas, but they will never doubt your sincerity."[39]

Although the fast against the H-bomb boosted morale in the pacifist movement, the exhilaration felt by Dellinger and the other men and women who lived together for a week at Inspiration House was cut short by the outbreak of war in Korea. Even more than in World War II, the peace movement was caught off guard by the coming of war. Protests were sporadic and poorly attended; publicity of any kind was rare; and the pervasiveness of anticommunist thought and culture intimidated even diehard militants. The typical protest against the Korean War in New York City, according to radical pacifist Jim Peck, consisted of "five stalwarts from the War Resisters League, including myself, and seven stalwarts from the *Catholic Worker*."[40]

It troubled Dellinger that the peace organizations had failed to protest the Korean War. Doing his part, he marched in small pickets, turned out antiwar leaflets at the print shop, and fasted to protest the war. Days before the outbreak of hostilities in Korea, the residents of Glen Gardner declared their rural co-op to be the "Glen Gardner World Citizens' Community," and the adults took part in a two-week fast in July against the Korean War. The Glen Gardner fasters then issued a statement condemning the Korean War as a fruitless, bloody conflict between the United States and the Soviet Union and warned against transforming "the United Nations into an agency of war on the side of the United States." They urged Americans to reject the Korean War and the cold-war policies that had resulted in Washington's sending troops overseas to fight the Communists: "We call upon all people everywhere to withdraw their primary allegiance from their present governments and to declare themselves World Citizens whose loyalty is to the World and who are unwilling to take part in the conflicts of nations."[41]

One particularly brutal confrontation at a demonstration against the Korean War tested Dellinger's nonviolent commitment. On June 20, 1951, David and a handful of demonstrators picketed New York's Times Square to mark the first anniversary of the eruption of hostilities in Korea. One of the speakers at the event was twenty-three-year-old Michael Harrington, an intense and brilliant socialist intellectual who had recently gravitated to the *Catholic Worker*. He described the Times Square gathering as "a motley little band." As Harrington watched Dellinger stepping up to the platform to speak, "a man came screaming through the curious crowd, yelling that we were a bunch of Commies." Dellinger replied that the demonstrators were pacifists opposed to the Korean War, not members of the Communist Party. The disgruntled man told Dellinger to "come down here so I can hit you and see if you really will turn the other cheek."[42] Dellinger did as he was asked. The first punch in the jaw knocked him out cold, and the "maniac" straddled the unconscious pacifist and began brutally pummeling him.[43]

When David returned to consciousness, he saw the assailant standing a short distance away, fists still clenched, ready for more. Dellinger's body ached all over; the sight in his right eye was blurry; and he could hardly move his jaw. Somehow, he hobbled back toward the platform and shouted, "I'm glad you hit me" to his beater. Dellinger carried over a broken picket sign to the man and encouraged him to continue the beating. Bayard Rustin yelled, "Dave, you're groggy and you don't know what you're saying." The furious man tossed the chunk of wood on the sidewalk, apologized to Dellinger, and swiftly walked away. "I lost all memory of what I thought I was doing," Dellinger recalled.[44] Physical damage from the confrontation had been extensive. A thorough doctor's examination revealed that Dellinger's jaw had been broken and his eye severely damaged. He also suffered from numerous abrasions and large bruises. Eventually, David was declared legally blind in his right eye as a result of the beating. He discovered afterward that his attacker had recently lost a son in the Korean War. The ordeal had a sobering effect on Michael Harrington, who later reflected on the surreal events: "I saw myself shuffling along in that pathetic little parade and I thought I looked like one of those cartoon figures with a placard announcing the end of the world."[45]

■

Ever since 1950, Dellinger and Ralph DiGia had repeatedly discussed the need to plan a dramatic, attention-getting action that would shine the spotlight on pacifist dissent. During the depths of the cold war, adherents of nonviolence had to think creatively and act boldly, Dellinger reasoned. The two men agreed that a bicycle ride from Paris to Moscow would be a vivid and exciting action that might revive the peace movement, which had been ailing since the start of the Korean War. Along the route the bicyclists would spread the gospel of nonviolence in the form of speeches and printed leaflets, and they would meet with local inhabitants at several stops along the way. In late 1950 and early 1951, Dellinger pitched the plan to Muste, Rustin, and other peace leaders and found them to be generally receptive to the idea. The lobbying paid off, and by the spring of 1951 the Peacemakers agreed to finance the undertaking. The bicycle journey initially consisted of Dellinger and DiGia, but it soon doubled in size to include Bill Sutherland and "a young dairy farmer from Iowa, a Quaker by the name of Art Emery."[46]

The so-called Paris-to-Moscow bicycle trip appealed strongly to DiGia, whose marriage was unraveling. But for Dellinger, the journey could not have come at a worse time. By 1951 the Glen Gardner community had plunged into a state of disarray. Most of its original inhabitants—the Andressens, the DiGias, and the Kuennings—had moved elsewhere. Igal Roodenko had opened his own printing press in New York City, and Bill Lovett's marriage was falling apart and he contracted tuberculosis, which meant a long stay at the nearby Glen Gardner sanatorium. The once robust Libertarian Press had almost stopped without any more printing contracts. Needless to say, Betty was worried about her husband bicycling across Europe. She had three children and a teenage foster son to take care of, and in the spring of 1951 she discovered she was pregnant with her fourth child.[47]

David considered giving up the European bicycle trip, but the beating he had endured at Times Square strengthened his resolve to accompany his three friends. He assured Betty he would return to Glen Gardner in a few months at the most, and he was so confident of being gone only a short time that he did not plan any backup support for his family in the event the trip took longer than expected. Perhaps, as he later suggested, the June beating clouded his reasoning. On July 9, 1951, Dellinger, DiGia, Emery, and Sutherland boarded a ship in New York City and arrived in France on July 21.[48]

"We got into Paris and had some contacts there. The plan was to go to the Soviet and German consulates and get permission to go into their countries and tell them exactly why we were going," recalled DiGia.[49] The four men checked into a small, inexpensive hotel, expecting to be in Paris for only a few days. Upon their arrival, they found a printer to run off stacks of a color leaflet listing their identities and the purpose of their mission in four different languages—English, French, German, and Russian. They also began contacting Soviet and German officials requesting travel visas. Days turned into weeks as the foursome waded through a sea of bureaucratic red tape, futilely attempting to gain permission from different governments to bicycle through various countries. On August 17, the four men held their first press conference to announce their plans to pedal across the continent, and the number of journalists present far exceeded their most optimistic expectations. In attendance were reporters from the *New York Times*, *Chicago Tribune*, and *Washington Post*; seven major French newspapers; and numerous French and American wire services. "We call for disarmament on both sides," the ambitious bicyclists announced, "and we ask the people on both sides to refuse to support the armaments of their governments."[50]

Ever optimistic, the men bought four ten-speed bicycles, complete with racks to carry their supplies. Dellinger took meticulous notes of the trip, recording every detail from visits to museums and historical landmarks to encounters with ordinary citizens. The four Americans met many different men and women, mostly amiable greeters from all walks of life. They enjoyed dinner invitations from locals, met the mayor of Paris, and gave Parisian youths stacks of their multilingual leaflets to post all over Paris. For Bill Sutherland, it was a poignant trip, as he discovered that France lacked the racism so pervasive in midcentury America. He met and talked with a few pan-African activists in Europe who tried to persuade him to come to Africa and take part in its nonviolent independence movements. All the pacifists were surprised by the amount of publicity that followed them. Press coverage of the bicycle trip was the most extensive that David had encountered since the trial of the Union Eight in 1940. Almost every day brought another interview with a newspaper or wire service reporter, and the four men repeatedly posed on their bicycles for photographers and newsreel cameras.[51]

On September 11, after two months of waiting, Dellinger, DiGia, Emery, and Sutherland commenced their bicycle trip without official approval. A headline in the September 12 *New York Herald Tribune* told the story: "FOUR U.S. PACIFISTS OFF FOR IRON CURTAIN."[52] The bicyclists pedaled out of the city toward Strasbourg on France's eastern border. On their way, they stopped in villages to rest and discuss their mission with locals. An enthusiastic barber in Vitry Le François asked for copies of their leaflet and gave them free haircuts. A motorcyclist in eastern France handed them three hundred francs and wished them luck. Not all encounters were so friendly, however. In a town outside Strasbourg, two "menacing" Frenchmen found Dellinger posting the color fliers and threatened him. But they backed away, giving him an opportunity to ride away quickly "in the opposite direction."[53]

On September 21 the men reached Strasbourg and went straight to the Allied High Command in Kehl, West Germany, just across the border from Strasbourg, hoping to secure visas to travel through West Germany. Their requests were denied. Back in Strasbourg, the men put up their tent on the banks of the Rhine near the Strasbourg-Kehl Bridge. A few hours later, a dozen police officers arrived, dismantled, and confiscated the tents and detained the pacifists at the local police station for several hours. This was a clear message to the pacifists: Leave Strasbourg or face deportation from France. At nightfall the police released the four men and returned their supplies. The pacifists camped in a grassy field that night and the next morning returned to the banks of the Rhine, near where the police had broken up their first camp, and once again erected their tents. The police returned, but instead of deporting the pacifists, they confiscated many of the color leaflets. Unable to obtain visas and menaced by local police, the pacifists camped on the banks of the Rhine for a week and fasted the entire time to draw attention to their plight. Area residents brought blankets, medicine, food, and other offerings to the camp, and each visitor received a Peacemakers leaflet. "They really wanted us to eat, to stop fasting," DiGia recalled. "Some of the people said, 'We can sneak you over the border into West Germany.' We turned down that idea right away because we knew that if we went across into Germany, we'd probably be deported and we'd never get a chance to make it into the Soviet Union."[54]

A bicycle trek through West Germany now seemed out of the question, and the prospects for entering the Soviet Union had grown dimmer as well. Undaunted, the men began heading toward Vienna on September 29, alternating between train and bicycle travel. Their hope was to persuade the Soviet embassy there to give them with visas to continue their journey into the Soviet Union. At the Austrian border they reached a U.S. checkpoint, staffed by American soldiers. DiGia later admitted: "We didn't tell the truth exactly. We said we were tourists. . . . We began talking about baseball with the soldiers, and they loved the game, and of course Dave's a huge fan too. And all the political stuff just faded away and they let us through."[55] The pacifists eventually rode into Vienna, where they had yet another wait ahead of them. They stayed in a rooming house owned by a sympathizer and visited the Soviet occupational headquarters at the Hotel Imperial, submitting a written request for a visa. The Soviets stalled for weeks, and time was running out. In mid-October a telegram arrived from the Peacemakers in New York City informing the four riders that their funds had run out. The organization had just enough money to buy them tickets back to New York City. DiGia stated glumly, "At that point, we knew we weren't getting into the Soviet Union."[56]

Although entry into the Soviet Union no longer appeared possible, the pacifists devised an alternative solution that would enable them to spread their message to the Soviets. In Vienna, they bought train tickets to the British-occupied Austrian town of Murzzuschlag, aware that one of the stops along the way was Baden, a Soviet-controlled Austrian city. On October 24, they boarded a train that departed at 11:15 A.M. and a half-hour later stopped at the Red Army headquarters in Baden. In an illegal move that could have landed them in a Soviet prison, the pacifists surreptitiously left the train without being seen by the occupational authorities. "In pairs we proceeded as nonchalantly as possible to the center of town," the men later wrote in a collective journal entry. "The first Russian soldiers we saw were officers."[57]

In the picturesque Austrian city, the four men dispersed, passing out colorful leaflets written in Russian to Red Army soldiers. The Americans spoke in a broken Russian they had learned while waiting in Paris and Vienna. Approximately sixty-five men and women, "mostly soldiers," received copies of the leaflets, "with a mixed attitude of friendliness and curiosity, even after they knew we were Americans."[58] The pacifists somehow remained calm and talkative under extraordinary pressure, even taking a moment to deposit a pile of leaflets on the front steps of the Red Army's military barracks. With few exceptions, the Russian soldiers were engaging and conversational, and several stopped what they were doing to read the leaflets. Although the Americans avoided anybody resembling a high-level officer, occasionally a heavily decorated Soviet officer appeared and watched them. After a few hours of distributing leaflets throughout Baden, three of the men gathered near the railroad depot to catch the next train. Black smoke in the distance indicated an approaching locomotive, but Bill Sutherland still had not come back. Minutes passed, the train drew closer, and the men at the station began to worry about their missing comrade. At the last minute, Sutherland appeared. "Let's get out of here," he said. "I've never been so scared in all my life."[59] Moments later, the pacifists were on the next train bound for the British Zone. Looking back on the Baden action, Sutherland recalled: "We were able to do it and get out of there before any higher-up could really figure out what was going on."[60] The pacifists set off to Paris to pick up their tickets to America. The Paris-to-Moscow bicycle trip was over.

On November 5, the four travelers arrived in New York City and held another press conference. The lack of enthusiasm among American journalists contrasted sharply with the almost daily coverage of the action by the European media. Although the four men attempted to put a positive spin on their trip, they had mixed feelings about the experience. "We didn't achieve our purpose in terms of actually riding into Russia. . . . We felt we had accomplished something, though, because of the publicity that the thing had gotten," remembered Bill Sutherland.[61] Undoubtedly, the most significant and dramatic part of the trip had been the brief excursion into Soviet-occupied Baden, which the pacifists emphasized. The bold act had enabled them to cross the Iron Curtain, as they had originally planned. As the four men stated, "We know also that, though it is possible the soldiers no longer have the leaflets, they must still have a memory of four American pacifists who came illegally across an artificial barrier to greet their Soviet brothers in a message of peace and friendship."[62] Before leaving for France, David had promised to participate in a Peacemakers-sponsored speaking tour, which delayed his return to Glen Gardner by a few more weeks. When Dellinger returned to Glen Gardner, he had been gone five months. He had missed birthdays and special events; each of his children had grown a little; and Betty was now seven months pregnant. The commune seemed more like a ghost town, with its cottages vacant and gardens overgrown. With no regular income, Betty had survived only by taking advantage of the commune's abundant natural resources. "I had no idea how I lived all the time he was gone," she recalled. "But we did have our garden and we had chickens, so we pretty much lived on eggs and vegetables and chicken."[63]

Years later, David openly admitted that the Paris-to-Moscow bicycle trip almost ruined his marriage. Betty was understandably upset about the duration of the journey, and David's guilt over being gone so long contributed to a sullen aloofness on his part. A disturbing pattern developed that hurt the relationship for decades to come: Betty would try to quarrel with David and he would not respond. "Every time there was a conflict, David walked away," Betty explained. "He wouldn't argue, he wouldn't discuss it. I think he didn't know how."[64]

The pacifist movement in America reached its lowest point after the Paris-to-Moscow bicycle trip. Burnout, a lack of direction and support, the Korean War, the Red scare, and internecine skirmishes all contributed to its decline. By 1952 it was clear to Dellinger that a small coterie of spirited pacifists would not be able to revive the American Left anytime soon. Since the late 1940s, internal problems and weaknesses had plagued the movement, and in 1949, Dwight McDonald's influential pacifist magazine *Politics* ceased publication owing to financial losses. Some activists left the movement to pursue other options. Predictably, the nation's few peace groups also diminished in size during the early 1950s. By 1952 the once promising Peacemakers was on the verge of bankruptcy, its account drained by the bicycle trek. Especially disheartening to Muste was the news that the organization had a six-month budget of $1,000, which had to be stretched to cover salaries and office space.[65] "It seems altogether likely," Muste noted in 1952, "that building a radical pacifist movement of any size will be a tougher and slower job in the U.S. than anywhere else."[66]

For steadfast adherents, these were discouraging days. Roy Kepler had been a founder of Peacemakers, coedited *Alternative* with Dellinger, and regularly attended protests against the Korean War and atomic weapons. But in 1949, Kepler took a national survey of groups affiliated with the Peacemakers, and the outcome troubled him. "By and large," he concluded, "[pacifists are] more interested in their particular field of study, their family, their record collections, their comfortable homes, their correct and genteel friends than they are in challenging people to think anew on the great issues of war and peace."[67] Kepler himself stepped back from political organizing in 1955 to open his own bookstore in Palo Alto, California. The store sold only paperback books, and it quickly became a legendary countercultural meeting place popular with Bay Area nonconformists, leftists, and beatniks. Roy often brought in prominent authors of recent books, such as the famed physicist Edward Teller, to give free talks to sizable crowds. It was at Kepler's Bookstore that a young Jerry Garcia, who later founded the Grateful Dead, landed his first job, and Joan Baez was one of Roy's best customers.[68]

Like Kepler and so many other cold war–era pacifists, Dellinger temporarily backed away somewhat, but not entirely, from political organizing. To secure a regular income, he took an office job at the War Resisters League for several months in 1952. The fourth Dellinger child, Danny, was born on January 21, 1952, at the Catholic Worker farm in Staten Island, New York. Aware of David and Betty's precarious financial situation, Dorothy Day had invited the family to move out to the farm to reduce David's commuting time to the WRL offices.[69]

Events in 1953 compounded David's frustrations with the American peace movement. On January 21, police in Pasadena, California, arrested Bayard Rustin for engaging in oral sex with two men in the backseat of an automobile at the Green Hotel. The lurid bust generated plenty of headlines and resulted in a humiliating ordeal for Rustin. At the time of the arrest, he was the FOR's field secretary and had gone to California to raise funds for a forthcoming trip to Nigeria. A. J. Muste, who had been like a father to Rustin, threatened to fire him unless he resigned from the FOR. Rustin agreed to Muste's terms and also wrote a letter of resignation from the executive committee of the WRL, but it was rejected.[70] "Bayard was in tears," recalled Glenn Smiley, an activist with the FOR in California. "He was most repentant over the homosexual incident, because of the grief it had brought to A. J. Muste."[71] In the summer, Roy Finch, who had risen to the position of chairman of the WRL, considered hiring Rustin to become the WRL's office secretary and program director. He solicited the opinions of various influential WRL members, including his close friend David Dellinger. Some respondents opposed hiring Rustin for the job, raising concerns about what they regarded as his reckless promiscuity. Longtime member Frances Witherspoon, who served on the WRL's advisory council, echoed the views of other troubled members in her objections. "Frankly, I feel that Bayard as Secretary at this juncture would be . . . a considerable liability, both because of the possibility of a recurrence of his difficulty, and because of the publicity the Western papers gave his case."[72]

Unlike Witherspoon, Dellinger adamantly supported hiring Rustin. His sensitivity to Rustin's dilemma was rooted in his own ambiguous sexual preferences. In an unpublished draft of his memoirs later omitted from the final version, Dellinger admitted that he had had an "intimate" relationship after "falling in love" with a fellow conscientious objector at Lewisburg Federal Penitentiary. He insisted that he had no sexual contact with the prisoner but said they enjoyed long conversations and "silences" with each other.[73] Dellinger never publicly stated whether he had had any homosexual encounters, but according to Betty, "he may've been interested in homosexual things," she remembered, "because young men just clung to him so often. His most intimate relationships were with young men. . . . They were good people, and I loved them. So it was never anything horrifying to me, it never had any negative connotations."[74] Apparently Dellinger underwent at least one personal ordeal that could have developed into a scandal similar to Rustin's troubles. In a 1986 letter to an acquaintance, David admitted that in 1951 police charged him with a "sexual 'misdemeanor.'" Without specifying the nature of the offense, he said the charge quietly haunted him for the next two decades. Years later, after reviewing declassified FBI documents, Dellinger discovered that federal agents attempted several times to tip off the media about the '51 incident, but without success.[75]

The murder of David's younger brother, Fiske, heightened David's awareness about the plight of homosexuals. Privately, David knew Fiske was gay. But when Fiske's killer, Richard Albrecht, told police that the murder occurred because Fiske propositioned him and the police reported these details to the press, Fiske's homosexuality became public knowledge. By the 1950s, Dellinger viewed the persecution of homosexuals as insidious. He therefore wrote a highly spirited defense of Bayard Rustin in September 1953, encouraging Roy Finch, in the strongest possible terms, to hire Rustin. He conceded that hiring Rustin might alienate some potential supporters but argued that it was worth the risk because Bayard was "the most creative nonviolent activist" in America. He found Rustin's political and organizational skills "truly inventive, courageous, and brilliant." The peace movement in general, and the WRL in particular, needed "new life and imagination," and Rustin "is the one person I can think of who can bring" such qualities to the WRL, Dellinger argued.[76] Weeks later, Rustin's supporters rejoiced at the news of his new full-time position at the WRL.

Another matter that troubled Dellinger in 1953 was the impending execution of the alleged atomic spies Julius and Ethel Rosenberg. Unlike Bayard Rustin's trying experience, the Rosenbergs' ordeal had no chance of a satisfactory resolution. At New York's Sing Sing Prison, the couple sat on death row in 1953 awaiting their execution, scheduled for June. In cold-war America, countless liberals and leftists, including most pacifists, remained silent about the case, and a few even supported the government. This bothered Dellinger, who believed the couple had been framed for their political beliefs. He routinely marched with handfuls of other pickets in New York's Union Square in the spring to protest the upcoming execution. Such a position put him at odds with much of the peace movement, thus adding to his growing dissatisfaction with it. Almost all pacifists opposed the death penalty, but unlike Dellinger, few regarded the Rosenbergs as martyrs. David wrote two articles about the couple, one before and one after the executions. Both appeared in the anarchist magazine *Individual Action*, edited by Dellinger's friend John Goldstein and printed at the Libertarian Press. The latter article included some of Dellinger's finest prose and was filled with despair. He extended the responsibility for the Rosenbergs' deaths to include the public, the legal system, the media, and the federal government. He concluded: "To our unspeakable shame, we murdered the Rosenbergs—instead of finding ways to mingle the love that slumbers in our hearts with the love that was so nobly developed in theirs."[77]

The executions of Julius and Ethel Rosenberg left Dellinger dispirited and frustrated. Around the same time as the Rosenberg execution, Dellinger said farewell to one of his closest friends and allies from his inner circle of pacifist comrades. Bill Sutherland decided to move to Africa in 1953 and work for Kwame Nkrumah's nonviolent pan-African liberation movement in Ghana. In 1955, George Houser, who had founded the American Committee on Africa two years earlier, moved to Africa as well, where he helped several nonviolent pan-African independence struggles across the continent and even worked with Sutherland on a few projects.

The loss of two such creative and tireless activists diminished the radical wing of the pacifist movement. But their departure did not lessen Dellinger's dedication to nonviolent direct action, and through the mid-1950s he continued searching for opportunities to protest that did not take him away from Glen Gardner for extended periods of time.

At first his search was to no avail. Indeed, toward the end of one particularly long, contentious, and unproductive Peacemakers meeting in 1952, Bayard Rustin proclaimed, "This is getting us nowhere."[78] His words could have described the nation's community of radical pacifists, who had been trying since 1940 to develop a viable mass movement to resist war and injustice, but by the mid-1950s, they appeared to be no closer to that elusive goal. History would soon turn in their favor, however. No one could have predicted the opportunity for dissent that lay ahead.

6

Winds of Change

My friend Dave Dellinger a few years ago put it this way: in the world
as it is today, you cannot be truly nonviolent if you are not revolutionary. Because if you are not revolutionary you're condoning the present
setup, which is basically one of exploitation and violence and militarism.

A. J. Muste

IN THE MID-1950S David Dellinger turned inward, focusing most of
his attention on family and work. Marital conflicts caused by the 1951
Paris-to-Moscow bicycle trip still stung, and the five months it took him
away from Betty and the children could not be replaced. Building a
community in the woods of New Jersey, far removed from the arms
race, suburban sprawl, and pervasive materialism of postwar America
seemed as essential to him as agitating for change in the streets of New
York City or Washington, D.C. "I believe it is crucial," Dellinger wrote
in 1958, "to renounce in our own lives property and privileges and
power (the things over which wars are fought) rather than merely call
for disarmament and a more humane society."[1] He spent much of the
decade working in his print shop, vacationing with his family in the
summer, watching his children grow bigger, and raising fruits, vegetables, and livestock at Glen Gardner. The pull of political action remained potent, however, and he often traveled to New York to speak at
rallies, attend meetings, and organize events. "I was all this time trying
to weigh dual responsibilities," he recalled, "one of them having five
children."[2] During this decade, Dellinger became increasingly selective
in his political commitments because he did not want to be away from
his family and community for extended periods of time. Two developments, however, drew him back into the fray: the creation of the highly
influential *Liberation* magazine in 1956 and the Cuban revolution in

1959. The epic civil rights struggle in the South, which turned the national spotlight on tactics of nonviolent direct action, also contributed to David's perception that the political atmosphere in America was undergoing a dramatic transformation.

In 1956, Betty received a call from the guidance counselor at her children's elementary school. A scuffle had broken out between her son Ray and another boy, and the administrator asked her to come to the school. Once again, David was gone, and Betty went alone to the elementary school to speak to the principal, who informed her that Ray and another boy had gotten into a fight after the boy called him a "traitor" and a "communist." Instead of turning the other cheek, Ray attacked the student until a playground monitor separated them. The principal sent Ray home with his mother for the remainder of the day so she could persuade him to avoid fighting in the future.[3] Ray was not the only Dellinger youth to fight back against schoolyard toughs in the 1950s. "I did have a few playground fights with narrow-minded bullies," remembered the Dellingers' eldest son, Patch, "but that is not a dominant part of the childhood experience."[4]

Even though such situations made Betty even more frustrated with David's frequent absences, she acknowledged that her husband had become more sensitive in the 1950s to her and his family's needs. For instance, David helped in the births of Natasha, Danny, and the last of the Dellinger children, Michele, born in October 1956. Indeed, the Dellingers did many things together as a family, with some of their happiest moments occurring in the 1950s and early 1960s, before the anti–Vietnam War movement began to absorb so much of David's time. Patch Dellinger remembered "reading Shakespeare together as a family. Going to chamber music concerts with my parents. Hiking in the woods. Hunting. Working in the family garden. Working in the print shop. Playing baseball. Marching to ban the bomb in the 1950's."[5]

Almost every aspect of family life at Glen Gardner had a political overtone. The Dellingers' frequent visitors included A. J. Muste, Dorothy Day, Bayard Rustin, and other pacifist luminaries. Family vacations often coincided with political events, as when in 1955 when the entire Dellinger clan attended an American Friends Service Committee Summer Peace Institute in Geneva, Wisconsin. During the gathering, the families stayed in cabins by the lake, and the children swam during the day while the adults attended nonviolence-training seminars.[6] The family counted on the stipends provided by peace organizations for participation in conferences and workshops, as finances were often tight in the Dellinger household and activism did not pay the bills. In good times, though, the printing press furnished a tolerable income, enabling the family to enjoy a modest lifestyle. David and Betty agreed that communal living was essential to their political beliefs. "A living community," Betty wrote in 1949, "offers the best opportunity for freedom from the regimentation of the public schools and development of a freer, truer education."[7]

One of the main reasons for creating the commune in the first place was to establish a network of pacifists who would take care of one another if a member was arrested or had to leave for an extended period. Unfortunately for the Dellingers, the reality turned out to be much more disappointing than the ideal. With the exception of the DiGias, the other residents only occasionally interacted socially with the Dellingers and, in Betty's words, "just tolerated our children."[8] Although later arrivals cared somewhat more about the collective group's well-being, the Dellingers never were close to any of the other commune inhabitants.

The children kept Betty's anxiety and depression at bay, and until 1951 she homeschooled them. This ended, however while David was in Europe on the bicycle trip, when the authorities demanded that Betty send her two sons, Patch and Ray, to the local elementary school. Still, as long as there were children in the house that needed looking after, Betty was content and tolerated David's political commitments. "Trying to find myself is really what I was trying to do. I was with a very strong man and I got lost a lot, at least I felt I did. As a mother I could always function."[9] Betty also sought something in life that was her own. In the early 1950s she attended religious retreats at a nearby Catholic monastery, and in 1952 she joined the Catholic Church and, for the next sixteen years, became active locally. The Catholic Church offered a community of kindred spirits, a spiritual haven, and an outlet for her volunteerism.[10]

Having radical nonconformists for parents in the 1950s proved at once to be both a blessing and a challenge for the Dellinger children. Routine cold war–era public school rituals, such as taking part in duck-and-cover atomic bomb drills or watching movies depicting the Red menace taking over the globe, conflicted with values the Dellinger children were taught at home. One particularly insensitive elementary school teacher announced to his class that the youngest Dellinger child,

Michele, was the daughter of "Reds." He routinely subjected her to questions about communism and life behind the Iron Curtain, insisting that she answer them without help from her fellow pupils. Although Betty protested to the teacher, she was unable to persuade him to cease his harsh treatment of Michele.[11]

Sometimes the Dellinger children simply wanted to fit in with the other children, as David learned when one of his sons told him that all the other boys in his class had toy guns. David stopped what he was doing, took his son into the woods, and found a chunk of wood. For the next hour Dellinger used a carving knife and shaped it into a respectable-looking wooden gun. On another occasion, when David disciplined one of his children for a minor wrongdoing, the child informed him that other kids' parents spanked them when they did something wrong. "Is that what you want?" asked David. The child nodded, and David obliged by giving him a "love tap"—a euphemism he concocted for a light swat. Years later, Patch Dellinger noted, "His children have been quoted as saying, 'Stop talking and hit me!'"[12]

Through much of the 1950s, David accepted a secondary role in political organizing so that he could spend more time with his family. Others, such as A. J. Muste, Bayard Rustin, Jim Peck, and the new rising star, Bradford Lyttle, who organized the Committee for Nonviolent Action (CNVA), assumed greater prominence. In the late 1950s and early 1960s, however, Dellinger reverted to his old habits. He began leaving Glen Gardner for weeks at a time, and Betty would try to maintain the routines as if he had never left, but her unhappiness was evident. Indeed, the children sometimes wondered whether their father cared more about political organizing than about his own family. "Dad was not always there when his family was growing up," remembered Patch, "but when he was there he made you feel as if you were the most important, intelligent, loved person in the world."[13] When Patch was in the seventh grade, he accompanied his dad on a ban-the-bomb march from New Haven to New York. For Patch, it marked the beginning of a lifetime of supporting the causes his father cherished. Other Dellingers also followed in their father's footsteps. As Patch put it, "My younger brothers and sisters went to many civil rights demonstrations with him, and we all went to Vietnam demonstrations with him and without him."[14]

■

On February 21, 1955, A. J. Muste wrote a lengthy report entitled "Proposal for a Bimonthly Magazine," in which he advocated creating a periodical that would

> try to reach out and speak to wide circles of students, labor people, Socialists, former Socialists and Communists, farmers, peace workers, pacifists, progressive church people—those troubled over the A-bomb and what it signifies. It should be serious in approach (not meant to exclude humor or liveliness) and deal with fundamental economic, political, cultural and ethical problems.

The publication, he asserted, should reflect the ideas of nonaligned, independent radicals and inspire creative and bold acts of resistance.[15] Muste also wrote a companion document entitled "Monthly Magazine Prospectus" which outlined the politics of his proposed periodical. The magazine should reject rigid, orthodox Marxism, an ideology that Muste believed "adopts the same old methods of force and chicanery characterizing the old regimes that had to be overthrown precisely because they embodied such evils." The magazine should also consistently provide a robust "critique of liberalism," an political outlook that, despite its admirable qualities of "humaneness and tolerance," had failed to "come to grips with war, poverty, . . . authoritarianism and other great evils of the world."[16]

In 1955 the time seemed right to launch such a periodical. Pacifists across the nation were mobilizing against the arms race and Jim Crow segregation in the South, and they would need a sensible, informative radical monthly to connect their movements together and help them make sense of developments. Muste saw Dellinger as a potential ally, and in the spring, David met A. J. at Muste's Manhattan office to discuss their possible collaboration on the project. The strained cordiality that had characterized their relationship in the 1940s had given way to an outwardly warm but still distant friendship by the mid-1950s. Despite some minor disagreements about the style and content of the proposed magazine, the two men agreed on its necessity. Dellinger went into the meeting with Muste with a cautiously optimistic outlook about the project and offered the use of his print shop. Like Muste, Dellinger wanted the magazine to serve as a vehicle for independent radical thought. "I don't want it to become a counter in the political struggle of old-line sects or tendencies," Dellinger wrote in 1957. "I want it to be a center for fresh and imaginative approaches of a wide variety of outlooks."[17] The War Resisters League (WRL) offered financial support, and in the summer of 1955 Muste and Dellinger began including in their planning meetings Bayard Rustin and Roy Finch, the latter by this time a professor of philosophy at Sarah Lawrence College.[18]

After months of planning and hard work, the first issue of *Liberation: An Independent Monthly* appeared in April 1956. Its contents reflected the creativity and eclecticism of the cold war–era independent radical left. Civil rights agitation in the South, nuclear disarmament campaigns, nonconformity in Eisenhower's America, and experimental poetry were common topics of discussion. The journal attracted some of the finest writers of the day, including James Baldwin, Gary Snyder, and Norman Mailer; activist luminaries such as Rev. Dr. Martin Luther King Jr. and Norman Thomas; and noted public intellectuals like William Appleman Williams and Lewis Mumford. In the 1960s, *Liberation* published pieces by some of the most influential Black Power, New Left, and feminist figures in the United States.

Ironically, *Liberation* emerged largely as a result of its chief competitor, Irving Howe's more moderate *Dissent* magazine. Muste had been a contributing editor to *Dissent* since it first appeared in early 1954 but had become increasingly dissatisfied with the rigid anticommunism of Howe and his supporters on the editorial board. Two *Dissent* editors, Muste and the militant labor activist and scholar Sid Lens, challenged the conventional wisdom of their fellow editors by writing pieces defending political alliances between communists who had renounced the 1956 Soviet invasion of Hungary and noncommunist radicals. Muste also called on nonaligned leftists to widen their circle to include members of the Trotskyist Socialist Workers Party (SWP). Such proposals offended Irving Howe's democratic socialist sensibilities. "Howe was appalled and said so," wrote his biographer Gerald Sorin.[19] Muste further alienated the *Dissent* editorial board by openly participating in a 1957 May Day rally that included communists and SWPers. As Sid Lens remembered, "I stopped writing for *Dissent* . . . and in the end Howe asked me to remove myself as a contributing editor. Muste, showing solidarity for my position, resigned." Lens moved over to *Liberation*, joining the editorial board in the late 1950s.[20]

Liberation rivaled *Dissent* as the most influential leftist publication in the United States in the late 1950s. Its very existence, and its endorsement of "third camp" radicalism distinct from both liberalism and Marxism, foreshadowed the rise of the New Left in the 1960s. Many copies of *Liberation* found their way into the hands of younger leftists—particularly college students and activists—who read its articles and were inspired by its daring, alternative reportage and ceaseless calls for resistance. For the Dellingers, *Liberation* became something of a family affair. Both David and Betty spent hours in the print shop. As Betty recalled, "I went into the office every day and did editorial, and . . . paste-up. Everything, whatever had to be done."[21] Occasionally the children worked in the print shop after school, helping keep the place tidy and produce the magazine. For the first time since it opened, the print shop furnished a steady, reliable income for the Dellinger family. Patch Dellinger remembered that his father "would work all night to finish a printing job on deadline and then collapse into bed the next day, or sometimes jump in the truck to deliver the job to New York."[22]

But sometimes the demands of *Liberation* exceeded the capabilities of the Libertarian Press. By 1960, most issues did not reach newsstands or subscribers until several weeks into the month of its publication date. The April 1960 issue, for example, did not appear until late April or early May. The slowdown was caused by the hospitalization of a Libertarian Press operator in the spring of 1960, the inability of its limited staff to keep up with the demands of a monthly magazine, and minor contractual problems. "We wonder," Muste wrote to Dellinger on March 24, 1960, "whether the only possible way to get back on schedule may be by having somebody else take over one of the issues, get it out approximately on time and then enable you . . . to get out subsequent issues on time." *Liberation* eventually overcame its scheduling problems, and the Libertarian Press continued to print the magazine until 1965.[23]

In the 1950s, the magazine had teetered on the brink of bankruptcy and appeared to be heading the way of its predecessors, *Direct Action*, *Alternative*, and Dwight MacDonald's *Politics*. Circulation rates were slow to climb. In October 1956, circulation hovered around 1,100, and although the number climbed to almost 2,000 three years later, it fell short of the 5,000 that staffers hoped to achieve by that time.[24] Then in 1957, the magazine hired David McReynolds, an energetic twenty-eight-year-old socialist pacifist from Los Angeles, as its sole staff person. In his role as "editorial secretary" of *Liberation*, McReynolds breathed new life into the magazine, devising creative ways of expanding the subscriber base and raising funds. Heavily influenced by Bayard

Rustin, whom he had met a few years earlier, McReynolds became a devoted disciple of Muste.

The editorial board of *Liberation*, McReynolds observed, "had an interesting breakdown between the anarchists who were Roy Finch and Dave Dellinger and the more Marxist position which was Sid Lens, Bayard, and A. J."[25] Finch's and Dellinger's anarchistic politics often clashed with Muste's unwavering socialist commitment. Muste was never fully aware of the extent of the tensions because Finch and Dellinger could sometimes be two-faced in their dealings with him. Petty jealousy also factored into the discord. Muste had gained national fame, which eluded Finch and Dellinger. For his part, Finch feared that *Liberation* would become too closely associated with Muste in readers' minds, which could undermine the magazine's claim to be independent. Given that radical periodicals in the 1950s typically developed around a cult of personality, his apprehension was understandable. Because *Dissent* revolved around Irving Howe, *Monthly Review* around editors Paul Sweezy and Leo Huberman, and *I.F. Stone's Weekly Reader* around Stone, its sole contributor, Finch worried that the same thing would happen with *Liberation*. With numerous pieces written by members of the WRL and by Muste himself, *Liberation* appeared to Finch to be evolving into a "Musteite" organ. "If you recall A. J.'s history," Finch wrote to Dellinger in July 1957, "he moved back and forth among the various sects and tendencies—maneuvering to get control of larger and larger blocs. . . . *Liberation*, which started off as an independent magazine quite apart from all that sort of thing has now been drawn into it. It becomes just another mouthpiece."[26] Dellinger was decidedly more sympathetic to Muste but nonetheless still harbored resentments and occasionally questioned Muste's judgment. In the summer of 1957, he counseled Finch:

> A. J. is not long for this world. I have often thought of the fact that you and I and Bayard have to be thinking of carrying on without him. His push, his contacts . . . have helped us get under way, but the basic tone of the magazine from the first had to be set by us . . . and we have to be getting the momentum to carry on without him.[27]

From 1956 to 1960 David immersed himself in producing *Liberation*, attending editorial board meetings and assuming the role of assignment editor. Each day he wrote letters and telephoned writers, soliciting articles, poems, and magazine covers. His own contributions to the magazine addressed an array of topics, from communal living to baseball. During his *Liberation* years, new friendships were made and old ones revived. As Dellinger wrote to Roy Finch: "After 40, I am establishing vital relationships with people, many of whom are not known within conventional pacifist circles . . . but an increasing number of whom are going to be helping out, I think."[28] In the spring of 1957, David met Staughton Lynd, son of the renowned sociologists Robert and Helen Lynd, at the Glen Gardner community. The two instantly became close friends. Since 1954, Staughton and his wife Alice had lived at a similar community, Macedonia, in rural Georgia. The Lynds moved to Glen Gardner and temporarily lived in a small cabin that had once been a chicken coop. Compared with Macedonia, which was an egalitarian and tightly knit communal experiment, Glen Gardner—by now referred to by its inhabitants as St. Francis Acres—was much more individualistic and fragmented. After six months the Lynds left Glen Gardner and eventually settled in Atlanta, where Staughton taught history at Emory University before later accepting a position at Yale. He remained in close contact with David and joined the *Liberation* editorial board in 1964.[29]

Working at *Liberation* also brought Dellinger closer to his longtime friends Muste and Rustin. Both men had been much more active than Dellinger in the 1950s, and their stories of civil rights campaigns and ban-the-bomb actions made him envious. Of particular interest to Dellinger were Rustin's firsthand reports of the 1956 bus boycott in Montgomery, Alabama. After listening to Rustin's accounts, Dellinger decided to visit the South, where he believed important things were happening. He did not visit Montgomery, but in the summer of 1956 he took his family to an interracial communal experiment known as Koinonia, near the small town of Americus, Georgia. Unlike many of his northern comrades, Dellinger did not view the South in stereotypical terms, as some distant, exotic land of deteriorating plantations and Ku Klux Klan nightriders. Because he had spent long periods of time in North Carolina during his youth, returning several times as an adult to visit relatives in the Appalachians, he believed that most ordinary white southerners were decent people who, if properly educated about the history of the South and the harsh realities of Jim Crow segregation, could become allies in the nonviolent freedom struggle.

The Koinonia settlement had recently been firebombed and shot at in the middle of the night because it had accepted African American families into the commune. Founded in 1943, Koinonia had a population of about sixty people in 1956. Its inhabitants, according to one account of the settlement, "share all the property and income communally, as they believe the early Christians did."[30] The recent attacks had left the residents shaken, and they called on other pacifists for assistance. David and Betty "stood nonviolent guard" late at night, reasoning that "if they had a light on and people were standing there, no attackers were apt to shoot or throw things." Night guard involved long periods of boredom punctuated by tense moments and occasional strange noises coming from the woods. Days passed with no more attacks, however, and the Dellingers prepared to return home. Toward the end of the trip, Patch begged his parents to let him stay in Georgia for his summer vacation and return to Glen Gardner later. It was a difficult decision, but because the Dellingers knew and trusted the families at Koinonia, David and Betty reluctantly agreed. David remembered, "He risked his life and we risked his life. And there's no way I can say now whether we were right or wrong in doing so. Just as I didn't completely know at the time what was right or wrong."[31]

Back in New York, Dellinger detected a shift in the nation's mood. The deep freeze of the cold war had thawed to a point that Soviet and American leaders now seriously considered the prospect of détente. The triumph of the Montgomery bus boycott, culminating with a U.S. Supreme Court ruling to desegregate buses, had energized and emboldened civil rights activists in the South. Civil disobedience enjoyed a new revival in the late 1950s when the recently created Committee for Nonviolent Action (CNVA) sponsored several nonviolent protest campaigns for nuclear disarmament at military bases and missile silos across America. Under the direction of Brad Lyttle, the CNVA led marches for peace and organized protests against civil defense air raid drills.

As an editor at *Liberation*, Dellinger wrote about—and sometimes participated in—some of the most momentous events of the day, and he was not afraid to criticize his fellow activists for what he regarded as errors in strategy and judgment. The September 1959 issue of *Liberation* contained one of his most influential pieces, entitled "Are Pacifists Willing to Be Negroes?" in which Dellinger took his pacifist comrades to task for not being sufficiently sensitive to the victims of white violence and for failing to work more closely with the civil rights movement. The article was a response to an article in the same issue by Robert F. Williams, the suspended president of the Monroe, North Carolina, chapter of the National Association for the Advancement of Colored People (NAACP). Williams criticized Martin Luther King Jr.'s nonviolent approach and advocated "armed self-defense" for African Americans when facing white violence. In contrast, Dellinger insisted on a "positive nonviolent campaign for the . . . liberation of the Negroes."[32]

All these experiences prepared Dellinger for the dramatic days ahead. "What I did in the fifties helped me play a role in the sixties movement," Dellinger told an interviewer. "For many of us, the sixties came out of those earlier types of experiences in which we stood up for what we knew was right."[33] He soon returned to full-time political organizing, inspired by events in the United States and in Cuba.

In the late 1950s, Havana, Cuba, was beset by corruption, betrayal, and violence. Besides presiding over a despotic regime, Cuba's autocratic dictator, Fulgencio Batista, personally profited from decades of support from Washington, D.C. By the eve of the revolution, Batista and his associates had embezzled millions of dollars. His security forces brutally repressed all forms of opposition in Cuba. In the countryside, living conditions were wretched and growing worse each year. But by the end of 1958 Batista's firm grip on power had weakened considerably. The armed revolutionaries of the July 26 movement had gained momentum in the mountains and sugarcane fields and now encircled Havana, defeating much larger forces of Batista's army in their march to the capital. In the early morning hours of January 1, 1959, Batista fled to Miami, and within forty-eight hours armed rebel forces swept into the city, greeted by cheering crowds. U.S. officials and journalists initially reacted to the 1959 revolution with cautious optimism. Few Americans knew anything about Fidel Castro, the charismatic young leader of the July 26 movement.

Like the fledgling civil rights movement in the South, the Cuban revolution stirred the American left, though some radicals were slow to back Castro. As Sid Lens observed, "It took a little while for leftist support to galvanize around the Cuban revolution, perhaps because few people thought Washington would revert to its ancient policy of gunboat diplomacy."[34] In the early months Dellinger took little notice of the

Cuban revolution. Finally, as relations between the United States and Cuba began deteriorating in the summer of 1960, the editorial board of *Liberation* showed interest in the revolution. In the fall, the board members agreed to send Dellinger to Cuba to record his impressions of the revolution for *Liberation* readers. He flew to Havana, Cuba, on October 27, 1960,[35] in a critical frame of mind, fully prepared to find fault with the Castro government. "As a pacifist and personalist (anarchist, if you prefer), I was not predisposed to like the Cuban Revolution . . . on my first trip in November 1960, when I spent three weeks on the island," Dellinger wrote.[36] "Not since I was in Spain in 1936, six short weeks after the outbreak of the Franco rebellion, have I been in such a heady atmosphere as that of Revolutionary Cuba."[37] After spending several days in Havana, Dellinger found an interpreter and an automobile and began a cross-country trek across the island to assess rural conditions. "I made a point of tracking down every kind of opposition to the regime (opponents are not hard to find) and spent hours at a time listening to religious, political, and economic objections to what is going on."[38]

Deeply moved by what he had witnessed in Cuba, Dellinger returned to the United States and wrote what many regarded as his finest contributions to *Liberation* magazine. The serialized account of his trip appeared in the December 1960, January, and March 1961 issues. The first article in Dellinger's account chronicled the turbulent history of U.S.-Cuban relations, highlighting the recurring U.S. invasions of Cuba since 1898 to suppress unrest on the island and Washington's policy of financing corrupt, autocratic leaders during the sixty years before the revolution. The second article explored Cuba's internal transformations carried out by the revolutionary regime in the areas of health care, education, and land reform. His final contribution described what he called "the campaign against Cuba," characterizing it as "a corrupt alliance of American financial and military interests with dispossessed and embittered members of the Cuban upper classes, some of whom derived their wealth from gross corruption that would not have been tolerated in the United States."[39] For Dellinger, the most difficult task was reconciling his support of the Cuban revolution with his commitment to Gandhian pacifism. In a critique underscoring his new approach to nonviolence, Dellinger faulted pacifists who "suffer from what seems to me to be an excess of puritanical zeal," as well as middle-class pacifists living in the affluence of postwar America who criticized the Cuban revolution for its violence. "Our children are not growing up illiterate and undernourished victims of a foreign imperialism," he argued. "We are not un-employed. Yet it does not seem to bother most of us that when we view the Cuban Revolution our main emotional drive . . . is against the vio-lence of those who have risen up in their suffering and the sufferings of their people to become Revolutionists."[40] Finally, Dellinger suggested that Batista's regime had been so repressive that it ruled out the possi-bility of a nonviolent resistance movement emerging in Cuba. Violence was an unfortunate but necessary means to an end for Castro's guerril-las, he insisted. But he predicted that once the revolution triumphed, the new regime would return to peaceful methods.

Although Dellinger's Cuba series became highly influential in American leftist circles, some *Liberation* supporters were less enthusias-tic. The most vehement protest came from fellow editorial board mem-ber Roy Finch, author of the magazine's first editorial on the Cuban rev-olution, in January 1959. But reports of human rights abuses in Cuba and allegations that Cuban anarchists and libertarians had been treated poorly by the government prompted Finch to reevaluate his initial, en-thusiastic assessment of the revolution. He thus felt that Dellinger's ar-ticles praised the regime too highly and lacked sufficient criticism. Ac-cordingly, he wrote a counterpoint piece for the March issue using high-lights of interviews with exiled, anti-Castro Cuban libertarian leftists conducted by Russell Blackwell of New York's Libertarian League. Cuba, Finch concluded, was "pretty well being taken over by totalitar-ian-minded people."[41] In May 1961, Finch resigned from the editorial board of *Liberation*, citing editorial differences over Cuba. The island had become a "state capitalist" totalitarian society, he declared, and he urged a peaceful "overthrow" of the Castro regime.[42]

Dellinger thought that Finch's position on Cuba was unreasonable. The U.S. government, not Castro, had drawn the battle lines, David be-lieved. In such a polarized cold-war climate, there was little that a com-mitted radical activist could do but back the Cuban revolution. The threat of an American invasion of the island necessitated accepting cer-tain unpleasant realities about Cuban society, which under normal cir-cumstances he would not hesitate to criticize. As far as Finch was con-cerned, Dellinger's stand on Cuba raised troubling questions about the sincerity of his commitment to nonviolence and human rights. Finch could not help but conclude that Dellinger had somehow been co-opted during his November visit to Cuba and had therefore abandoned his authentic and independent voice. Contact between the two men ceased, bringing an end to a friendship that had begun almost a quarter of a century earlier at Yale. Maggie Finch, widow of Roy Finch, looked back on the unfortunate break and explained:

> Roy was extremely bright. He was a philosopher and he could understand all kinds of things, but he lacked a certain warmth or gentleness or softness that Dave had. . . . I always imagined Dave was perhaps more of a forgiving kind of person and therefore he could understand more things about Cuba that would put it on the good side. And Roy would just sort of close his eyes and think of it as a communist country and that was the end of that.[43]

Other members of *Liberation*'s editorial board were more sympathetic to Dellinger's position. Sid Lens had traveled to Cuba at the same time that Dellinger had, and while not as partisan in his conclusions, he was equally impressed by what he had seen. A. J. Muste's concern over Cuba grew out of his commitment to the antinuclear movement. He feared that the island might become a flash point in the geopolitical cold war between the superpowers. Though unsure of Castro, Muste repeatedly signed statements urging the U.S. government to lift its embargo against Cuba and avoid intervention. Bayard Rustin, meanwhile, largely avoided the Cuba question, focusing most of his attention on civil rights campaigns.

In 1961, David joined the newly organized Fair Play for Cuba Committee (FPCC), which historian Van Gosse described as "a hodgepodge of self-radicalizing liberals, black nationalists or those considered to be such, Trotskyists and other Old Leftists on their way into the New, and young people somewhere between a purified liberalism, neo-Marxism and all-purpose radicalism."[44] By late 1961, Dellinger was on the FPCC's executive committee, along with the African American poet LeRoi Jones, who was serving as its president, and Trotskyist activist Nat Weinstein.[45]

Dellinger also founded another organization, the ad hoc Nonviolent Committee for Cuban Independence (NVCCI). Although the NVCCI was never as large as the FPCC, it enjoyed the legitimacy of several pacifist endorsements, including sponsorship by the *Catholic Worker*, the Committee for Nonviolent Action, the Peacemakers, and the War Resisters League. Along with Dellinger, the NVCCI's membership included such noted pacifists as Muste, Jim Peck, Ralph DiGia, Barbara

Deming, Dorothy Day, Al Uhrie, George Willoughby, Robert Steed, and Richard Gilpin. The impetus for its creation was the United States' ill-fated Bay of Pigs invasion on April 17, 1961. Even before the election of John F. Kennedy as president in November 1960, the Central Intelligence Agency and the Eisenhower administration had been planning an invasion of the island by sixteen hundred Cuban exiles. The exiles were promised U.S. air and naval support and were told by American intelligence experts that the invasion would trigger a widespread public uprising inside Cuba. But the invaders landed at a swamp, where there were no mountains for refuge, and the revolutionary forces swiftly routed them.[46]

The Bay of Pigs invasion triggered a wave of protests across the United States. Demonstrations were held in New York City, Los Angeles, San Francisco, Chicago, Washington, D.C., Boston, Tampa, Philadelphia, Detroit, Cleveland, New Haven, Seattle, and Baltimore.[47] The NVCCI conducted its own action, a two-week vigil and fast from April 30 to May 13 outside the CIA headquarters in Washington, D.C. (before the agency relocated to Langley, Virginia). The NVCCI released a statement denouncing U.S. policy toward Cuba and called on Castro to "look with compassion and forgiveness upon the misguided invaders." David Dellinger was one of ten protesters who participated in the round-the-clock action on the lawn next to the CIA, which at times attracted a mixed crowd of sympathizers, foes, and indifferent observers. On the third day of the action, police arrested seven out of the ten demonstrators, including Dellinger, charged them with "disorderly conduct," and booked them into the Washington district jail. In the meantime, the combination of fast and vigil at the CIA headquarters continued, with about seventy-five people joining the three original fasters who were not arrested. "We were released in time to join the closing demonstration," Dellinger remembered, "at which approximately two hundred and fifty people walked from the CIA past the White House to a public rally, which was attended by four hundred persons."[48]

By the fall of 1962, the possibility of nuclear war loomed with the Cuban missile crisis. Once again, the peace movement mobilized, marching in several American cities and attracting a crowd of ten thousand at the United Nations on October 21. By the end of October, the worst of the crisis had passed, and the superpowers had avoided a nuclear confrontation. Nevertheless, the event underscored divergent views in the American peace movement. At an emergency meeting during the early stages of the Cuban missile crisis, Bayard Rustin criticized all the nations involved—the United States, Cuba, and the Soviet Union—as equal provocateurs.[49] A split developed between those who accepted Rustin's position and more radical activists such as David Dellinger, who believed that the crisis arose largely as a result of the U.S. government's aggressive anti-Castro policies, which predated the Bay of Pigs invasion.

In the early 1960s, David Dellinger stood at the confluence of several emerging protest movements, and being an editor at *Liberation* offered him a vantage point from which to view the gathering forces.[50] By the early 1960s, sit-ins, freedom rides, and mass arrests in the South indicated the spread of nonviolent direct action to a part of the country where its adherents least expected to find it. Dellinger felt a kinship with the youthful Student Nonviolent Coordinating Committee (SNCC), which organized many key civil rights campaigns. "SNCC was a grassroots participatory democracy organization," he explained, "so it was much closer to my beliefs than Martin Luther King was."[51]

Likewise, in the late 1950s and early 1960s the peace movement had grown bolder in its tactics. The Committee for a Sane Nuclear Policy, more widely known as SANE, was the nation's most influential antinuclear organization. Founded in 1959, SANE adopted a cautious liberal approach, organizing respectable rallies and lobbying campaigns while rejecting civil disobedience. But in many respects the CNVA's smaller, headline-grabbing protests overshadowed SANE's efforts.

Although David Dellinger abstained from CNVA's early campaigns, he wrote about them in *Liberation*. Ultimately, though, no other event in this period stirred Dellinger's activist impulses like the Cuban revolution. Indeed, he was so enthralled with it and so convinced that an American invasion of the island was imminent that he neglected developments on the other side of the globe, in Southeast Asia.

7

The Birth of a Movement

He was one of the few who made the transition from the old left to the new starting in the 1960s. Maybe that's because he wasn't really part of the old left, . . . or maybe because serious nonviolence meant engaging creatively and respectfully with diverse people. But Dave didn't spend a lot of time wondering if he was a schachmanite or deutscherite or stalinoid or any of the categorical junk that made it hard for the old left to get down with the new.

Tom Hayden

ON EASTER SUNDAY 1963, David Dellinger attended the Easter Peace Walk in New York City, an event sponsored by the Committee for a Sane Nuclear Policy (SANE) and other peace groups and scheduled to coincide with the annual Easter "ban-the-bomb" marches in Britain. Seven thousand protesters gathered at the United Nations Plaza near the East River to listened to peace luminaries denounce the arms race and call for the ratification of an atmospheric nuclear test ban treaty between the United States and Soviet Union. Most of the placards and banners at the demonstration condemned nuclear testing and arms production and drew attention to the looming threat of World War III. A few signs, however, mostly along the periphery of the gathering, called for peace in Vietnam and a withdrawal of U.S. military forces from Southeast Asia. At the time of the 1963 Easter Peace Walk, SANE was dominated by cautious peace liberals like Norman Cousins, Norman Thomas, Homer Jack, and Clarence Pickett. Besides fearing the presence of radical elements at SANE-sponsored protests, especially communists and Trotskyists, they worried that signs protesting the Vietnam conflict at a ban-the-bomb march would cloud the main issue and confuse the media, public, and authorities about the purpose of the Easter gathering.[1]

Accordingly, SANE representatives asked such influential participants as Dellinger and Bayard Rustin to confiscate the signs and warn
the carriers to avoid the issue of Vietnam at this event. Rustin politely
approached the sign carriers and tried to convince them of the error of
their ways, but Dellinger refused to discourage them. Dellinger also
stuck closely to his prepared speech, but toward the end he called on the
audience to organize against the threat of U.S. intervention in Vietnam.
Afterward, a man from SANE told him he "would never again speak at
one of their rallies" again.[2]

For moderates in the peace movement, there was little to be gained
by adding Vietnam to their list of protest grievances. It was a faraway
land whose history and culture remained inscrutable in the minds of
most Americans. President John F. Kennedy had successfully convinced
much of the public that he was striving to limit the American military
presence in Vietnam and that the conflict against Ho Chi Minh and the
Vietnamese communists could be won. At the time of the 1963 Easter
Walk for Peace, Americans had heard primarily positive reports by U.S.
officials and the press about the progress being made in Vietnam. As far
as the leaders of SANE were concerned, protesting American intervention in Vietnam was a foolish move, typically the work of young radicals affiliated with Students for a Democratic Society (SDS) and irresponsible militants like Dellinger. Even those people who dared speak
out against the escalating war in Vietnam exercised caution and kept
their rhetoric mild. "At the beginning of the sixties," explained
Dellinger, "I think a lot of people were naive about the war and thought,
'Well, if you get the right sort of information through to President
Kennedy or President Johnson, then they will understand that it really
isn't working, that there are various negative aspects about it.'"[3] Within
a few years, however, the anti–Vietnam War movement grew bolder
and gained new adherents across the nation, eventually becoming a
mass movement that eventually defeated President Johnson.

In the wake of the Cuban missile crisis, Brad Lyttle, the head of the
Committee for Nonviolent Action (CNVA), began organizing an action
that would combine the concerns of three key movements of the early
1960s activist left: civil rights, peace, and Cuban solidarity. By the early
spring of 1963, CNVA workers were busily putting the finishing
touches on an upcoming march, the Quebec-Washington-Guantanamo
Walk for Peace. The demonstrators planned to walk thousands of miles

by foot, picket near military bases, march through racially segregated Georgia, and eventually reach Miami. From there, they intended to sail to the U.S. naval base at Guantanamo, Cuba, to "picket, vigil or fast for the abandonment of the base."[4] Pacifists hoped that the long peace march would inspire other activists and convince the American public of the efficacy of nonviolent, direct action.[5]

In May 1963 the peace walk began with little media fanfare, as it coincided with the civil rights movement's epic Birmingham desegregation campaign. The Birmingham demonstrations began during Easter week in April 1963. At first they were small and poorly publicized, which worried Martin Luther King Jr. "The press is leaving, we've got to get something going," an alarmed King urged his staff.[6] Finally, on May 1, the movement's full assault against segregated Birmingham began in earnest when students from the city's black schools—at the urging of King and the Southern Christian Leadership Conference (SCLC)—marched through downtown. Under the direction of the city's police chief, Bull Connor, the police responded by releasing attack dogs on the protesters and aiming high-pressure hoses at them while news photographers and television cameras captured the event on film.[7] Dellinger was visiting Birmingham that spring to cover the campaign for *Liberation* and found that support for the nonviolent desegregation campaign was widespread among the city's African American residents. "One local Negro leader told me, 'You might as well say that we never heard of Gandhi or nonviolence. But we are determined to get our freedom. And in the course of struggling for it, we came upon nonviolence, like gold in the ground.'"[8]

After returning home from Birmingham, Dellinger turned his attention to the Quebec-Washington-Guantanamo Peace Walk, which he backed enthusiastically. Despite his support of the walk, his family and work commitments took priority at this time and prevented him from taking part in the entire march. In 1962 Patch had left home to attend Swarthmore College near Philadelphia, and Ray soon departed for Yale. At Swarthmore, Patch's roommate was Michael Ferber, a pacifist from Buffalo who later went on to become a leading figure in the Boston anti–Vietnam War movement. In the late 1960s, Ferber gained notoriety as a defendant in the case of the Boston Five, a trial of prominent antidraft activists that included the pediatrician Dr. Benjamin Spock and the Reverend William Sloane Coffin. When Ferber arrived at Swarthmore, he was still relatively new to politics and was pleased to discover several pacifist volumes, including Gandhi's autobiography, sitting on Patch's bookshelves. "Within a month or so," Ferber recalled, "I think the whole Dellinger family came to visit Patch in college and I was invited over to meet the family and I was quite taken with the whole group of them. . . . Here was this dedicated family that expected their dad to be in jail half the year and they somehow carried on." During one of David's visits to Swarthmore, he encouraged Ferber to contribute articles to *Liberation*. Ferber had recently been arrested in a series of civil rights protests, and Dellinger wanted to publish the young activist's account of the action. This marked the beginning of a long, close bond between the Dellingers and Ferber. Michael and Patch served as best man at each other's weddings, and Michael regarded David as a mentor.[9]

At Glen Gardner, Betty and David still were struggling at the Libertarian Press to finance the commune, barely making ends meet. The production of *Liberation* often fell behind, and each month it arrived late at the magazine stands and in subscriber's mailboxes. Making matters even more difficult was the magazine's paltry budget, and payments for printing costs seldom arrived on time. A. J. Muste referred to the problem in a 1961 letter pleading for help from one of *Liberation*'s biggest donors: "Just now we are far enough behind with our printing bill to cause real hardship to Dave Dellinger and his family."[10] Fortunately, help soon arrived. Wealthy supporter Mary Meigs sold her stock in the American Tobacco Company for $5,000, which she donated to *Liberation* and the CNVA. "I'm glad to get rid of it," she wrote Muste, "and glad to see it translated into peace action."[11] On many occasions, donations furnished temporary reprieves for the Dellingers, but *Liberation* was always in a precarious position financially.

In the summer, Dellinger monitored the progress of the Quebec-Washington-Guantanamo Peace Walk from his office at Glen Gardner, and he joined the walkers whenever the opportunity permitted. During one of his outings on the route, Dellinger befriended Marv Davidov, an exuberant and colorful radical pacifist from St. Paul, Minnesota, and the two formed a close friendship that lasted for the rest of David's life. "I found in him a mentor whom I listened carefully to," Davidov noted, "because there wasn't an ounce of repression in the guy. He was lively, . . . he was fully engaged in life, and I learned incredible subtleties about nonviolence from him."[12] Davidov came from a working-class Jewish family, grew up in the Midwest, and, by the early 1950s, had developed "liberal" leanings. A stint in the U.S. Army radicalized him, transforming him from a "conformist" who thought little about politics into a dedicated left-wing pacifist. He served "nineteen months in the army, the last month in the stockade, and then they threw my ass out, which was an exciting and liberating day for me." He resumed his life as a university student but spent most of his time involved in peace and civil rights protests in downtown Minneapolis throughout the late 1950s and early 1960s. In 1961, he walked past a building at the University of Minnesota where activists were holding a planning meeting for the upcoming freedom rides. Days later, he boarded a bus going to Jackson, Mississippi, with six other white Minnesotans to protest the segregation of interstate travel facilities. Davidov received his nonviolence training from the activist (and future U.S. congressman) John Lewis and was eventually arrested in Jackson for entering a "Negro waiting room" at the local Greyhound bus terminal. Davidov went to prison for several weeks, first at the Jackson city jail and then at the Mississippi State Penitentiary, where hundreds of black and white activists filled the cells and sang "freedom songs." "At the time, I thought, 'This is what I was meant to do. There's no place on earth I'd rather be than right here, right now, singing with these wonderful people.'"[13]

For several days in August, Dellinger marched alongside Davidov and the other peace walkers but left later in the month to attend the historic March on Washington. Bayard Rustin, chief organizer of the March on Washington, had given Dellinger a backstage pass to hear Rev. Martin Luther King Jr.'s "I have a dream" speech. By the time of the march, Rustin was a full-time civil rights activist, and for months he had worked to build an effective gathering in the nation's capital. "I came out of prison realizing that talking to individuals about being good is a pile of crap," Rustin remarked. "You've got to have a social organization that helps people to bring out the goodness in them, not one that brutalizes them."[14] King spoke in the early afternoon, and the crowd encircling the Reflecting Pool now numbered a quarter of a million. Dellinger found King's speech to be "pedestrian and labored, a severe disappointment after the magnificent 'letter from a Birmingham jail.'" The crowd also appeared listless, Dellinger observed, until King "threw aside the prepared text from which he had been reading and launched into his inspirational dream melody, a theme he used in a couple of previous speeches and now brought to rhythmic heights. He came alive for the first time and so did everyone else."[15]

In the fall, Dellinger divided his time between family, the Libertarian Press, and CNVA activities. The Quebec-Washington-Guantanamo Peace Walk remained relatively uneventful and generated few newspaper headlines until the walkers reached Georgia in October 1963, which was still firmly controlled by white segregationists. Harassment began in Lawrenceville, a small town just east of Atlanta, with the arrest of participant Ken Meister, who was charged by police with being "reckless" after a local motorist backed into him. Meister refused to pay bail and served a month in jail.[16] In Griffin, Georgia, forty miles south of Atlanta, local agents with the Georgia Bureau of Investigation injured protesters with electric cattle prods for leafleting in African American neighborhoods and then proceeded to make several arrests. Peace walkers faced similar harassment in Macon City when they attempted to distribute leaflets in the predominantly black parts of town. Such activity violated the town's anti-leafleting ordinance, and six of the walkers were arrested and placed inside six-by-six-and-a-half-foot "sweat boxes." Back in New Jersey, David Dellinger heard the shocking news of President John F. Kennedy's assassination in a Dallas motorcade on November 22. Hours later, he received a call from a worried Brad Lyttle, who reported that the authorities were going to release the pacifists from local jails on November 23. The police told Lyttle they could not guarantee their safety in southwest Georgia after Kennedy had been assassinated by Lee Harvey Oswald, who was rumored to be a "pro-Castro Communist."[17] Oswald allegedly had been active in the New Orleans chapter of the Fair Play for Cuba Committee, although Dellinger and other Fair Play members had never met him.[18]

At Lyttle's request, Dellinger went to Georgia to assess the crisis and offer advice. Shaken by recent events, the peace walkers had moved to a motel in Atlanta. Lyttle had suspended the walk for two weeks and in the meantime consulted with Dellinger and A. J. Muste about what to do next. By late November, the peace walkers—accompanied by Dellinger—left Atlanta, once again walking south toward Macon and then Albany, which had been a key civil rights battleground since 1961. In early December, the walkers approached Albany, about 175 miles south of Atlanta, a town whose segregationist chief of police, Laurie Pritchett, had been hardened by years of civil rights agitation in his community. In the fall of 1961, the civil rights movement had targeted Albany as the center of one of its most important desegregation campaigns. Activists from the National Association for the Advancement of Colored People (NAACP), Southern Christian Leadership Conference (SCLC), and SNCC protested segregation in Albany's public places, including schools and libraries, and held peaceful marches in the city. Chief Pritchett, who prided himself for having read King's writings and studied movement tactics, oversaw the mass arrests of protesters in Albany. "We can't tolerate the NAACP or the SNCC or any other nigger organization to take over this town with mass demonstrations," he declared.[19] Chief Pritchett's nonviolent but decisive response to the Albany movement was a brilliant maneuver that effectively neutralized the campaign. By the summer of 1962, the Albany struggle had lost much of its momentum.

More than a year later, Brad Lyttle arrived in Albany ahead of the CNVA peace walkers to assure Chief Pritchett that "the purpose of the walk was not to create dissension or public disturbances." In his discussions with Pritchett, Lyttle emphasized the peace walk's antiwar purpose. Their goal "was to ask men and women everywhere . . . to turn, if they can, from social customs based upon violence to those rooted in truth, justice and respect for one another."[20]

Despite Lyttle's pleas, Pritchett regarded the walkers as undesirable troublemakers invading his community, just as the SNCC agitators had done two years earlier. Meanwhile, at several points along the peace walk route, participants faced hostile crowds of local citizens who regarded them as dangerous interlopers. Despite the numerous confrontations with angry residents, the peace walkers tried to remain nonviolent and calm. One of the walkers, Barbara Deming, had covered the civil rights movement for the left-wing *Nation* magazine. Deming had lived a remarkable life. She quit her comfortable job as a film analyst at the Library of Congress in 1944 to write poetry, short stories, and essays and to teach drama at various schools. In the late 1950s, she traveled to India and began reading Gandhi's works. In 1960 Deming became involved with the CNVA, putting to use her skills as a writer and teacher, and she publicized the group's actions in *The Nation*. During the peace walk, Deming and Dellinger became good friends, and eventually she joined him on the editorial board of *Liberation*.

After days of marching alongside Deming and others, Dellinger returned to Glen Gardner but continued monitoring the march through regular telephone communication with Lyttle and A. J. Muste. As the peace walkers approached Albany, Brad Lyttle negotiated with town officials over acceptable terms under which they could enter the city limits. The authorities feared that a racially integrated peace march would embolden local activists and create more agitation. They therefore insisted that peace walkers could enter Albany only if they did not distribute leaflets in African American neighborhoods, shopping areas, the downtown, or along any major thoroughfare in the city. Most important to Pritchett was that the men and women of CNVA stay away from Oglethorpe Street, which divided Albany's white and African American sections. Two days after the negotiations between Lyttle and Pritchett, the first walkers entered Albany and were immediately arrested after marching straight into a busy shopping area. The charges against them included "failure to follow the parade permit, disorderly conduct, and refusal to obey an officer."[21] A few days before Christmas 1963, police arrested fourteen of the walkers and placed them in the city jail. The activists refused to pay bail and engaged in a fast, which Lyttle described as a "silent prayer to God to soften the adversaries hearts and let the march continue."[22]

At Lyttle's request, Dellinger returned to Georgia in early February to assist in the effort. In Albany, he "picketed the jail, was roughed up, arrested, and spent eight days in jail, fasting with the others."[23] Besides Dellinger, the police arrested six other local protesters who had also turned out to picket, including Barbara Deming. "As I approached him," she wrote, "I saw the look of struggle on his face; his chin began to tremble; he told me, 'When I see you, I can't help crying.' As we hugged, a queer little rippling explosion of sobs burst from him for a moment, then he recovered his calm."[24]

After eight days, a thin and unshaven Dellinger was released from jail, along with most of the other imprisoned activists. He found Muste, who had recently arrived in town. Muste knew the peace walkers intended to return to Albany to demonstrate and leaflet, so he persuaded Dellinger to help negotiate with the town's black and white leaders. On February 21, one week the freed peace walkers left Albany, they were back in town, picketing and leafleting again, this time concentrating their efforts on Oglethorpe Street, where Pritchett had explicitly forbidden leafleting. By nighttime, the police had taken twenty-four protesters to the jail. Representing CNVA, Dellinger visited the Albany jail that night to talk to the peace walkers.

Within days of the second series of mass arrests, Dellinger and Muste, working closely with city officials and local African American leaders, reached an agreement allowing the peace walkers to pass out leaflets in areas that previously had been off limits and permitting certain participants who had been approved by authorities to carry protest signs through the town. Upon their release from jail, the activists went straight out to the streets of Albany to hand out leaflets, this time without interference from the Albany police. Both the CNVA organizers and the civil rights movement activists celebrated the agreement as a triumph. The Quebec-Washington-Guantanamo Peace Walk—which had begun as yet another largely ignored peace march—had accomplished something remarkable, relying entirely on nonviolent tactics. Such success had eluded the combined efforts of SNCC, the SCLC, the NAACP, and Rev. Dr. Martin Luther King Jr. "The 'impossible' had happened," rejoiced Brad Lyttle.[25]

Like much of the rest of America, Dellinger paid little attention to events unfolding in Vietnam in the late 1950s and early 1960s. But his experience at the 1963 Easter peace walk in New York City—his refusal to confiscate signs critical of U.S. involvement in Vietnam and his last-minute decision to comment on Vietnam in his speech—stirred his interest in the conflict on the other side of the world. Unlike A. J. Muste, who had spoken out against the incremental but steady escalation of U.S. advisers and military personnel in Southeast Asia for years, Dellinger had largely ignored Vietnam before 1963. In doing so, he failed to notice the benchmarks of America's deepening involvement: Washington's decision to aid France in its war against the Vietnamese communists in the late 1940s and early 1950s; the Vietminh's stunning victory over the beleaguered French garrison at Dien Bien Phu in 1954; the Geneva Conference that same year, which partitioned Vietnam into a communist north and a noncommunist south; and the steadily increasing number of U.S. military advisers in the region throughout the late 1950s and early 1960s. But his attention gradually shifted to Vietnam. "After Easter weekend 1963," he recounted, "I began to find out more. Of course, when I investigated, I found out that the United States had intervened in Vietnam as early as 1945. . . . But I didn't know any of that until after . . . 1963."[26] In April 1964, Dellinger added his name to CNVA's "Declaration of Conscience," which announced its "refusal to cooperate with the United States Government in the prosecution of the war in Vietnam."

But Dellinger did not spend much time on anti–Vietnam War organizing until 1965. For much of 1964, he remained fearful that an American invasion of Cuba was imminent. He visited Cuba for a second time from April 29 to May 21, 1964, crisscrossing the island as he had in 1960, once again meeting with Cubans from all walks of life to report their stories in *Liberation*. Back in the United States, he resumed work in the Cuba solidarity movement. On May 29, a few days before his return to Glen Gardner, the Quebec-Washington-Guantanamo Peace Walk reached Miami, one year and three days after leaving Quebec City, though after Albany the rest of the march was anticlimactic. At their arrival ceremony in a Miami park, speakers praised the peace walk, and the crowd—which included walkers and local supporters—sang civil rights freedom songs.

Next, the walkers planned to sail a twenty-four-foot boat the ninety miles to Havana, Cuba. But the plan was stalled in Miami for several months when the authorities denied the walkers' right to sail to Cuba, claiming that the trip violated the McCarran Internal Security Act. Dellinger went to Florida in mid-July, along with Muste, to help the activists arrange their voyage. In Miami, he found the CNVA peace walkers waiting to sail to Cuba. The local chapter of Women Strike for Peace (WSP) organized a public forum at the Methodist Center on the local university campus and asked Dellinger to speak.

Earlier in the day, a right-wing Cuban exile radio station had announced the event and encouraged listeners to attend the proceedings. The presence of so many hostile Cuban expatriates made for a harrowing and unforgettable evening for Dellinger, Davidov, and the many peace activists in attendance. A shouting match ensued between irate members of the audience who wanted to hear Dellinger speak and angry Cubans who intended to disrupt the talk. The debate became so intense that the coordinator of the Methodist Center began turning the lights in the room on and off and ordered the audience and speakers to leave. People began filing out of the large room. Davidov and a few other activists escorted Dellinger to the parking lot and their car. Outside, a large gathering of Cuban exiles were waiting, still furious about Dellinger's speech. "There were lights from the parking lot," Davidov explained, "no cops around. These thirty-five guys, twelve of us, and everybody was leaving." As Dellinger walked toward the car, a young Cuban came running out of the darkness and punched him in the back.

Almost instantly, Dellinger turned to the youth and extended a hand of friendship, and reluctantly, the Cuban shook hands with the man he had just struck. For the next several minutes, Dellinger and the youth talked quietly while peace activists and Cuban exiles watched. Later, Davidov learned that the boy who hit Dellinger was the son of a Bay of Pigs participant who was now in a Cuban prison. The kid asked David to see if anything could be done to help his father. "Dave said, 'Give me your address and phone number.'"[27] Afterward, two carloads of Cuban exiles pursued Dellinger's car for several blocks through the streets of Miami. The driver, a WSP activist, engaged in some evasive speeding, and as Dellinger recounted, "after a few U-turns and other maneuvers to keep us in the well-lit area where there are lots of people on the streets," the exiles gave up and drove away.[28]

After returning home in late July, Dellinger kept track of U.S.-Cuban relations and continued to fear the worst. The developments in South Vietnam, however, forced him to turn to Indochina. In early August 1964, President Lyndon Baines Johnson went on national television to claim that two U.S. Navy destroyers had been attacked by North Vietnamese PT boats. Before the "Tonkin Gulf incident" and resolution, protests against the United States' intervention in Vietnam were sporadic and poorly publicized. In 1963, the year the U.S.-backed Saigon regime brutally cracked down on nonviolent Buddhist protesters, there were several small demonstrations. Then, beginning with Thich Quang Duc in June 1963, a few Vietnamese Buddhists resorted to the extreme tactic of self-immolation as a means of resisting the autocratic government. Back in the United States, antiwar stalwarts began organizing rallies and pickets against U.S. intervention. The most notable early demonstrations took place on July 25, 1963, when the WRL picketed the home of South Vietnam's permanent observer to the United Nations, and in October, when activists protested a visit by Madame Ngo Dinh Nhu, sister-in-law of South Vietnam's autocratic leader, Ngo Dinh Diem.[29] Within a few weeks of the October protest, Diem, having outlived his usefulness to Washington, was assassinated in a coup orchestrated by pro-U.S. generals in the South Vietnamese military.

Pacifist groups such as the WRL, FOR, and CNVA began mobilizing before August 1964. Tom Cornell, the pacifist organizer of the small June 25, 1963, protest in New York City, conceded that "we never had a demonstration of more than 250 people until the war got going."[30] Dellinger attended his first anti–Vietnam War demonstration on June 3,

1964, when pacifists gathered outside the White House to protest U.S. intervention in Indochina. He greeted his old friends Muste and Ralph DiGia and was introduced to newcomers Joan Baez and Daniel and Philip Berrigan, two brothers who were Catholic priests. Baez, who would soon be going to Berkeley to support the free speech movement on the University of California campus, sang folk songs, and the protesters listened to speakers, who included Dellinger.[31]

By the middle of the decade, Dellinger took notice of what he referred to as "the new spirit that was developing" in the United States, which coincided with the escalation of the Vietnam War.[32] More than any of his contemporaries, David Dellinger felt a genuine rapport with youthful American radicals, many of whom he had influenced during his years as an editor and writer at *Liberation*. In that capacity, he had interviewed college-age African American activists in Alabama and Georgia, talked with New Left insurgents in the sugarcane fields of Cuba, and met pacifists in their twenties living in New York City. He could easily relate to their restlessness and impatience. Indeed, in many of the SDS or SNCC militants, Dellinger could see a reflection of himself in his twenties. Especially exciting to him was SDS's Economic Research and Action Project (ERAP), which sent student leftists into cities such as Chicago, Cleveland, Newark, and Trenton to develop "an interracial movement of the poor."[33]

The SDSers listened to Dellinger's antiwar speeches, read his articles in *Liberation*, and solicited his advice about tactics and goals. "The few older figures whom the new generation seems to respect," wrote New Left journalist Jack Newfield in May 1965, "come out of the radical pacifist tradition."[34] In *"Democracy Is in the Streets,"* a history of SDS, author James Miller noted that such early SDS leaders as Dick Flacks and Tom Hayden were influenced by the *Liberation* writers. This new generation gradually became receptive to Dellinger's pacifist gospel, which made David—now approaching age fifty—feel like he had been given a new lease on life.

For Dellinger, bridging the generation gap was the crucial first step toward building a viable antiwar movement. In late 1964 and early 1965, the success of that movement was uncertain. The earliest events were sparsely attended and seldom generated headlines. At the 1964 Democratic National Convention in Atlantic City, four hundred pacifists gathered outside the convention hall on August 25 for a daylong vigil to protest the U.S. government's Vietnam policies. Four months later, the first major nationwide anti–Vietnam War demonstrations took place on December 19, 1964, in San Francisco, Minneapolis, Chicago, Miami, Austin, Sacramento, Philadelphia, Washington, Boston, and Cleveland. The largest crowd assembled in New York City to hear Norman Thomas, A. J. Muste, A. Philip Randolph, and Dave McReynolds denounce the war. Two weeks later, the *CNVA Bulletin* declared 1965 to be "The Year of Vietnam."[35] In the last week of 1964, the leaders of SDS began organizing what became the first large-scale national protest against the Vietnam War. They set a target date of April 17, 1965, the Saturday before Easter.

Although he was not actively involved in organizing the April 17 march, Dellinger stayed abreast of its planning during the winter and spring. Months before the April event, moderate peace leaders pressured SDS to exclude the Communist Party (CPUSA) and the Trotskyist Socialist Workers Party (SWP) from the protest. The SDS organizers refused, leading to a split in the incipient peace movement. A debate ensued, which eventually became a long-running dialogue about the tactics, scope, and purpose of the antiwar movement. The debate lasted throughout 1965 and much of 1966. As the struggle to end the Vietnam War gained momentum, so too did the battles within the antiwar movement. "The movement of the 1960s was composed of hundreds of groups and grouplets in hundreds of communities," explained Sid Lens, "loosely tied together by a vague leftism that was neither Marxist nor anti-Marxist, that never bothered to spell out an ideology."[36]

Most of the early conflicts pitted cautious peace bureaucrats, who wanted to exclude certain radical organizations and tone down the movement's militant rhetoric, against advocates of a more open, nonexclusionary policy, who were more receptive to confrontation. The opening shot in the battle came from the moderates, who believed that SDS's nonexclusionary policy of allowing communists and members of the party's youth group, the DuBois Clubs, to participate in organizing activities was the "kiss of death" for the antiwar movement.[37] To movement moderates like pacifists Robert Pickus and Norman Thomas, as well as the leadership of SANE and FOR, the decision by SDS to allow communists to take part in the April 17 march was risky. For example, Pickus—a World War II veteran, antiwar organizer, and an old friend of Dellinger—referred to SDS's radical analysis of the Vietnam War and capitalism as "so much pure crap."[38] To Pickus and other liberals, the radicals in the movement were blinded by their antipathy to all things

American. Allowing communists into antiwar coalitions, Pickus insisted, threatened to marginalize a movement that had the potential to blossom into a thriving mass protest struggle. Pickus and other moderates thus founded an organization, Turn Toward Peace (TTP), that they hoped would promote a more cautious agenda for the movement, by condemning what its leaders regarded as the reckless militancy of young radicals.

In the spring of 1965, the directors of TTP convinced several respected peace luminaries to sign a statement denouncing SDS's upcoming April 17 march. Just days before the event, newspaper headlines painted an unflattering portrait of SDS as a group of headstrong militants whose march had become "Red-dominated." An article in the *New York Post* described the TTP's efforts to derail the march.

> On the eve of this weekend's "peace march" on Washington, several leaders of the peace movement have taken note of the attempts to convert the event into a pro-Communist production. In a joint statement, Norman Thomas, A. J. Muste, H. Stuart Hughes, Robert Gilmore, Bayard Rustin and others have pointed out that President Johnson's April 7 speech "suggested the possibility of a healthy shift in American foreign policy" toward a negotiated settlement.[39]

Later, A. J. Muste insisted in a *Village Voice* interview with Jack Newfield that he was pressured to sign the TTP statement by Bayard Rustin, who, Muste claimed, "wanted to torpedo the march because he thought communists had taken over in some places."[40] TTP's efforts to undermine the SDS march as a "communist-dominated" event before it even happened infuriated Dellinger, who knew that the presence of card-carrying CPUSA members in the small, fragile antiwar coalition was insignificant at most. Dellinger had made clear his dislike of the Communist Party, particularly its leaders, whom he regarded as Machiavellian and out of touch with ordinary Americans. In a response to a 1970 request to explain his position on the CPUSA, Dellinger wrote:

> Despite my disagreements with the Communist Party—my opposition, really, in terms of both politics and lifestyle—I am always nervous about Red baiting. I think that ideas should be examined on their own merits, rather than in terms of their origin or associations with specific groups. I have never hesitated to speak on the same platform

as Communists, welcome them into the . . . [movement] on the basis of
our non-exclusion policy, or defend their civil and political rights.[41]

For Dellinger, the most demoralizing aspect of Turn Toward Peace's
attempt to sabotage the SDS march was that it underscored Bayard
Rustin's political shift. For almost twenty years, Dellinger and Rustin
had attended the same planning meetings, committed civil disobedience together, been hauled off with each other in paddy wagons, co-
founded organizations, and worked side by side at *Liberation* magazine.
But in the early 1960s Rustin began to change. Since immersing himself
in the civil rights movement, he slowly—almost imperceptibly to some
of his closest friends—became more moderate. Unlike such ex-radicals
as John Dos Passos and Irving Kristol, who made a 180-degree turn in
their politics, Rustin did not gravitate to the conservative end of the political spectrum. Rather, he stopped at the liberal center but desperately
tried to keep civil rights issues separate from anti–Vietnam War grievances. At the time of the 1963 March on Washington, which he organized so brilliantly, his political realignment already was under way.
Early in the war he voiced misgivings about American intervention in
Vietnam, but throughout 1965 and 1966 his criticisms became more
muted and eventually silent. But Rustin's transformation from dove to
hawk was never complete. Instead, he adopted the liberal position of
advocating negotiations among the U.S. government, the Saigon
regime, and the Communists. This position contrasted sharply with
Dellinger's advocacy of immediate withdrawal, which Rustin found irresponsible and unreasonable. Increasingly, Rustin refrained from criticizing the war, but he frequently lashed out at antiwar activists for
what he regarded as their failure to criticize Vietnamese communism
sufficiently. "By 1966," wrote Rustin's biographer John D'Emilio, "he
had disappeared completely from the precincts of peace activism. He
remained mostly silent on the issue and detached from the struggle."[42]

The extent of Rustin's transformation became apparent in the February 1965 issue of *Commentary* magazine, in his influential article
"From Protest to Politics: The Future of the Civil Rights Movement." As
the title suggests, Rustin now recommended a shift in tactics for leftists,
to abandon conventional protests and instead to try to win allies in the
labor movement and government in order to build a more robust and
influential civil rights coalition. "The difference between expediency
and morality in politics," he wrote, "is the difference between selling

out a principle and making smaller concessions to win larger ones. The leader who shrinks from this task reveals not his purity, but his lack of political sense." The United States, he argued, had arrived at a historic moment that required progressives to reject "intransigence and refusal of all compromise" and instead to develop a "program for racial equality . . . so intertwined with progressive economic and social policies as to make it impossible to choose one without the other."[43]

Months before the article appeared, Dellinger sensed that he and Rustin were moving apart. "From Bayard, I have learned many things, in the course of sharing prison cells and lonely, difficult battles," he admitted in 1965.[44] At a chance encounter between Dellinger and Rustin at New York's LaGuardia Airport on July 3, 1964, the two pacifists engaged in a lively conversation. Rustin was on his way to the White House to attend the ceremony at which President Lyndon Johnson would sign the 1964 Civil Rights Act. The two activists sat together on the same airplane to Washington, D.C., and Dellinger tried to persuade Rustin to come to a peace rally scheduled for the same day. Rustin refused, saying he did not want to combine civil rights and antiwar issues. Their conversation convinced Dellinger that his old comrade had "gone over the hill."[45] At a *Liberation* editorial board meeting in the summer of 1964, Rustin contended that progressives had a duty to support Lyndon Johnson's presidential candidacy. His comrades were aghast. "At *Liberation* magazine," remembered Sid Lens, "three of the four members of the editorial board, Muste, Dellinger, and I, took the traditional position of supporting neither major party candidate. But Bayard Rustin came out four-square for Johnson."[46]

The loss of such a close friend saddened Dellinger. But he also did not want Rustin to have the last word with his lengthy *Commentary* treatise calling for a cessation of protest activities. So David, along with A. J. Muste, began exerting behind-the-scenes pressure on Staughton Lynd to respond to Rustin's arguments. At the time, Lynd was an assistant professor in the history department at Yale and an associate editor at *Liberation*. He had positioned himself on the front lines of numerous civil rights and antiwar political struggles and was less reluctant than Dellinger or Muste to go after Rustin. Lynd explained:

> I think what happened was that A. J. and Dave were very much upset by Bayard's new departure but that having known him so long they found it difficult to denounce him. And they rather encouraged me to

do that. . . . So I wrote an article . . . that did denounce Bayard and created a lot of controversy.[47]

Lynd's attack on Rustin, entitled "Coalition Politics or Nonviolent Revolution?" appeared in the June/July 1965 issue of *Liberation*. He accused Rustin of embracing a "kind of elitism" and seeking to create a "coalition with the marines." He expressed fear that the day would come when "men like Rustin will become the national spokesmen who sell the line agreed on behind doors to the faithful followers waiting in the streets." Worst of all, Lynd insisted that Rustin had abandoned his authenticity in his quest for respectability and access to power. "Rustin," wrote Lynd, "has permitted himself to drift into that posture which once evoked epithets such as 'labor lieutenant of capitalism.'"[48]

Lynd did not anticipate the counterattacks from such respectable figures as Michael Harrington, Irving Howe, and Norman Thomas. Curiously, Rustin stayed out of the exchange and even remained an associate editor of *Liberation* for several months after the attack. The attacks against Lynd continued for a few months. His most outspoken critic from the left was David McReynolds, who vehemently "objected at the time to Lynd's critique of Rustin," although years later he expressed regret that Rustin had abandoned radical politics.[49] In the summer of 1965, McReynolds took his fellow pacifists to task for what he viewed as their intolerance and mean-spiritedness toward Rustin. "I think A. J. Muste, as well as Dave Dellinger and Staughton Lynd, have treated Rustin in a way that is basically indecent," McReynolds concluded.[50] In early 1966, Rustin quietly resigned as associate editor of *Liberation* and went to work for the A. Philip Randolph Institute, a respected liberal civil rights advocacy organization in New York City. For Dellinger, Muste, and Lynd, the imbroglio over Bayard Rustin represented something much more significant than singling out an erstwhile ex-radical who had second thoughts. Rather, they treated the matter as an unpleasant but necessary ideological contest. Rustin, they believed, had fired the opening shots in the debate, with his public pronouncement that protest activism was not as effective as building alliances with establishment politicians and labor leaders. For their part, the pacifists at *Liberation* showed that they were willing to fight back against any adversaries in print, even someone who, for decades, had been one of their own.

∎

April 17, 1965, was an unforgettable day for the thousands of protesters who gathered for SDS's march on Washington, the first large-scale, national antiwar gathering of the 1960s. A new sense of urgency filled the antiwar movement after the Johnson administration, with the backing of Congress, had begun round-the-clock air strikes over North Vietnam in February and had sent the first ground combat military personnel to South Vietnam the following month. Even before the SDS march, much smaller events had taken place in cities and towns throughout America, and the number of new antiwar organizations across the country was growing.

The April 17 march emboldened antiwar activists to think about the possibilities of the newly emerging movement. After the SDS march, Dellinger became increasingly busy and remained so for the rest of the decade. He now was the editor in chief of *Liberation*, a position that gave him tremendous visibility on the left. Invitations to speak began pouring in from across the country. Organizers of rallies, public lectures, university forums, community debates, and church events requested his presence. Meanwhile, newly formed antiwar organizations rented space at 5 Beekman Street in lower Manhattan, near City Hall Park, which also housed the *Liberation* offices. Before long, 5 Beekman became the East Coast's nerve center for the thriving antiwar movement. In May, Dellinger traveled to the University of California in Berkeley, long a haven of collegiate radicalism and a campus that just months earlier had been the battleground of the free speech movement. Aside from energizing Dellinger with its youthful spirit, huge crowds, and contagious fervor, the Berkeley teach-in assumed a critical significance in the early phase of the antiwar movement. In Berkeley, Dellinger met with other strategists to discuss the movement's future. It all was happening so quickly, and some organizers feared that the new energy was not being properly harnessed or channeled. Seasoned activists like Dellinger recognized the need to build a strong coalition that could advance the cause effectively. Since its inception, the antiwar movement had always been strikingly diverse, with numerous organizations emerging, some lasting only briefly and others for the entire duration of the war. Of utmost importance to Dellinger in the spring and summer of 1965 was forging a national alliance out of the many disparate strands of activism. For a time it appeared that in the months after its highly successful April 17 march, SDS was poised to assume a prominent role in coordinating the struggle. But to the shock of many observers, SDS abdicated its leadership position in the anti–Vietnam War movement at its national convention in Camp Kewadin, Michigan, in June 1965. After concluding that antiwar work was too narrowly focused and not sufficiently radical, the SDS leaders decided instead to devote their efforts and resources to building a nationwide poor people's movement. It was a decision that many SDSers later regretted, and it was one of the factors that led to the organization's premature collapse in the late 1960s.[51]

By the summer of 1965, the leadership vacuum in the antiwar movement threatened to jeopardize its continued success. Now, more than ever, Dellinger believed, the movement needed guidance and leadership. Press coverage and activist reports from the field indicated that President Johnson's escalation of troops in South Vietnam in the spring and summer had triggered numerous small protests in communities across the country. Dellinger worried that such efforts often lacked a clear focus on Vietnam and instead celebrated dissent for its own sake. Reflecting on these developments, he wrote:

> I wonder if there is not some terrible sense in which the American peace movement is . . . in danger of role-playing, as we go through the motions of meetings, protests, and the necessary debates over strategy and tactics without quite believing in the primacy of ending the war. The victims become abstract, the day-to-day obscenity of events in Vietnam affects us only remotely, and we overestimate the intensity of our commitment by comparing it with the relative placidity of life-as-usual in temporarily sheltered middle-class white America.[52]

With the momentum of the Berkeley teach-in behind him, Dellinger began working with others to build a coalition. On June 20, he, along with Lynd, Robert Parris Moses, and other independent antiwar activists, met in Washington, D.C., to organize what became the Assembly of Unrepresented People, a combination of conference and protest that was intended to link together the civil rights struggle and the Vietnam War. They scheduled it to be held in Washington from August 6 to 9 and took out ads in the left-wing *National Guardian* newspaper to promote it. Even before the event began, Roy Wilkins, executive director of the NAACP, felt sufficiently threatened by the prospect of the assembly to write a letter to the *New York Times* urging people to avoid it. As

Wilkins explained, "We simply advised our units that a meeting was set up and to place its main emphasis on opposition to the war in Vietnam, and not civil rights."[53] In August, two thousand persons gathered for the assembly, which was a series of educational workshops about a variety of interrelated topics, including civil disobedience, Native Americans, free universities, communal living, neocolonialism, the Puerto Rican independence movement, the civil rights movement, South Africa, and, most important, the war in Vietnam. The conference was relatively uneventful until the last day, August 9, when about eight hundred participants marched to the Capitol. Dellinger, Lynd and Moses walked together, and as they neared the Capitol, a group of Nazi hecklers tossed a container of red paint all over the trio. The three men continued marching unfazed. Photographers on the scene captured on film the image of the paint-splattered activists, and it appeared on the cover of *Life* magazine shortly thereafter. At the Capitol, Dellinger and about 350 assembly participants engaged in mass civil disobedience by reading a "declaration of peace" and then crawling between the legs of police officers who blocked their entrance to the building. Police began beating and hauling limp protesters to jail in what became the first mass civil disobedience action of the Vietnam War. In jail, the hundreds of incarcerated prisoners, including Dellinger, listened to radio bulletins about the looting and rioting going in Watts, a predominantly African American area of Los Angeles. But they were encouraged to learn that on the same weekend as the assembly, hundreds of activists in Oakland, California, had taken part in mass civil disobedience at the Oakland Army Terminal in an attempt to halt troop trains leaving the center. Most of the protesters in the Washington jail were temporarily held, fined, and then released. But Dellinger received a forty-five day jail term and a substantial fine. By contrast, the Nazi hecklers who threw the paint were released on $10 bail. As an act of solidarity with Dellinger, the other jailed activists refused to pay their fines and vowed to remain in behind bars until police released their pacifist comrade. Within a few days, Dellinger was a free man.[54]

Beyond the publicity it generated, the most important outcome of the assembly was that it gave birth to the first successful antiwar umbrella coalition, the National Coordinating Committee to End the War in Vietnam (NCC), consisting of thirty-three antiwar organizations. By mid-August, NCC activists were already organizing their first demonstration, "The International Days of Protest," two days of direct action set to take place on October 15 and 16 in New York City and the San Francisco Bay Area.

For the thirty-six-year-old public school teacher Norma Becker, a single mother of two children, the Assembly of Unrepresented People was her first exposure to the antiwar movement. In the spring, Becker had organized the Teachers' Committee for Peace, and in her limited spare time she actively recruited supporters in the New York City area. Although she admitted being a "novice" to the antiwar struggle, Becker had spent two summers volunteering in the south for SNCC.[55] Born and raised in New York City, Becker grew up in a left-wing Jewish household and plunged into politics while still a teenager by supporting Progressive candidate Henry Wallace's presidential campaign in 1948. As a young girl she once regarded the United States as "a glowing democracy of kindness and compassion and justice and truth" but eventually concluded that "Manifest Destiny and global dominance were the driving forces in American foreign policy," and "the Vietnam War . . . seemed more of the same."[56] The months Becker spent volunteering for SNCC in Mississippi in 1963 and 1964 "converted" her to pacifism.[57]

Attending the Assembly of Unrepresented People in Washington, D.C., gave Becker an opportunity to establish connections with likeminded peace activists. In late August, the newly formed NCC called on antiwar groups across the country to organize their own actions as part of the upcoming International Days of Protest. Becker came up with the idea of marching up Fifth Avenue as a show of strength and patriotism to counter the prowar parades that regularly were held there. She remembered telling a friend, "Well, they march those missiles down Fifth Avenue for the Loyalty Day parade. Let's march down Fifth Avenue."[58]

Becker created her own organization to plan the march, the Fifth Avenue Peace Parade Committee, which she hoped would ultimately serve as an umbrella coalition for New York City's antiwar movement. It was a bold idea, and Becker needed the help of other local peace groups to see it through. She scheduled a planning meeting and sent invitations to a number of organizations, including SANE, Women Strike for Peace, the Women's International League for Peace and Freedom, the War Resisters League, the Socialist Workers Party, the Communist Party, and various university groups and labor unions. The meeting was held shortly after Labor Day, and the turnout exceeded her expectations. Becker arrived and met David Dellinger for the first time, and he agreed to cochair the meeting with her. "Well, that meeting was mind-boggling," she recalled. The gathering became bogged down when the representatives of the many groups in attendance could not agree on a slogan to print on the march placards. The debate became heated. Sitting in the corner of the room, the elderly father of the anti-war movement, A. J. Muste, wearing his trademark gray fedora hat and narrow tie, quietly observed the proceedings. Becker recalled: "We reached a point where there was dead silence. Out of sheer naiveté, I said, 'Look, if the people in this room can't agree, I'll call twenty other people.'" Toward the end of the meeting, Abner Gruauer of SANE proposed a slogan that everybody in the room could agree upon: "Stop the War in Vietnam Now."[59]

Dellinger and Becker instantly formed a bond of friendship and mutual respect, and together, they remained on the front lines of some of the largest anti–Vietnam War events. Becker recalled:

> I thought he was an articulate, principled, honest, warm, nonsectarian, nondogmatic. He believed strongly in what he believed in, but it was not in a sectarian, dogmatic belief. He was open . . . and quite willing to acknowledge that we didn't have all the answers and we had to learn as we went along.[60]

As a single mother, Becker often took her children to long planning meetings, where they read, drew pictures, and engaged in other quiet activities. She remembered when her children first met Dellinger and Muste, in the early days of the movement:

> On one occasion, we had to go to 5 Beekman for something, and I had to bring my children. My son was twelve and my daughter was ten. We walked in and I was so impressed. Dellinger immediately stood up and greeted my children, and A. J. with his smile said, "Well, I'm much older than Dave, so I'm not going to stand." They began talking to my children and asking them all sorts of questions, and carried on a long conversation with them. I was so struck with the respect and recognition they gave to two young children. . . . That was, I thought, a very telling incident about their personal character.[61]

The International Days of Protest was the first test of the newly formed antiwar coalition. On October 15, Dellinger and about five hundred other people gathered on a crisp autumn day for a "speak-out" at New York's Whitehall Street Induction Center to picket and listen to speeches. David Miller, a young Catholic Worker scheduled to speak, decided at the last minute to burn his draft card instead. The act electrified the cheering audience, and it made Miller the first person to publicly burn his draft card since Congress passed a law earlier in the summer making the destruction of draft cards a felony.[62] The next day, twenty thousand marchers, including clergy, students, homemakers, and the elderly, walked up Fifth Avenue to the United Nations Plaza. Along the way, some were pelted by eggs, punched by counterdemonstrators, or doused with red paint. Elsewhere, in cities such as Austin, Cleveland, and Oakland, protesters were beaten, taunted, screamed at, roughed up, or threatened by various groups, including Nazis, Hells Angels, Republicans, and the new Committee to Support American Fighting Men.[63]

The Fifth Avenue Peace Parade, which was planned as a follow-up to the International Days of Protest, took place in New York City on March 26, 1966. Fifty thousand people marched to Central Park and cheered A. J. Muste, the honorary parade chairman, when he welcomed them to the event. "The protest," reported the *New York Herald Tribune* the following day, "had a different complexion from the one last October 16. . . . Although most of the sponsors were the same, the marchers this time seemed to represent much more of a cross section of Americans."[64]

Despite having spent so many years at or near the epicenter of political struggles, Dellinger was not able to grasp the depth or breadth of the transformations occurring in American society during the 1960s, although he did understand that a nationwide "awakening" was under way.[65] As historian Maurice Isserman observed, "SDS kept its guard up with representatives of the Old Left but maintained cordial relations with pacifists like Dave Dellinger."[66] Still, Dellinger found little solace in the developments of 1965. The summer and fall brought more newspaper headlines and television broadcasts about America's deepening involvement in Indochina. At the end of 1965, more than 200,000 U.S. troops were stationed in Vietnam, a figure that continued to climb throughout 1966. Dellinger and his fellow pacifists would have gladly traded their newfound prestige for avoiding the bloody war unfolding in Vietnam. That option, however, was not available, leaving only the possibility of militant, nonviolent resistance, which demanded unity from a disparate array of people. "What held the movement together," Dellinger remembered, "was the fact that the emergency was so great and the knowledge of what was happening in Vietnam was so overwhelming. . . . There was that pressure of events that was forcing us to stay together."[67]

8

Gandhi and Guerrilla

His way of never giving in was to continue the conversation but always maintain his position.

Grace Paley

TODAY THE PEACE MOVEMENT has an historic opportunity," wrote David Dellinger in 1966, "to move from its perpetually repeated 'beginnings' to a new stage of historical relevance."[1] Never before had Dellinger felt so optimistic about the prospects of militant, nonviolent direct action in the United States, and the accomplishments of the anti–Vietnam War movement since 1965 only strengthened his commitment. In only a year, a mass protest had taken shape, and a variety of peace organizations were coexisting within a robust national coalition. The presence of American combat troops in Vietnam since the spring of 1965 contributed to the activists' sense of urgency. "The massive demonstrations and the smaller, more radical protests against the war in Vietnam have not succeeded as yet in altering basic government policy in Vietnam, but they have not been wasted and they should be expanded," Dellinger noted in 1966.[2] Although some cautious peace bureaucrats took exception to the politics and rhetoric of militants like Dellinger, most liberals and leftists put aside their differences and joined forces. The antiwar movement continued to expand, replenished with fresh faces and buoyed by a spirit of youthful vigor and endorsements from eminent figures such as Rev. Martin Luther King Jr. and Dr. Benjamin Spock.

In late 1965 and 1966 Betty Dellinger began to see less and less of her husband, as meetings, protests, and the demands of *Liberation* magazine dominated most of his time. Whenever possible, she and the children went with him to demonstrations and other events, but usually she took care of the family back in Glen Gardner while he immersed himself in his causes. "I believed in what he was doing," she explained, "and I wanted him to go, but then I would be angry anyway when he came back."[3] For the Dellinger children, going stretches of time without seeing their father seemed like a normal part of growing up. According to Patch Dellinger, "For the record they were equal partners, but in fact a tremendous amount of the family dynamic revolved around Dad's trips and projects and other things fit in around those. There is no doubt that my mother and probably my younger brothers and sisters suffered from this."[4] Patch and Ray were university students by this time, and Natasha soon moved out and married, which left Danny and Michele still living at home. Staughton Lynd and his wife, Alice, worried about the Dellingers. More than any of the Dellingers' other friends and acquaintances, the Lynds understood how full-time activism could destroy family life.

> Betty . . . went through a time of great stress and depression. This period represented a moment when Dave chose to put the cause ahead of family, which I've done often enough, but which I step back from at an earlier point than did he. When I began to sense that my marriage was coming under stress from going out of town, making speeches about the war, going to Hanoi, or whatever it might be, I stopped doing those things. Dave didn't.[5]

Even though Dellinger later regretted the extent to which he allowed political organizing to take over his life, in 1966 he was too driven by events in Vietnam and too involved in the antiwar movement to consider any other options. Like many of his comrades, Dellinger was at once pleased with the accomplishments of the antiwar movement and also troubled by its predictability and inability to raise the stakes with bold and creative new actions. The movement could not afford to stand still. SDS's April 17, 1965, march on Washington had been an electrifying moment, and after that, the teach-ins, campus rallies, pickets, and large-scale mass protests invigorated the war's opponents. But they quickly lost their news value. The problem, Dellinger argued in late 1965, lay in the widespread feelings of powerlessness and disfranchisement among ordinary people. "Oddly enough, there is considerable evidence that the war could be stopped, if even a small percentage of those who disapprove of it could get past their sense of hopelessness and focus actively on that objective."[6]

To achieve this end, Dellinger tried to unite the many disparate antiwar organizations across the country. In 1965, the National Coordinating Committee (NCC), which Dellinger had been instrumental in creating, temporarily served as the umbrella organization for a variety of antiwar groups. But at the beginning of 1966 the NCC sputtered to a halt following a poorly attended national steering committee meeting in Milwaukee, and in the summer of 1966 the NCC was replaced by another ad hoc coalition, the November 5–8 Mobilization Committee. The creation of the new committee owed much to the organizing talents of Doug Dowd, an economics professor at Cornell University in Ithaca, New York, and Sidney Peck, a sociology professor at Case Western Reserve University in Cleveland, Ohio. Already a central figure in the antiwar movement, Dowd was chairman of the nation's largest teach-in organization, the Inter-University Committee for Debate on Foreign Policy, as well as a World War II combat veteran. While stationed in the Pacific, he developed an interest in Southeast Asian affairs after meeting covert U.S agents who had helped Ho Chi Minh's forces against the Japanese in Vietnam. Later, as a professor and author, he attracted radical students at Cornell who revered him for his willingness to speak out when few other professors dared to do so. In 1960, Dowd, along with other faculty members and students, organized one of the earliest campus movements—even before the war began—to oppose U.S. intervention in Southeast Asia. A few years later he assumed a key leadership position in the teach-in movement. "Between 1965 and 1966, it had gotten to the point where the student audiences were quite large and almost always against the United States being involved in any way in Vietnam," Dowd recalled.[7] But the success of the teach-in movement proved to be its own undoing. Before long, Pentagon and State Department officials refused to attend teach-ins to defend the government's Vietnam policies. "It really was getting damn hard to find anybody to go against you," Dowd said. "What we needed always was government people. You could get another professor to go against you, but most people didn't care about that."[8]

In the summer of 1966, Dowd and other academics in the Inter-University Committee stopped organizing teach-ins and shifted their time and energy to building a new national coalition to replace the moribund NCC. With the help of Sid Peck at Case Western Reserve, Dowd organized a meeting of antiwar leaders at the Case Western campus to form the November 5–8 Mobilization Committee. Eventually the committee would change and be renamed. Now, however, it functioned as the nation's main antiwar coalition and provided coherent and cohesive guidance for the nationwide peace movement.

Born in Maryland in 1926, Sid Peck was the youngest of six children in a poor immigrant family that eventually settled in St. Paul, Minnesota. After World War II, he attended the University of Minnesota, with help from the GI Bill, and there met his future wife, Louise, while working on Progressive Party candidate Henry Wallace's 1948 presidential campaign. He eventually received his doctorate in sociology and accepted a teaching job at Case Western Reserve in 1964. Like Dowd, Peck was active in the teach-in movement, which became his point of entry into the antiwar movement. As he noted,

> In June of 1966, my teach-in committee invited representatives of national organizations to come to Cleveland to talk about how we could help to unify the developing antiwar movement. . . . We did have a meeting in Cleveland in July that A. J. Muste attended, and that led to another meeting in September of 1966.[9]

A third academic, Robert Greenblatt, a thirty-year-old assistant professor of mathematics at Cornell, also helped form the mobilization committee. As a youth Greenblatt had survived concentration camps in Germany and Austria and resettled with his family in the United States in 1949. By 1966 he had become "very active in the 'Teach-In' movement," which reflected his "deep commitment to educate Americans about the tragic errors of our Vietnam policies." The following year, Greenblatt "left his Cornell post in order to work full time for the antiwar movement."[10]

The committee's initial gathering at Case Western Reserve in September accomplished several goals, the most important being the establishment of a nonexclusionary policy enabling all groups and individuals opposed to U.S. intervention in Indochina to participate in the antiwar coalition. Chief among the supporters of the nonexclusionary policy was A. J. Muste, who had experienced a turnaround since the spring of 1965 when he supported the exclusion of Communist Party members from SDS's April 17 march. In addition to voting for the nonexclusionary policy, the hundreds of men and women assembled for the September meeting in Cleveland scheduled the next national mass protests for November 5 through 8.[11]

Ironically, David Dellinger had little to do with the formation of the anti–Vietnam War coalition in Cleveland, even though he eventually led it. His tight schedule in the spring and summer of 1966 simply did not permit his immediate involvement. Throughout the year, he cochaired several gatherings of the Fifth Avenue Peace Parade Committee, along with Muste and Norma Becker. By this time the parade committee consisted of ninety-three peace groups in the New York City area. Dellinger also agreed to speak at the committee's next New York City demonstration on August 6. In the meantime, invitations continued to arrive. One he readily accepted came from a group of Japanese antiwar leaders requesting his presence at an August peace conference in Tokyo. While coordinating his travel itinerary to Tokyo, Dellinger figured that as long as he was in Asia, he might as well go to Indochina. He convinced the editorial board of *Liberation* to help finance a trip to both North and South Vietnam in exchange for a series of articles.[12]

In the months before his Asia trip, Dellinger took a strong interest in the case of the Fort Hood Three, a trio of soldiers based at Fort Hood, Texas, who refused the government's orders to serve in Vietnam. The three men—James Johnson, age twenty, an African American; Dennis Mora, twenty-five, a Puerto Rican, and David Samas, twenty, of Lithuanian Italian descent—held a well-publicized press conference, organized by Dellinger, at New York's Community Church on June 30. Dellinger stood with Muste and Black Power militant Stokely Carmichael at the conference while the three men read a statement: "We have decided to take a stand against this war, which we consider immoral, illegal and unjust. . . . We intend to report as ordered to the Oakland Army Terminal, but under no circumstances will we board ship for Vietnam. We will face Court Martial if necessary."[13] After the press conference, Private First Class Johnson elaborated on his reasons for refusing to serve in Vietnam: "In my case, the fact that I am Negro makes the fact of U.S. involvement even more acute. The Negro in Vietnam is being called upon to defend a freedom that in many parts of this country does not exist for him."[14]

As head of the Fort Hood Three Defense Committee, David regularly visited the men in the stockade, bringing them books, magazines, letters, and gifts from well-wishers in the antiwar movement. He also launched a speaking tour on their behalf, lecturing about their case in several cities, primarily in the East. Meantime, the three privates announced plans to file a lawsuit challenging their orders to fight in Vietnam on the grounds that the war was illegal. Federal agents and local authorities, alarmed by the amount of press surrounding the case, began a campaign of harassment against the men. On July 7, Dellinger drafted a telegram protesting the intimidation, cosigned by Becker and Muste, and sent it to Attorney General Nicholas Katzenbach, Secretary of Defense Robert McNamara, and the press. The telegram mentioned various specific incidents. For instance, in Modesto, California, police had recently visited the family of Private Samas, at the urging of "higher authorities." The Modesto police pressured the private's parents to persuade their son to testify against his friends in exchange for a discharge from the army and his freedom. Dellinger's telegram concluded: "The peace movement will continue to aid in every possible lawful way anyone, civilian, soldier, sailor or Marine, who opposes this illegal and immoral war."[15] The Fort Hood Three were eventually court-martialed and jailed for two years in Leavenworth, Kansas, where Dellinger repeatedly visited them to offer his sympathy and encouragement. Their courage in the face of adversity inspired activists, and their heavily publicized case was one of the first instances that peace leaders joined dissenters in the military.[16]

In August, Dellinger went to Japan and North and South Vietnam. In Tokyo he attended a conference organized by Beheiren, a Japanese abbreviation for the Japan Peace for Vietnam Committee. There he met peace activists from around the world, including the Japanese novelist and human rights advocate Oda Makoto. He also met the scholar-activist Howard Zinn, who came to the conference with his wife, Roslyn. Zinn and Dellinger developed a close relationship that lasted for the rest of David's life.[17] Although Dellinger went to several conference sessions, his fondest memory of the Beheiren meeting was the time he spent with Oda.

In late August, Dellinger flew to Saigon. For days he toured the city, interviewing students, intellectuals, Buddhist monks, farmers, and former members of the Saigon regime. Almost everybody he encountered opposed the war, the repressive pro-U.S. regime in Saigon, and the presence of American troops. Even one Saigon official risked purge or possibly even death by confiding to Dellinger,

We have had a war since 1939. My hair has become gray. War, always war, and everyone suffers. And since the United States is insistent on continuing the war, I have come to feel that it would be better to form a new government . . . one that would initiate a cease-fire. . . . It would have to be a new nationalist government for peace.[18]

When his two weeks in Saigon were up, Dellinger flew to Phnom Penh, capital of neighboring Cambodia. Its neutralist government, under the popular king Norodom Sihanouk, had normalized relations with Hanoi and Peking and was at odds with Washington over the Vietnam War. Dellinger could not stay long in Cambodia, as he planned to travel to Hanoi from Phnom Penh aboard a chartered airplane. His original travel plans were scrapped, however, following the recent disappearance of a chartered airplane flying from Phnom Penh to Hanoi. Indeed, the incident resulted in a temporary cancellation of air travel between Hanoi and the rest of Southeast Asia, which meant Dellinger had to fly from Phnom Penh to Moscow, then to Beijing, and finally Hanoi.[19]

Dellinger made the most of the opportunity by sightseeing in Moscow. In mid-October, he flew to Beijing and traveled around the city and nearby towns. At the end of October, Dellinger finally boarded a plane that took him to Hanoi. The trip lasted much longer than he anticipated it would. Ironically, one year earlier—in the fall of 1965—Dellinger had declined an invitation to visit the North Vietnamese capital as part of a fact-finding mission with Staughton Lynd and academic Herbert Aptheker because he feared their trip would take him away from his family and work too long.[20] "I wanted to be at home . . . and declined the invitation. Staughton, as a result, chose Tom Hayden," Dellinger remembered.[21]

Reaching Hanoi on October 28, Dellinger found a nation reeling under intense, round-the-clock bombing by American airplanes. Although American planes bombed the outskirts of Hanoi, they did not strike the city itself. Because of the extent of the bombing in the countryside, officials in the Hanoi government were reluctant to allow Dellinger to leave the city. When he did venture out, with a driver and interpreter, he finally had an opportunity to assess the damage. The destruction that Dellinger found in the North Vietnamese countryside shocked even him, a longtime antiwar activist. He had arrived in North Vietnam doubting the official reports of the wholesale carpet bombing of civilian populated areas. "Something, perhaps my own type of Americanism, rose up inside me and I tried to deny that Americans would knowingly bomb and strafe civilians, at least as part of deliberate government policy."[22] South of Hanoi, he discovered that few towns had been spared the horrifying devastation of American bombs. Over and over again he saw the smoking ruins of what had once been civilian neighborhoods, which contradicted reports by high-level U.S. officials who insisted the bombing was surgical and precise and targeted only North Vietnam's infrastructure and war production facilities.

These cataclysmic scenes left Dellinger shaken, and the fact that his own country was responsible only made his despair worse. At one point during his travels through the countryside, Dellinger got a taste of what the Vietnamese had endured for the past several months. At night, in the tiny hamlet of Nam Ngan, he and his fellow Vietnamese travelers were walking outside when planes flying overhead suddenly began dropping bright flares. Seconds later, massive, earthshaking fireballs burst across the landscape, rising into the sky, and causing Dellinger to leap into a ditch by the road. Although the bombs came close, Dellinger and his Vietnamese companions emerged unscathed.

Nguyen Vinh Vy, an official who met Dellinger in North Vietnam and later became a negotiator for the government, remarked to him, "America has always been on the side of the oppressed people. They always stood up for them. How did it happen that this time they've turned around and suddenly become aggressors and try to put down a legitimate government?" Dellinger found Vy's question naive but did his best to answer it, explaining that the United States had a long history of slavery, genocidal policies against Native Americans, exploitation of ordinary people, and wars of conquest, such as the Mexican War. However, he hastened to add, "There have always been two sides of America, and one is the idealistic side that a lot of people believe in at a time like this."[23] But Dellinger found it difficult to be idealistic under these circumstances. Several things troubled him deeply about this war, particularly the use of antipersonnel weapons by American planes over remote villages inhabited mainly by civilians. If the purpose of the bombing was to target factories and infrastructure, as Johnson and McNamara insisted, why were fragmentation bombs being used, which, when dropped, opened up and released three hundred smaller bombs? The bombs were ineffective against bridges, factories, electrical plants, dikes, and the like, but highly lethal when unleashed on human beings.

Back in Hanoi, Dellinger had the opportunity to sit down and talk with North Vietnam's premier Pham Van Dong, a revolutionary known for his calm, soft-spoken demeanor. With the help of his interpreter, Do Xuan Oanh, Dellinger asked Pham a series of questions. Suddenly, without fanfare or warning, a short and lean balding figure with a wispy goatee entered the room. Dellinger stood and shook hands with Ho Chi Minh, the father of the modern Vietnamese independence movement. The American pacifist and the Vietnamese revolutionary took an instant liking to each other. Ho sat across from Dellinger, and the conversation immediately became more animated. Ho laughed several times and gesticulated dramatically when he spoke, while Pham sat silently, nodding his head reverentially and chuckling softly from time to time. Ho told his visitor about the time he lived in New York while working as a seaman before World War I. "I served as a house boy for a family in Brooklyn. They were very nice," he reminisced. Later in the conversation, Ho reminded Dellinger, "When you go back, say that I worked for very nice people in Brooklyn, and they paid me forty dollars a month, and now I am president of Vietnam, and I get paid forty-five dollars a month." At one point, Ho expressed sympathy with American GIs, particularly the prisoners of war being held in Hanoi. "I feel very sorry for them," he said. "They come over here thinking they are saving the world from some horrible thing called communism. . . . And they get over here, and they find out that even the anticommunist Vietnamese don't want them here."[24]

On November 15, Dellinger said farewell to his Vietnamese hosts and began his long trip home. Throughout the 1960s, 1970s, and 1980s, Dellinger visited both North and South Vietnam several times. But like his first trip to Cuba in 1960, his first one to Vietnam left the longest-lasting impression on him. At the end, Dellinger identified even more strongly with the Vietnamese revolutionary struggle and vowed to defend it, despite its reliance on violent means. He also made no secret of his newfound admiration for Ho Chi Minh. "I'm a totally nonviolent activist, but I found out that I had more in common with Ho and Pham Van Dong than I did with some of the peace leaders in this country," he recalled.[25] Most important, Dellinger came to regard movements for social justice at home as inseparable from liberation struggles overseas. "Self-determination in the countries presently occupied by the American military-industrial complex and self-determination within the United States go hand in hand," he concluded.[26]

Low morale plagued the antiwar movement back in the United States. The struggle appeared to be losing its momentum, and in the fall of 1966 the zeal of its participants gave way to disappointment. Nonetheless, the war continued to expand, with new units being deployed, and no amount of protest seemed to slow its steady escalation. A. J. Muste counseled his fellow activists not to be disheartened. "The feeling of letdown, of hopelessness . . . is in the final analysis something to be ashamed of," he said. "Did we really think the job would be easy?"[27]

On November 26, Dellinger cochaired a gathering of coalition representatives at the Case Western Reserve campus in Cleveland. In attendance were 180 people representing more than seventy local and national groups opposed to the war. At the meeting, mobilization leaders announced their most ambitious event yet: the Spring Mobilization to End the War in Vietnam, which would really be two marches, one in New York City and the other in San Francisco, on April 15, 1967. Support for the proposed event was enthusiastic and unanimous. According to conventional wisdom, April was an ideal time to schedule protests. After months of being cooped up, activists would emerge from their winter doldrums refreshed and ready to take to the streets. "The question," announced Sid Peck at the opening of the meeting, "is whether or not we . . . have developed the roots and ties in our communities to organize within a six-month period this kind of dramatically concentrated expression of opposition to the war."[28] Once again, mobilization leaders renamed their coalition, this time calling it the Spring Mobilization Committee to End the War in Vietnam. Participants in the Cleveland conference chose A. J. Muste as the chair and Dellinger as the vice chair.[29] Other officers were Sid Peck, Robert Greenblatt, and Edward Keating, founder of the leftist *Ramparts* magazine.

Dellinger had high hopes for the Spring Mobilization. No longer on the periphery of American society in marginal enclaves of like-minded radical pacifists, he now had both influence and the opportunity to use the coalition in a way that would reach far greater numbers of people than he had ever imagined possible. In Dellinger's mind, this new movement represented the apogee of what he had spent his life fighting. A self-deprecating man, he was painfully aware of his past mistakes, yet he knew that history was shifting in his favor. "Whatever mistakes we made in the antiwar movement—and we did of course, make them—people turned out anyway, people came, because there were historic reasons why the country was step by step turning against the war."[30]

The Mobilization drew supporters from all walks of life, including trade union members, women, homemakers, small business owners, white-collar workers, scientists, college professors, students, and physicians. Their politics also spanned the political spectrum, reflecting both the strengths and the weaknesses of the movement. As Norma Becker noted: "We had a wide range of political outlooks. The only thing we had in common was our opposition to the war in Vietnam."[31] Consensus was the cement that held the coalition together. It was essential that representatives from all the organizations in the Spring Mobilization Committee—which by the end of January 1967 totaled more than 150 national, regional, and local antiwar groups—agree on all of the major decisions made at the meetings. The various constituencies posed different challenges for Dellinger and the other Mobilization leaders. Overall, Dellinger got along well with liberals in the coalition in the months leading up to April 15. Prominent liberal antiwar groups, including the American Friends Service Committee and Women's Strike for Peace, had tremendous influence within the Mobilization. But liberals were far from monolithic, and the more staunchly anticommunist ones avoided the Mobilization. The war also caused rifts between moderate liberals like Robert Pickus, an unwavering critic of the antiwar movement, and more progressive liberals like Dr. Benjamin Spock, who believed strongly in forming close alliances with militants and favored dramatic protests. A struggle raged for months within SANE in 1966 and 1967, resulting in a split that pitted Spock and his followers, who supported the Spring Mobilization, against Norman Cousins and other SANE leaders who shunned ties with the coalition, fearing that it was too much influenced by communists. The moderates won and SANE did not officially endorse the April 15 march. A frustrated Dr. Spock, who later resigned from SANE, complained, "The conservatives literally want us to pause and make a little speech criticizing Ho Chi Minh every time we criticize Lyndon Johnson."[32]

The Mobilization attracted liberals for whom ending the war was a higher priority than anticommunism. Because of the coalition's nonexclusionary policy, liberals in the Mobilization knew they would be working alongside some of the Old Left radicals. Still, even the nominal presence of Communist Party members (and some ex-members) worried potential supporters like Martin Luther King Jr., who was considering speaking at the April 15 New York demonstration but feared reports of "Red" influences. It took months to convince him that communists constituted an insignificant presence in the Mobilization.[33]

Over the years, Dellinger had worked closely with liberals, forming alliances and friendships, although he had never hesitated to state that he was no liberal. Instead, he referred to himself as a "revolutionary," a label that upset some liberals. "I'm not a liberal and I never wanted to be one," he once remarked. "Most liberals accept our economic system, even though I appreciate that they are at least questioning some aspects of the status quo."[34] At the same time, Dellinger grew annoyed with the abrasive, knee-jerk antiliberalism that had become increasingly fashionable among certain elements of the New Left. The few New Leftists who were in the coalition he described as "disturbingly compulsive characters," who were "so wounded in their inner selves by the mounting stupidity of the cold war or by other baneful aspects of our culture, that they have become seriously unbalanced emotionally and bring to their peace activities powerful personal drives that conflict with the spirit of nonviolence."[35]

The most formidable challenge to Dellinger's leadership came from a disciplined and intensely ideological cadre of Socialist Workers Party (SWP) members. At every Mobilization planning meeting, he could count on SWPers attempting to dominate the proceedings. A Trotskyist revolutionary organization founded in 1938, the SWP never grew beyond a few thousand members and even sustained losses during a federal assault in the 1950s, but most of its followers remained firmly committed. Typical of the adherents who immersed themselves in antiwar work was the brilliant young activist Peter Camejo, a Berkeley radical who became a key figure in the national coalition. "I totally believed that the SWP had all the answers to all the questions. I was a cultist of the SWP," Camejo maintained.[36] Among the SWP's several offshoot organizations were the Young Socialist Alliance and the Student Mobilization Committee to End the War in Vietnam. Within the antiwar movement, the leader of the Trotskyists was Fred Halstead, a burly, good-humored, and thoughtful man from a solidly blue-collar background. A cloth cutter by trade, Halstead grew up in California, where his parents were union organizers and supporters of Eugene Debs. He joined the Industrial Workers of the World in his youth, served in the navy during World War II, and in 1947, while still in his early twenties, joined the SWP. He moved from California to New York that year and became a staff writer for the *Militant*, the SWP's weekly newspaper.[37] Doug Dowd remembered: "He [Halstead] was very tough, and a good leader. . . . He was somebody who, to put it in very old-fashioned terms, when he gave you his word you could count on it."[38]

The SWPers regarded their involvement in the antiwar movement as part of a larger mission to spread the socialist revolution to the American masses. "I am a socialist," proclaimed SWPer Harry Ring at the November 26 Cleveland meeting, "and I think the best way to end the war, and the thing that I give top priority to, is abolishing the capitalist system."[39] Like Dellinger, the Trotskyists called themselves "revolutionaries," yet their definition of the term was more theoretical. As disciplined Marxist-Leninists, they did not smoke dope, listen to rock music, or engage in free love, all of which they regarded as decadent and bourgeois. The SWP had formed a position on nearly every matter imaginable. Particularly frustrating to Dellinger was that SWPers rejected civil disobedience as counterproductive and potentially alienating to the "masses," especially to union members and moderates. Civil disobedience, Halstead and his colleagues reasoned, had no place at any sizable antiwar protest. "The purpose of these mass demonstrations," Halstead maintained, "is to provide a visible form in which dissent on the war can manifest itself; and to provide a form whereby new sections of the population can become inovlved."[40] SWP members urged all dissenters to obey the law and spread the revolutionary gospel to workers, soldiers, and poor people. Sometimes the official SWP line left Dellinger flabbergasted. For example, when the Fort Hood Three met with Halstead and Dellinger in the summer of 1966 seeking advice on what course of action to take, Dellinger advised resisting service in Vietnam. Halstead offered a strikingly different opinion, more in line with the SWP's position: "I told them that in their place I wouldn't do the same, that I would go to Vietnam, which would only be a year, and spread the antiwar message as best I could over there."[41]

SWPers irritated Dellinger, especially their tactics of outlasting other delegates at meetings, sometimes well past midnight, in an effort to dominate the decision making, and often taking credit for the coalition's successes. Other coalition leaders, including Norma Becker, A. J. Muste, and Doug Dowd, also occasionally became frustrated with the SWP's machinations while at the same time welcoming the contributions of individual members like Halstead. "They could be a pain in the ass," Dowd admitted.[42] Looking back on the SWP's contributions in the 1960s, Dellinger commented:

Since the SWP regularly packed meetings with delegates . . . none of
whom identified themselves as members of the SWP but all of whom
were directed by an SWP floor leader, it was not always easy for a
coalition of over 150 . . . organizations to make a decision that ran
counter to a decision already made in the SWP caucus.[43]

Despite making his antagonisms known later, Dellinger remained outwardly friendly to Halstead. "We had our differences but our relations
were still cordial," Halstead said of Dellinger.[44]

Civil rights activists also were vital to the Spring Mobilization to
End the War in Vietnam. More than any other previous mass demonstration, the April 15 Mobilization drew on the energies of the African
American freedom struggle and bridged the gap between the civil
rights and the antiwar movements. Just before Christmas 1966, the Mobilization—with Dellinger's blessing—hired a new national director,
Rev. James Bevel, a thirty-year-old Baptist minister who since 1963 had
served as the action program director of the Southern Christian Leadership Conference. The move was a masterstroke in a behind-the-scenes
struggle that had been going on for months to persuade Martin Luther
King Jr. to denounce the war. Bevel was close to King and, along with
other key aides, pressured him to take a stand against the war. Dellinger
knew King, but not particularly well. Unlike Bayard Rustin, Dellinger
had never been an indispensable player in the civil rights movement, although he once ghostwrote an article for King. King also invited
Dellinger to travel to the Bahamas to help him write his memoirs, but
he declined. Despite their mutual respect, King and Dellinger did not
have a close friendship. Not surprisingly, Dellinger thought King was
too cautious, although he recognized the significance of King's participation in the April 15 march. The Mobilization thus found in Bevel the
link it needed to reach King. After spending time with Bevel and meeting with Andrew Young, another King lieutenant, Dellinger sent a message to the civil rights leader. The time for King to take a stand on the
war "is long overdue," Dellinger told Young, "and if he fails to act now
history will pass him by and from now on his influence will be mini-
mized."[45] King apparently listened and by February had promised to
speak at the April 15 event in New York City.

The momentum of planning for April 15 was temporarily interrupted by the sudden death of A. J. Muste on February 11, 1967, from

heart failure, shortly after being admitted to St. Luke's Hospital in New York City. He was eighty-two. Muste's death represented a tragic setback for the Mobilization in particular and the antiwar movement in general. Some of Muste's comrades, including Dellinger, had worried about his deteriorating health. But with the escalation and intensification of the Vietnam War, Muste had refused to scale back his agenda. In his last year of life, he had gone to Vietnam twice, and during his final weeks, he took part in radio interviews, committee meetings, speaking engagements. and court hearings for earlier acts of civil disobedience. News of Muste's death saddened Dellinger. Although their relationship had been rocky at first, over the years it evolved into one of mutual respect, and toward the end of Muste's life it became genuinely warm. Muste's death suddenly elevated Dellinger to a vital leadership spot in the antiwar movement. "When A. J. Muste died in 1967," remembered David McReynolds, "he had been the glue for the anti–Vietnam War movement. Dave took on that post, an enormously valuable and difficult task, as the only person who could do it."[46]

For the January 1967 issue of *Liberation*, which came out after Muste's death and on whose cover was a photograph of him at an antiwar demonstration, Dellinger wrote an obituary for Muste. The final passage read:

> To some it may seem that A. J. died too soon, and to all who knew and loved him or valued his work, any time would have been too soon. But we can rejoice that he lived 82 years and left a heritage in which radical personal commitment and an insistence on the necessity for nonviolent revolution were combined with a deep respect for those with whom he differed politically or philosophically. He managed to work creatively with those who shared only a part of his philosophy or strategy, without sacrificing the integrity of his own deepest beliefs or being prevented from engaging in actions that stemmed from them. It was part of his greatness that he could feel that he was right without becoming self-righteous or demeaning those who could not share in all his activities and attitudes. It was enough for him that they walked part of the way with him and that while walking together he and they could probe and examine and analyze so that each might learn from the other.[47]

Despite cold weather, gray skies, and intermittent rain, crowds of demonstrators began arriving at Central Park on the morning of April

15. Never before had a mass protest been so large or diverse. At approximately 11 A.M., one hour before the march began, a group of about sixty young draft resisters gathered to burn their draft cards and the draft cards of more than a hundred other men who could not be present. David Dellinger stood among the surrounding crowds of curious onlookers, plainclothes police officers, FBI agents, and journalists. He intended his presence as a show of solidarity. Leading the draft card burners was a young Cornell University student, Bruce Dancis, whose father had been a conscientious objector in World War II. His action marked the beginning of a nationwide draft resistance movement.[48]

Early in 1967, a group of college students, several from Cornell, had asked Dellinger whether they should publicly burn their draft cards at the upcoming April 15 protest. As a former conscientious objector, Dellinger believed such an act of resistance would embolden other young draft evaders. He therefore asked the Mobilization leaders to allow the draft-age men to burn their federal government-issued draft cards on the podium between speeches. But the issue threatened to divide the Spring Mobilization Committee, as David McReynolds explained:

> A struggle ensued over whether the draft-card burning would be part of the main event or entirely separate. When it became clear that the moderates would suffer heart attacks if we did not work out a compromise, we agreed that draft-card burning would take place before the main rally started, and that it would be separated from the area of the main rally.[49]

The key opponent of allowing the draft-card burners to perform their protest on the main podium was Sid Peck. Earlier, he and other Spring Mobilization leaders had promised the SWP and representatives of Martin Luther King Jr. that draft-card burning would not be an official part of the April 15 event. The decision infuriated Dellinger, who had opposed it at a Spring Mobilization steering committee meeting. Many of the draft resisters were nervous young men, he reasoned, who needed the support of the coalition. Peck, however, felt that including the draft-card burners in the main event would fracture the fragile alliance. It would drive away King, he feared, not to mention the small army of SWPers who were performing much of the drudge labor. Peck also enjoyed the support of a large segment of the coalition. Only a few other militant pacifists, including Norma Becker, Ralph DiGia, and David McReynolds, backed the draft resisters. Peck and Dellinger clashed repeatedly over the matter, which strained a relationship that had been distant since the day they met in the fall of 1966. "What Dave pushed for . . . was the burning of the draft cards at the stage of the demonstration at the UN," recounted Peck. "That was a total violation of the agreement that had been reached, and I'm a stickler for agreements. When you make an agreement with a handshake, you keep your word."[50] According to Dellinger's version of events, a group of the draft resisters attended a Spring Mobilization steering committee meeting and demanded an opportunity to ignite their cards on the main stage. According to Dellinger, the group "used the personal endorsements of the burning by Norma Becker and myself as an argument to support their plea. This upset some of the . . . [Spring Mobilization] members, and . . . Sidney Peck, a stalwart organizer and idea person, surprised me by calling for my replacement as chair."[51] Despite his split with Dellinger, Peck openly expressed his admiration for Dancis and the other resisters and acknowledged that as a result of their efforts, "the draft resistance movement increased substantially."[52]

The April 15 protest was so enormous that by 5 P.M., as a torrential downpour began soaking the thousands of protesters at the United Nations plaza, the last contingents of marchers still had not left Central Park and therefore missed the speakers at the UN. King remarked to Dellinger that the crowd appeared larger than the one at the 1963 March on Washington. The events of April 15 amounted to an incredible achievement for the antiwar movement, and overall the extensive and largely sympathetic media coverage showed an image of diversity and respectability to the rest of the nation.[53]

The Spring Mobilization to End the War had immediate symbolic importance, as it resulted in a mainstreaming of the antiwar movement. The war's opponents had put aside their differences and showed that they could reach the rest of the nation. A. J. Muste would have been proud of the event. After April 15, Dellinger's thoughts about an antiwar strategy changed. Now in a more militant frame of mind, he began proposing bolder, more dramatic types of confrontation, especially acts of civil disobedience that would result in mass arrests. His heightened militancy coincided with a public relations campaign by the Johnson administration, which was busily trying to convince the American people that victory in Vietnam was imminent. At the beginning of 1967, there were 340,000 U.S. troops in South Vietnam, a number that steadily increased throughout the year. In 1967 alone, 9,419 Americans died in military actions in Southeast Asia.[54] Despite the rising death tolls, President Johnson repeatedly insisted that America was winning the war in Vietnam. After April 15, Dellinger often spoke of the need "to forge a creative synthesis of Gandhi and guerrilla."[55] It seemed clear to him that war makers had no intention of listening to an antiwar movement grounded in political moderation. Coalition representatives met repeatedly after April 15 to establish strategies and plan future protests. At a June 17 administrative committee meeting in New York City, antiwar organizers transformed the ad hoc Spring Mobilization into a new, permanent organization: the National Mobilization to End the War in Vietnam.[56] Activists called it the Mobe. By the late spring, plans already were under way for the next major event, set to take place in Washington, D.C., in October. Even though the Mobe organizers met regularly, some activists felt it was not enough given the gravity of events in Vietnam. "One of our big problems is that we didn't meet as often as we should have," recounted Doug Dowd, who sat on the Mobe's steering committee. "Our main defect was that we'd have a big demonstration and it would be a great success, then we'd all go home and a few months later we'd start planning for another one."[57]

After the Mobe was formed, Dellinger was elected to serve as its chairman, and under his direction, the coalition took a more militant turn. In one of the group's earliest official statements to the press in May, he set the tone for upcoming protests. "Central to any . . . direct action must be a program for the ever-growing number of people who are ready to cease cooperating with the policies of destruction and genocide and equally ready to commit themselves to building for peace and equality."[58]

In the summer, Dellinger hired Bay Area activist Jerry Rubin to be the project coordinator for the upcoming October protests. It was a move that later alienated a number of people in the coalition because of Rubin's outrageous behavior and over-the-top rhetoric. Dellinger and Rubin first met at the teach-ins on the University of California's Berkeley campus in 1965, long before Rubin became a well-known Yippie icon. At Berkeley, Dave found Jerry to be a deeply dedicated and earnest organizer, and Rubin considered it an honor to be asked by Dellinger to come to New York to help coordinate the October protests. Born in 1938 to a truck driver father in the Teamsters and well-educated mother, Rubin grew up in a working-class Cincinnati neighborhood. After attending Oberlin College and graduating from the University of Cincinnati, Rubin worked as a sports reporter for a Cincinnati newspaper in the early 1960s. Following the death of his parents—his father died in 1960, his mother in 1961—Jerry went to Israel with his younger brother, Gil, who was now under his care. After meeting Jewish leftists in Israel, he returned to the United States radicalized. He entered the graduate program in sociology at Berkeley in 1964 but dropped out after six months to become a full-time activist.[59]

By the time Dellinger approached him in the late spring of 1967, Rubin had been a full-time antiwar activist for two years. Adapting to the local counterculture scene, Rubin had abandoned his suits and ties and clean-cut image in favor of long hair, a bushy beard, tight-fitting turtleneck sweaters, and faded corduroy pants. From his years as a journalist, he had a strong sense of the theatrical and much media savvy. When Dellinger asked him to come to work for the Mobe in New York City, Rubin jumped at the chance. He remembered, "I was pretty tired of Berkeley, and I was just thrilled that Dave Dellinger and the steering committee had voted to bring me there as project director."[60]

In June, Dellinger and Rubin discussed the October protest over dinner in New York City. Dave told Jerry that the Mobe was planning a march on Congress as part of an effort to "bring the war to the war makers." Rubin suggested an alternative scenario: "You know, this March on Congress, Dave, doesn't really make sense to me. People don't see Congress as the enemy. They elect Congress. There's no point to be made by doing that. We should march on the Pentagon."[61]

Although Dellinger found Jerry Rubin a welcome newcomer to the national coalition, others were not so impressed. When Rubin began appearing in the Mobe offices during the summer of 1967, most seasoned activists regarded him as an upstart. Rubin once lectured Fred Halstead about why protesters should target the Pentagon instead of the Capitol building, arguing that Native Americans regarded five-sided objects like the Pentagon building as symbols of evil. Rubin left the Halstead speechless. Halstead later revealed, "As it turned out, Rubin didn't even know the Pentagon wasn't in the city of Washington but across the Potomac River in Virginia."[62]

While the Mobe organizers prepared for the October protests, Dellinger made several overseas trips directly related to his antiwar work at home. In late 1966, Ralph Schoenman, a young American activist and assistant to Bertrand Russell, invited him to serve as a member on the Russell War Crimes Tribunal. The idea of conducting extensive war crimes hearings in Europe came from Schoenman, a Brooklyn-born, Princeton-educated radical. Schoenman wanted to bring in a variety of people—such as physicians, aid workers, religious volunteers, Vietnamese civilians, and combatants from all sides—who could testify about the systematic occurrence of "atrocities" in the Vietnam War. Presiding over the sessions was the French philosopher Jean-Paul Sartre, who introduced the speakers and maintained order. Schoenman hoped the tribunal would provide those testifying with a highly visible public forum in which to share their accounts.[63] Dellinger enthusiastically backed the hearings and recruited other peace activists to join him in Stockholm for the May proceedings. Staughton Lynd, however, turned down the offer, fearing that the tribunal had adopted "Stalinist" tactics by refusing to explore the violence committed by communist forces. "My position," Lynd explained, "is that an action defined as a 'crime' remains criminal no matter who commits it."[64] Lynd's stance marked a parting of ways with Dellinger over the use of violence by Third World liberation struggles, which Lynd was more reluctant to defend than Dellinger was. Dellinger then found two other Americans to sit on the tribunal: SDS leader Carl Oglesby and leading Black Power proponent Stokely Carmichael.

In May, the first tribunal opened in Stockholm, and the testimony was so extensive that the organizers planned a second gathering in Copenhagen in November. Dellinger believed the tribunal's findings would have a decisive impact back in America. But he greatly misjudged the potency of the Russell tribunal. In fact, its findings did little to shape public opinion back home and had virtually no influence on the government's Vietnam policies.[65] From the outset, the proceedings suffered from a limited budget, repeated clashes between Sartre and Schoenman, a lack of focus, and a shortage of high-profile witnesses. Not a single American soldier who had served in Vietnam testified at the Stockholm gathering. At the second tribunal in Copenhagen, three American soldiers testified, but they alone could not adequately speak for the entire American military presence in Southeast Asia. Very few Americans noticed or cared about the Russell tribunal's findings.

Other overseas commitments kept David Dellinger out of the country for weeks at a time during the planning phases for the October Pentagon march. At the end of April, he received a telegram from the Viet-

namese Peace Committee, a Hanoi-based nongovernmental organization, alerting him to the intensification of the American air war over
North Vietnam. From May 26 to June 9, Dellinger and Nick Egleson,
then president of SDS, traveled to several provinces in the southern part
of North Vietnam to inspect the damage. In September, Dellinger went
to Bratislava, Czechoslovakia, to attend a meeting organized by Tom
Hayden that brought together Vietnamese revolutionaries and American antiwar activists. Both sides hoped the conference would provide a
forum to discuss the future of the war and the prospects for ending it.
Most of the thirty or so Americans in Bratislava were SDSers. Dellinger
was one of the few older activists to receive an invitation to the event,
indicating his powerful influence in New Left circles. Like the Russell
tribunal, the Bratislava meetings inspired those present but had no impact on public opinion back in the United States.

Returning to the United States, Dellinger increased his involvement
in the antiwar movement in the summer and early fall, chairing numerous meetings and appearing more regularly at the Mobe headquarters. Posters and promotional materials for the upcoming October
protests promised militant action. By late September and early October,
everything appeared to be coming together. Organizers rented sound
systems, lined up speakers and musicians, sent out mass mailings,
bought ads in newspapers across the country, and granted interviews to
local media. "Whatever our differences," Dellinger wrote in the October issue of *Mobilizer News*, the Mobe's official newsletter, "let us remember that we are united in the overriding goal of ending the war in
Vietnam."[66]

Since it began, the planning for the Pentagon march had been beset
by problems. Jerry Rubin failed miserably as the project coordinator for
the Mobe, managing to alienate almost everybody in the Mobe offices
with his often sanctimonious and abrasive personality. Weeks after arriving in New York City, he dropped out of the job he was hired to do
and immersed himself in the Greenwich Village scene with his newfound political soul mate, Abbie Hoffman. Abbie and Jerry formed an
enclave of other countercultural radicals and formulated their own,
separate, protest at the Pentagon, which involved bringing in a Native
American shaman to levitate the building ten feet off the ground in
order to "exorcise" it of its "evil spirits." Media coverage of the
Rubin/Hoffman levitation plans was extensive. As Paul Krassner, edi-

tor of the *Realist* magazine and a friend of the duo, wrote, "We applied for a permit, then told the press that the government would allow us to raise the Pentagon no more than three feet off the ground, and the press actually reported the quote."[67] This sort of media attention did not benefit the Mobe, and many insiders questioned Dellinger's leadership abilities after he hired Rubin. Dellinger conceded that "Rubin didn't do the work he had come to do"[68] but stopped short of admitting that the hiring had been a mistake. Even Dellinger's closest allies in the movement grew to dislike Jerry Rubin. Doug Dowd spoke for many in the coalition when he stated, "Jerry Rubin just wanted to be in the public eye all the time. . . . The guy was an asshole, really childish."[69]

Worse than the Rubin imbroglio was the threat of a split in the coalition over the militant tactics and tone of the upcoming Pentagon march. One segment of the Mobe feared that the planning for the October protest had been hijacked by confrontational leftists determined to cause a huge clash with authorities. On August 28, the Mobe held a press conference in New York City to discuss the Pentagon march and reveal their plans to the media. They announced that on the weekend of October 20 and 21, a series of massive protests would "shut down the Pentagon." The antiwar movement planned to fuse "Gandhi and guerrilla" and combine mass action with civil disobedience. "We will fill the hallways and block the entrances. . . . This confrontation will be massive, continuing, flexible, surprising." At the same press conference, Jerry Rubin revealed his plans to raise the Pentagon "three hundred feet in the air." Dellinger then added this grave warning: "There will be no government building left unattacked."[70]

Nervous about plans to "confront the war makers," SANE and the Women's International League for Peace and Freedom refused to endorse the march, although the league reversed its decision at the last minute. And as the march drew closer, the SWP and Women's Strike for Peace came close to withdrawing their endorsements as well.[71] In August, Harold Feldman of the Philadelphia chapter of Veterans to Peace wrote to Dellinger criticizing the new direction of the antiwar movement. Feldman feared that militant "direct actions" would only alienate the public. "Are you out to win?" he asked Dellinger. "Or are you simply out to demonstrate your moral superiority in defeat and ruin?"[72]

The crisis extended to the editorial offices of *Liberation*, where David McReynolds resigned from the editorial board. It was not the

prospect of mass civil disobedience at the Pentagon—which he supported—that drove McReynolds away. Rather, he quit in June after
eleven years at *Liberation* because he felt Dellinger exerted too much authority over the magazine's contents and had strayed too far from his
original pacifist ideals.[73] McReynolds decried

> pacifists who, while rejecting the "macho" stereotype of American
> men, count arrests as a manly act, and feel that someone who has been
> arrested twenty times has more virtue than someone who has been ar-
> rested only once, and spent the rest of his or her time taking care of a
> family or volunteering in a Catholic Worker house.[74]

Similarly, *Liberation* contributor and veteran radical pacifist Charles
Bloomstein asked that his name be removed from the masthead. In his
June 27 letter of resignation, he wrote, ""I no longer consider *Liberation*
to be a pacifist magazine and feel that its present trend is taking it further from that position."[75]

Not easily discouraged, Dellinger took these obstacles in stride. He
constantly assured moderates of his intention to remain responsible
and hold the coalition together, even if it required compromise. As
Doug Dowd explained, "His main virtue was in the way he thought
and acted and talked and behaved with respect to everybody else. He
was always somebody who brought people together who were on the
edge of breaking apart, which was almost always, of course."[76]

In Washington, D.C., government officials created another impedi-
ment by refusing to grant any permits until the Mobe renounced civil
disobedience. Mobe representatives Dellinger, Rubin, Halstead, and
Robert Greenblatt attended long meetings over a period of several days
with Harry Van Cleve, lawyer for the General Services Administration,
which oversaw the maintenance of all federal property. After much
haggling and threats of unruly protests if they were denied a permit,
Van Cleve offered a compromise. The marchers would receive a permit
to gather near the Lincoln Memorial on October 21 for a peaceful assembly involving speakers and music, followed by a march across Arlington Memorial Bridge to the Pentagon. The protesters would then be
allowed to conduct a demonstration in the Pentagon's north parking
lot, a thousand feet away from the main building. Following the rally in
the parking lot, demonstrators would be granted access to the Pentagon
mall closer to the building for additional protests after 4 P.M. The Mobe

representatives accepted Van Cleve's offer, except for Jerry Rubin, who favored "wholesale disruption" without permits.[77]

The mood in the nation's capital was tense on the morning of Friday, October 20, 1967. Guarding the Pentagon and various points throughout the city were eighteen hundred National Guard troops, four battalions of military police totaling about three thousand men, two thousand District of Columbia police officers, and contingents from the Eighty-second Airborne Division. "Permits for the rallies, the march, the picketing and vigils on the mall of the Pentagon have been assured us," Dellinger informed activists across the nation in the *Mobilizer Newsletter* mailed out a week before the protest. "Problems may arise, but serious trouble is unlikely."[78]

On the night of October 20, as thousands of demonstrators streamed into Washington, the *CBS Evening News* broadcast a lengthy interview with David Dellinger. Wearing a suit and tie, with his partially balding head glistening in the lights, the pacifist spoke softly to the nation, proclaiming that the events of the following day would amount to more than "a polite registering of disapproval." He described the war in Vietnam as "uncivil disobedience" and vowed that it would be met with a decisive and confrontational protest at the Lincoln Memorial and the Pentagon.[79] The next day, the *New York Times* ran a lengthy biographical sketch of the man it described as the "Cool Protest Leader."[80] Now a prominent figure in a mass protest movement, Dellinger's vision of "Gandhi and guerrilla"—a meeting of nonviolence and militant resistance—was about to be put to the test.

9

The Road to Chicago

His life sounds like a protracted, quiet, undiminishingly affectionate argument with those of the young who strain against his pacifism. His conduct in Chicago earned him wider notice and trust from the young radicals than he has ever had; but, if it is the largest constituency in his life, it is also the most volatile, the most subject to bursting forth in directions that alarm him.

Murray Kempton

Our position is that whoever the candidates are, and whatever the platforms, that we must stay in the streets and stay in active resistance or else there will be no peace. Either in the ghettos or in Vietnam.

David Dellinger

In 1968 the name Chicago won a significance far beyond date and place. It became the title of an episode, like Waterloo, or Versailles, or Munich.

Theodore H. White

ON SATURDAY, OCTOBER 21, 1967, the normally placid atmosphere of the Pentagon was interrupted by the chants of about fifty thousand people who reached its north parking lot in the midafternoon. Under Defense Secretary Robert McNamara's orders, armed troops encircled the building. An outer row of U.S. marshals also guarded the premises as the first line of defense against protesters whose goal was reportedly to "shut down" the Pentagon. Sharpshooters on the roof were prepared to act in the event of a crisis. The troops, marshals, and phalanxes of military police guarding the government structure kept remarkably cool as the first wave of demonstrators approached, chanting slogans and carrying placards and banners. "The front ranks indeed included many troublemakers, who used every device to provoke the troops to violence," remembered McNamara.[1]

The march was the result of almost six months of planning by antiwar leaders in a coalition that at times teetered on collapse. The Mobe overcame this internal strife thanks largely to Dave Dellinger, Sid Peck, Fred Halstead, Norma Becker, and other talented leaders who emphasized compromise and consensus. Their efforts finally bore fruit at the Pentagon on October 21 with the enormous march that by midafternoon was inching toward the building. According to Sid Lens, "The agreement with the government called for entering the north Pentagon parking lot at a certain gate, but within a few minutes the fence was breached in three or four places and what was to have been a single march became a confused welter of Indian lines."[2] At the front of the line, Dellinger, Peck, and other Mobe leaders tried to keep the crowd together at least until it arrived in the parking lot. Demonstrators carried placards ranging from the respectable ("Negotiate") to the inflammatory ("Where Is Oswald When We Need Him?").[3] The Pentagon march soon deteriorated into a confusion of teargas, police clubbing protesters, hippies chanting, paddy wagons racing in all directions, and thousands of leaderless participants milling around the parking lot well into Sunday. Whereas government officials judged the day's events a dismal failure, Mobe leaders declared it a victory. As Dellinger hoped, it set the tone for future protests and turned out to be a rehearsal of the clashes between police and peace activists in the streets of Chicago less than a year later.

In the weeks leading up to the Pentagon protest, Dellinger's greatest challenge was preventing a split between the militants and the moderates. Particularly galling to supporters of traditional tactics were the antics of Jerry Rubin, Abbie Hoffman, and their followers. One of Hoffman's closest friends, Stew Albert, who moved to New York City with Jerry Rubin in the summer of 1967 to help with the antiwar organizing, briefly edited the Mobe's nationally circulated newsletter, the *Mobilizer*. His stint as editor came to an abrupt end, however, when he decided to run a tongue-in-cheek piece by Keith Lampe, a friend of Rubin and Hoffman, calling for a nationwide "loot-in" of rioting and trashing in communities across America. The article never appeared in print, and Mobe moderates fired Albert as *Mobilizer* editor.[4] By the summer, the media were focusing on the more colorful activists and their attempts to synthesize the counterculture and insurgent street politics. Hoffman, in particular, loved the attention, and the more he received, the more outrageous he became. Dellinger stood by in bemused silence and watched the younger Greenwich Village radicals issue extreme manifestos and conduct wild press conferences. "I trusted Abbie's and Jerry's sincerity and dedication," he said, "even though their lifestyle was different than my lifestyle or the people I was used to working with."[5]

Somehow Dellinger managed to keep the critics of Hoffman and Rubin in the fold, but it was not easy. Barbara Deming's idea of dividing the events of October 21 into two parts—a demonstration at the Lincoln Memorial without civil disobedience followed by a march to the Pentagon at which activists would defy the authorities en masse—probably prevented a destructive split in the Mobilization. Cochairing the plans for the Pentagon march with Dellinger was the well-known pediatrician Dr. Benjamin Spock, who represented the Mobe's more liberal tendencies. Spock added an air of respectability to the proceedings. "My usefulness to the peace movement," Spock acknowledged, "is in recruiting people from the middle of the road. I'm quite realistic about that. But I'm willing to cooperate with anyone who's halfway responsible who wants to end this terrible war."[6]

Mobe leaders timed the Pentagon march to coincide with a series of protests across the country known as "Stop the Draft Week." The week began on October 16 when fifty young men burned their draft cards in front of an audience of four thousand people at Boston's Arlington Street Church. An additional 250 other young men presented their cards to Yale Chaplain William Sloane Coffin, who eventually gathered nearly a thousand draft cards from across the nation and delivered them to the Justice Department. Officials there refused to accept them. On the same day as the emotional Arlington Street Church gathering, peaceful protests were held in Oakland, California, aimed at halting operations at the Oakland induction center. At the steps of the center, where new recruits were processed and shipped out on trains, police carted off nonviolent resisters by the hundreds. Later in the week, thousands of angry protesters clashed with police in the streets of Oakland, overturning cars, smashing windows, and tipping over barricades. Police used teargas and nightsticks to drive back crowds of demonstrators, some of whom picked up the canisters of teargas and hurled them back at the police lines. Meanwhile, at the University of Wisconsin in

Madison, police clashed with activists who were protesting the recruitment of students by Dow Chemical, the manufacturer of napalm, the incendiary jelly widely used by the U.S. armed forces in Vietnam. This led to a clash between the demonstrators, most of them students, and the police, in full riot gear and armed with teargas and attack dogs. Against this backdrop of increasing tensions, more than 150 influential figures, including noted writers, clergy, and professors, signed and published "A Call to Resist Illegitimate Authority," which appeared in several publications, including the *New York Review of Books* and *The New Republic*. The statement excited and emboldened war resisters everywhere. Written by Arthur Waskow and Maurice Raskin of the Institute for Policy Studies, a left-wing think tank, the "Call" declared that the Vietnam War was unjust, illegal, and immoral and that Americans had an obligation to resist it. "Many of us believe that open resistance to the war and the draft is the course of action most likely to strengthen the moral resolve with which all of us can oppose the war and most likely bring an end to the war."[7]

On October 21, a hundred thousand people streamed into the mall near the Lincoln Memorial and the Washington Monument for the largest antiwar demonstration to date in Washington, D.C. The people at the march were predominantly white and middle class; indeed, "the vast majority looked as if they had decamped temporarily from Ivy League campuses," noted a correspondent from the *Times* of London.[8] Crossing the stage to introduce the speakers, David Dellinger was suddenly attacked by three American Nazi Party members who rushed onto the platform. One of them leaped on him and began pummeling him. Rev. William Sloane Coffin pried off the assailant, and a group of young Mobe marshals restrained the Nazis until the police hauled them away in a patrol wagon.[9] Slightly shaken, Dellinger joked to the audience that the attackers must have wanted to steal the check he had just finished writing to the company that furnished the sound system. He then introduced Dr. Spock, who delivered the most rousing speech of the day. The real enemy, Spock said, "is Lyndon Johnson, whom we elected as a peace candidate in 1964, and who betrayed us within three months, who has stubbornly led us deeper and deeper into a bloody quagmire."[10]

For the next two hours, speakers and performers whipped up the crowd. Finally, Dellinger stepped up to the microphone and when the applause subsided, he announced, "This is the beginning of a new stage of the American peace movement in which the cutting edge becomes active resistance."[11] He called on Americans in cities and communities across the country to launch new resistance movements against the war. Today's march, he emphasized, represented an overdue shift "from protest to resistance." "We said we would disrupt the Pentagon," he announced into the microphone, "and I believe it is already being disrupted."[12] One of the thousands of people in the Mall that day was the activist and writer Marty Jezer, who listened intently to Dellinger's speech but was not entirely captivated by what he heard. "Dave never knew when to end a speech. He'd come to a great and obvious ending and you'd start applauding and he'd go on; he'd do this two or three times in every speech. His voice had a whiney quality to it. He was not a great orator."[13]

Several times over the loudspeaker Dellinger announced that those who wished to do so could participate in the march to the Pentagon at the end of the rally. At 2:15 P.M., about fifty thousand people began moving down Boundary Channel Drive, packing the road so tightly that some demonstrators found it difficult to hold up their banners and placards. The marchers surged forward toward Memorial Bridge, crossing the Potomac as army helicopters hovered overhead. The crowd crossed the bridge slowly, nobody knowing what awaited on the other side. At the front of the line the notables gathered. Poet Robert Lowell, novelist Norman Mailer, and literary critic Dwight MacDonald locked arms together, along with lesser known figures like Sidney Lens, Monsignor Charles O. Rice of Pittsburgh, and Noam Chomsky, a professor of linguistics at the Massachusetts Institute of Technology. Dr. Benjamin Spock and Rev. William Sloane Coffin also marched at the front of the line.

Dellinger walked close to Cordell Reagan, a former SNCC activist who was supervising the highly disciplined parade marshals who were to preserve order along the route.[14] The trouble began even before the thousands of people reached the Pentagon. A small contingent of ultraleftists broke off from the march after crossing the bridge. Scurrying into the forest, they ran carrying a National Liberation Front flag toward the Pentagon, eventually reaching the U.S. marshals and MPs surrounding the complex, who swiftly routed them.[15]

Around 4 P.M. the marchers arrived at the Pentagon. Using a bullhorn, Dellinger began guiding people into the north parking lot, where a rally was scheduled to take place before the mass civil disobedience.

But some impatient activists had heard enough speeches and music and wanted to bypass the rally and head straight for the building. The group made their way over to the building, where, to the sound of a trumpet and a drum, hundreds of men and women formed a line, holding hands and chanting in unison.[16]

At the same time, a large group of militants calling themselves the "Revolutionary Contingent" also left the parking lot rally and charged toward the building, heading straight for a line of heavily armed federal personnel. They were quickly beaten back. At another location along the Pentagon steps, Norman Mailer rounded up a ragtag army of luminaries and lesser-known protesters and went straight for an unprotected Pentagon entrance, but a swarm of MPs arrested and hauled them away.[17]

Upon learning about the clashes near the main building, Dellinger, along with march coordinator Brad Lyttle and a few other Mobe officials, headed toward the Pentagon. Meanwhile, Norma Becker and Sid Peck remained in the north parking guiding thousands of marchers, who were still arriving and looking for leadership and direction. Suddenly, Becker saw panicked demonstrators fleeing from the Pentagon, some carrying their battered and beaten comrades. "Bloody heads were coming down, one after the other," Becker remembered. "They had been hit with rifle butts or clubs. Within minutes, it was clear that there was a pattern: Almost everyone who came down with a bloody head was a female, a young college girl."[18] Dellinger neared the Pentagon, speaking into the bullhorn, beginning his planned teach-in for the troops, which he hoped would also calm the more militant protesters. "You are our brothers!" he called out. "Join us!"[19] His words were at odds with the actions of the more abrasive demonstrators, who angrily chanted slogans and screamed obscenities near the MPs and U.S. marshals. Jerry Rubin repeatedly called the guards "fascists." Some hecklers even threw objects at them. But by all accounts, most of the protesters at the Pentagon that afternoon were orderly and respectful to the soldiers. George Dennison, a young pacifist journalist, echoed the heartfelt empathy of many activists toward the MPs and U.S. marshals guarding the building. "Many were Negro," he wrote, "almost all were young. These were not violent faces, but those of boys from small towns and city slums, many with an unfinished, hangdog look of profound uncertainty in the conduct of life."[20] Dellinger likewise encouraged protesters to support the soldiers at the Pentagon, reminding the crowd through his bullhorn that they were not the enemies. One of the most famous and enduring images of the Pentagon march is that of a young man slipping flowers into the rifles of MPs, a practice widely repeated by the demonstrators.[21]

Near the Pentagon, the MPs intentionally opened large gaps in their line that the resisters could easily penetrate. Their purpose was to lure the demonstrators into restricted areas, where they would immediately be arrested and taken away. A number of people fell into the trap. As early evening neared, Dellinger, along with Monsignor Rice, Dr. Spock, activist Maris Cakars, and other demonstrators crossed the MPs' line and came within yards of one of the entrances to the Pentagon. The doors of the building suddenly opened, and a long column of fresh troops in riot gear moved outside and formed a new line in front of Dellinger. He continued his teach-in through the bullhorn when a sergeant commanded, "All right, push 'em out now!"[22] Dellinger fell to his knees and kept speaking through his megaphone, imploring the troops to join the siege. Other activists immediately fell down and covered their heads and genitals, a position pioneered by SNCC in the early 1960s. "I don't know how to explain what happened next," Dellinger recounted. "I had never before been hit and kicked by so many people so many times. . . . A swarm of government marshals rushed us from the opposite direction, flailing and beating us with clubs."[23]

Bloody, bruised, and dazed, Dellinger went limp as the soldiers carried him away. The federal troops deliberately avoided Dr. Spock, however, who had fallen to his knees with his hands behind his head, clearly waiting to be arrested. "Dave, they won't arrest me!" Spock cried out amid the din of screams and helicopters flying overhead. "Apparently he was too popular a figure to be included in the list of disreputable people who would appear in the next day's news accounts," Dellinger remembered.[24] U.S. marshals took Dellinger inside the building to a holding dormitory in the basement where dozens of other battered demonstrators were waiting to be removed from the premises. By the end of the weekend, authorities released Dellinger, fined him fifty dollars, and gave him a thirty-day suspended jail sentence on the condition he would not return to the Pentagon "with the intention of committing an illegal act."[25]

While he was detained with the other protesters, Dellinger missed some of the most dramatic moments of the siege at the Pentagon. By the late afternoon and early evening, the north parking lot had become a scene of chaos and confusion. The company that owned the sound system used by the Mobe abruptly shut it down and hauled it away in a truck, leaving the organizers with only a handful of battery-powered bullhorns. Thousands of people wandered aimlessly—hungry, cold, and tired. Men and women in the parking lot began panicking when the chartered buses that were supposed to take them home were diverted to other parking areas by Pentagon authorities who did not bother informing the Mobe organizers of their decision. "It became so frantic," remembered Sid Peck. "We were trying to give people guidance as to where their buses were because they wanted to go back. There was a lot of mix-up and . . . we just had two bullhorns because the sound system was gone."[26]

By nightfall, most of the protesters had left, although a few thousand remained. Floodlights bathed the area in an ethereal yellowish glow, and helicopters flew overhead while sharpshooters kept watch on the roof of the Pentagon. At midnight, the lines of MPs and marshals once again fanned out and began arbitrarily clubbing demonstrators. The marshals arrested Hoffman, Rubin, and several of their Greenwich Village comrades. Doug Dowd was pleased to see authorities dragging away the defiant Rubin. Earlier in the evening, Dowd had watched as Rubin, standing behind the thousands of protesters who were gathered near the soldiers, "began throwing fiery pieces of wood over the heads of the crowd at the marshals" to provoke an attack. "If I could've gone after him right then, I would have," Dowd recalled.[27] The round of arrests that began at midnight were not triggered by any confrontations but, rather, by the impatience of the MPs and marshals. Sid Peck appeared with a bullhorn and reminded the authorities that the Mobe still had a permit to protest until Sunday night. The troops returned to their lines, leaving Peck and Norma Becker with the unenviable job of assisting the wounded. Sometime later, in the wee hours of the morning, a few protesters spontaneously began singing the Christmas carol "Silent Night." The chorus began softly but steadily grew louder as more people joined in. Peck felt himself getting choked up at the sound of the singing. It was a poignant end to a long and brutal day. "I can't tell you how proud I was of those people who were there and got arrested or stayed throughout the night," he reflected.[28]

Although David Dellinger won fame in antiwar circles for his dramatic arrest that day, the real hero of the weekend was Sid Peck. He proved to be one of the few Mobe stalwarts who exhibited leadership during the siege, and he never forgave Dellinger for essentially abdicating his role as an authority figure. When Dellinger was needed, he "was nowhere to be found," Peck recalled. As far as Peck was concerned, this represented Dellinger's "typical pattern. . . . He was not involved in organizational matters, the day-to-day stuff."[29] As chairman of the Mobe, Dellinger should have exercised his influence to help protect the thousands of protesters on the Pentagon grounds and keep the violence to a minimum. Instead, early in the protest, he knowingly penetrated a prohibited area in order to get arrested, a brave but also self-aggrandizing act that highlighted his shortcomings as a leader. "He never really regarded himself as a leader," reasoned his friend Noam Chomsky.[30]

Nevertheless, after the death of A. J. Muste in February, Dellinger accepted the prominent position of Mobe chairman, a leadership role that he performed admirably in the months leading up to the Pentagon march but not so effectively during the siege itself. His temperament and style were well suited to the small anti–Korean War and ban-the-bomb picket lines of the early 1950s but faltered at the Pentagon. Although the anarchist in Dellinger believed that the predominantly young protesters were perfectly capable of leading themselves, he ignored certain realities. Newcomers to the antiwar movement lacked the experience and insights of movement veterans and longed for guidance. As one dispirited young marcher complained to *Newsweek*, "The Mobilization for Peace leadership wasn't around to keep order. It was disorganized, disorderly and ineffective."[31] Civil disobedience and clashes between the troops and protesters continued well until the Mobe's permit expired at midnight on Sunday. By the end of the siege at the Pentagon, 683 people had been arrested, fifty-one had received jail sentences, more than $8,000 in fines had been issued, and countless numbers of demonstrators had suffered injuries.[32]

David Dellinger judged the weekend to be a rousing triumph for the antiwar movement. Mass civil disobedience had been put to the test on the steps of the Pentagon and it had worked, he insisted. Now the time had come for the movement to apply those tactics to the upcoming political conventions in 1968 to take advantage of the extensive media coverage.

Government officials and the media offered a less flattering portrait of the Pentagon march, however, emphasizing the skirmishes instead of the many peaceful moments. The tone was set weeks before the march, when Attorney General Ramsey Clark warned that the demonstrator's sponsors consisted of "extreme left-wing groups with long lines of Communist affiliations."[33] On October 26, White House political adviser Fred Panzer echoed the sentiments of many in the Johnson administration when he observed, "The speeches at the Memorial, I am sure, set the stage for the violence at the Pentagon."[34] Members of Congress were equally critical. Senator Barry Goldwater characterized the march as "a hate-filled, anti-American, pro-Communist and violent mob uprising."[35] Congressman Gerald Ford of Michigan and two other Republican congressmen speculated in *U.S. News & World Report* that the march had been "cranked up in Hanoi."[36] Even the more restrained media assessments took the protesters to task for being overly confrontational. NBC commentator David Brinkley found the march to be "a coarse, vulgar episode by people who seemed more interested in exhibitionist displays than any redress of grievances."[37] *Newsweek* played up Dellinger's visits to Hanoi, described the march as an example of "the derangement of the American scene in the '60s," and warned that the event "ended with blood on the steps of the Pentagon."[38] A *Washington Post* reporter underscored the futility of the protest. "They came and they confronted and by the end of the day everyone was fulfilled and nothing changed. The war goes on."[39]

The Pentagon march probably failed to convert any hawks to doves. Most Americans condemned the protesters while ignoring the violence of the MPs and marshals. Nor did the march substantially disrupt the Pentagon's operations, as Dellinger and other antiwar leaders hoped it would. As Defense Secretary Robert McNamara later reflected,

> I could not help but think that had the protesters been more disciplined—Gandhi-like—they could have achieved their objective of shutting us down. All they had to do was lie on the pavement around the building. We would have found it impossible to remove enough of them fast enough to keep the Pentagon open.[40]

Still, the march jolted the public's collective consciousness. No other previous antiwar protest had been so dramatic or offered so much startling network television footage. The weekend siege gave Americans the distinct impression that the country's centers of power were under siege and that "business as usual" had been interrupted on a large scale. The nation's confidence was shaken, and doubts about President Johnson's claims of a quick victory in Vietnam deepened. By showcasing the "cutting edge of resistance" in such an emotional and heavily publicized fashion, the antiwar protesters, perhaps without knowing it, had suddenly expanded the scope of debate over the war and emboldened moderate doves across the country to express their dissent more openly.

The march also rattled officials at the highest levels of government. Historian Melvin Small found that the Pentagon march "contributed directly to the fatigue, anxiety and frustration that many of the Johnson officials felt as they realized in the late fall of 1967 that their Vietnam policies were failing."[41] The October event set in motion a chain reaction of unanticipated events: it emboldened Senators Eugene McCarthy and Bobby Kennedy to run in the Democratic primaries as peace candidates in 1968; it was the first of many demoralizing blows that led President Johnson to announce his decision not to run for reelection in late March of that year; and it sparked the planning for the protests at the 1968 Democratic National Convention in Chicago.

Dellinger spent little time nursing the wounds he suffered at the Pentagon before resuming his breakneck pace. He now commanded a speaking fee, by no means large, but enough to help support his family. Dellinger had finally hired a personal assistant, Barbara Webster, to help coordinate his full schedule. Between his speaking engagements and his regular income from the Mobe and *Liberation*, the Dellinger family no longer hovered quite so close to edge of poverty. David also scaled back his hours at the Libertarian Press in Glen Gardner, now spending most of his time on antiwar organizing. "After the October event," he remembered, "there were a lot of people who kept saying, 'Well, where do we go next?' . . . So at that point we talked about the convention."[42]

In the meantime, federal authorities stepped up their surveillance of Dellinger. Since 1956, the FBI, with the cooperation of other federal, state, and local agencies, monitored, infiltrated, and, in some cases, harassed leftist organizations as part of its Counterintelligence Program (COINTELPRO). However, throughout the 1950s and much of the 1960s, the FBI largely ignored the radical pacifists, dismissing them as marginal. But that changed in 1967, when FBI director J. Edgar Hoover put Dellinger on the FBI's watch list. A classified memorandum sent on October 23, 1967, from the bureau's headquarters to agents in the field stated, "New York office should endeavor to obtain further particulars concerning the activities of Dellinger, especially remarks made by subject in Washington on 10/21/67."[43] Even before the October 21 siege, an extensive network of federal agents were conducting clandestine surveillance operations. Not surprisingly, Dellinger's file grew fat over the years after the federal authorities classified Dellinger as part of their COINTELPRO "New Left" surveillance operations. Although the FBI felt particularly threatened by younger radical activists of the New Left, they also broadened their investigation to include seasoned movement leaders such as Sid Peck, Dave Dellinger, Norma Becker, and Doug Dowd. A memo sent to Hoover from undercover agents in the Newark office in May 1968 warned about the activities of New Left militants. "These individuals are apparently getting stronger and more brazen in their attempts to destroy American society. . . . It is believed therefore that they must be destroyed or neutralized from the inside."[44]

The FBI was not the only agency taking an active interest in Dellinger. A few days after the Pentagon march, the CIA began preparing an ambitious and extensive study entitled "International Connections of the U.S. Peace Movement." Of most interest to the agency was the extent of foreign communist involvement in the antiwar movement. The CIA report described Dellinger as a "tireless, peripatetic, fulltime crusader," which the pacifist likely would have regarded as the highest compliment.[45] In mid-November, the CIA completed the document and forwarded it to the White House for President Johnson to review. Much to Johnson's disappointment, the report found that except for trips to Hanoi by peace activists like Dellinger, there was no sign of any involvement in the American antiwar movement by foreign governments or communist organizations. "On the basis of what we now know," the report concluded, "we see no significant evidence that would prove Communist control or direction of the U.S. peace movement or its leaders."[46]

After the Pentagon march, even the most energetic FBI agent would have had a difficult time keeping up with Dellinger, although he did take a much-needed break from the movement in late December 1967. Dellinger had grown weary of round-the-clock organizing and wanted to spend time with the people dearest to him. The entire Dellinger clan gathered at Glen Gardner on New Year's Eve for a belated Christmas celebration. The family had added two more members: Patch's wife, Lissa, and Natasha's newborn daughter, Michele. It was a joyful time. During the day, the entire family drove into Manhattan to marvel at the

Christmas lights, shop, and visit friends. Upon returning to Glen Gardner, Dellinger retrieved a bundle of letters and packages from his mailbox at the end of the mile-long dirt road that led to his house. Inside the house, David noticed a package wrapped in brown paper with the initials "V.C." scrawled prominently above the return address of the Fifth Avenue Peace Parade Committee. He knew the initials "V.C." stood for Viet Cong and immediately felt uneasy about the package, although he did not want to alarm his family. He opened the package to find a bottle of Johnny Walker Red Scotch. Slowly easing the bottle out of the package, he saw wires and explosive powder inside a small container underneath the bottle. Dellinger motioned to Patch to go outside with him. "It's a bomb," Dave quietly told his startled son, and the two carefully deposited the package in a snowdrift in the woods, where it remained until Dellinger telephoned the bomb squad the following day.[47]

The New Year's Eve bomb scare was not Dellinger's first brush with death threats at Glen Gardner. Two years earlier, on October 6, 1965, vandals broke into the Libertarian Press print shop and ransacked the facility, smashing the equipment, demolishing the linotype machine, and crippling the main printing press. In large red letters his visitors wrote "NEXT IT WILL BE YOU" on a large table.[48] After that, the editors of *Liberation* began contracting with a different printer to produce the magazine. The demands of antiwar work, however, forced Dellinger to cease his involvement in the Libertarian Press, and he began considering moving to New York City. His anxiety intensified when a postal inspector informed him that two other mail bombs addressed to Glen Gardner had injured two postal workers at the central mail-processing center. The mail inspector vowed to find the culprit or culprits who sent the incendiary parcels, but in the highly polarized atmosphere of the period, Dellinger feared the worst. "It increased my suspicions that the government was behind sending the bombs and made me think that it was making sure that the investigations didn't go too far," he wrote.[49]

By 1968 there were many reasons to leave Glen Gardner and few to stay. Long gone were the idealistic notions of creating a nonviolent community in the New Jersey woods. David already was spending a great deal of time in New York City organizing for the Mobe and editing *Liberation*. Betty could not find a teaching job and concluded that she had been "blackballed" in New Jersey as a result of David's high-profile political commitments. The two youngest Dellinger children, Michele and

Danny, announced to their parents, "We are not going back to school again in this area."[50] They were tired of being singled out as "communists" and ostracized by other students in their class. As Betty recalled, "We said we could no longer live in that area because of the prejudice against us because of his activities. We thought in New York City it would be more anonymous."[51] With David's blessing, the three remaining Dellingers still living at Glen Gardner moved to an apartment on Eastern Parkway in Brooklyn in the spring of 1968 to begin a new and dramatically different chapter in their lives. Glen Gardner had become an albatross. Dellinger owed $2,490 in local property taxes, and although he probably could have come up with the money to pay off his debts, he found little incentive to do so. On September 12, 1968, Dellinger put up his thirteen acres of land for sale to pay off his back taxes, an anticlimactic ending for his twenty-year-long Gandhian experiment in the woods of New Jersey.[52]

Now based in New York, Dellinger turned to planning the upcoming demonstrations in Chicago with the help of two high-profile SDS veterans, Tom Hayden and Rennie Davis, who had begun working for the Mobe in late 1967 as field organizers. Representing the militant wing of the antiwar movement, Davis and Hayden hoped that a massive confrontation at the Democratic National Convention would highlight the deepening fissures in American society over the Vietnam War and embolden Democratic doves. They dismissed the Republican Convention planned for Miami as a lost cause, concluding that the party was too dominated by hawks. According to Dellinger, the original idea for the Chicago protest was to conduct "a loose counterconvention, decentralized and diversified in contrast to the rigid, overcentralized and authoritarian convention of the Democrats."[53] The Mobe's Administrative Committee met on December 27, 1967, in New York City to discuss plans for Chicago. Dellinger advocated mass direct action and civil disobedience. As Sid Lens explained, 'We expected Johnson to run for another four-year term, and in that case we were confident of a massive turnout since it had become axiomatic that the president could go almost nowhere without encountering blistering hostility."[54]

Not all Mobe organizers were convinced that confrontational protests were appropriate during a national political convention. Fred Halstead, who by this time had emerged as one of the Mobe's leading moderates, urged peaceful mass demonstrations in the spring, followed up nationwide actions on Hiroshima Day—August 6—as an alternative to the convention protests. He called on his comrades in the Mobe to hold a conference as soon as possible to discuss future actions. Dellinger scoffed at Halstead's proposal: "Every time there's a conference there's also a power scramble which with time could cause a fiasco."[55] The Mobe steering committee remained divided about Chicago, but through their stubbornness, the radicals prevailed and pressed on with their plans in the early months of 1968.

Smaller Mobe planning meetings were held throughout January and February, establishing the groundwork for the Chicago protests. In the early weeks of 1968, Davis and Hayden drafted a report entitled "Discussion on the Democratic Convention Challenge," which they distributed to Mobe steering committee members and staffers. Hayden and Davis, both newcomers to the Mobe, were a study in contrasts. Hayden was a movement celebrity long before Chicago, thanks largely to his influential 1962 Port Huron Statement, a powerful critique of the cold war, racism, and corporate capitalism that gave voice to the incipient New Left in America. He spent the 1960s working in a succession of political struggles. In contrast, Rennie Davis came from the farmlands of the Blue Ridge Mountains in rural Virginia. His father, John C. Davis, was a professor of economics who had served as a member of President Harry Truman's Council of Economic Advisers before retiring to a quiet farm in the countryside. Davis attended Oberlin College in Ohio, developed a strong interest in leftist politics, and founded the Progressive Student League. "From 1960 onward," Davis said, "I considered myself a full-time activist in what was then called the 'student movement,' and later just the 'movement.'"[56] By the time he went to work for the Mobe at the end of 1967, Davis had a long history of movement organizing, including serving as the director of SDS's Economic Research and Action Project (ERAP), a planner for the Center for Radical Research, and a key leader of Jobs for Income Now (JOIN), a militant poor people's lobbying organization. Dellinger and Davis formed an instant bond. There was something about the quiet SDS organizer from the Blue Ridge Mountains that strongly appealed to Dellinger. Later, during the famous conspiracy trial of the Chicago Eight, Dellinger admitted that of all the defendants, "I was closest to Rennie Davis."[57] By contrast, Tom Hayden turned out to be a constant source of frustration for Dellinger, mainly due to Hayden's unwavering militancy and penchant for reckless tactics. "I have what you might call a love-hate relationship with Tom Hayden," he later remarked.[58]

In February, with Dellinger's backing, Davis opened a Mobe office in Chicago to plan the protests. On March 22, activists gathered for a Mobe convention, to allow the many different groups in the coalition to issue position papers concerning the protests at the Democratic National Convention. The longest paper came from Davis and Hayden, who used the conference to announce their plans for Chicago: "The summer would be capped by three days of sustained, organized protests at the Democratic National Convention, clogging the streets of Chicago with people demanding peace, justice and self-determination for all people."[59]

Dellinger backed the Davis/Hayden plans. Delegates from the newly formed Youth International Party, the Yippies for short, also were enthusiastic about protesting at the convention. Abbie Hoffman, Jerry Rubin, Paul Krassner, Stew Albert, and other Yippies announced plans to hold a "Festival of Life" at the convention, which they envisioned as a mixture of free love, dope, rock music, and street demonstrations. Dellinger quietly encouraged the Yippies and grew closer to Hoffman at the conference, but Hoffman and his comrades were bitterly disappointed that other Mobe activists did not seem to take them seriously. "We were treated like Niggers, you know," Hoffman wrote four months later, "like we were irrelevant."[60] Other conference participants were lukewarm about the Davis/Hayden proposal. Doug Dowd, one of Dellinger's closest allies in the coalition, had grave doubts. As he recalled, "Hayden was making plans for . . . eight months ahead as though there was a kind of straight line going from January to August."[61] Similarly, the Mobe's so-called Black Caucus, consisting of twenty-five African American activists, issued a position paper indicating their indifference, arguing that the proposals on the table had failed to advance their cause. By the end of the conference, Dellinger was disappointed by what he perceived to be the Mobe stalwarts' "lack of interest" in the Chicago protests.[62] Nonetheless, the uneasy Mobe delegates voted to move ahead with plans for the Chicago demonstrations. To appease the moderates, the activists approved a proposal to conduct peaceful, nonconfrontational marches across the country on April 27, and they also decided not to formally endorse any particular presidential candidate.

The turbulent events of 1968 further transformed the upcoming protests in Chicago. The enormous communist-led Tet offensive throughout South Vietnam in January and February shook U.S. policymakers and shocked the nation. Despite President Johnson's prowar public relations blitz in the fall of 1967, the film footage coming out of Vietnam during Tet showed a fierce and determined enemy seizing cities, provincial capitals, and towns across the country. Although U.S. forces quickly rebuffed most of the communist advances, it took weeks for the marines to dislodge North Vietnamese army and Vietcong troops from the ancient walled citadel at Hué. Despite a decisive American victory, public morale plunged along with Johnson's standing in the polls. The president obviously could not fulfill the promises of a rapid victory that he made in late 1967, and the nation's confidence was now badly shaken. By the early months of 1968, Johnson could not travel anywhere in America without confronting crowds of protesters attacking his Vietnam policies. On March 12, Senator Eugene McCarthy, an antiwar Democrat running in the presidential race against Johnson, lost to him by only a few thousand votes in the New Hampshire primary. Soon afterward, Senator Robert Kennedy's decided to enter the race as well. Johnson ignored General William Westmoreland's requests for additional troops, and on March 31 he announced to a stunned nation that he would not run for reelection.[63]

Antiwar activists across the country, including Dellinger, rejoiced when they heard Johnson's announcement. However, in his customary cautionary tone, Dellinger warned activists to remain vigilant and avoid "the trap of" electoral politics. "The powerful forces that got us involved in Vietnam are still in basic control of our country," he wrote. "They have suffered a setback but until they are repudiated there is a danger of further military adventures at home and abroad."[64] Despite Johnson's decision not to run again, Dellinger, Davis, and Hayden continued to press ahead with their plans.

In early April, Dellinger and Hayden flew to Washington, D.C., to meet with Averell Harriman, then an ambassador-at-large attending the Paris peace talks with North Vietnam, and Sargent Shriver, a former Peace Corps director and now the U.S. ambassador to France. As key figures in the Paris negotiations, Harriman and Shriver wanted to talk to Dellinger and Hayden about conditions in North Vietnam and the prospects for peace in the region. Because Shriver had been one of Dellinger's classmates at Yale, they treated each other warmly despite their political differences. The meeting was held on April 5, the day after the assassination of Martin Luther King Jr. Radio and television reports played and replayed King's "I have a dream speech" as riots erupted in more than a hundred cities across the nation. The worst one was in Washington, D.C. On the way to Harriman's office, Dellinger and Hayden watched rioters running through the streets and damaging property. Hayden later wrote, "Outside the windows of Harriman's office, one could see flames and smoke shooting up over the nation's capital and fire trucks and squad cars rushing everywhere."[65] In the following weeks, Dellinger wrestled with depression and pessimism. Around the world, including in the United States, the violence appeared to be rising, and the tired pacifist—now nearing age fifty-three—began questioning his ability to influence events.[66]

The murder of Martin Luther King Jr., followed two months later by the assassination of Robert Kennedy while campaigning in Los Angeles, left Dellinger bereft. As an anarchist, Dellinger had always eschewed electoral politics and rejected the prospect of working within the progressive wing of the Democratic Party. Still, his sorrow following Kennedy's assassination was heartfelt. "One does not have to agree with a man politically to be shocked by his premature and brutal death," he wrote. He grouped Kennedy with King and the recently murdered California Black Panther Bobby Hutton as victims of a "violent" and "dehumanized society."[67]

Everywhere Dellinger looked in 1968, he saw American society unraveling. Mass sit-ins at Columbia University on April 23 rapidly escalated into an eight-day takeover of the institution by radical students. With mounting anxiety, Dellinger watched a small, violence-prone minority within the antiwar movement growing bolder, carrying Viet Cong flags at demonstrations and chanting "Ho, Ho, Ho Chi Minh!" The Pentagon march had raised the stakes. Now antiwar activists believed that whatever they did, it had to be bold and dramatic or nobody would listen. The spring brought more protests. On April 3, the Resistance, an antidraft organization, returned thousands of draft cards to the U.S. government. In late April, the Student Mobilization Committee organized the largest student strike in U.S. history, involving hundreds of thousands of students from high schools and universities across the country. On May 17, Fathers Philip and Daniel Berrigan and a small group of Catholic antiwar activists entered the Catonsville draft board office in Maryland, and using a combination of blood and napalm, they destroyed three hundred draft files before they were stopped and arrested.[68]

With nationwide protests reaching a crescendo, few people noticed the peaceful Mobe protests taking place across the country on the weekend of April 26 to 28. On Saturday, April 27, more than 120,000 people marched through New York City, and around 20,000 rallied in San Francisco. Seven thousand protesters in Chicago, demonstrating without a permit, clashed with police in riot gear. At the New York City rally in Central Park, Dellinger introduced Coretta Scott King, who approached the microphone wearing a black dress. "Mr. Dellinger, my dear friends of peace and freedom," she began, "I come to New York today with a strong feeling that my dearly beloved husband, who was snatched suddenly from our midst slightly more than three weeks ago now, would have wanted me to be present today."[69] Other prominent speakers followed; musicians sang antiwar ballads; and, in a sign of election-year loyalties, 30 percent of the people in Central Park that afternoon wore Eugene McCarthy campaign buttons. Yet despite the best efforts of antiwar organizers, protests like this one lacked the potency of previous similar actions. Even the leftist *National Guardian* noted that the April 27 march had a "rather sluggish pace"; *Time* magazine insisted that the protest simply "fizzled"; and the *Washington Post* dismissed the throng at Central Park as "strangely lifeless."[70]

After April 27, Dellinger turned his attention almost exclusively to the Chicago protests and the numerous obstacles yet remaining. City officials refused to issue permits. Coalition people bickered about the most effective means of demonstrating. Communication between the Mobe offices in New York and Chicago was patchy at best. Publicly, Dellinger tried to show that the Mobe was united. But privately, he feared that Hayden, who exercised a strong influence over the younger militants, planned to turn the Chicago protests into a violent clash with the police. Dellinger had reason to be concerned. After the assassination of Bobby Kennedy, Hayden was looking for a showdown with the authorities. He had become irrational, even mildly insane, some people thought. Although Hayden and Davis assured Dellinger that the Chicago protests "would be nonviolent," their promises gave him little peace of mind, and many moderate activists expressed their concerns to him. He wrote: "In my recruiting trips around the country, the two questions I was always asked were: (1) Is there any chance that the police won't create a bloodbath? (2) Are you sure that Tom and Rennie don't want one?"[71]

Dellinger worried that Hayden, who had an undeniably charismatic personality, would undercut the nonviolent character of the Chicago demonstrations. Rumors swirled in the weeks leading up to the convention that street fights between protesters and police were imminent. The conventional wisdom in New Left circles was that violence in Chicago was inevitable. "It should be clear to anyone who has been following developments in Chicago," editorialized the *New Left Notes*, "that a nonviolent demonstration would be impossible."[72] Fueling the flames were the Yippies, who, in the words of Jerry Rubin, planned to "camp out, smoke pot, dance to wild music, burn draft cards and roar like wild bands through the streets."[73] Such statements made Dellinger's job even more difficult. Despite his struggle to keep the coalition together and prevent violence, several groups in the Mobe were advising their members to avoid Chicago completely. Indeed, nervous Democratic Party liberals in the Mobe feared that any turmoil in Chicago would undermine Eugene McCarthy's bid for the presidency. At a secret meeting, apparently held without consulting Dellinger, Hayden assured Sam Brown, a McCarthy campaign organizer and antiwar activist, that if Senator McCarthy appeared poised to receive the Democratic Party nomination, the Mobe's leaders would reconsider conducting protests. Dellinger, as well, tried to alleviate the McCarthy backers' fears. In a preconvention editorial in the *Chicago Tribune*, he told the McCarthy camp that the "teach-ins, street demonstrations and active resistance" would strengthen "McCarthy's bargaining power" and result in his being "taken seriously" at the convention.[74]

Under the direction of the city's mayor, Richard Daley, the forces of law and order were mobilized for a gigantic conflict. Daley was determined to make sure the Democratic National Convention ran smoothly for President Johnson's handpicked successor, Vice President Hubert Humphrey, whose unwavering support of the war had aroused the anger of the antiwar activists. Daley was not afraid to use force to crack down on the demonstrations, and he enjoyed widespread support from Chicagoans, most of whom felt that their city was under siege by hippies and radicals. Indeed, the Yippies' outrageous antics only strengthened Daley's determination.

More than any other participants in the antiwar movement, the Yippies had become the darlings of the press, and their outrageous statements only boosted the coverage of their antics. Thus, when Mobe organizers predicted that 100,000 protesters would go to Chicago and the Yippies anticipated half a million, Daley accepted such wildly overblown estimates at face value. The mayor placed the city's 11,900 police on twelve-hour shifts, requested a thousand FBI and Secret Service agents from Washington, and invited 7,500 army troops, complete with riot gear, to be airlifted from Texas, Oklahoma, and Colorado. The governor assigned six thousand National Guardsmen to safeguard the city in the event of a riot. Responding to Yippie threats to put LSD in the Chicago water supply, Mayor Daley called for twenty-four-hour police patrols along the perimeters of Chicago's water filtration plants. He ordered the fronts of all jeeps to be equipped with long steel planks wrapped in barbed wire to clear protesters out of the streets. Daley even directed his own undercover organization, the Chicago Department of Investigation, to send agents to New York City to disrupt the antiwar effort. After the convention, one of the agents, John Clarke, revealed that Daley's small army of saboteurs undermined the Mobe's plans to raise funds and charter buses: "As a result of our activities in New York, instead of 200 busloads of demonstrators coming to Chicago, they ended up with eight carloads, totaling 60 people."[75]

For Dellinger, the greatest challenge in the final weeks leading up to Chicago was securing permits from city officials. From August 5 through 23, Mobe organizers spent every day in meetings with police, Justice Department officials, representatives from the mayor's office, and attorneys for the city. By August 18, it was becoming clear to Dellinger that the city would grant only one permit for a peaceful rally at Grant Park, to be held on the afternoon of Wednesday, August 28. Then, on Wednesday, August 21, Raymond Simon, a staffer in Daley's office, met with Dellinger, Davis, and Hayden and extended an offer. Peaceful parades would be allowed between 1 P.M. and 4 P.M. and only along the streets near Lake Michigan, several miles away from the International Amphitheater where the Democratic Party would be meeting. Although Hayden dismissed the offer as "ridiculous," Dellinger tried to be diplomatic. Calling the proposal "completely unsatisfactory," he nonetheless conceded, "We are encouraged that at last the city has at least made an offer that recognized the right of the people to demonstrate."[76]

In the summer of 1968, Betty asked her second oldest son, Ray, to go with his father to the demonstrations. Ray was twenty-two, had just completed his undergraduate education at Yale, and "was the most [politically] active" of the Dellinger children.[77] In mid-August, Ray drove to Chicago to meet his father and attend the demonstration. It was an experience that neither man would forget.

Based solely on body count, Chicago was a disaster. By all estimates, the number of people who traveled to the city to participate in the convention protests did not exceed ten thousand.[78] Moreover, ten years after the event, army sources informed CBS News that one in six demonstrators in Chicago that week was a government agent.[79] These numbers fell far short of the hundred thousand predicted by the Mobe. Film footage of Mayor Daley's police forces sent chills through the movement. Some revolutionaries even managed to scare people away with their visions of an apocalyptic bloodbath. In early August, the underground Chicago newspaper *The Seed* warned, "Many people are into confrontation. . . . The Man is into confrontation. . . . Chicago may host a Festival of Blood. Don't come if you expect a five-day Festival of Life, music and love."[80] Such violent rhetoric intimidated even the bravest souls.

Nonetheless, Dellinger still hoped to keep the protest peaceful. Before the convention, he talked to his friend Stewart Meacham, a widely respected former pastor and head of the American Friends Service Committee.

> If you want to know how you can help me and the others that are closest to the planning of this, you will get as many people there as you can who have had experience with nonviolent demonstrations where there has been the threat of violence, where there have been some people engaged in violence or where the police are hostile or where you are coping with agents provocateurs.[81]

But despite Dellinger's efforts, few pacifists wanted to risk going to Chicago and facing Daley's police force. Initially, the low turnout of protesters disappointed the Mobe activists. But all the elements were in place for a showdown that would become a momentous historical event.

Mobe activities commenced on Thursday, August 22, the week before the convention, with a heavily publicized "school for protesters" in Lincoln Park, which Dellinger attended. To become protest marshals, hundreds of male and female volunteers received training in self-defense and crowd management. Long rows of activists were taught to form so-called skirmish lines to confront the police nonviolently and to guide the demonstrators.

From the perspective of impatient militants, three years of nonviolent protests had failed to stop the Vietnam War. In the parks, coffee shops, apartments, and street corners where radicals met during the week of the convention, their talk turned to confrontation. Typical of the younger activists who had grown impatient with nonviolent tactics was Mobe organizer Linda Morse. A close associate of Dellinger's, Morse had maintained a Gandhian outlook since joining the antiwar movement in 1965. But during that tumultuous week in Chicago, "I changed," she explained, "from being a pacifist to the realization that we had to defend ourselves. A nonviolent revolution was impossible. I desperately wish it was possible."[82]

As he had done in the past, Dellinger led by example, adhering to Gandhian techniques while avoiding moralistic lectures. Since the early 1960s, the younger New Left radicals had looked up to him as a role model because of his ideological flexibility and nonjudgmental acceptance of different lifestyles. On such matters as the Cuban revolution and the Vietnam War, he rejected the pacifists' rigid, doctrinaire position by proclaiming his solidarity with armed liberation struggles. This anarchical eclecticism made him a hero among younger militants of the era, and he exercised that influence whenever and wherever possible to prevent violent confrontations in Chicago.

Unlike the Pentagon march, much of which Dellinger missed because of his early arrest, he was extremely cautious in Chicago, carefully avoiding arrest. But there was little he could do to forestall the inevitable onslaught of police violence. On the opening day of the convention, Monday, August 25, the police arrested Tom Hayden twice, the first time in Lincoln Park and the second time while trying to enter the Conrad Hilton Hotel. In response to the arrests, Rennie Davis led fifteen hundred chanting antiwar activists to the Chicago police headquarters, where Hayden's bail was posted and he was released that day. Hayden later disguised himself and went underground in an effort to outmaneuver the Chicago police, who were actively pursuing him. For the remainder of the day, Dellinger faced the difficult task of trying to shift the spotlight back to the antiwar protests. He attended an afternoon rally in Grant Park, a long, narrow, grassy park situated between Michigan Avenue to the west and Lake Michigan to the east. The central landmark in Grant Park was the statue of the Civil War major general Jonathan Logan mounted on a horse. Around 5 P.M., hundreds of protesters surrounded the statue and several began climbing on it carrying Vietcong and red flags. A horrified Dellinger watched as police stormed into the gathering of protesters and began swinging their clubs.

In the evening, people in the park turned on their radios and listened to Mayor Daley deliver the speech that officially opened the 1968 Democratic National Convention. At Lincoln Park, although fights occasionally broke out between protesters and counterprotesters, the Mobe marshals intervened to stop them. With the curfew approaching, a group of activists constructed a thirty-five-foot-long barricade to prevent police from entering to the east. At 11 P.M., more than a thousand people were still in the park. The police moved in and street battles raged until early in the morning. In some neighborhoods, journalists and innocent bystanders who had nothing to do with the protests were beaten by the police. Even some local residents were forcibly removed from their porches by furious cops. "Many people were very seriously hurt, not only by the clubs, but by mace," he explained.[83]

The battles continued to rage on Tuesday, and few observers took note of the nonviolent march in the early afternoon. At a gathering sponsored by the American Friends Service Committee and other pacifist groups, around one thousand people marched from a northside church to the amphitheater without incident. The police halted them at Thirty-ninth and Halsted, half a mile north of the convention site, the closest any march had come to the proceedings. The marchers then switched to a peaceful picket line that lasted until 10 A.M. the next day, when police ordered the crowd to disperse. About thirty picketers were arrested with a minimum of force. Even though the protest received little publicity, it convinced Dellinger that nonviolence could work in Chicago.

Following the pacifist march, the arrival of the Black Panthers at the convention site in the afternoon offered a dramatically different kind of protest. Around 7 P.M., an audience of three thousand listened to Bobby Seale, the leader of the Black Panther Party, speak at Lincoln Park. He came at the invitation of the Mobe and counseled all present to use violence as a means of self-defense against the police. Dressed in black, wearing a black beret, and surrounded by similarly attired supporters, Seale addressed the cheering crowd: "If a pig comes up to us and starts swingin' a billy club and you check around and you got your piece—you gotta down that pig in defense of yourself! We're gonna barbecue us some pork!"[84]

Feeling uneasy about Seale's speech and the increasingly hostile climate in Chicago, Dellinger and his son Ray decided to attend the upbeat "Unbirthday Party" for President Johnson, organized by the Yippies. African American activist/comedian Dick Gregory spoke, as did Beat author William Burroughs, who likened the police to "vicious guard dogs."[85] Phil Ochs performed "I Ain't Marching Anymore," a perennial crowd favorite. For the Unbirthday Party, the Yippies wanted to do something light and fun to take people's minds off the dreariness of previous convention protests. David and Ray savored the rare moment of not having to look over their shoulders for police.[86]

For Dellinger and the antiwar movement, the most important day of the convention week was Wednesday, August 29, nomination day at the convention. Thanks to Dellinger's efforts, the Mobe had been able to secure a protest permit for a mass rally at Grant Park on Wednesday afternoon, although city officials refused to issue a marching permit. Because the protest permit was the only one they had been able to obtain, the Mobe leaders wanted to make the rally the focal point of that day. Early in the day, helmeted, club-wielding police appeared at Grant Park, distributing leaflets informing the resisters that even though the rally was legal, they could not march through the city streets.

The first protesters began arriving at the park in the early afternoon as Mobe volunteers set up the stage and performed sound checks at the bandstand. The keynote speaker that afternoon was the writer and former SDS leader Carl Oglesby, an electrifying orator who had stunned audiences three years earlier at SANE's national protest in Washington, D.C., with his critique of the role of liberals in planning and executing the Vietnam War. The decision to ask Oglesby to speak was made at the last minute. Upon discovering that Oglesby—who had come as an observer, not a speaker—was in the crowd, Dellinger sent Mobe operatives to retrieve him. Dellinger, "looking frazzled, told me they needed speakers to fill some time before some other speakers showed up, so would I [Oglesby] please do a turn. Well, okay, fine."[87] Shortly after the rally began, three young men appeared at the base of the flagpole near the band shell and tried to lower the American flag. Horrified antiwar activists panicked, knowing such an action would unleash the wrath of the police.

A hundred police formed what Oglesby described as a "spearhead-shaped phalanx formation" and surged forward into the crowd, "their line of march bristling on both sides with riot sticks."[88] Rennie Davis ran to the flagpole to prevent further trouble. A line of Chicago police rushed toward the Mobe activist with clubs swinging, yelling "Kill

Davis! Kill Davis!" The police began beating Davis senseless, clubbing him in the head, arms, back, and legs with the heavy wooden weapons. His head had been split open and he would later receive numerous stitches, and his face and clothing were covered with blood. "I realized my shirt was just becoming blood, and someone—I don't know who—took my arm and took me to the east side of the band shell and I laid down. . . ." Gazing up at the blue sky, Davis could hear part of Oglesby's speech and then he lost consciousness.[89]

The Chicago police formed a long line and began closing in on the legal mass rally at Grant Park, clubbing everyone in sight. Worried Mobe organizers looked to Dellinger for guidance. With Ray by his side, Dellinger discussed a variety of options with Mobe organizers. After a brief conference, Dellinger approached the microphone and, as one witness recalled, presented "a sustained appeal to the crowd not provoke any violence and asking the police to withdraw."[90] Meantime, Mobe marshals warned the people on stage—among them, Allen Ginsberg, Norman Mailer, and Jean Genet—that the police were moving into the crowd with clubs swinging. As the police advanced and the odor of teargas wafted onto the stage, the Mobe leaders told the crowd that anyone wishing to do so could join an illegal nonviolent march to the amphitheater to protest. But their announcement was cut short when a scuffle broke out between Dellinger and Tom Hayden. It began when Hayden, his assistant Tom Neuman (stepson of leftist philosopher Herbert Marcuse), and a group of their followers encircled Dellinger menacingly and demanded control of the microphone. "Hayden tried to remove me, physically, from the platform," Dellinger recounted.[91] From Hayden's point of view, it had been irresponsible for Dellinger to ask the crowd to passively allow the police to beat them. A critic of pacifism, Hayden firmly advocated violence as a retaliatory measure to counter aggression. As he explained:

The police attacked a peaceful crowd, as I predicted they would, and tried to cordon us off at the bandshell in order to prevent us from getting to Grant Park across from the Hilton. I thought Dave's idea of a nonviolent march would be ineffective in ever getting us to the park across from the hotel, and might lead to mass arrests even before the convention got underway that evening. I told him and I told the crowd to try to get out of the bandshell area and make their way to the hotel district. In Dave's mind, such mobile street tactics were in violation of his concepts of nonviolence. He didn't have a feel for what was going on in the streets, or the mood of the young people.[92]

Exhausted and fearing that his death was imminent, Hayden behaved like a hunted animal, lashing out at enemies real and imagined. At this moment, an equally stressed Dellinger wished some of his old pacifist comrades were there to help him, but he faced Hayden alone. "I said, 'Fuck you, Tom Hayden! That's not the way we operate. We're a coalition, and there's a . . . difference in our views. I'll give you the microphone and you can say what we ought to do, then I'll say what we ought to do.'"[93] Hayden eventually got hold of the microphone and roared into it:

> This city and the military machine it has aimed at us won't permit us to protest in an organized fashion. Therefore, we must move out of this park in groups throughout the city, and turn this overheated military machine against itself. Let us make sure that if the blood flows, it flows all over the city. If they use gas against us, let us make sure they use it against their own citizens. If the police run wild, let them run wild all over Chicago—not just over us sitting in the park. If they are going to disrupt us and our march, let them disrupt the whole city.[94]

But Hayden failed to articulate a concrete plan of action to the audience other than offering a few words about fighting their way out of the park. The police continued to club their way toward the band shell, kicking over benches, shouting obscenities, and taunting protesters. People ran in all directions. Thousands of protesters deserted the tear-gas-filled park, many fearing for their lives.

A short distance away, the atmosphere inside the convention hall had also become tense, reflecting deep divisions in the Democratic Party. In the afternoon, delegates adopted a pro-Johnson administration plank that praised the president's efforts to achieve peace in Vietnam and encouraged continued negotiations between Washington and Hanoi. By a small margin, the pro-Johnson plank won, prompting the doves in the convention hall to erupt into a chorus of "We Shall Overcome." The mood grew ugly, and at one point the police assaulted CBS news correspondent Dan Rather. In the late afternoon, back at Grant Park, Dellinger mobilized the remaining three thousand people to march to the convention hall. The crowd gradually funneled out of the park behind Dellinger, Peck, Mailer, Genet, and Ginsberg. Ginsberg recalled hearing Dellinger speaking into a bullhorn at the moving throng: "This is a peaceful march. All those who want to participate in a peaceful march please join our line. All those who are not peaceful please go away and don't join our line."[95]

In order to reach downtown, the crowd had to cross one of many bridges spanning a deep and wide railroad channel that lay between the park and the rest of Chicago, but the police had blocked all the bridges in the immediate vicinity. A few Mobe leaders, including Dellinger and Sid Peck, negotiated for more than an hour with police officials. Thousands of protesters sat down and began singing songs and chanting. When they had accomplished nothing, Dellinger addressed the crowd by bullhorn, advising them to disperse and proceed on their own to the Hilton Hotel, where the Mobe planned to conduct further demonstrations. Dellinger walked with the bullhorn, repeating the message at several points down the line, and waited until the last protester had left. David and Ray walked alone, eventually reaching the Balbo Bridge, where nervous young National Guard troops allowed them to pass. Arriving at Michigan Avenue, Dellinger found a telephone and "called Elizabeth at home to reassure her that Ray and I were okay."[96]

Most of the people from the aborted Mobe march crossed the railroad tracks at the Jackson Street Bridge, joined a legal march sponsored by Rev. Ralph Abernathy's Poor People's Campaign, and made their way to the Hilton. By 7:30 P.M., more than seven thousand protesters were packed into the streets by the hotel near the intersection of Michigan and Balbo. A wide line of blue-shirted, blue-helmeted police prevented the demonstrators from going any farther.

Spotlights illuminated the crowd as they chanted, "The whole world is watching! The whole world is watching! The whole world is watching!" Although their words may have been an exaggeration, news cameras in the streets of Chicago were beaming the confrontation to the television sets of 90 million American viewers, from Maine to California. Shortly before 8 P.M., the so-called Battle of Michigan Avenue commenced. It was twenty minutes of fury as police beat and gassed the protesters out of the intersection of Michigan and Balbo. One of the most savagely beaten protesters that night was Sid Peck, who endured several severe clubbings. Elsewhere, a group of terrified spectators were pushed through a large plate glass window at the Haymarket Inn, a restaurant in the Hilton. "The window gave way," the *New York Times* reported, "sending screaming middle-aged women and children through the broken shards of glass."[97] A *Life* magazine correspondent wrote about a "well-dressed woman" who witnessed a fifteen-year-old youth being beaten by the police and "spoke angrily to a nearby police captain." The police sprayed "something in her face with an aerosol can," clubbed the woman, and pushed her into a paddy wagon.[98] At Lincoln Park, where many of the protesters regrouped, journalist Nicholas Von Hoffman described the madness:

> Shrieks and screams all over the wooded encampment area. . . . Rivulets of running people came out of the woods across the lawn. . . . Next, the cops burst out of the woods in selective pursuit of news photographers. Pictures are unanswerable evidence in court. They'd taken off their badges, their name plates, even the unit patches on their shoulders to become a mob of identical, unidentifiable club swingers.[99]

The actual Battle of Michigan Avenue lasted until the police cleared the intersection, but explosive street fights continued all over Chicago well into the early morning.[100]

Although not yet officially over until it adjourned at ten minutes after midnight on Friday, the Democratic National Convention drew to a climactic and bloody close on Wednesday night. Inside the convention hall, there were more scuffles, more screaming matches, more feuds between doves and hawks. Despite receiving his party's nomination to be the Democratic presidential candidate, Hubert Humphrey's was a Pyrrhic victory that would doom him in November. The ranks of the antiwar movement quickly expanded as thousands of disillusioned "Clean for Gene" activists, infuriated that Senator McCarthy was out of the race, joined the Yippies and Mobe protesters in the streets the following day. The bloody protests in Chicago finally petered out on Friday.

In the aftermath of the riots, the media were not kind to Mayor Daley. "The blame has to be taken to the top," editorialized the *Washington Post*. "Brutes ought not to be put into police uniforms. Chicago has been disgraced by them—and even more by those responsible for their barbarity."[101] Added *New York Times* columnist Tom Wicker: "The truth was, those were our children in the streets, and the Chicago police beat them up."[102] After the riots, an independent commission headed by prominent Chicago attorney Daniel Walker, head of the Chicago Crime Commission, issued a report based on the testimony of 3,427 eye-witnesses and FBI and police records. The Walker Commission concluded:

> During the week of the Democratic National Convention, the Chicago police were targets of mounting provocation by both word and act.... The nature of the response was unrestrained and indiscriminate police violence on many occasions, particularly at night. That violence was made more shocking by the fact that it was often inflicted upon persons who had broken no law, disobeyed no order, made no threat.... To read dispassionately the hundreds of statements describing at first-hand the events . . . is to become convinced of the presence of what can only be called a police riot.[103]

Polls taken after the protest found that a majority of Americans sympathized with the Chicago police and their treatment of the protesters. According to a thorough study by two television analysts, most viewers who watched the police violence on television "adjusted the television images to fit their own preconceived beliefs."[104] Moreover, the convention protests bolstered the popularity of Richard Nixon and his promise to restore law and order across the land.

David Dellinger chose to accentuate the positive. Even if most Americans supported the police, "millions of people have been educated and horrified by this experience," he told a *Chicago Daily News* reporter at the end of the convention.[105] The passage of time did not diminish his enthusiasm, and after the convention Dellinger began to sound like the street-fighting revolutionaries he distrusted.

> The triumph of Chicago was the triumph of street protesters who displayed courage, imagination, flexibility and fraternal solidarity as they refused to knuckle under to the police.... There is a heady sense of manhood that comes from advancing from apathy to commitment, from timidity to courage, from passivity to aggressiveness.... There is an intoxication that comes from standing up to the police at last.[106]

In the short run, the Chicago Democratic National Convention may have aroused sympathy for the struggle of law enforcement officials against "hippie" agitators. But Dellinger understood that added to the other national traumas of 1968, the convention protests gave millions of people the impression that the Vietnam War had triggered a war at home. Even the most hawkish Americans eventually conceded that any hope for a stable America depended on finding a peaceful resolution to the conflict in Southeast Asia.

At the end of the convention, the Dellingers returned home. David was proud of Ray, who had prevented his father from being clubbed by police on at least two occasions. In many ways, Chicago represented the pinnacle of David Dellinger's leadership career in the 1960s. He had wielded enormous influence at the convention protests. But he also had learned a crucial lesson that week: in the increasingly polarized climate of 1968 a small but vocal cadre of young militants—fueled by a week of ferocious police beatings—had rejected his Gandhian philosophy and raised troubling questions about the efficacy of nonviolence. Undaunted, Dellinger maintained his pacifist convictions, even as a more radicals entertained the possibility of violent resistance. During the Chicago conspiracy trial in 1969/1970, Dellinger became famous as the elder, conservatively dressed father figure being tried. The trial took a heavy emotional and physical toll on him, and in the streets of America the movement he helped forge in 1965 began to wane as the war in Vietnam slowed to a brutal end.

Dellinger's immediate family in the late 1920s. Seated: Dellinger's younger sister Nancy (left) and mother Marie (right). Standing: His father Raymond (left) and younger brother Fiske (right). *Courtesy, Natasha Singer Collection.*

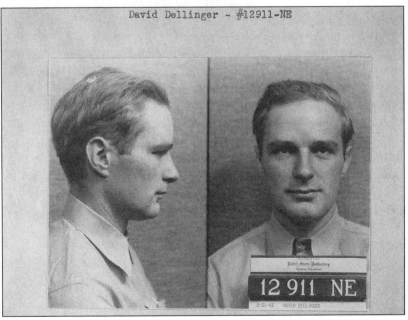

Dellinger's prison mugshot, taken at the time he entered Lewisburg Federal Penitentiary, August 31, 1943. *National Archives.*

Posing with his children and in-laws in a 1950 photograph. Dellinger is second from left. To his left is his foster son, Howie Douglas. The children (below) are Patch, Ray and Natasha Dellinger.
Courtesy, Natasha Singer Collection.

Camping on the Rhine in France during the Peacemakers-sponsored Paris-to-Moscow Bicycle Trip for Peace, 1951. Left to right: Art Emery, David Dellinger, Ralph DiGia and Bill Sutherland. *Courtesy, Elizabeth Peterson Collection.*

Snapshot taken for a Dellinger Family Christmas card in 1962. Clockwise from left: Danny, Ray, Patch, Natasha, Dave, Michele and Betty Dellinger. *Courtesy, Elizabeth Peterson Collection.*

At a press conference in New York City with A.J. Muste shortly after returning from Vietnam, November 22, 1966. *AP Worldwide Photos.*

Dellinger in one of his cherished quiet moments, holding his first granddaughter Michele, 1968. *Courtesy, Natasha Singer Collection.*

At a Mobe press conference during the Democratic National Convention, August 1968. *AP Worldwide Photos.*

Addressing an antiwar rally in Pennsylvania, the day before the killings at Kent State, May 3, 1970. During his speech, Dellinger called for "not a protest, but a paralysis of the war making machine." *AP Worldwide Photos.*

At a press conference with Cora Weiss, co-chair of the Committee of Liaison with Families of Servicemen Detained in Vietnam, December 22, 1970. Weiss and Dellinger released a list to the media containing the names of 339 American prisoners of war held in North Vietnam. *AP Worldwide Photos.*

At a demonstration outside a courthouse in New Haven, Connecticut, on May 20, 1971, to show his support during the trial of Black Panthers Bobby Seale and Ericka Huggins. *AP Worldwide Photos.*

Speaking at a press conference at Kennedy Airport, August 9, 1972, after returning from Paris. The effects of a recent fast are evident in this photograph.
AP Worldwide Photos.

Addressing a crowd on a college campus in the mid-1970s. *Courtesy, Natasha Singer Collection.*

Dellinger is standing third from right with the Rotunda 19, a group of Vermont activists on trial in 1986 for committing civil disobedience in protest against the U.S. government's Central America policies. *Courtesy, Elizabeth Peterson Collection.*

At a 1993 rally in Columbus, Ohio. Standing to the left of Dellinger is his foster son, Howie Douglas, who lived with the Dellingers in the late 1940s and early 1950s. *Courtesy, Elizabeth Peterson Collection.*

Blocking a gate with other protesters at a 1998 civil disobedience action to protest the Vermont Yankee Nuclear Power Plant in Vernon, Vermont. Shortly after this photograph was taken, Dellinger and several other protesters were arrested and carried away by the state police. *Courtesy, Elizabeth Peterson Collection.*

David Dellinger and Elizabeth Peterson, 2001.
Courtesy, Elizabeth Peterson Collection.

Speaking at a peace rally in Tokyo in 2002. Not long after this photograph was taken, Dellinger's Alzheimer's Disease intensified, bringing an end to his speaking engagements. *Courtesy, Elizabeth Peterson Collection.*

10

Disrupting the Holy Mysteries

I think he's one of the most conservative radicals that you would ever meet. He dresses neatly and is very polite.

Betty Dellinger

Dellinger doesn't look like . . . a revolutionary. He is going a little bald, and he was wearing a good tweed jacket, and he looked like Yale '36, Republican family, grandmother in the D.A.R.—all of which he is. . . . Unlike the young play-actor revolutionaries, he knows revolution is grim business, which exacts a grim price.

Stewart Alsop

I thought he was a dirty old man who was trying to lead a bunch of kids down the garden path.

Thomas Foran, U.S. attorney and
Chicago Eight prosecutor

CHICAGO 1968 WAS a turning point not only for the antiwar movement but for Dellinger's personal life as well. After Chicago, ultraleft elements of the movement became even more emboldened. Coincidentally and paradoxically, antiwar sentiments spilled out of the traditional centers of dissent—Chicago, New York, and San Francisco—and into the heartland, sowing the seeds of opposition to the Vietnam War in communities across America. By the late 1960s and early 1970s, the movement had become increasingly decentralized and localized, reinforcing perceptions of a nation divided. At the center of many of these struggles was David Dellinger. Parting ways with those of his comrades who regarded Chicago as a disaster, Dellinger celebrated the protests as a fresh starting point for the antiwar movement. "As we lick our wounds and analyze the political lessons of the battle of Chicago," he wrote days after the protest, "we must not lose sight of the urgency of a continuing, many-faceted program to challenge the status-quo of war and racism. . . . Now we must reunite our forces and proceed with the tasks ahead."[1]

The five-month-long Chicago conspiracy trial became the defining moment in Dellinger's life. It transformed him into a national media icon, cemented his leadership position in the antiwar movement, and elevated respect for him in radical circles. It is safe to say that all roads in David Dellinger's life led to and away from the Chicago conspiracy trial. Even though the long and rigorous ordeal failed to quash his activism, its long-term effects were primarily negative. The momentary fame he gained from it came at a terrible price, as it wreaked havoc with his health and personal life, which was exactly what his enemies wanted.

Dellinger's performance at the convention protests earned mixed assessments. Many of the younger activists celebrated him as a hero at antiwar gatherings and in the pages of underground newspapers. "He was a true leader," remembered *Realist* editor and Yippie Paul Krassner, "who tried to maintain a nonviolent stance because there were so many different factions that went to Chicago. . . . He believed in confronting the warmakers, but it was always done in an idealistic and non-threatening way."[2] Mobe leaders were less enthusiastic in their appraisals. Doug Dowd thought that although Dellinger had acted admirably in Chicago, the protests ultimately reversed the momentum of the antiwar movement. Because the Mobe was so divided in the summer of 1968 over the necessity of the demonstrations, the coalition failed to enlist a significant number of demonstrators to go to Chicago. These divisions continued to plague the Mobe until its demise in 1969. "By 1968 on, really from Chicago on," Dowd remembered, "the movement began to go downhill, except for a brief moment in the fall of 1969. . . . In my judgment, Chicago was a total disaster for the . . . peace movement in terms of the long run and how it went down to the people of the United States."[3]

As far as Sid Peck was concerned, Chicago yet again highlighted Dellinger's inability to provide real leadership in mass demonstrations. Although Dellinger handled the chaotic scene at Grant Park on Wednesday afternoon as well as might be expected, he made no attempt to help control the massive, televised crowd outside the Hilton that night. Moreover, the Mobe had failed to mobilize the crucial moderate and pacifist segments of the movement, Peck noted. "Going ahead in Chicago, even though I agreed it was the right thing to do, certainly alienated the pacifist formations." While Peck noted that Dellinger was "strongly in support of nonviolent civil disobedience," he hastened to add that the Mobe did not agree on the effectiveness of either nonviolence or civil disobedience.[4] In Dellinger's defense, the week of convention protests was so frenetic and packed with activities that no one individual could have hoped to provide leadership consistently in all events.

In the aftermath of the Chicago, Dellinger reevaluated some of his long-held Gandhian assumptions. His refusal to condemn the radical left's calls for violent self-defense against authorities placed him at odds with the more orthodox pacifists. In the long run, the inability of Dellinger and other antiwar leaders to consistently call into question the existence of military institutions in American society even as they condemned the Vietnam War diluted the pacifist message of the movement, according to Brad Lyttle, a more traditional pacifist than Dellinger. "It is my view," he concluded, "that the failure to try to strengthen the arguments for pacifism, and make pacifism part of the platforms of peace organizations, may be the most important reason why the peace movement in the U.S. has had so little influence."[5]

Committed to carrying on business as usual after the convention protests, Dellinger attended an important Mobe administrative committee meeting on September 17 in Washington, D.C., to plan the organization's fall and winter agenda. To follow up on Chicago, Dellinger and other Mobe organizers envisioned scores of scattered, decentralized demonstrations across the country. The largest and most ambitious demonstration planned by the Mobe, the so-called counterinaugural protest, was scheduled for inauguration day in Washington, D.C., in January 1969. The counterinaugural was Dellinger's idea. He wanted Richard Nixon, the victor in the 1968 presidential race, to understand that regardless of the election's outcome, the antiwar protesters planned to remain in the streets until the end of the war.

The most alarming news at the September Mobe meeting was an announcement that a judge in Illinois planned to indict Dellinger, Tom Hayden, Rennie Davis, Jerry Rubin, and Abbie Hoffman on charges of conspiracy to cause a riot at the Democratic National Convention. For the next few months, rumors swirled about a conspiracy trial, but little concrete information surfaced. On December 5, Dellinger testified before the House Committee on Un-American Activities in Washington, D.C. Jerry Rubin had already appeared before the committee dressed in American Revolution attire. Although Dellinger respectfully answered questions, he also turned the committee into a bully pulpit from which to denounce the Vietnam War.

It took a long time for the antiwar movement to rebound from Chicago. Protest actions in the fall of 1968 and winter of 1969 were sluggish and poorly attended at best. Antiwar activists aggressively dogged Hubert Humphrey and Richard Nixon on the campaign trail, marching and chanting wherever the candidates appeared. In the November elections, even though Nixon defeated Humphrey by only a razor-thin margin, the Democrat's loss registered scarcely a ripple in many antiwar circles. Because Humphrey kept his misgivings about the war private, he made it difficult for the public to distinguish his position on the war from Nixon's.

On Nixon's inauguration day—January 20, 1969—the Mobe held its counterinaugural. For three days, from January 18 through 20, thousands of protesters attended workshops, rallies, and marches, and on the final day, about fifteen thousand people flocked to the cold, muddy counterinaugural ball to hear rock bands and speakers inside a huge circus tent. On a dreary morning, crowds of protesters carrying signs began pelting the presidential limousine with rocks, sticks, and other debris as it drove in a motorcade up Pennsylvania Avenue. Such hostilities antagonized the new president, who entered the White House detesting the antiwar movement. But even though they outraged Nixon, the counterinaugural protests could hardly be judged a success. Dellinger, blinded by his own chronic optimism, thought otherwise. Even the modest-size crowds at the actions convinced him that the antiwar coalition was healthy. His perpetually sunny outlook was one of his weaknesses as a leader: his refusal to examine any indicators of decline.

At the February Mobe meeting, Dellinger backed a proposal to proceed with a series of protests on April 5 and 6 in key cities across the country. During the first weekend in April, fifty thousand protesters assembled on a gray, wet day in New York's Central Park for a mass rally. In Chicago, around thirty thousand people marched in a peaceful rally that failed to trigger violent police reprisals. Four thousand gathered in Atlanta, and antiwar actions took place throughout San Francisco for two days. But despite the decent turnouts, the rest of the nation paid little attention to the April protests. The leftist *Guardian* emphasized the "incredible boredom of the ritual parade, while the *Village Voice* categorized the events as part of the "annual rite of righteous indignation."[6]

As Dellinger and thousands of other resisters took part in the counterinaugural activities, President Nixon's newly appointed attorney general, John Mitchell, began the process of indicting the leaders of the previous year's Chicago protests. On March 20, 1969, a federal court in Chicago indicted eight men—Rennie Davis, David Dellinger, John Froines, Tom Hayden, Abbie Hoffman, Jerry Rubin, Bobby Seale, and Lee Weiner—on several felony charges. The two most significant accusations were conspiring to cross state lines "with the intent to incite, organize, promote encourage, participate in, and carry on a riot," and, once in Chicago during the convention, "inciting, participating in, and carrying out a riot."[7] The charges carried a sentence of up to ten years in prison and $20,000 in fines. But the indictments surprised no one. In the weeks leading up to the March 20 indictments, there had been much talk in movement circles about the likelihood of a trial. As early as October 1968, the FBI director, J. Edgar Hoover, had advised his subordinates in the bureau that he wanted to see "approximately twenty principal leaders and activists of various New Left organizations . . . charged under the federal anti-riot law for their Chicago activities." Hoover hoped that such a prosecution would "seriously disrupt and curtail the activities of the New Left."[8]

When the indictments finally came, the choice of the eight activists was not accidental or random. According to radical journalist Andrew Kopkind, who covered the Chicago trial for the alternative magazine *Hard Times*, each man represented a key segment of the movement:

> The Chicago all-stars—the original eight defendants were picked for their symbolic value and leadership roles: Bobby Seale, the Panther; Tom Hayden and Rennie Davis, the SDS veterans; Abbie Hoffman and Jerry Rubin, the anarcho-Yippies; Dave Dellinger, the Mobilization coalitionist; John Froines, the activist professor; and Lee Weiner, the street organizer and second-level cadre.[9]

John Froines, a chemistry professor at the University of Oregon, and Lee Weiner, a sociology professor at Northwestern University, were Mobe marshals during convention and had nothing to do with the actual planning of the Chicago protests. Rather, the two academics were accused of teaching the protesters to make bombs, a charge later refuted. Seale's involvement was limited to only a brief stay in Chicago and a few speaking engagements.

The charges outraged the defendants. Before the conspiracy indictments were issued, the eight men had never gathered together as a group in the same place. Even impartial observers with no sympathies for the defendants or their views characterized the violence at the 1968 Democratic National Convention as a police riot. More ominously, the eight activists were being tried under a draconian law that severely limited free speech. According to this law, any person publicly advocating "violence," "confrontation," or "militant action" before the convention—even months before it—could be blamed for any violence that occurred during the convention week, regardless of whether they were in Chicago or had anything to do with encouraging the violence. Furthermore, the evidence against Dellinger and the others came largely from government and police informants. For instance, FBI informer Carl Gilman submitted evidence to the court based on notes he took at a speech that Dellinger delivered in San Diego on July 12, 1968. According to Gilman's notes, Dellinger told the crowd, "Burn your draft cards. Resist the draft. Violate the laws. Go to jail. Disrupt the United States government in any way you can to stop this insane war. . . . I am going to Chicago to the Democratic National Convention where there may be problems. . . . [Applause] I'll see you in Chicago."[10] Dellinger never specified what "problems" he anticipated, but Gilman speculated the pacifist meant that protesters going to Chicago felt uneasy about the reception they expected to receive.[11]

In response to the indictments, Dellinger issued a blistering statement. He turned the tables against the government, as he often did throughout the trial, calling the indictment "immoral." It exposed, in his view, the lengths the government would go to crush the antiwar movement:

> It is hypocrisy for an administration which has refused to withdraw its troops from Vietnam and therefore bears responsibility for the death of 453 Americans in a single week to indict us for traveling to Chicago to demand an end to the war. The government that uses napalm to incinerate little children has huffed and puffed and tried to save its

honor by indicting us on trumped-up charges of teaching the use of incendiary devices.[12]

By April 1969, Dellinger had turned most of his attention to the trial. He often had to excuse himself from meetings, antiwar rallies, and speaking engagements, spending the spring and summer months with the other defendants and their attorneys discussing legal strategies. Initially, the Chicago Eight planned to secure the services of Charles Garry, a militant "people's lawyer" from San Francisco often hired by the Black Panthers. Garry had been Bobby Seale's first choice for attorney. Tom Hayden preferred his old friend Leonard "Lenny" Weinglass, a soft-spoken New York lawyer who had developed a close bond with Hayden when the two worked for New Left organizations in Newark. Famed civil rights attorney William Kunstler also volunteered his services and received an enthusiastic endorsement from Davis, Hoffman, Rubin, Froines, Weiner, and Dellinger. When the defendants met with the legal team for the first time in the spring, Garry presented them with a bill for $375,000 and vowed he would not tolerate any disruptions or outbursts during the trial.[13]

Garry suddenly parted ways with the Chicago Eight lawyers in early September after his doctor advised him that he needed a gall bladder operation. Although the defense attorneys asked for a six-month delay until Garry recovered, their requests were denied. Garry's departure meant that the job of chief counsel went to Kunstler. Assisting him in the Chicago Eight case were Weinglass and leftist attorney Gerald Lefcourt, a close friend of Hoffman and Rubin. In the pretrial meetings, Dellinger and Kunstler took an instant liking to each other. "Kunstler was no radical," Dellinger wrote, "but from talking with him I was impressed that he had a compassionate heart, lots of courage—as demonstrated by his work in the South on civil rights cases—and was intrigued with the issues involved in our case."[14] Kunstler was largely responsible for casting Dellinger as the elder father figure of the trial.

From the outset, the defense faced an uphill battle against the highly combative judge, Julius Hoffman, who was determined to hold an orderly trial. As Kunstler recalled, "Judge Hoffman viewed the defendants and defense attorneys as the enemy, and since he believed he represented the lawful authority of the United States, he was certain he was always correct and just."[15] All the motions by the defense, including a request to postpone the trial because of excessive publicity, were denied. The prosecution, meanwhile, resorted to heavy-handed tactics. FBI files obtained a decade after the trial through the Freedom of Information Act revealed that "the Chicago Police and possibly the FBI had surreptitiously attended and/or surveilled several meetings of the defendants and their counsel. It appears that information obtained in this manner . . . was forwarded to Assistant United States Attorney Richard Schultz, one of the prosecutors."[16] Declassified FBI documents also revealed a collusion during the entire trial among Judge Hoffman, the FBI, and the prosecution team.[17]

Long before the trial began, the eight defendants and their attorneys decided to politicize the case in an effort to put the government on trial. They took advantage of the media circus in Chicago. A small army of journalists, television camera operators, and photographers regularly followed the defendants, and the eight defendants and their lawyers conducted press conferences before and during the trial to articulate their strategies. Dellinger frequently commuted back and forth between Chicago and New York, and family members often traveled to Chicago to stay with him. In late 1969 and early 1970 he began a cross-country university campus lecture tour, typically charging $1,000 for a speaking engagement. The "conspiracy defendants" and their lawyers appeared on about five hundred campuses, which became a vital source of their defense funds.[18]

For Betty Dellinger, having a celebrity as a husband presented new challenges. "He wouldn't want to go out to dinner," she recounted, "because everywhere he went, people would walk up to him and say, 'Oh, you are David Dellinger.' Even if we would pick out-of-the-way places, there would be somebody there who would recognize him. He was like a movie star. It was very hard."[19] In Chicago, both sides of the heavily publicized legal battle believed they were on the verge of making history. "It's going to be a combination Scopes trial, revolution in the streets, Woodstock Festival and People's Park, all rolled into one," raved Abbie Hoffman. Judge Hoffman wondered whether "the trial of the century" was about to begin, while an American Civil Liberties Union official anticipated it would "be the most important political trial in the history of the United States."[20]

On the morning of September 24, the trial commenced. Beforehand, Dellinger admitted that he "didn't even know some of the people with whom I was accused of having conspired, including Bobby Seale." At the trial it took a while for Dellinger to become acquainted with the Black Panther. Underneath Seale's gruff and tough-talking exterior, Dellinger soon discovered a deep reservoir of warmth and humanity, and he enjoyed getting to know him.[21] Dellinger also became friends with Seale's twenty-one-year-old assistant, Fred Hampton, who regularly appeared at the courtroom to support Seale. The more Dellinger got to know Hampton, the more he was convinced that the young Black Panther was "a unique and extraordinary young man, like no one else I've ever known."[22]

Jury selection began September 24, with attorneys on both sides interviewing hundreds of prospective jurors over the next two days. During the process, Judge Hoffman forbade the defense attorneys from asking any questions remotely related to politics, which jeopardized meaningful interviews with potential jurors. The defense and prosecution finally settled on a jury of ten women, mostly suburban homemakers, and two men. On the morning of September 26, assistant prosecutor Richard Schultz and defense attorney William Kunstler delivered their opening statements. Schultz told the court that the government intended to show that the defendants had "crossed state lines . . . with the intent to riot" and to "create a situation in this city where people would come to Chicago . . . [to] riot." He identified Dellinger as the ringleader of the Chicago protests. "Now, as to the defendant Dellinger's participation during convention week," Schultz announced, "Dellinger was the principal architect."[23] Kunstler, by contrast, argued that the conspiracy charges represented a chilling effort by the government to repress protest. "Dissent died here for a moment during that Democratic National Convention," he proclaimed. "What happens in this case may determine whether it is moribund."[24]

In the early weeks of the trial, the defendants lightly mocked the proceedings by propping their feet on the table, passing around bags of jelly beans, occasionally making editorial comments and one-liners, and laughing at testimony they found absurd. The more militant among them brought North Vietnamese flags and pictures of Che Guevara. Abbie and Jerry dressed in judge's robes and, on Bobby Seale's birthday, brought a birthday cake into the courtroom, which the marshals promptly seized. The duo dismissed the trial as absurd and mocked it at every turn. When prosecutor Schultz introduced Abbie Hoffman to the jury, the anarchical activist blew the jurors a kiss, which Judge Hoffman told them to disregard. Some of the defendants remained more reticent. Tom Hayden hoped to play the whole affair straight to win the sympathy of the jury. Initially Bobby Seale remained quiet and disciplined, reading Frantz Fanon to pass the time in court. Throughout the early months of the trial, David Dellinger said little, but by mid-October he began engaging in acts of disruption that grew bolder and bolder as the trial progressed. His first act of open defiance occurred on October 15, when he stood at the front of the courtroom at the beginning of the day wearing a black armband and read aloud the names of Americans and Vietnamese killed in the war. When Judge Hoffman entered the courtroom, he ordered Dellinger to stop. Explaining that his actions were in solidarity with the nationwide Moratorium against the Vietnam War, which had begun that morning, Dellinger referred to the judge as "Mr. Hoffman." "I am *Judge* Hoffman, sir," the judge retorted. "I believe in equality, sir, so I prefer to call people mister or by their first name," Dellinger replied. As the jury entered the room and took their seats, Dellinger announced, "Before the witness resumes the stand, we would like to propose . . . a moment of silence."[25] The judge refused and ordered Dellinger not to interrupt.[26]

The legendary sparring between Judge Hoffman and Bobby Seale began in mid-October. Seale, who still wanted Charles Garry to be his lawyer, refused to allow Kunstler and Weinglass to represent him and asked the court's permission to defend himself. The judge denied Seale's request. Seale refused to compromise, insisting that he either wanted Garry or would represent himself. Tensions between the Black Panther and the judge peaked at the end of October. Each day brought a new verbal skirmish. "You're making it very difficult for me, Mr. Seale," Judge Hoffman said, to which Seale shot back: "You are making it difficult for me, Judge Hoffman." Other exchanges electrified the courtroom. "Let the record show," Judge Hoffman announced, "that the defendant Seale has refused to be quiet in the face of the admonition and direction of the Court." "Let the record show," Seale forcefully countered, "that Bobby Seale speaks out in behalf of his constitutional rights to defend himself, his right to speak in behalf of himself in this courtroom."[27]

Numerous contempt citations failed to silence Seale. In court, Dellinger repeatedly and emphatically stated his support for the Black Panther. "I think you should understand," Dellinger told the judge on October 22, that "we support Bobby Seale in this." And then, looking at his silent codefendants, Dellinger quickly added, "At least I do."[28]

Such shows of solidarity only intensified Judge Hoffman's antagonism toward Seale. On October 29, Seale called Hoffman a "racist" and a "fascist" and pointed to the painting of George Washington and referred to him as a "slave owner." "What about Section 1982, Title 42 of the code," Seale protested, "where it says the black man cannot be discriminated against in my legal defense in any court in America?"[29] With that, Judge Hoffman, visibly furious, called for a recess and then ordered the marshals to bind and gag Seale. As they moved toward him, Dellinger leaped in their way to block access. A marshal kneed David in the testicles and pushed him aside while the others chained Seale's hands and feet to the metal chair and stuffed a piece of muslin into his mouth.[30]

Throughout the remainder of the trial, Dellinger refused to stand when Judge Hoffman entered the room, each time receiving a contempt citation. Each morning the marshals carried Seale into the courtroom, with a tight gag covering his mouth and heavy chains securing his arms and legs to the chair. Several times he almost choked or passed out because of the gag. On one occasion Seale remembered "the blood began to stop coming to my head. That was too much. I started shaking my head."[31] Outside the federal building, hundreds of demonstrators gathered each day, chanting "Free Bobby! Free Bobby!" Courtroom sketches of the Black Panther chained and gagged stirred protest around the world, with critics condemning Seale's treatment as barbaric and racist. With his hands cuffed, Seale scrawled a terse message on a yellow pad for his fellow defendants to read at a noon press conference. "TELL BROTHERS AND SISTERS TO COOL IT EVERYWHERE. JUST SPREAD THE WORD ABOUT HOFFMAN AND INJUSTICE OF U.S. COURTROOM."[32]

Telegrams and letters of protest inundated Judge Hoffman's office. Dellinger advocated boycotting the remainder of the trial, even if meant the revocation of his bail. At the end of October, he and his codefendants met in a crowded room with attorneys, legal aides, and supportive family members. Already fissures had formed among the defendants. A split pitted Hayden and Froines—who sought to minimize the outbursts and respect the decorum—against Rubin, Hoffman, and Weiner, who advocated maximum disruption. Caught in the middle, Dellinger and Davis tried to maintain a united front. "Dave was actually the most outspoken in the courtroom," remembered Froines. "Tom and I took a more conservative course, and David was the person who argued that we really had to be, in a sense, conscientious objectors in the courtroom as much as in the streets of Chicago and elsewhere."[33]

The Yippies—Abbie and Jerry—were as disruptive as Dellinger, but in a more absurd and irreverent way. By the late fall, they even proposed meeting with Hollywood producers to make a movie about the trial. Frictions sometimes exploded into yelling matches, and Dellinger often intervened to keep the peace. Chicago activist Bob Lamb, who volunteered as a full-time assistant to the defense and had befriended Dellinger the previous year, remembered the nonviolent elder being the cement that held the conspiracy together. "Dave was respected by one and all of the attorneys and defendants. . . . There was conflict between the defendants on strategy and Dave tried to bridge the gaps."[34]

Still, Hayden resisted Dellinger's call to boycott the trial to protest Seale's treatment. He, unlike Dellinger, was not willing to subject himself to a lengthy prison sentence. "Dave's a pacifist," Hayden remarked, "and pacifists don't have much sense of reality. So he can do what he wants, but the rest of us have to act more responsibly."[35]

What separated Dellinger from Hayden—and indeed, from the rest of the defendants—was his willingness to go to jail if necessary. There was nothing that Judge Hoffman or the U.S. prison system could do to him that had not already been done before, he reasoned. Yet compromise was also part of his nature, and in the face of growing pressure from his codefendants, he abandoned his plans to boycott the trial, although he intended to remain outspoken in Judge Hoffman's chamber.

On October 30, marshals first delivered Bobby Seale bound and gagged to the courtroom. He repeatedly writhed in his chair, rattled his chains, and attempted to shout through the gag. Eventually Judge Hoffman ordered the marshals to attach a larger and tighter gag to the rebellious defendant. "Others joined me in trying to protect him," Dellinger recounted, "but even so he was beaten and hit in the balls and stomach a number of times; some of us were slugged and mauled while trying to protect him."[36] On one occasion, Dellinger shoved some marshals who were closing in on the chained defendant. "We later asked him how he, a pacifist, could be so rough," Stew Albert jokingly recalled, "and he said, with a twinkle in his eye, that shoving can be a form of nonviolent resistance if it's done to stop evil."[37]

The firestorm of controversy ignited by the court's method of restraint finally overwhelmed Judge Hoffman. On the afternoon of November 5, he declared a mistrial for Seale and ordered a separate trial for him. At that point, the Chicago Eight became the Chicago Seven, and the case dragged on for another four months. Judge Hoffman sentenced Seale to four years in prison for sixteen separate counts of contempt, each carrying a four-month sentence. By 1971, however, the government had dropped all charges against Seale, including the separate charges of involvement in the torture and murder of Alex Rackley, a Black Panther suspected of being a government informant. Once again, the evidence against Seale proved to be too flimsy. "In the end," wrote Abbie Hoffman's brother Jack, "it was Seale who set the standard for rest of the defendants. He showed courage in the courtroom as if it were a battlefield and taught his codefendants that you can't reason with the enemy."[38]

Repeated efforts by Dellinger, Abbie Hoffman, and Jerry Rubin to defend Seale in the courtroom, both physically and verbally, won them the respect of African American militants. Black Panther leader David Hilliard lauded the three defendants for trying "to help him" but condemned Tom Hayden for staying out of the conflict. Hayden's neutrality made Hilliard "even angrier than usual at the antiwar movement's refusal to recognize and relate to our persecution."[39] But Bobby Seale never forgot Dellinger's support, and the warmth between the two men was still evident when they embraced at a 1988 Chicago protest reunion. "Dave was a true revolutionary humanist whom I have always admired," he recalled. "He was the main Chicago codefendant to support my . . . [constitutional] rights."[40]

Outside the courtroom, the antiwar movement enjoyed a revival. For the first nine months of 1969, there were no mass mobilizations. But the Moratorium protests in the fall invigorated the movement and signaled a restoration. In mid-November, Judge Hoffman allowed the defendants to attend an antiwar demonstration in Washington, D.C. Between 250,000 and 500,000 people gathered for the November 15 Mobilization against the War. In an area of the Mall west of the Capitol, the crowd listened to speeches by Senator Eugene McCarthy, Dr. Benjamin Spock, Dick Gregory, and Senator George McGovern. John Denver, Arlo Guthrie, Pete Seeger, and Mitch Miller supplied the music. Dellinger spoke in the late afternoon. The crowd cheered wildly as he, flanked by Jerry Rubin and Abbie Hoffman, approached the microphone. The enthusiastic applause may have been a reflection of Dellinger's newfound fame as a Chicago conspiracy trial defendant. In a move reminiscent of the 1967 Pentagon march, Dellinger told the crowd that he intended to lead a separate march to the Justice Department to protest the war and the trial of the Chicago Seven. This time he managed to obtain a permit.[41]

In the late afternoon thousands of marchers streamed out of the Mall and followed Dellinger to the Justice Department. Chanting demonstrators hauled a tall papier-mâché caricature of John Mitchell, Nixon's attorney general, down Constitution Avenue. Much to Dellinger's disappointment, however, ultraleft militants transformed the peaceful march into a display of righteous indignation. A scattered but highly visible minority of marchers carried red and blue Vietcong flags, and some men and women began chanting, "Stop the trial!" and "Free Bobby!"[42] Long rows of police equipped with full riot gear and gas masks waited on the front steps of the Justice Department with clubs ready. From inside his office, Attorney General Mitchell watched as protesters chanted, waved their banners, and encircled the building. After a few protesters broke some windows, the police charged, clubbing the demonstrators and throwing teargas canisters into the throng.

Dellinger's march to the Justice Department angered moderates in the antiwar movement, particularly the youthful Moratorium staff who had recently transferred to the antiwar movement from Eugene McCarthy's failed 1968 presidential campaign. Although the November 15 march had been organized by the New Mobe to coincide with nationwide Moratorium protests, the last thing that the Moratorium activists wanted was yet another peaceful mass protest closely identified with their efforts to deteriorate into a violent clash. John Schultz, who has written more about the Chicago protests and Conspiracy Trial than any other author, noted that long before November 15 support for the Chicago Seven was lukewarm in the Moratorium milieu. "I myself did not want to tell the defendants that the organizers of the October 15 . . . Vietnam Moratorium Day demonstrations at some of the largest universities in the Chicago area refused to announce or give any support to the Conspiracy Eight from their stages," he wrote. "The students in the Moratorium audiences wanted the music and the dance the way people in the old revival meeting wanted the release of ecstasy and tears, and probably . . . one in five considered themselves revolutionaries."[43]

Back in Chicago, the prosecution's case dragged on through the rest of November. The three star witnesses who formed the heart of the government's case—Irwin Bock, William Frappolly, and Robert Pierson—were agents who had infiltrated the ranks of the antiwar movement.

Predictably, they portrayed the defendants—including Dellinger—as destructive conspirators united for the purpose of causing massive riots in Chicago to disrupt the convention. The prosecution called its last witness on December 5. Three days later the defense began.

The defense attorneys tried to fashion a deliberate and coherent narrative of the 1960s protest movements. Their witnesses included poets Allen Ginsberg and Ed Sanders; musicians Arlo Guthrie, Country Joe McDonald, Phil Ochs, Pete Seeger, and Judy Collins; historian Staughton Lynd; authors Norman Mailer and William Styron; comedian Dick Gregory; LSD guru Timothy Leary; Congressman John Conyers; and civil rights leaders Jesse Jackson and Julian Bond. Even Chicago mayor Richard Daley testified. Less combative than he had been during the convention, the mayor laughed when Abbie Hoffman challenged him to step outside and settle their differences.

The broad range of famous witnesses did little for the defendants. Judge Hoffman overruled the introduction of any social or historical context that might have helped clarify the defendants' actions. He helped the prosecution team convince the jury that the protests were actually a prolonged, massive riot that took place in a vacuum, cut off from the war in Vietnam and social conditions at home. The judge refused to allow the testimony of such vital defense witnesses as the Reverend Ralph Abernathy, successor to Martin Luther King Jr. as head of the SCLC, and the former U.S. attorney general Ramsey Clark. To make matters worse, once the dramatic ordeal of Bobby Seale ended, the press cut back their coverage. Dellinger privately grew despondent, sometimes doubting whether pacifism would survive the turmoil. "I continued to stand for nonviolence," Dellinger recalled, but at times it seemed like "people weren't listening."[44]

His concern over the mounting violence grew with the sudden rise of the Weathermen, an ultraleft faction of the SDS. On June 18, 1969, SDS held its last national convention in Chicago. For the past few years the SDS had been mostly a paper organization, but from its ashes emerged an ultraradical faction: the Revolutionary Youth Movement, later known as Weathermen (and, later, the more gender-neutral Weather Underground). The Weathermen eschewed the counterculture, called for building "worker-student" alliances, referred to themselves as "Marxist-Leninists," and encouraged young activists to commit to revolutionary resistance to end the Vietnam War. At first, Dellinger welcomed the Weathermen into the antiwar coalition. In fact, he and Rennie Davis brought a group of young activists from the Weathermen faction, including Mark Rudd and Kathy Boudin, to the founding conference of the New Mobilization to End the War in Vietnam on July 4 and 5, 1969, at the campus of Case Western Reserve University in Cleveland.[45] Dellinger initially hoped that the Weathermen would become reliable allies in the antiwar struggle.

The Weathermen held their infamous "Days of Rage" protest in Chicago during the conspiracy trial. Hundreds of them assembled in Chicago between October 8 and 11 and invited Tom Hayden to speak at a night rally. Unaware of their plans to go wild in the streets, Hayden appeared at Lincoln Park and addressed the crowd through a megaphone. He gazed out at hundreds of youths, most of them "helmeted, wearing heavy jackets, carrying clubs and NLF flags." The situation, Hayden feared, was about to turn ugly.

Both Hayden and Dellinger had pleaded with the Weathermen to keep their protests nonviolent. The night before the outbreak of the Days of Rage, Dellinger, William Kunstler, and Fred Hampton met with Weatherman Mark Rudd in an effort to convince the ultraleft faction to call off the protest. The meeting turned ugly when Rudd accused the Panthers of lacking sufficient revolutionary fervor. Hampton "floored him with a single angry blow," Dellinger recalled, forcing him and Kunstler to intervene to prevent a fistfight.[46]

The Weathermen went ahead with their plans anyway. "Tom [Hayden] and Dave Dellinger were trying to tone us down, put the brakes on what we were organizing," remembered Weatherman Jeff Jones.[47] The Weathermen charged out of the park that cold autumn night, clubs swinging, fists clenched, chanting, "Revolution's begun! Off the pig! Pick up the gun!"[48] For the next several hours hundreds of youths ran through the streets of Chicago, breaking windows, kicking over garbage cans, knocking over bystanders, bashing automobiles, and, in some cases, charging into police lines. Marauding Weathermen swept into the elite neighborhoods of the Gold Coast, shouting revolutionary slogans, scaring local residents, and targeting fancy hotels and high-rise Lake Shore apartments. All night and into the morning, the Chicago police raced from one call to the next. As Dellinger later wrote,

> I was there as a disgusted observer and saw that a disproportionately high percentage of the cars wrecked were Volkswagens and other lower-priced cars. Inevitably, the police guarded best the main streets,

which housed the swankier establishments. The Weathermen soon swept down an unguarded side street, attacking small shops, proletarian beer halls and lower-middle-class housing.[49]

As irrational as the Days of Rage rampages were, they lacked the savagery of the government's repression, perhaps best displayed on December 4, 1969, in the murder of Black Panthers Fred Hampton and Mark Clark. In a predawn raid by the Chicago police and FBI agents, Hampton and his close friend Clark were killed in what police claimed was a Panther-instigated shootout. Inconsistencies in the official version of events immediately surfaced. To "neutralize" Hampton and Clark, the police and FBI relied heavily on FBI informant William O'Neal, head of security for the Chicago Black Panthers. O'Neal gave the authorities floor plans of Fred Hampton's apartment, told them where he kept his guns, and reported his movements during his final days. In late November, the FBI began planning a raid on Hampton's apartment, ostensibly to arrest him for possession of illegal weapons, despite O'Neal's final report indicating that all of Hampton's weapons were properly registered.[50] The FBI disregarded the information and moved ahead with plans for the raid. O'Neal cooked Hampton's final supper on the night of December 3 and slipped the Black Panther a powerful sleeping drug. At 4:00 A.M. a large force of Chicago police stormed Hampton's apartment. The police fired almost a hundred shots, killing Hampton as he slept in his bed. The sole bullet discharged by Clark was a reflex shot that fired as he reached for his shotgun, only to be riddled with police bullets before he could use it. Several other Panthers in the apartment, including Hampton's pregnant fiancée Deborah Johnson, were shot as well but survived. The surviving Panthers were charged with aggravated assault and attempted murder, and their bail was set at $100,000. Police later gave O'Neal a bonus of $300 for his assistance.[51]

News of Fred Hampton's violent death reached Dellinger later that morning. "It was one of the saddest moments of my life," he recounted.[52] Defense attorneys asked Judge Hoffman to postpone the trial for a day of mourning, but he refused. At night the Chicago defendants met with local Black Panther leaders at the party's headquarters, which had recently been shot up and ransacked by the Chicago police as part of a nationwide crackdown on all local Black Panther chapters. During the meeting, the Panther security chief William O'Neal approached Dellinger, who was unaware at the time that O'Neal had acted as a government informant. O'Neal told him, "Now, Dave, you understand why we had to pick up the gun, why everyone has to pick up the gun. Now you can see why even you, Dave, have to pick up the gun."[53] Years later, O'Neal committed suicide by leaping off a bridge into oncoming traffic.[54]

Deeply shaken by the deaths of Fred Hampton and Mark Clark, by the beginning of 1970 Dellinger assumed a more combative posture in the courtroom. Judge Hoffman's enmity toward Seale now shifted to Dellinger, who supplied the trial with much of its drama in the final weeks. The time had come to speak truth to power, he reasoned. Tensions in the courtroom reached a breaking point in early February. Judge Hoffman became incensed when he heard that Dellinger had recently delivered a strident speech at Marquette University in Milwaukee, denouncing the judge and the trial. Hoffman was poised to revoke the pacifist's bail and send him to the Cook County jail. All he needed was an appropriate provocation, which came on February 7 while assistant prosecutor John Schultz was questioning deputy police chief James Riordan. The police official wrongly testified that Dellinger had led marchers carrying Vietcong flags to downtown Chicago on Wednesday, August 28, 1968. "Oh bullshit," Dellinger mumbled quietly. "That's an absolute lie."[55] Judge Hoffman promptly dismissed the jury for the remainder of the afternoon and terminated Dellinger's bail. The courtroom fell into disorder as seated observers in the back of the courtroom stood and cried out in protest and struggled with the marshals. Upon hearing that her father was about to go to jail, thirteen-year-old Michele Dellinger burst into tears. Rennie Davis announced, "I associate myself with Dave Dellinger completely, 100 percent. This is the most obscene court I have ever seen." "Everything in this court is bullshit," added Jerry Rubin. Abbie Hoffman scolded: "You're a disgrace to the Jews. You would've served Hitler better."[56]

Judge Hoffman ignored the insults and refused to revoke the bail of the other defendants. Recalling the courtroom uproar at that moment, John Schultz wrote in his account of the trial, "Throughout the disorder, David Dellinger sat with an appearance of release, of peace. It was marvelous to believe that all of this resulted from the use of the word 'bullshit' once and once only and quietly."[57] As the marshals hauled away Dellinger to the Cook County jail, Michele Dellinger cried, "Don't take my father away!"[58] Abbie Hoffman raced to her side, embraced her, and assured her, "Don't worry. Your daddy's going to be fine."[59]

Dellinger fully embraced his status as prisoner, and early each morning police escorted him to the courtroom. Dellinger's "bullshit" remark rekindled the media frenzy. All eyes were once again on Chicago. But Dellinger's use of the word caused a minor crisis. Editorial boards met in newspaper offices throughout the United States. The mainstream press assiduously steered clear of printing the word. The *New York Times* opted instead to borrow a term coined by Judge Hoffman: "an eight-letter barnyard epithet."[60]

The case finally went to the jury on Saturday, February 14, 1970. After the jury left the courtroom to deliberate, Judge Hoffman began contempt proceedings, handing down sentences that ranged from two months for Lee Weiner to more than four years for attorney William Kunstler. Dellinger received the most charges of any defendant: thirty-two contempt citations, which translated into a sentence of two and a half years.

When given the opportunity to respond to his punishment, Dellinger stood and faced the court. He started his address with a discussion of the treatment of Bobby Seale and the contempt citation he received in October for supporting the Moratorium's protests. Judge Hoffman angrily cut him off:

> The Court: I hope you excuse me, sir. I ask you to say what you want to say in respect to punishments. I don't want you to talk politics.
>
> Dellinger: You see, that's one of the reasons I have needed to stand up and speak anyway, because you have tried to keep what you call politics, which means the truth, out of this courtroom, just as the prosecution has.
>
> The Court: I will ask you to sit down.
>
> Dellinger: Therefore it is necessary—
>
> The Court: I won't let you go any further.
>
> Dellinger: You want us to be like good Germans, supporting the evils of our decade, and then when we refused to be good Germans and came to Chicago and demonstrated, now you want us to be like good Jews, going quietly and politely to the concentration camps while you and this court suppress

freedom and truth. And the fact is that I am not prepared to do that. You want us to stay in our place like black people are supposed to stay in their place—

The Court: Mr. Marshal, I will ask you to have Mr. Dellinger sit down.

Dellinger: —like poor people were supposed to stay in their place, like people with formal education are supposed to stay in their place, like women are supposed to stay in their place—

The Court: I will ask you to sit down.

Dellinger: Like children are supposed to stay in their place, like lawyers—(to Kunstler and Weinglass) I thank you—are supposed to stay in their places. It is a travesty of justice and if you had any sense at all you would know that the record you read condemns you and not us. . . .

The Court: Mr. Marshal, will you please ask him to keep quiet.

The Marshal: Be quiet, Mr. Dellinger.

Dellinger: I sat here and heard that man Mr. Foran say evil, terrible, dishonest things that even he could not believe in—I heard him say that and you expect me to be quiet and accept that without speaking up. People no longer will be quiet. People are going to speak up. I am an old man and I am just speaking feebly and not too well, but I reflect the spirit that will echo—

As Dellinger spoke these words, a state of utter pandemonium erupted in the courtroom. Marshals restrained the 54-year-old pacifist, but he still managed to get in a few more words above the deafening din. "The court," he cried, "is in contempt of human life and dignity and truth and justice."[61]

On February 18, the jury returned with its verdict. They acquitted all the defendants of the conspiracy charges but convicted Dellinger, Davis, Hoffman, Rubin, and Hayden of crossing state lines with intent to riot. Each man received the maximum sentence of five years in prison and a fine of $5,000. Claiming they were harmful to society, Hoffman revoked their bail, which meant that their prison terms would begin immediately. The verdict touched off a series of demonstrations across the country known as "Day After" protests, with crowds as large as 25,000.

Returning to his Cook County jail cell, Dellinger prepared for an-other long imprisonment. Then, two weeks after the verdicts, an ap-peals court overturned Judge Hoffman's bail ruling, and the five men were released from jail. After more than a month behind bars Dellinger was a free man. Meanwhile, the Chicago conspiracy case entered the long appeals process. On May 11, 1972, the Seventh Circuit court re-versed Judge Hoffman's contempt charges, preparing the way for a new hearing before a different judge. In November 1972, an appellate court overturned all the convictions, citing numerous errors by the prosecution. Finally, in November 1973, Judge Edward Gignoux of Maine, specially appointed by the government to review the case, up-held thirteen contempt charges against Dellinger, Hoffman, Rubin, and Kunstler but concluded that nothing would be gained by sending the four men to jail.[62]

Book publishers expressed an interest in Dellinger's memoirs; radio and television stations asked him for interviews; and invitations poured in from college campuses. Mindful of the legal fees associated with the conspiracy trial, Dellinger began to assemble a collection of ar-ticles that he had written since the early 1940s, to publish as a reader. The Chicago Seven attorneys, working for "movement wages," charged $500,000 for their services, much of which was ultimately paid by wealthy donors and movement organizations. But Dellinger still faced a variety of expenses associated with the trial, and he needed the money that came from speaking engagements and book contracts. Just as the government officials hoped, the trial diverted funds and energy away from the antiwar movement. "It could be said the trial took too much money, time and attention away from fighting the government," Dellinger later reflected. "But we tried to compensate by turning the trial into something useful. We got a huge response when we traveled and spoke around the country weekends and evenings."[63]

At a time when elements of the radical left had drifted toward vio-lent resistance, Dellinger's faith in the power of peaceful tactics re-mained steadfast. More than any of his codefendants, he repeatedly used the trial as a platform to propagate a distinctly Gandhian doctrine. As Leonard Weinglass remembered,

Dave taught me the difference between being a dissident pacifist as opposed to a passive pacifist. He always made it clear that being a pacifist does not mean you do nothing. It might mean you do not engage in violent behavior, but you certainly behave in a militant, non-violent way where it's called for.[64]

Don Rose, a political strategist with the Democratic Party and a legal consultant for the protesters during the Democratic National Convention, shared Weinglass's view. At a crucial juncture in the history of the movement, he remembered, Dellinger somehow managed "to keep a balance among those who were committed to nonviolence and those for whom violence was a tactic."[65]

The trial of the Chicago Seven reflected the deep cultural divisions in America, a nation marked by years of racial upheaval and mounting antiwar struggles. Backlashes against the defendants were as numerous as supportive shows of solidarity. In the early weeks of the trial, the *Chicago Tribune* encouraged "patriotic citizens" to "fly the American flag daily throughout the trial" to show their support for Judge Hoffman and the prosecution.[66] President Richard Nixon rewarded Judge Hoffman by inviting him to the White House.

After the verdicts, the nation's most respected political commentators and legal observers tried to make sense of the Chicago conspiracy trial but disagreed about its significance. It immediately became fashionable to treat the trial as one of the events contributing to the decline of the 1960s activism. "The defendants' antics," noted *Time* magazine days after the verdicts, "have outraged many Americans who now deplore dissension more than ever."[67] Conservative columnist William F. Buckley applauded Judge Hoffman's tough stance against the "Maoist assault" of the defendants and predicted that the Chicago Seven would soon fall into obscurity, assuring *National Review* readers that "there is nothing more passé than last year's martyr."[68] Years later, chroniclers of the era still regard the trial as a severe blow to 1960s radicalism. In 1994, legal history scholar James W. Ely Jr. wrote: "Due in some measure to the Chicago prosecution, the movement began to wane. . . . Whether the conspiracy trial was intended to achieve a political result may be debated, but the proceedings unquestionably helped to still militant protest."[69]

Nonetheless, the widely held belief that the Chicago conspiracy trial contributed to the demise of dissent was challenged by the equally prevalent notion that it jump-started the ailing antiwar movement. Even though the personalities of the courtroom drama often overshadowed the defendants' antiwar message, the trial reached a far wider audience than did the most successful antiwar demonstrations. The sometimes abrasive and outrageous behavior of the defendants undoubtedly alienated a broad segment of the public. But like the most effective antiwar protests, the conspiracy trial weakened the public's confidence in government and the judicial system. In the early days of the trial, *New York Times* columnist Tom Wicker commented that ever since the Democratic National Convention, "things seem sharper now, more pointed, more dangerous. Mr. Nixon may tell us to lower our voices, but we are raising them instead."[70]

Daniel Patrick Moynihan, a social scientist (and, later, senator) admired by both Democrats and Republicans, regarded the trial as a disaster for American society. "The trial of the Chicago Seven was a terrible setback to the cause of social stability," he argued. "Authority was made to look foolish, incompetent, impotent, corrupt. Of all the people who buy judgeships in Chicago, how could we have chosen Hoffman?"[71] Looking back from the vantage point of 2004, Harvard law professor Alan Dershowitz reflected,

> I have often wondered how differently the case would have come out had the trial judge been a dignified, fair, and self-confident jurist. I suspect the defendants and their trial lawyers would have come off looking like fools had the judge given them a fair trial. But he did not, and by his obvious unfairness he made the defendants look good, at least in comparison to him.[72]

The trial's impact on the movement may have been ambiguous, but its effects on David Dellinger's personal life were unquestionably deleterious. Removing him from the antiwar movement for an extended period effectively reduced his influence in the national coalition. Jay Craven, later one of Dellinger's closest friends and confidants, explained: "Once the media identified the Chicago Eight as leaders, they put them outside the experience of the people in the movement and alienated them." Dellinger, he argued, was essentially "thrust into a position of being a leader without accountability. There was no mechanism, no feedback from, no dialogue with the rank and file. It played into a general backlash in the movement against all the leaders of the 60s."[73] Dellinger's family life also suffered. David was away from Betty for long periods of time, and his daughters experienced the traumatic ordeal of witnessing the harsh treatment of their father in the court-room. During the trial, Ray Dellinger even changed his last name to "Sundance." He desperately wanted his own identity and could no longer cope with living in his father's shadow. "So I told Ray how much I loved him," David recalled, "how proud I was of him, and that I thoroughly agreed with his change of name."[74] After the Chicago conspiracy verdicts, the Dellingers' marriage fell apart; David's physical health continued to deteriorate; and there was little he could do to forestall the decline of the protest movements. But he stuck tenaciously to his radical vision of peace and social justice, even as history veered sharply in a different direction.

11

Staying the Course

> Never cancel a rally or meeting. That's the golden rule of the movement. If even one person has troubled to come, carry on as if there are 1000. Every individual counts and bearing witness counts.
>
> David Dellinger

NO OTHER DECADE transformed David Dellinger's life as significantly as the 1960s. When it began, he still lived in the shadow of A. J. Muste, working as one of several editors of an increasingly influential but still marginal leftist magazine, and he was barely known outside radical pacifist circles. But by the close of the decade, he had become a leader in one of the largest mass protest movements in American history, a defendant in the famous—some say infamous—Chicago conspiracy trial, and a widely demanded speaker on college campuses across the nation. Although the era that Dellinger came to know as the "sixties" did not necessarily begin in 1960 or end in 1970, a precipitous decline of the sort of activism that he championed was evident by the early 1970s. So embedded in antiwar work and so optimistic was Dellinger that he hardly noticed it until the movement was nearly dormant by the mid-1970s. At the same time, Dellinger's health and marriage took a turn for the worse.

Reasons to be discouraged abounded in mid-1970s: Ultraleft factions were self-destructing. Old comrades were scaling back their commitments or dropping out of the movement altogether. Federal officials were continuing their crackdowns. And a broad segment of the American public—weary after years of catastrophic warfare in Southeast Asia and upheaval at home—found solace in President Nixon's decision to withdraw American troops from Vietnam and pursue "peace with honor." The public's hunger for order and calm persisted even as Nixon's presidency collapsed under the crippling weight of the Watergate scandal. Against this backdrop, Dellinger did his best to stay true to his ideals. He continued his crusade, albeit on a smaller scale, long after the last American military personnel had left South Vietnam in 1975. He launched a magazine called *Seven Days*, which he hoped would become the *Newsweek* of the American left. He changed from organizing anti–Vietnam War protests in the first half of the decade to staging antinuclear protests in the late 1970s. In his private life, he finally realized what a terrible mistake he had made by ignoring his marriage for so long. Although he tried to repair his relationship with Betty, he soon discovered that reconciliation required the same level of commitment and determination as had his public struggles to eradicate war, poverty, and racism.

On April 30, 1970, President Nixon announced the American invasion of Cambodia in a televised speech to the nation, triggering a storm of upheaval across the nation. The first demonstrations began on the night of his speech, and within four days student strikes were under way at more than a hundred schools. Eventually 350 colleges and high schools went on strike. The night before Nixon's announcement, Dellinger attended a New Mobe meeting with about twenty others at Norma Becker's home to plan the upcoming "spring offensive." Part way into the meeting Dellinger answered a telephone call alerting the organizers that in Southeast Asia a joint U.S. and South Vietnamese invasion force was marching eastward into Cambodia.[1] After hearing the news, participants at the New Mobe meeting unanimously decided to conduct a series of mass protests at the White House on May 9.

In early May, Dellinger spent several days participating in demonstrations at his alma mater, Yale University.[2] He then went to Washington, D.C., for the May 9 national demonstration, an event that, despite short notice, drew 100,000 people. At the time, the New Mobe was broke and beset by several internal divisions, the worst being between Fred Halstead and his supporters in the SWP against Dave Dellinger and his fellow direct actionists. The hostility between Halstead and Dellinger threatened to tear apart the coalition. During the previous two years, the two men had hardened their positions, and neither was willing to compromise. Halstead found Dellinger's anarchical position to be inimical to the coalition, arguing that Dellinger encouraged "impatient" and "reckless militancy" by advocating "the tactic of small-group sallies" without any long-term strategy. "The harm came," Halstead insisted, "from his attempts to subordinate mass mobilizations to these peripheral activities and his insistent efforts to impose such methods on the movement as a whole."[3]

Dellinger fired back at the SWP in *Liberation* and other periodicals, assailing Halstead and his comrades as undemocratic, condemning them for packing meetings with obedient party members, and denouncing their opposition to civil disobedience. He denied Halstead's charge that he was attempting to "subordinate" mass protests to smaller civil disobedience actions. Instead, he asserted in the *Village Voice* in the spring of 1970 that "such activities as work stoppages, draft-board disruptions, and other organized attempts to paralyze the war machine . . . [would] add power and variety to the movement's assortment of tactics."[4]

In the days leading up to May 9, the planning meetings became little more than forums for emotional debates. Moderates were pleased that they had received permits from the government to hold a mass rally in the Ellipse, a vast, circular, grassy area near the White House, and they firmly rejected all proposals for civil disobedience. Radicals, in contrast, called for militant resistance and accused their opponents of equivocating. The coalition's unraveling could not have come at a worse time. National opinion polls indicated plunging support for the Vietnam War, and communities across America were increasingly receptive to protest. In September 1970, a record 55 percent of Americans polled called for a complete withdrawal of troops from Southeast Asia as soon as possible.[5] The times demanded a unified antiwar movement. Still, Halstead and Dellinger were unwilling to put aside their differences, and the New Mobe succumbed to sectarianism. Nowhere was this destructive tendency more evident than at the May 9 protests.

By 1 P.M. around 120,000 people showed up at the Ellipse to listen to three hours of speakers and musicians. For this event alone, four thousand marshals had been specially trained by the New Mobe to prevent violence and maintain order. It was hot and humid, and many demonstrators in the audience were overcome by heat exhaustion. One after another, a long line of speakers—a mixture of senators, antiwar luminaries, and lesser-known New Mobe operatives—denounced Nixon's invasion of Cambodia. The protest lasted into the late afternoon; the speeches droned on under the sweltering sun; and people began to leave the Ellipse before it ended. A headline in the *Washington*

Post blared, "It Was Just Too Hot for Revolution," while *Time* called the event a "letdown" and a "canned antiwar rally."[6]

Unknown to the audience, a quarrel broke out backstage between Halstead and Dellinger. Dellinger wanted to announce that he planned to lead a march up Fifteenth and Seventeenth streets to the White House for anyone interested in committing civil disobedience. A frazzled Brad Lyttle, who had usually sided with Dellinger in the past, now backed Fred Halstead and at one point broke down and wept during the bickering. This was not the time or place, Lyttle and Halstead argued, to commit civil disobedience. Dellinger disagreed, knowing that twenty thousand people in the audience that day were prepared to do so. But Halstead and Lyttle refused to back down and ultimately threatened Dellinger. "If I urged people to join me in civil disobedience," recalled Dellinger, "which is what I wanted to do, they were going to cut the microphone."[7]

At 4:00 P.M., Dellinger spoke, calling on the crowd to join his march but refraining from mentioning anything about "civil disobedience," and thus few people understood the purpose of the action. Dellinger's march therefore was a flop. It was disorganized, poorly directed, and involved only a thousand or so people. Lacking a clear focus, it ultimately broke apart. Overall, the May 9 mass mobilization in Washington, D.C., acquired the dubious reputation as one of the most poorly organized and inept protests in the history of the antiwar movement. Not only was the main rally judged to be an overlong and uninspiring rehash of past national gatherings, but the paltry attempts at mass civil disobedience afterward quickly fizzled.

The New Mobe died on May 9, and the coalition builders went in different directions. So divided were the surviving remnants that it took them almost a year to mount another successful national mobilization. The remaining activists scrambled to rebuild coalitions. The SWP and some of its allies founded the National Peace Action Coalition (NPAC) at a conference in Cleveland in June. NPAC stayed under the firm control of the Trotskyists for the remainder of the war. Not to be outdone, the radical pacifists and like-minded antiwar activists, including Dellinger, met for the Strategy Action Conference in Milwaukee in September and formed the National Coalition against War, Racism and Repression (NCAWRR), nicknamed by its detractors the "coalition against everything."[8]

Dellinger, Rennie Davis, Sid Peck, Brad Lyttle, Cora Weiss, and David McReynolds became the leaders of the new coalition. In February 1971, NCAWRR became the People's Coalition for Peace and Justice (PCPJ). But the tired organizers planned only relatively small events for the fall and instead looked ahead to the spring of 1971 for large mobilizations. Meanwhile, student strikes continued into the fall; liberal antiwar groups such as SANE, FOR, and Clergy and Laity Concerned (CALC) campaigned for dovish political candidates running in the 1970 midterm elections; and GIs and antiwar Vietnam veterans initiated numerous actions.

Within weeks of the May 9 demonstration, President Nixon withdrew U.S. forces from Cambodia. He continued to favor a gradual "Vietnamization," the steady withdrawal of U.S. troops from South Vietnam, to be replaced by soldiers from the Army of the Republic of Vietnam (ARVN). Together with Vietnamization came an intensification of the air war and the allocation of billions of dollars in military and economic aid to bolster the vulnerable Saigon regime. These changing policies in Indochina took away much of the wind from the sails of the antiwar movement. Many activists stepped back and pondered the future; some left the movement altogether. Not surprisingly, by the summer and fall of 1970, Dellinger was burned out. "None of us can escape our share of shame," he wrote, "for not having been able to overcome the difficulties that enervated and partially isolated the antiwar movement at a time when the antiwar sentiment of the country was growing by leaps and bounds."[9]

Equally vexing to Dellinger was the emergence of small revolutionary sects throughout the country, especially the Weathermen. After walking out of the Cook County jail in March 1970, he was shocked to hear about a deadly explosion that had ripped through a Manhattan townhouse owned by the father of one of the Weathermen. The militants had been careless with their incendiary devices, and the explosion killed two men and a woman, all of whom Dellinger had known. After that, there were hundreds of bombings, carried out by numerous ultra-left factions, across America. Nearly all of them were carefully orchestrated to take place in the middle of the night and claimed surprisingly few lives but still caused millions of dollars of property damage. These tactics, Dellinger feared, reflected a growing nihilism in the antiwar movement. Nonetheless, it also became fashionable for both conservative foes of the antiwar movement and moderate doves to dismiss the Weathermen as mere thugs. Dellinger avoided such denouncements, understanding the radicals' desperation even as he deplored their methods. Rather than condemn them, he attempted to persuade the Weathermen he knew to return to the nonviolent antiwar fold, but with limited success. By the fall, though, his patience with the Weathermen had worn thin, and he voiced his frustrations in the pages of *Liberation*: "It is time that the no longer New Left take a serious look at where it was going and what it is becoming." Opponents of the Vietnam War, he insisted, must "stop playacting at violent revolution."[10]

In the summer of 1970, Dellinger and Rennie Davis began planning the most ambitious mass civil disobedience event ever, the May Day protests, in Washington, D.C., adhering to the conventional wisdom that spring was the best time to hold large demonstrations. They also established yet another group, the May Day Collective (also known as the May Day Tribe), to organize the actions. Almost a year of planning and preparation went into the spring protests, and virtually no detail was overlooked. By this time, the members of the May Day Collective believed that traditional national mobilizations no longer sufficed. No longer encumbered by domineering Trotskyists, Dellinger and Davis planned to carry out direct, nonviolent action in the very center of American power. They managed to gather a small army of dedicated activists to volunteer full time for the May Day Tribe. In the summer of 1970, Davis traveled to numerous antiwar conferences and college campuses pitching the idea of May Day demonstrations and seeking support for his plans. One of the young people he brought into the fold was the nineteen-year-old Boston University student Jay Craven. Craven had briefly met Dellinger in early 1970 when he had come to speak at Boston University, and he had become acquainted with Davis around the same time. "One of the strongest images of my lifetime," Craven later recounted, "will be the sight when the door opened, of Dave Dellinger sitting in an overstuffed chair, smoking a cigar and drinking a glass of cognac . . . looking every inch the Godfather."[11] Craven worked full time for the May Day Tribe throughout the winter of 1971, organizing alongside Davis, Dellinger, and Michael Lerner, one of the Seattle Eight activists indicted for draft resistance and the future editor of *Tikkun* magazine. They produced a short documentary entitled *Time Is Running Out*, narrated by singer Joni Mitchell, about the history of the Vietnamese people and their resistance against foreign domination.[12]

They also printed the *May Day Tactical Manual*, which they distributed to those activists across America planning to organize local delegations to attend the May Day demonstrations. The Tribe's extreme anarchical politics leaned toward decentralized turmoil. As the manual stressed, "The aim of the May Day action is to raise the social cost of the war to a level unacceptable to America's rulers. To do this we seek to create the spectre of social chaos while maintaining the support or at least toleration of the broad masses of American people."[13]

Dellinger wore two hats in early 1971, as a leader of the PCPJ and a co-coordinator of the May Day protests. Jay Craven explained: "Dave's contribution was the commitment to civil disobedience, whereas Rennie tended to be more of the feet on the ground with young constituencies and mobilizing them. And Dave worked with the traditional peace movement, wrote about all of this, and was in all of the meetings to decide strategy."[14] He also supported the People's Peace Treaty, a grassroots effort by Vietnamese and American students and peace groups to fashion a treaty to end the war in Southeast Asia and establish social justice at home. Gradually, the itinerary for April and May began to take shape. The antiwar veterans in the Vietnam Veterans Against the War (VVAW) organization planned to open the spring offensive on Monday, April 19, with a week of lobbying, guerrilla theater, camping out on the Mall, marches, and a medal-throwing ceremony. On April 24, two legal mass rallies, sponsored by NPAC, would be held in Washington, D.C., and San Francisco. In February, the Nixon administration supported a South Vietnamese invasion of Laos. But peace advocates expecting an explosion of activism like that following the invasion of Cambodia were disappointed. The turnout at nationwide antiwar demonstrations was dismal. Dellinger and Davis were disheartened by a poorly attended rally at the White House, fearing it was an omen of things to come.

While Dellinger was preparing for April 24 and the May Day protests, the army of antiwar veterans in the VVAW invaded Washington, D.C. They established a huge campsite in the Mall on Sunday, April 18, in preparation for their weeklong protest, Dewey Canyon III, named after two earlier invasions of Laos (codenamed Dewey Canyon I and II). Dellinger had met several VVAWers at previous demonstrations and had befriended the national coordinator, Al Hubbard, while the two of them served on the PCPJ coordinating committee. During the following week, the veterans lobbied, marched, performed guerilla theater, addressed crowds at famous Washington landmarks, conducted nonviolent civil disobedience, and testified before Congress. The authorities recognized the special clout of the VVAWers and tried unsuccessfully to undermine their momentum. President Nixon received hourly updates on their protests, and the U.S. Supreme Court ruled during the week that the veterans could not sleep in the Mall. On the night of Wednesday, April 22, the VVAWers voted to defy the court and sleep at their campsite. While the veterans waited nervously to see whether the police would arrive and haul them away to jail, Dellinger showed up at the tent city to a warm welcome. "If you go to jail, I'll go with you," he told a crowd of cheering veterans.[15] But under secret orders from President Nixon, the District of Columbia police did not arrest the veterans, leaving the door wide open for their medal-throwing ceremony.[16]

On Friday, April 23, a thousand or more decorated and honorably discharged Vietnam veterans lined up at the Capitol Building, surrounded on all sides by thousands of observers. One by one, the veterans approached the microphone, made a short statement, and then turned and hurled their medals and other war-related items in the direction of Congress. Most of the stalwarts in the antiwar movement anticipated that the VVAW's demonstrations would serve as a prelude to the April 24 march and the May Day protests. But as it turned out, the VVAW's self-described "limited incursion into the country of Congress"—though it never surpassed more than a few thousand participants—was arguably the antiwar movement's most influential act of resistance. A Pennsylvania newspaper described it as "the smallest yet the most meaningful and perhaps the most effective of all the peace demonstrations Washington has seen."[17] The *Akron Beacon Journal* editorialized: "Whatever their number, they at least are speaking what they themselves believe. Their testimony must inevitably carry more weight than the protests or endorsements of those who have never seen this war first-hand."[18]

The next day—Saturday, April 24—hundreds of thousands of protesters assembled at the Ellipse for a march to the Capitol. It turned out to be the antiwar movement's largest mass march and rally. At 11:00 A.M., one hour before the march was originally scheduled to begin, people spilled out of the Ellipse and proceeded slowly down Pennsylvania and Constitutional avenues to the Capitol. From sidewalk to sidewalk, marchers of all ages and from all walks of life packed the streets, chanting and singing and carrying placards and banners. They filled the west lawn of the Capitol and flooded into the Mall. Eventually, their numbers reached half a million (some estimates ran as high as 750,000). The rally lasted for five hours. David Dellinger, Coretta Scott King, Rev. Ralph Abernathy, Congresswoman Bell Abzug, Senator Ernest Gruening, and VVAW leader John Kerry all spoke. The rally in San Francisco attracted an unprecedented 250,000 people. In total, almost a million people protested that day.

Although protests continued in Washington during the week between April 24 and the May Day actions, the relative interlude gave Dellinger, Davis, and other May Day Collective members more time to coordinate their plans for the following week. The purpose of May Day, Dellinger explained, was to "shut down the city this time." As one of the lead organizers of the event, he regarded himself as a "reconciler . . . trying to increase human understanding between competing groups, both within the movement and between the movement and those outside."[19] But anyone familiar with the May Day Tribe knew that Rennie Davis, not David Dellinger, ran the show. Dellinger was more of a figurehead, and Davis could be a real wild card. He was enigmatic, and nobody quite knew what to expect of him. Although he had been less prone to violence than Tom Hayden had been in the months leading up to the 1968 Democratic National Convention, he nevertheless remained susceptible to apocalyptic rhetoric. "Rennie . . . was very sharp and so reserved that I could not be sure what he really had in mind," remembered David McReynolds.[20] Still, Dellinger assured prospective allies that May Day would be nonviolent and a huge success. "I went to Brooklyn to talk to Dave Dellinger," explained McReynolds, "who said he felt quite sure that Rennie would remain nonviolent. Pretty sure, but not absolutely sure."[21]

The May Day events opened on the night of Saturday, May 1, with a free, all-night rock concert next to the Jefferson Memorial, attended by fifty thousand young people. It ended abruptly at dawn when police revoked the permit for the park because of the widespread use of drugs. Most of the attendees, exhausted after a long night of music and partying, willingly left the park, although two hundred stayed behind and were arrested.[22] The May Day protests began in earnest on the morning of May 3. Around fifteen thousand radicals surged into Washington from all directions, many wearing handkerchiefs and goggles or army surplus gas masks over their face to protect them from teargas and mace. Riot police, reinforced in several locations by federal troops, awaited their arrival. David Dellinger's exact role in the protest remains difficult to determine. The anarchical nature of the May Day protests (they were intended to be "decentralized and leaderless," wrote Noam Chomsky in the *New York Review of Books*),[23] the record number of people arrested for civil disobedience, and the general state of confusion in Washington were a recipe for chaos. As was the case at the 1967 Pentagon march, Dellinger was instrumental in planning the May Day action but seems to have disappeared from the picture quite early in the actual protests. He did not assume an important leadership role during the three days of upheaval. To the credit of the May Day organizers and participants, however, incidents of property damage in the demonstrations were rare and isolated, and at no point did May Day ever degenerate into another Days of Rage.[24]

On the first day, the protesters obstructed bridges and major thoroughfares, blocked entrances to key government buildings, and held illegal antiwar demonstrations in several locations. When the police arrived, most of the protesters fled. But by 8:00 A.M., police had arrested more than two thousand, and the clashes continued all day. At a press conference that afternoon, Rennie Davis made a disastrous decision that ultimately helped undermine the massive civil disobedience campaign. He told reporters, "We want to make clear that we failed this morning to stop the U.S. government."[25] Police promptly arrested him as he left the press conference. A number of May Day participants were dumbfounded by Davis's deflating announcement. "It was ridiculous, I couldn't believe he said it," remembered Sid Peck.[26] During the same press conference, to counter Davis, May Day organizer Jay Craven declared the protest so far a "success" and a "victory" for the antiwar movement.[27] But the damage had been done; Davis's words set the tone for the remainder of the May Day actions. Few people wanted to risk their health and livelihood for a "failed" demonstration.

By the end of the first day, the police had arrested 7,200 people, setting a record for a single day of civil disobedience in the nation's capital. On May 4 and 5, the protests continued throughout Washington, D.C., but not on the same scale as the opening day. By midweek, the May Day protests had petered out. Although they made front-page headlines in newspapers and top stories on network news, the press's conclusion was that May Day actions did not benefit the antiwar movement. "May Day, living up to all expectations," fumed syndicated liberal columnist Mary McGrory, "got the worst reviews of any demonstration in history. It was universally panned as the worst planned, worst executed, most slovenly, strident and obnoxious peace action every committed."[28] Other reactions varied, depending on the source. The Nixon administration applauded police and federal troops for maintaining order. Civil libertarians attacked the repressive police dragnets for arresting so many innocent people. David Dellinger and other radical antiwar activists regarded the event as a successful conclusion to the spring offensive. Dellinger even proclaimed: "From April 24 to Mayday (May 3) 1971, the antiwar movement produced ten days that shook the world."[29] Little did he realize that it would be the antiwar movement's swan song. "The era of mass anti–Vietnam War demonstrations," wrote historian Melvin Small, "came to a close in the spring of 1971."[30]

The new cohort of activists entering the movement in the late 1960s and early 1970s—people who had missed out on the Port Huron Statement, the Berkeley Free Speech Movement, and the early antiwar protests— knew David Dellinger primarily as the elder defendant in the Chicago conspiracy trial. To the older movement veterans, he was the "old-line" pacifist who helped sow the seeds of the current revolt. There was, however, another side of his political commitment that was often overshadowed by his work in the coalition. Between 1969 and 1972, Dellinger tried his hand at citizen diplomacy, traveling to Paris and North Vietnam and serving as a conduit between the Hanoi government and the families of American prisoners of war (POWs) back in the United States. He eventually helped secure the release of several American POWs from North Vietnamese prisons, thanks in part to his tireless, behind-the-scenes work.

During his earlier visits to Vietnam in 1966 and 1967, Dellinger had established ties with officials in the Hanoi regime and the thriving Vietnamese peace movement. He also interviewed American POWs and sympathized with them, perhaps because of his own ordeals in prison. In addition, he had met several Vietnamese revolutionaries during his 1967 trip to Bratislava, Czechoslovakia, and had stayed in contact with them over the years. "We were deeply stirred by the great demonstrations in Chicago (which the press rightly called 'The Battle of Chicago,')," wrote Le Phuong, a Vietnamese peace activist whom Dellinger had met in Bratislava. "Please send to all our most affectionate greetings of solidarity and friendship."[31] Dellinger promised his Vietnamese friends that he would use his newfound prominence to help broker a peaceful settlement to the war. Throughout the 1960s, many antiwar activists acted as citizen diplomats, almost always with positive results.

In 1967, Tom Hayden negotiated the release of three prisoners of war held captive by the National Liberation Front in South Vietnam. The following year, Dellinger, at the request of his close friend Do Xuan Oanh of the Vietnam Peace Committee, organized a two-person delegation to secure the release of additional POWs. In 1968, the Vietnam Peace Committee sent a telegram to Dellinger stating, "In celebration of our New Year Tet holiday, we are preparing to release three captured American pilots to the American peace movement. Please send responsible representative for reception and discussion."[32] Dellinger persuaded two trusted friends, Professor Howard Zinn of Boston University and Jesuit priest Daniel Berrigan to go to North Vietnam to facilitate the release of three American pilots. The POWs, along with Berrigan and Zinn, returned home to a warm reception in the United States. A similar delegation, headed by Stewart Meacham of the American Friends Service Committee, persuaded the Hanoi regime to free three more POWs. In the summer of 1969, Dellinger used his connections with Hanoi—especially his close friendship with Premier Pham Van Dong——to conduct negotiations with the North Vietnamese delegation to the Paris peace talks. Wrote Dellinger's close friend Do Xuan Oanh in early 1969: "In the present situation, your presence is more important than ever. You will provide an important voice, that of the peace movement, and you are trusted by the Vietnamese people."[33]

Months before his 1969 Paris trip, Dellinger received communiqués from officials in the Hanoi government, as well as from independent Vietnamese peace activists, requesting his help. "At different times, I was asked to take part in the POW release," he recounted. "Once I received a teletype message asking me to come over to release some POWs."[34] Peace talks between American and Vietnamese leaders had been under way in Paris for more than a year before Dellinger flew there on July 8. Negotiators representing the communist North Vietnamese government, the noncommunist Saigon regime, and the Johnson and Nixon administrations met from 1968 until 1972 to settle on terms of peace. When David arrived in Paris, he was under indictment for the Chicago Democratic National Convention protests. In a rare move that underscored his growing leverage, State Department officials went to Chicago in advance of his trip to persuade Judge Julius Hoffman to lift the travel restrictions imposed by the Chicago indictments to enable him to fly to Paris.[35]

On July 9, representatives of the North Vietnamese delegation whisked Dellinger away to an "undisclosed" location to discuss the fate of a group of POWs that Hanoi officials were considering releasing. He spent a few hours talking to Colonel Ha Van Lau, deputy leader of the Hanoi delegation. The colonel regarded the release of POWs as a good-faith gesture that would present a more positive image of the regime to the American people. By selecting a citizen diplomat who also happened to be a peace activist, the North Vietnamese hoped to heighten the prestige of the antiwar movement. Dellinger, too, regarded the meetings as a possible coup for the movement. He met with Colonel Lau twice, and after they established the terms of the POWs' release, Dellinger spent an hour meeting with Henry Cabot Lodge, who was both the chief U.S. negotiator and the U.S. ambassador to South Vietnam, on July 10. "Ambassador Lodge gave me assurances that there would be no interference with free transport provided by the antiwar movement for the released prisoners," Dellinger told the press.[36]

Their efforts to free the POWs led to a friendship between Dellinger and the antiwar activist Cora Weiss. The two had known each other since the mid-1960s, when Weiss began attending antiwar coalition planning meetings as a representative of Women Strike for Peace. The daughter of wealthy radical philanthropists Sam and Vera Rubin, Cora first was attracted to progressive politics in the 1950s while she was a student at the University of Wisconsin in Madison. During her sophomore year she collected student signatures on a petition to recall Senator Joseph McCarthy. For a time during the late 1950s and early 1960s, her activism focused on supporting African liberation struggles and opposing radioactive fallout from nuclear testing. Weiss never shied away from controversy, but within activist circles her politics were considered decidedly moderate. "I guess decency and justice came with my genes," she explained. "I've always participated in efforts to improve the quality of life and create an atmosphere of decency, to prevent conflict here as well as abroad."[37] In the early 1960s she sought an organization that rejected civil disobedience and radical rhetoric. She joined Women Strike for Peace (WSP) and served as a delegate from the organization to the national antiwar coalition. "I will say, retrospectively, that it was never easy for us inside that coalition," she recalled. "And it was over class reasons and gender reasons, both. We were women and we weren't poor and black. There was real resentment. But we played, in the end, a pivotal role because we insisted on making any action safe for new people. So they couldn't have *just* civil disobedience or they couldn't have *just* risk-taking and strident actions." Movement stalwarts, she remembered, "saw us as being in the political center, even though the rest of the country didn't."[38]

Camaraderie was slow to develop between Dellinger and Weiss. At first Dellinger found her politics too moderate, while Weiss concluded that he was hopelessly out of touch with women's experiences. "That was before Betty, Dave's wife, had succeeded in influencing him to become a little more quote—feminist—unquote," she remembered.[39] Slowly, steadily, a mutual affection deepened. Weiss served as the cochair for the gigantic November 15 Mobilization protest in Washington, D.C., which brought her into regular contact with Dellinger. A trip she made to Hanoi in late 1969 with fellow WSPers Ethel Taylor and Madeline Duckles supplied a much-needed human face for the war. In Hanoi, Weiss repeatedly met with high-level officials, who allowed her to mediate between the POWs in North Vietnam and their families in America. In addition, when she left for home, she brought with her a bundle of mail from 132 prisoners in Hanoi to their friends and loved ones. During the Chicago conspiracy trial, Weiss and Dellinger discussed the POWs and what the antiwar movement could do to help them. "We heard complaints in this country . . . that the mail wasn't getting through to the American POWs," Dellinger remembered, ". . . and that they weren't hearing from their loved ones. We told the Vietnamese that if it was true, it was a disgrace. They said it wasn't true."[40]

Both activists believed that the movement could play an important role in securing the release of more prisoners and acting as a conduit between the POWs and their families. Weiss contacted numerous families of captured American servicemen and found widespread support for the formation of a new organization to represent their needs. In January 1970, with the conspiracy trial still under way in Chicago, Weiss rented a cluster of offices in New York City and formally established the Committee of Liaison with Families of Servicemen Detained in North Vietnam (usually shortened to the Committee of Liaison).[41] "It was a cooperative effort," remembered Weiss. "Dave Dellinger and I were cochairs and initiated the committee. . . . I think there were no more than six of us altogether on the board. I became the executive director and ran the office. It was all done on a shoestring."[42]

For the next two years, the Committee of Liaison regularly ferried sacks of mail back and forth between the Untied States and Hanoi. By identifying itself so closely with families who had loved ones imprisoned in North Vietnam, the committee attained a level of respect that eluded many other antiwar groups. Moreover, officials in Hanoi trusted the key players in the committee and allowed them an unprecedented degree of freedom to perform their tasks. Several times a year delegations of committee supporters traveled to North Vietnam to deliver mail, investigate the treatment of POWs, and bring mail back to the United States. (The committee also lodged complaints about mistreated POWs while simultaneously denouncing the Nixon administration whenever the air war over North Vietnam intensified.) In 1970 alone, the committee shipped 3,671 letters between the two countries and made eighteen large mail deliveries.[43] On December 21, 1971, Dellinger and other committee members held a press conference announcing that volunteers had received a single delivery of 1,001 letters from Vietnam—the largest single shipment of letters from POWs yet during the war—in time for the Christmas holidays. The committee revealed as well that in the large shipment, "983 letters were from men detained in North Vietnam. Eighteen were from U.S. servicemen held by the Provisional Revolutionary Government in the South. It is the first time mail has been received from men held in the South." Dellinger read a statement rejoicing at the sizable shipment of mail while lamenting recent developments in the war. "In the past ten days," he announced, "six planes have been shot down. Four new prisoners are known to have been captured and two more are listed as MIA. The peace talks have been cancelled this month."[44]

The Committee of Liaison's high point came in September 1972. At the beginning of the month, Weiss and Dellinger went to Paris to meet with members of the North Vietnamese delegation. Topping their agenda was a discussion of the possible release of three American fliers—Major Edward Elias, Lieutenant Norris Charles, and Lieutenant Markham Gartley—from a Hanoi POW camp. The atmosphere at the peace talks was tense. Since May, American planes had been bombing targets in North Vietnam around the clock in an effort to pressure the regime to agree to the terms backed by the American delegation at the Paris peace talks. Weiss remembered that when she and Dellinger "went to Paris to make arrangements for the POW release," the two activists keenly felt the gravity of the moment and came to regard their actions as necessary to "end a wrong war that had absolutely no legitimacy morally or legally."[45]

At the Paris meetings Dellinger was in the middle of a month-long fast to protest the war and pressure Hanoi to release the POWs.[46] On September 2, he held a press conference to reveal the committee's plans to escort the three POWs back to the United States. He announced that a group of prominent antiwar figures and families of the POWs would go to Hanoi to escort the newly freed men back to the United States on commercial flights. This was necessary, Dellinger explained, to prevent military authorities from "kidnapping" and "brainwashing" them before they could meet with their families and the press.[47] In the United States days later, Weiss and Dellinger selected their fellow travelers: Princeton professor and human rights activist Richard Falk; Rev. William Sloane Coffin; Olga Charles, the wife of POW Norris Charles; Minnie Lee Gartley, mother of POW Markham Gartley; and Father Harry Bury and Marianne Hamilton of the International Assembly of Christians. Accompanying the travelers was the Pulitzer Prize–winning Associated Press correspondent Peter Arnett, who planned to file wire stories about the trip. For more than a week, the delegation stayed in a hotel in downtown Hanoi, awaiting the release of the three POWs. Conditions in the battle-scarred nation had worsened since Dellinger visited five years earlier. Only 27,000 American troops remained in Vietnam, yet the air war over North Vietnam had escalated sharply. Five air raid alerts sounded on Dellinger's first day in Hanoi alone. American planes repeatedly flew over the city, triggering mass evacuations. On one outing, the bombing sent Dellinger and other Committee of Liaison delegates scurrying into roadside ditches to take cover. Dellinger noticed far more bomb craters in the countryside than he had on his previous journey to North Vietnam.[48]

The North Vietnamese released the three POWs in late September to the Committee of Liaison delegation. The newly freed trio attended a packed press conference to answer questions. They, especially Markham Gartley, who had developed antiwar views while in prison, wanted to avoid U.S. military authorities. But the U.S. military wanted custody of the three men and pursued the Committee of Liaison delegation as far as Vientiane, Laos, despite Dellinger's warnings that continued military interference would undermine the likelihood of negotiating more POW releases in the future. The three ex-POWs and the Committee of Liaison delegation flew to Copenhagen, stopping in Beijing and Moscow on the way, with military officials in pursuit. The former POWs remained with the Committee of Liaison delegation until they arrived in New York on September 28. Intense pressure from authorities resulted in two of the POWs—Gartley and Charles—being taken away by armed forces personnel to military hospitals, despite the emotional and angry protests of family members.[49] Although the saga of the POWs generated front-page headlines in the *New York Times* and other newspapers across the country, the excitement faded quickly.

In Paris, the long agonizing quest for peace waxed and waned. In the fall of 1972, when it appeared to President Nixon that the North Vietnamese were stalling, he ordered round-the-clock bombings of Hanoi, Haiphong, and the surrounding regions. Although the strategy horrified observers around the world, it also pressured the North Vietnamese to meet the American demands. On January 27, 1973, U.S. Secretary of State Henry Kissinger and North Vietnamese negotiator Le Duc Tho signed the Paris Peace Accords. To the joy of antiwar activists, among the treaty's many provisions was the withdrawal within sixty days of the remaining 27,000 U.S. troops still in South Vietnam. Hanoi released the POWs in the spring.

In early October 1971, Marie Dellinger asked her son to come to Boston. Raymond Dellinger was in the hospital, and his doctors did not think he would live much longer. David dropped everything and went to Boston with his family, arriving to find his father frail and bedridden. Over the years David and his family had returned to Massachusetts and North Carolina for occasional Dellinger family reunions, but the ideological chasm that separated father and son had strained their relationship. Although David's parents remained devout Republicans, they did not abandon their son, and in time they grew more accepting of his unorthodox lifestyle. Indeed, many of David's pacifist experiments would have ended much sooner had it not been for Raymond's constant and generous financial support. "They're old now," David told his former Yale classmate Stewart Alsop during the Chicago conspiracy trial, "and they're worried about me going to jail again. . . . For a while they would send money, but of course I gave it away, so they stopped."[50]

David often cited his father as being the most important influence on his political beliefs. "I always felt that my politics were in a sense a carrying-out of the kind of attitude that he instilled in me toward human beings," he recounted.[51] When David arrived at his father's bedside, they sat together reminiscing about the old days in Wakefield. Raymond and Marie had moved out of the large Shumway Circle house in the 1940s into a much smaller house, and in the late 1960s they had moved yet again into a nursing home. But Raymond still had fond memories of coming home to Wakefield in the evenings from the law firm and seeing his children. Now hunched over Raymond's bedside, David reminded him of the time when the family was having dinner at a restaurant and the waitress accidentally spilled some sauce, but his father accepted responsibility so the waitress would not get in trouble. Raymond smiled and replied yes. Then he looked at David and stated, "I'm proud of the way you've lived your life."[52]

Raymond Dellinger died a few days later, on October 12, 1971, just a week before what would have been his eighty-fourth birthday. During the packed funeral service, David realized how beloved he had been. "As a sign of my mother's new attitude," he recalled,

> she asked me to speak at his funeral, crowded as it was bound to be— and was—with conventional Republican civic and business leaders, as well as many of the poor people whom my father befriended. My mother had become proud of me too. . . . I did speak, but my voice broke in the middle of what I was trying to say and I had to stop earlier than I had intended.[53]

After his father's death, David and Betty spent two months in Hawaii in the spring and summer of 1971, far away from the demands of the antiwar movement. Now in his mid-fifties, David could not maintain the same frenetic schedule of his youth. In August 1971, he retreated to a remote cabin in the woods of Vermont. "I read hard, think hard, struggle hard over writing, exercise hard and even undergo withdrawal feelings as I am reducing smoking to a bare minimum," he wrote to a friend. As a sign of the growing rift in his marriage, David did not invite Betty to the cabin. He confided in his friend, "One of the things that has regenerated and reinvigorated the relationship between Betty and me is re-discovering the importance of being apart as well as together, and not feeling guilty or remiss about being so."[54]

But it was not "being apart" from Betty that was a challenge for David. He rarely spent much time with her, and now, after thirty years of marriage, their relationship had grown distant. Undoubtedly, the rise of the feminist movement contributed to their discontent.

Sexism was pervasive in the antiwar movement as well. For years, women typed letters, ran errands, licked envelopes, answered telephones, delivered packages, and, at the end of the day, performed domestic duties at home. Meanwhile, men dominated the speakers' platforms at mass antiwar mobilizations, with the occasional token female luminary or congresswoman adding her voice to the protests. At the January 1969 counterinaugural protest, antiwar activist Marilyn Webb dared raise the issue of women's oppression in a speech that she considered mild. Standing on stage before a crowd of tens of thousands, she proclaimed, "Women must take control of our bodies. We must define our own issues." A few men in the audience began hooting and whistling, and hecklers shouted, "Take off your clothes!" and "Take her off stage and fuck her!" The sexist gestures triggered a huge brawl, and Dellinger accused Webb of "causing a riot."

Dellinger's performance at the counterinaugural protest was far from his finest moment. He not only warned Marilyn Webb to stop causing a riot, he asked her to tell the other "women to stop, they were going on too long." His behavior continued to worsen in the presence of the feminist antiwar activists on the platform. When a group of women at the counterinaugural asked the protesters to clear off the stage because it was on the verge of collapsing from all the people standing on it, Dellinger misrepresented their pleas in front of the large audience. "The women," he announced, "have asked all the men to leave the stage except the Vietnam vet who has earned the right to be there." By the early 1970s, some radical feminists were criticizing Dellinger and other movement leaders.[55]

In the spring of 1970, Dellinger's oldest daughter, Tasha Peterson (who had taken Betty's maiden name) moved into a militant feminist communal house in Washington, D.C. A year later Tasha immersed herself in the activities of "Those Women," a militant lesbian sect that embraced radical politics and rejected middle-class heterosexual feminist values.[56] Her decision caused both her parents to reevaluate previous assumptions about feminism. Like Tasha, Betty Dellinger felt the pull of women's liberation struggles. Although she did not share Tasha's militancy, she still developed new expectations and confronted old resentments. Betty began attending consciousness-raising seminars in New York and acknowledging the anger that had long been raging inside her. She spent years in therapy sorting through her feelings and making sense of her past. "I didn't know who I was anymore because he was getting so well-known. If you said the name 'Dellinger' anywhere, their eyes changed and they didn't see you anymore—they saw David. I felt like a shadow—I wasn't existing as a person anymore."[57] At the time of the Chicago trial, Betty began to consider her options.

> I was thinking of moving—all of the defendants from the trial had gotten together at Bill Kunstler's house, up in Westchester somewhere. . . . And I talked to Kunstler's wife, and she was having some of the same problems I was. He was just never there, and when he was home, he couldn't even see her. I was just part of the furniture, that's all.[58]

Sometime in the early 1970s, Betty Dellinger reclaimed her childhood name: Elizabeth Peterson. She no longer wanted to be Betty Dellinger, living in the shadow of her activist husband. It was a bold move for a woman who had previously been so mild mannered and eager to please. In the fall of 1972 Elizabeth arrived at the painful decision to leave David "to find myself. . . . We started out with an equal relationship, but over the years I gradually became just a caretaker. So I decided that we would start new again."[59] Elizabeth gave her youngest daughter, Michele—the only Dellinger still living at home—the option of coming with her. Michele declined, choosing to live with her father instead. Elizabeth moved into a basement apartment of a building owned by one of William Kunstler's daughters. Elizabeth recalled: "I knew I had to confine myself to really figure things out, and I decided not to have a phone because I wanted people to come to my house if they wanted to see me. My children, I told them to come over. And I left Dave a note, 'You have to take care of the bills now I'm gone,' because I had taken care of all the bills up until that time."[60]

For the next several years, Elizabeth fashioned her own identity apart from David. Whenever she saw him, he tried to persuade her to move back with him, but she resisted. To make ends meet, she found a job at a day care cooperative that paid a modest but regular salary. Leaving David also meant leaving the antiwar movement. Although Elizabeth still vehemently opposed U.S. involvement in Indochina, she was shocked by the way that other women in the movement treated her. "When I did leave David, they said, 'You're crazy . . . there are all these women just waiting for him.' So I got no support from the women in the movement."[61]

The Dellingers' marriage collapsed only a year after his father's death. In addition, David faced a series of debilitating health problems that in the early 1970s had taken him out of the antiwar movement for long stretches at a time. Throughout 1972 a malfunctioning gall bladder led to a whole host of physical problems until doctors finally removed it. His gall bladder operation prevented Dellinger from accompanying Rennie Davis to the signing of the Paris peace treaty in January. Next doctors removed a severely ruptured appendix, followed by an operation to take out tissue infected by an acute case of peritonitis. A hernia resulted in yet another operation and hospital stay, and while staying in Cape Cod, he tore ligaments in his knee, forcing knee surgery.

Physical problems removed Dellinger from peace activism at time when the antiwar movement was ailing as well. With the draft abolished and the president withdrawing troops from Vietnam, the activists' sense of urgency subsided. Signs of the decrepit state of the antiwar movement were evident at both the Democratic and Republican political conventions of 1972. Dellinger attended both events, in different capacities. The Democratic National Convention in Miami that July offered a glaring contrast to the events in Chicago four years earlier. This time, Abbie Hoffman, Jerry Rubin, and Tom Hayden were inside the convention hall instead of protesting in the streets. Dellinger, in the middle of a fast to protest the war in Indochina, went to Miami ostensibly to make sure that the Democratic platform included a strongly worded peace plank. He also carried messages from the North Vietnamese to the Democratic candidate, Senator George McGovern, inviting him to participate in the peace talks. "The Democratic convention was a party, from beginning to end," remarked writer/activist Jay Levin. "Lots of kids who'd been on the streets in 1968 were now delegates. Abbie and Jerry were greeted as heroes."[62]

The next month, Dellinger returned to Miami, still engaged in a fast he had begun more than a month earlier. He came to take part in a series of disorderly and largely ineffectual protests at the Republican National Convention. The scene in Miami was hectic and confused. Clusters of radicals camped in Flamingo Park at night and resisted during the day. Only the VVAW, with its silent marches and guerrilla theater, was still able to orchestrate protests that generated publicity. Some estimates of the turnout ran as high as ten thousand—a number comparable to that in Chicago four years earlier—but the demonstrations in

Miami were poorly organized and decisively beaten back by police using mace and teargas. "I doubt if there was two thousand people," remarked a Miami police officer. "And half the demonstrators were undercover people."[63] Cheering Republicans inside the convention hall were hardly aware of them.

All this time Dellinger's influence was shrinking. Most of the newcomers to the movement knew little about him or his earlier fame. In November 1972, the *Chicago Tribune* referred to Dellinger and the other Chicago conspiracy trial defendants as "a bunch of has-beens, transitory symbols of a fleeting era which most Americans, including the campus dissenters whom the seven pretended to represent, would just as soon forget."[64]

Fueling such negative and simplistic perceptions was the fate of several of the Chicago Eight defendants. In late August 1973, police arrested Abbie Hoffman while he was attempting to sell three pounds of cocaine.[65] The judge in the case set bail at ten thousand dollars, which was paid by the Abbie Hoffman and Friends Defense Committee. While out on bail, Abbie went into hiding and eventually moved to Fineview, New York, near the St. Lawrence River, where he adopted the pseudonym "Barry Freed" and championed environmentalist causes. Throughout the 1970s, he remained close to Dellinger, and the two stayed in regular contact for the rest of the decade. Jerry Rubin, too, maintained a warm relationship with Dellinger throughout the 1970s. But Rubin also drifted away from the movement. After the Chicago trial, Rubin's rants became more irrational, culminating with his disturbing celebration of the mass murderer Charles Manson after visiting the psychopath in prison. Rubin's political drift away from radicalism began shortly after that, and by 1972 he conceded that he had "become more conservative."[66] Rubin eventually settled in San Francisco, where he began living a "very moderate life based on low expectations."[67]

Likewise, Tom Hayden's priorities shifted. Living on the West Coast, he married actress Jane Fonda and began working full time for the moderate Indochina Peace Campaign (IPC), a key organization in the later antiwar movement. The IPC, bankrolled by Fonda's sizable war chest, sponsored traveling antiwar rallies, complete with speakers, singers, and other entertainers. From time to time, Dellinger worked with the IPC, and his friendship with Jane Fonda grew warmer even as he remained wary of Hayden.

Two years later, Dellinger strongly criticized Hayden for abandoning protest politics to run for the U.S. Senate seat in California held by John V. Tunney. By 1976 Hayden had moved on to a new phase of his life, which he described as a "transition from protest to power, from arguing political realignment to making it happen."[68] Dellinger, more anarchical now than ever, wrote an editorial in the *New York Times* denouncing Hayden's view that the Washington political establishment had been cleansed in the wake of Watergate. "Nothing has happened," Dellinger wrote, "to justify this shift from the politics of Power to the People back to the discredited politics of Power to a Handful of Politicians in Washington Elected by the People, not even if the candidates include enlightened veterans of the struggles of the 60s."[69]

For Dellinger personally, the most disheartening defection was Rennie Davis's decision to become a follower of the fifteen-year-old Indian guru Maharaj Ji. In the late 1960s and early 1970s, Dellinger and Davis had been extremely close politically. Some even considered Davis to be Dellinger's disciple. As the mastermind of the May Day protests, Davis was saturated by media exposure in the spring of 1971. Few other activists experienced the same constant and intense level of beatings, teargassings, and jail time that he so stoically endured. The final straw came at the Republican National Convention, when Davis, forty-two days into a fast and marching alongside Dellinger to the convention hall, was struck in the chest by a flying teargas canister. Dazed, poisoned, and frail, Davis shortly thereafter embarked on a spiritual odyssey. He accompanied a friend to India and spent time at a Himalayan retreat inhabited by other Americans living with the young teacher Maharaj Ji. Sudden enlightenment came to Davis, prompting him to abandon his New Left radicalism. The conversion cost him numerous friendships. "Here was my best friend in front of me," remembered Hayden, "present in form only, his mind gone somewhere else."[70] Abbie Hoffman thought Davis had gone crazy. Dellinger was mature enough to remain open minded about the abrupt transformation. Unfortunately, Davis wrongly interpreted Dellinger's tolerance to mean that he was "open to the teachings," so Davis began proselytizing. Months after Davis attempted to convert him, Dellinger remarked, "I can't understand it. . . . Rennie smiled and told me our meeting was meant to be, but I don't see how he could have the idea that I was ripe for conversion."[71]

Dellinger's fellow stalwarts in the antiwar movement proved more durable. Sid Peck, Fred Halstead, Norma Becker, Sid Lens, Brad Lyttle, Cora Weiss, and Doug Dowd continued organizing demonstrations throughout the 1970s. President Nixon's landslide presidential victory over George McGovern in November 1972 did not slow their efforts. On January 20, 1973, Dellinger and other leaders in the coalition joined about 100,000 people at the second counterinaugural demonstration to protest the inauguration of Richard Nixon.

Between the signing of the Paris Peace Accords at the end of January and the fall of Saigon in April 1975, a diminished but lively antiwar movement maintained pressure on the Nixon administration to cut aid to the Thieu regime in South Vietnam and to cease the bombing of Cambodia. PCPJ and NPAC folded not long after the peace treaty, but other protests flared up elsewhere. Revelations of the Watergate scandal and Nixon's attempt to cover it up fueled a thriving, grassroots "Impeach Nixon" campaign, in which Dellinger played a small but recurring role. On May 11, 1975, the final mass antiwar rally took place in Central Park. Fifty thousand people came out to celebrate the end of the war in Southeast Asia. Dellinger spoke at the Central Park rally. "We've worked hard for this day," Dellinger told the cheering crowd. "The war is over!"[72]

Even before the Vietnam War finally ended, Dellinger began searching for a new direction. By the mid-1970s he was sensing a shift in the national political scene, although what many people called "the sixties" he merely regarded as a moment when the struggles for social justice and the celebrations of free thought gained wider-than-usual audiences. Following Gandhi, he concluded that it did not matter whether thousands of people agreed with him or nobody did. Instead, he needed to continue speaking truth to power, regardless of the size of the crowd at a demonstration.

Writing absorbed much of David Dellinger's time for the remainder of the decade. His main project beginning in 1972 was a book about the antiwar movement. Partly an autobiographical account, partly an analysis of nonviolent tactics, partly an attempt to explain and justify his decisions as a leader, and partly a hodgepodge of previously published *Liberation* articles, the book was not so much a conventional history of the antiwar movement as it was an extended essay. Following Barbara Deming's suggestion, he called it *More Power Than We Know: The People's Movement toward Democracy*. It was his second book, after his 1970 *Revolutionary Nonviolence,* a collection of his *Liberation* articles and earlier pieces dating back to World War II.

Even before *More Power Than We Know* was published, Dellinger turned his attention once again to radical journalism. *Liberation* still appeared on newsstands, and Dellinger now sat on its "editorial collective," but by the mid-1970s it was in its final throes. Dellinger's heart was no longer in the magazine, and each month featured fewer of his pieces.

What the left needed, Dellinger decided, was a new magazine. In 1974, he began building support among like-minded journalists to launch a leftist weekly magazine, complete with illustrations. Dellinger then drafted a statement of purpose, which included likely contributors and a breakdown of expenses. He called the magazine *Seven Days* and envisioned its being a biweekly filled with news and information for a variety of progressives. He wanted *Seven Days* to represent the best of both worlds. Handsomely laid out with plenty of color, its content would reflect the finest contributions from both well-established radical journalists and new, up-and-coming talent. Although he condemned the mainstream press as being dominated by corporate interests and advertisers, he also found the "the radical press . . . too blatantly ideological or rhetorical to be palatable to most audiences."[73]

Along with a few other younger radical journalists, Dellinger created a nonprofit group, the Institute for New Communications, and rented a large office in New York City. Fund-raising became his highest priority. In early 1975 he began soliciting funds for the magazine, targeting left-leaning Hollywood celebrities such as Peter Fonda, Jon Voight, Dustin Hoffman, and Steve Allen. Checks began trickling in, some as large as $10,000.

In the early months of *Seven Days,* everything fell into place. Firm commitments to contribute pieces came from Seymour Hersh, Susan Sontag, Ram Das, Elinor Langer, and Rita Mae Brown. Money—some donated, some lent—arrived daily. Film critic Peter Biskind, author Barbara Ehrenreich, and numerous others joined the *Seven Days* staff, though most of the magazine's articles came from freelance writers. In its pages appeared articles about California governor Jerry Brown, nuclear power, American Indian activism, Third World liberation movements, Bruce Springsteen and the E Street Band, President Jimmy Carter's hawkish policies, the Trilateral Commission, layoffs of steelworkers, and the environmentalist movement. Correspondents reported from as far away as Zaire, Pakistan, Iran, the Soviet Union, Indonesia, Japan, and Peru. Each issue also contained photographs and cartoons. Dellinger was proud of his creation. But as he had often done in the past, Dellinger chose to ignore warning signs, especially the demise of several important alternative periodicals in the mid-1970s, including *New Times*, *Ramparts*, *Politicks*, and, of course, *Liberation*. He was determined to make *Seven Days* into an enduring radical magazine. "At last," he told prospective readers in a pitch letter, "there's a major national newsmagazine that fills in the gaps and tells you what's really going on."[74]

In the late 1970s, while not promoting or editing the magazine, he tried new varieties of political activism. On July 4, 1976, Dellinger was one of several speakers at the People's Bicentennial Rallies in Philadelphia, a series of protests commemorating the two-hundredth anniversary of the United States. The main rally attracted a crowd of 30,000.[75] Then he worked hard throughout the summer to organize a march on the 1976 Democratic National Convention in New York. A peace parade the following October brought together two thousand protesters in Washington, D.C., and gave Dellinger a welcome opportunity to march alongside his close friend Sid Lens from the Mobe days.

For many nonviolent activists, including Dellinger, the struggle for nuclear disarmament replaced the anti–Vietnam War movement. In 1977, David gathered with antiwar movement comrades Lens, Norma Becker, and Sid Peck to create the Mobilization for Survival, an antinuclear coalition that called for nuclear disarmament, a halt to the arms race, an end to nuclear power, and a shift from military spending to human needs.[76] A wave of activism in the spring culminated with a mass rally at the United Nations building on May 28, 1978, scheduled to coincide with the United Nations conference on disarmament. The antinuclear protests of the late 1970s usually drew smaller crowds than had even the most modest anti–Vietnam War rallies.

Dellinger did not assume a key leadership position in the antinuclear coalition, as he had in the anti–Vietnam War movement. Rather, his determination to see *Seven Days* succeed outweighed his desire to return to coalition work. But the magazine repeatedly faltered. In the fall of 1977, *Seven Days* temporarily ceased publication and remained dormant for several months owing to insufficient funds. In early 1978, *Seven Days* resumed publication after a hiatus of almost half a year. The number of subscriptions surpassed fifty thousand in the summer, still a far cry from the quarter-million subscribers to *Mother Jones* but promising nevertheless. Dellinger reckoned that more high-profile contributors would bolster subscriptions. In May, he begged Arthur Miller to submit an article, but the playwright politely declined. "To be honest with you," Miller told Dellinger, "I'm not at all convinced that such a magazine, financed by 'the people' can very long compete with corporate giants whose resources give them something speciously or actually new to offer in every issue."[77]

Soon, letters detailing *Seven Days*'s questionable business practices began flooding in. In August 1978, San Francisco literary agent Ken McEldowney wrote to Dellinger asking why two of his clients, Karen and Warren Sharpe, had not yet been paid for an article of theirs that had appeared in the April 19, 1977, issue. "People should be paid for the work they do," McEldowney suggested, "and if for some legitimate reason payment can't be made on time workers deserve the courtesy of a letter explaining what the problem is."[78] San Francisco–based writer and activist Michael Castleman was even more blunt in his complaint that fall about the magazine's nonpayment of funds: "I was deeply saddened, and disappointed. A leftist magazine abusing its workers . . . the shame of it. I'm upset with you. I want my $95. Immediately. The next letter will be from my attorney."[79] Some investors began requesting the repayment of earlier loans. One backer who hoped to be reimbursed for the $2,000 he had lent a few years earlier wrote, "I'm sorry to do this, but I would like to make an investment for which I will need the money."[80] Another lender noted, "I'm writing about that loan I made to the direct mail fund. The two years are up, and I hope the loan can be repaid."[81]

Through its own ineptitude, *Seven Days* damaged its reputation among up-and-coming leftist journalists, who by the end of the decade increasingly began to steer clear of the magazine. The editor of *Mother Jones*, Adam Hochschild, however, found *Seven Days* "readable, lively and to the point." In January 1979, he met with Dellinger and reviewed the magazine's budget. He admitted he could not understand how the magazine had survived for so long. Hochschild wrote: "We publish 10 times a year; the new *Seven Days* would, if I read you right, publish 24. How it would manage to do that on less than half of the money we've spent I do not see. . . . I'm awfully skeptical."[82]

By the summer of 1980, it became apparent to Dellinger and his fellow staffers that the magazine would soon fold.[83] Dellinger sent a letter to all *Seven Days* subscribers announcing that *The Nation* would honor the remainder of their subscriptions. Thus ended *Seven Days*, a colorful yet short-lived experiment in radical journalism. Barbara Ehrenreich, Peter Biskind, and other full-time staffers moved on to more prestigious commitments. Dellinger chose not to look back, and he rarely mentioned *Seven Days* in conversations, interviews, or correspondence. Indeed, in his 1993 autobiography, *From Yale to Jail*, Dellinger discusses his involvement with *Liberation* in great detail but does not once refer to his five years at *Seven Days*.[84]

Now in his sixties, Dellinger took stock of his life. His mother had died in January 1976. "I have given up smoking," Dellinger wrote to his friend Tom Hirsch in August 1975 from the remote wilderness of Vermont, adding that the money he saved abstaining he planned to spend on "fresh fruit."[85] He boasted in a letter to his Vietnamese friend Do Xuan Oanh that he had lost forty pounds during and after his 1975 trip to Hanoi, due to a new exercise regimen. "I've never felt better. I find I can breathe more easily and I feel at one with nature," he wrote.[86] In addition, Dellinger found a generous financial supporter in Carol Bernstein Ferry, a rich New Yorker who had grown close to David over the years and gave him money when he fell upon hard times.[87]

In 1976, David and Elizabeth began their long and painful journey toward reconciliation. Therapy had helped Elizabeth make sense of her complex emotions and troubled relationship with David. In fact, nearly everybody in the Dellinger clan sought counseling to help them understand their unusual upbringing.

At first, David and Elizabeth went on walks through Central Park or strolled through museums. "I didn't really feel happy meeting with him over a meal," Elizabeth remembered, "because my stomach had had ulcers, and I'm very sensitive about being in a bad situation. It wasn't healthy for me to eat with him when we were separated."[88] They told each other about developments in their lives, and David listened carefully to Elizabeth's grievances. Their tensions persisted, however, and quarrels were not unusual. "We went for walks in the botanical gardens, so we could separate and cool down if we got into something hot," Elizabeth recounted.[89] A breakthrough came in late 1975 when Peterson moved into Dellinger's Brooklyn apartment. But for almost five years, they more closely resembled roommates than an intimate couple and they often spent extended periods apart. Still, the odd living arrangement was a step toward reconciliation.

By 1980 they had few reasons to remain in New York. When the Vietnam War ended and the protest struggles were waning, Dellinger had stayed in the city to edit and manage *Seven Days*. The final issue appeared in July, a few weeks before his sixty-fifth birthday. Although David's health had improved since the early 1970s, his body could no longer withstand the long jail stints and the beatings associated with mass civil disobedience. He thus wanted to move somewhere quiet, where woods and streams were abundant, where he could plant vegetables, write his memoirs, and raise hell on a local level. Elizabeth, too, was ready to go but planned to commute to the New York City adoption agency where she had worked since 1977. Increasingly, the couple looked to Vermont. For years it had been one of David's favorite getaway destinations. By this time, Jay Craven had become a close confidant of Dellinger, and he helped David and Elizabeth move. He explained, "Dave felt like he had to get out of the city to repair the links with his family, to find a place where he could write and think, a place like Vermont where there is still a progressive tradition, and spirit of rural independence and local democracy."[90] Dellinger did not intend to retire, however. This move, he insisted, would instead mark a new beginning.

12

Making Peace in Vermont

He's a complex, complex man and incredibly dedicated. I hated him and I loved him from hour to hour. He is one of the most humane people in the world but he is also so sure of himself.

Nina Kraut (Dellinger's attorney in the 1980s)

He was predictable in a very good sense: His integrity was always intact. His nonviolence was outstanding and it kept him on an even keel in a wonderful way. He was never cynical, probably knowing that if the country gets cynical and withdraws, the special interests really move in. He wasn't a barrel of fun but then most self-styled revolutionaries are not.

Rev. William Sloane Coffin

Charlie Parker said, "Jazz comes from who you are, where you've been, what you've done. If you don't live it, it won't come out of your horn." It's the same with the revolution.

David Dellinger

DELLINGER WANTED TO MAKE CLEAR that moving to Vermont in 1980 in no way represented a withdrawal from a lifetime of radical social justice activism. "I didn't come up here to retire," he insisted. "I came here so I can live closer to nature. I cut my own wood. I have a garden. And I remain an antiwar activist."[1]

The 1970s offered a transition period that enabled Dellinger to pull back from building coalitions and organizing mass movements. But at the end of the decade he still was visible in progressive circles because of his capacity as the editor and manager of *Seven Days*. Then, the demise of the magazine reinforced Dellinger's desire to move to Vermont, and in 1977, he accepted a position teaching writing at Goddard College in Plainfield. His move to Vermont coincided with a rightward shift in American politics. The disturbing trends that had begun under President Jimmy Carter's administration—the abandonment of détente, a sharp escalation of the arms race, cuts in social welfare programs, and the government's deepening procorporate ethos—accelerated dramatically during the Reagan administration.

Nonetheless, Dellinger continued to accentuate the positive, despite sometimes overwhelming evidence to the contrary. In his mind, the spirit of the 1960s had never really subsided. In April 1980, he wrote, "From the teach-ins, demonstrations, and planning conferences I have attended around the country during the past few months, I am convinced that the movement for peace and justice is . . . stronger . . . than it was during the first few years of opposition to the Vietnam War."[2] Even in the face of Ronald Reagan's 1980 presidential victory, Dellinger declared, "Most people have not moved to the right. I never have felt that things died down as much as everyone said after the '60s."[3] But his decision to leave New York City nonetheless signified a refocusing of his political activism. In the 1980s and 1990s, no longer a leader of national protest movements or an editor of a leftist magazine, Dellinger lost much of his mass audience. Since he had always felt uneasy about his leadership role, he welcomed the change. He lived the remainder of his life in Vermont, agitating against militarism, fostering friendships with local activists, devoting time to his family, working in his garden, chopping wood in the winter, and—whenever the opportunity arose—"speaking truth to power."

David Dellinger and Elizabeth Peterson moved into a restored schoolhouse in rural Vermont in the fall of 1980, where they lived for a year. At first, David canceled many of his lecture engagements—a vital source of income—so he could write his memoirs and spend time with Elizabeth. He did continue teaching night courses in Goddard College's Adult Education Program. The following year, the Dellingers bought a house on thirty acres of land near Peacham, a small village in northeastern Vermont. Peacham was an out-of-the-way community ("a small cluster of white houses around a church spire," as one local journalist described it), close to the Interstate but far from any large cities.[4] Dellinger blended in quietly, greeting townspeople with a friendly "hello" or a nod of the head whenever he went into town to buy groceries or pick up mail from his P.O. box. He typically introduced Elizabeth first, referring to himself simply as "Dave." For a few years, locals thought his name was Dave Peterson. "Their first reaction to the news that David Dellinger, the 'architect of violence at Chicago,' was moving into their town drew a lot of testy remarks around the post office," noted Jay Craven.[5]

Even though Dellinger did not seek out trouble in Peacham, he did not avoid it. In early 1984, some residents of Peacham objected to the leftist politics of thirty-three-year-old Rev. Richard Hough-Ross, the minister at the local Congregational church. The clergyman supported sanctuary for Salvadoran refugees, opposed the United States' military involvement in Central America, and denounced the proliferation of nuclear arms, views that divided the community. But David Dellinger supported Hough-Ross and resumed his weekly church attendance as a show of solidarity. Some locals welcomed the minister's dissenting views. "He must be doing something right. Church membership is higher than ever," remarked a parishioner. But a vocal minority denounced Hough-Ross and his supporters, particularly Dellinger. Church deacon Peg Newburn commented, "Now that David Dellinger has joined the church, I think a lot of people are going to leave."[6] Although Hough-Ross weathered the storm, the debate over his politics revealed the community's ideological fault lines.

Eventually, most Peacham residents warmed up to Dellinger, thanks to his disarmingly friendly and nonconfrontational personality. A former State Department official and longtime Peacham resident who befriended Dellinger later explained, "It's fair to say that the uneasiness has gone away. Now he's been pretty well accepted into the community."[7] Dellinger loved teaching and eventually took a second teaching position at Vermont College in Montpelier. Not surprisingly, his non-hierarchical teaching style invited debate and discussion, and at the conclusion of each semester he received almost unanimously positive teaching evaluations.

Writing also absorbed significant amounts of Dellinger's time. Sporadically since the mid-1970s, he had been working on his autobiography. Dellinger intended to write a two-volume narrative of his life and to find a major commercial press to publish it. But he was repeatedly distracted: "I'm unable to find the time to do half of the things I want to," he wrote to his friend Birch Shapiro in 1988, "such as reading certain books, writing friends, answering letters and phone messages, or doing nearly as much on my autobiography as I want to."[8]

Once again, nonviolent direct action lured him away. The politics of the Reagan era greatly troubled Dellinger: the intensification of the arms race, the deepening poverty, and the looming threat of military intervention in Central America. In his lectures, he cautioned young listeners to avoid the "trap" of electoral politics, and in a speech he delivered during the 1984 presidential campaign, Dellinger declared, "Most of the important social gains are not made by electoral politics." When an audience member asked him about President Reagan, he stated, "I hope he's not reelected. But if he is, don't panic. What happens in society depends more on the way we live."[9]

This position placed him at odds with the largest and most visible leftist organization in the country, the Democratic Socialists of America (DSA). The DSA grew out of a merger in 1982 between the moderate Democratic Socialist Organizing Committee, headed by Michael Harrington and Irving Howe, and the more radical New American Movement, founded in the early 1970s by Staughton Lynd, Barbara Ehrenreich, and other prominent New Leftists.[10] Dellinger and Harrington first met in 1951 at an anti–Korean War protest at Times Square where Dellinger was severely beaten by a counterdemonstrator. Harrington, however, rejected the politics of radical pacifism and embraced a solidly social democratic outlook. By the 1980s, most DSAers, including Harrington, campaigned for liberal Democrats and supported their reform efforts in Washington, D.C. But the anarchistic Dellinger bristled at such an agenda and continued throughout the Reagan era to defend the dramatic protests and uncompromising militancy of the 1960s. "We may have made a lot of mistakes in the 1960s, but that era was a miracle of human endeavor. It was a burst of humanistic energy that came out of the blue. . . . It opened up a lot of consciousness before it began to go astray."[11] Nonetheless, some of Dellinger's closest friends from the New Left and the antiwar movement joined the DSA. Despite his disagreements, Dellinger remained on good terms with Michael Harrington and mourned when the socialist leader died in 1989. As Dellinger explained, "He thought the best way to work was in the Democratic Party, to turn it into a more progressive organization. I felt it turned him into a more conservative person. He and I were good friends right to the end."[12]

In the early 1980s, the arms race dominated Dellinger's attention. On June 3, 1979, he attended an antinuclear rally at the site of the Lilco nuclear power plant, which was still under construction. More than fifteen thousand people participated in the protest, and Dellinger, along with Pete Seeger and Jerry Rubin, was arrested for trespassing in a restricted area.[13] In January 1982, he received a telephone call from Norma Becker requesting his help in planning the June 12 march for disarmament in New York City. Once again, he was back in business. The event was endorsed by religious groups, labor unions, and peace organizations, including SANE. While Dellinger relished the opportunity to meet new activists and work alongside familiar veterans, he confronted the same frustrations he faced in the 1960s. That is, most of the leading organizers of the event refused to acknowledge any global crises other than nuclear war. As Dellinger remembered: "We were told not to discuss the war in Lebanon or Central America or any other issues. It was like trying to get rid of war without talking about the causes of war."[14]

The June 12 march surpassed the highest expectations of its organizers, turning out to be the largest march in the history of New York City, drawing 750,000 protesters. At Central Park, Dellinger introduced speakers and made announcements. He was about to deliver a speech when rock star Bruce Springsteen made a surprise visit to the stage. At the organizers' urging, Springsteen agreed to sing, and in exchange, Dellinger and several other speakers gave up their allotted speaking time.[15]

Buoyed from the experience of June 12, Dellinger turned his attention to a matter he considered equally pressing: Central America. For decades, Washington, D.C., had backed various autocratic regimes in the region. A turning point came in July 1979 when the leftist Sandinista rebels in Nicaragua overthrew the tyrannical dictator Anastassio Somoza, whose family dynasty had been financed by Washington for almost a half century. The Sandinistas ushered in an idealistic revolution, more democratic than the Cuban experiment but less vulnerable than Salvadore Allende's social democratic government in Chile. On November 16, 1981, President Reagan quietly approved $20 million in funds for an army in Honduras consisting of men who had previously been soldiers in Somoza's widely reviled national guard.[16] This was the first of many aid packages for the so-called *contras*. The government in El Salvador became more repressive, with rightist politicians and generals staging a series of coups and countercoups while paramilitary "death squads" with ties to the regime assassinated students, labor leaders, religious figures, and other dissidents in the capital, San Salvador, and throughout the countryside. In response, the Farabundo

Marti National Liberation Front (FMLN) began waging a guerrilla war against the Salvadoran government. American aid flowed steadily into the regime, and U.S. military advisers trained Salvadoran officers in counterinsurgency techniques.

At first, Dellinger and his fellow Vermont activists targeted Washington's El Salvador policies. They conducted a series of highly publicized civil disobedience actions at General Electric's main Vermont plant in Burlington, which manufactured rapid-fire Gatling guns that were shipped to the Salvadoran government. As part of the Peace and Justice Coalition, Dellinger helped organize a series of demonstrations that began in the fall of 1982 and continued throughout the rest of the decade. The protests ultimately had the desired effect. GE continued to scale back its production at the facility until 1989, by which time the manufacture of Gatling guns had nearly ground to a halt.[17]

In the fall of 1984, Dellinger traveled with a delegation of American activists to Nicaragua to assess the achievements of the Sandinista revolution. Visits by American delegations were commonplace in the 1980s and helped build opposition in the United States. Across America, activists stepped up the struggle against the covert war in Nicaragua, with marches, rallies, and civil disobedience.

Before his Nicaragua trip, Dellinger participated in one of the most dramatic anti-*contra* protests in the United States. It began as a modest-size rally of about 150 people in Winooski, a town next to Montpelier. On the afternoon of Friday, March 23, 1984, the demonstrators picketed outside the local offices of Republican U.S. Senator Robert Stafford, who had voted for military aid to El Salvador and funding for the Nicaraguan *contras*. The protesters asked Senator Stafford to reconsider his stand on funding the Salvadoran government and *contra* war in Nicaragua. At the very least, they wanted him to hold a public meeting explaining his position, especially since recent polls indicated that 75 percent of the state's population disagreed with such policies.[18] It seemed like a reasonable request, as Vermont's other senator, Patrick Leahy, and its representative in the House, James Jeffords, each had held public meetings to explain their stances. When Senator Stafford did not respond, forty-four of the activists, including Dellinger, occupied his offices.

The protesters assumed that Senator Stafford would promptly evict them from the premises. but he surprised everyone by waiting a few days to respond. Thus, for the entire weekend, the so-called Winooski

44 took over Stafford's office. Before it ended, the takeover by the Winooski 44 made headlines across the nation as well as the nightly newscasts. The police finally arrived around 11:00 A.M. on Monday and informed the protesters that if they did not leave the offices, they would be forcibly removed and arrested for unlawful trespass. Although some of the protesters were dragged out by police, Dellinger willingly walked out, having fulfilled his purpose of calling "attention to the senator's support . . . of terrorist death squads in El Salvador and brutal acts of rape, torture and murder in Nicaragua by agents of the CIA and by U.S.-trained and financed former members of the Somoza National Guard."[19] In the fall of 1984, the case of the Winooski 44 went to trial. Attorneys for the defendants presented a "necessity defense," arguing that the actions of the protesters represented an effort to prevent a greater harm from occurring. The argument won the jury, and the defendants were cleared of all charges.[20]

The Winooski 44 case elevated Dellinger in the Vermont peace movement. Unlike the anti–Vietnam War movement days, Dellinger abstained from the planning, believing that the time had come for younger and more energetic activists to take their turn. But he did speak at Central America anti-intervention protests in cities across the country, and he served as an adviser in the fall of 1986 to four veterans of World War II and the Vietnam War who fasted for more than a month in protest against the Reagan administration's Nicaragua policies.[21] Dellinger also made several trips to jail in the 1980s for protesting his government's policies.

While Dellinger was on trial in the fall of 1987 for one of his protests, physicians in California discovered that his son Ray had cancer. The second oldest of the Dellinger children, Ray had changed his last name to Sundance during the Chicago conspiracy trial and eventually settled in Berkeley. Upon hearing the news, Dellinger scaled back his speaking engagements to be with Ray. Ray's condition deteriorated in the summer, and it became apparent he would not recover. Early in his treatment, he told his father, "You know, Dad, I always felt that you understood some things I didn't because you faced death in prison. Now I am beginning to think I understand those things."[22] Ray faced his death with the same sort of fearlessness that enabled David to endure his ordeals in the past. David later wrote to a relative: "We are happy . . . that when he knew he was going to die—as indeed we all must, and Elizabeth and I not long from now—he worked it through until he found peace inside himself."[23] Ray died on October 18, 1988, at the age of forty-two. The grief-stricken father wrote: "Now, we hope, he lives comfortably 'on the other side.' And continues to grow."[24] After Ray's death, Dellinger stopped traveling for a while to spend time with his family. He canceled or postponed "everything else for the next few months, in order to be with my wife and two of my other children who moved to Vermont."[25] Then, little by little, David resumed his old speaking schedule. He spent several weeks at the University of Illinois in March 1989, where he gave lectures about the 1960s and worked with local activists, but nothing could completely erase the sorrow. Beneath his warm exterior, David grieved the loss of his son for the rest of his life.

In the 1980s and 1990s, the "sixties" enjoyed a revival of sorts, and Dellinger benefited from the windfall of renewed interest. Between 1986 and 1996, David's speaking engagements remained an important and steady source of income for the Dellingers. David also worked on his memoirs, rewriting and revising drafts. Earlier in his life, he had been an advocate of small publishing houses, but this time he hoped to reach a broader audience. He coedited one book in the 1980s, *Beyond Survival*, a critique of the arms race, and wrote *Vietnam Revisited*, an account of the Vietnam War inspired by his visit to the country in April and May 1985 to celebrate the tenth anniversary of the revolution. The small, leftist, Boston-based South End Press published both books, but Dellinger intended to aim higher with his memoirs. "I decided to go to a bigger publisher this time because South End Press books are not reviewed in the *New York Times*," he explained. "I just sort of wanted to get this book out. There were so many misunderstandings about Chicago and wrong attitudes."[26] Accordingly, he signed a contract with Pantheon, a large and respected commercial publisher.

Friendships that Dellinger had formed in the 1960s continued to be important to him, especially his relationship with Abbie Hoffman. After Hoffman's 1973 cocaine bust, Dellinger constantly helped him with emotional and moral support. Marty Jezer recalled: "When Abbie was underground and going crazy, Dave was one of the people who went up to his hideout in Canada and tried to help him."[27] He also made repeated visits to Fineview, New York, where Abbie worked as an environmentalist for several years under the pseudonym Barry Freed. When Hoffman considered resurfacing in 1979, he first consulted a group of his closest comrades, including Dellinger. On September 4, 1980, Hoffman, still wanted for selling cocaine in 1973, resurfaced and publicly surrendered to law enforcement officials in Manhattan. Most people hardly recognized him. Gone were the frizzy hair and the countercultural clothing. His hair now was shorter and grayer, and he had a beard and moustache. Hoffman's return to society touched off a media frenzy.

In the 1980s, Hoffman's life paralleled Dellinger's in many respects. Both men wrote frequently; both relied on income from speaking tours; and both sought to debunk popular misconceptions about the legacies of the 1960s. As Abbie's wife Johanna Lawrenson put it, "Abbie and Dave disproved the myth that Sixties grew more conservative as they got older."[28] One of the most distressing developments for Hoffman was the discovery that Jerry Rubin had become a highly successful Wall Street entrepreneur. According to Abbie's brother Jack, the transformation of Jerry Rubin represented "the worst betrayal of Abbie's life."[29] Jerry Rubin had exploited his status as a 1960s radical and, in the process, became the archetype for the myth that the 1960s activists had "sold out." As Rubin proclaimed, "In America you've got to follow the dollar, right? And . . . I've always been a sort of mainstream person."[30] When Hoffman learned about this, he said he wanted nothing to do with his onetime comrade, although he went on a nationwide tour with Rubin, joining him in sixty debates over eighteen months. The debates attracted huge crowds. At $5,000 per debate, Hoffman could not afford to say no. But as Hoffman's close personal friend Kinky Friedman remembered, "He lost those debates. The audience was cheering for Abbie and they laughed at Abbie and championed him, but they went out and did what Jerry Rubin said."[31]

David avoided the feud between Hoffman and Rubin. Unlike many veterans of the 1960s, he refrained from attacking Rubin. Over the years, Dellinger and Rubin went in different directions, and by the late 1970s they saw little of each other. Hoffman, by contrast, grew closer to Dellinger. In 1986 Hoffman once again generated widespread media coverage when, with Jimmy Carter's daughter, Amy, he protested the CIA's recruiting at the University of Massachusetts. They were arrested and charged with trespassing and disorderly conduct. At their trial in April 1987 the jury found them not guilty of the charges. The CIA protests were Abbie's last big effort. Although he continued writing, touring, and making public appearances, some of his feistiness had begun to fade.

Toward the end of his life, Hoffman communicated regularly with Dellinger, either over the telephone or in person. As Dellinger recalled,

> After August 1985, he would telephone me between eleven and twelve at night once every week or two. He also sent me a lot of letters. He was enthusiastic about how things were shaping up. He said wherever he went, he got a huge crowd of young people, and they were eager to hear what he had to say.[32]

David saw Abbie often; one of their last visits together was in August 1988 when they met in Chicago to commemorate the twentieth anniversary of the 1968 Democratic National Convention. They shared the stage at public panels and attended demonstrations together. "In Chicago in 1988 at the twentieth reunion, . . . [Hoffman] was nuts. Manic," remembered Stew Albert. "He was in pain. He would talk beyond his time limit and interrupt on panels."[33] But David was too preoccupied with Ray's cancer to notice Abbie's acute depression. Until the end, Dellinger insisted that Abbie was fine, despite widespread claims to the contrary by Hoffman's friends and family members. "I know he wasn't depressed in the sense of being discouraged, as the media claimed," Dellinger insisted.[34]

On April 12, 1989, Hoffman's body was found inside his apartment in New Hope, Pennsylvania. According to the coroner, he had swallowed 150 phenobarbital capsules and chased them down with a bottle of Glenlivet.[35] When Dellinger learned the news, he asserted that powerful figures had played a role in Abbie's death. Publicly, he claimed that Abbie had fallen victim to "the same forces that killed John F. Kennedy and Martin Luther King. He was a little too dangerous."[36] He pointed to Hoffman's protests against the CIA in recent years, particularly his highly publicized trial with Amy Carter. He reminded reporters that Hoffman had been injured in an automobile accident in June 1988 and "told me that he wondered if someone had been playing with the brakes."[37] After Hoffman's death, Dellinger shared this paranoid scenario with anybody who would listen, even repeating the allegations at a memorial service held in Abbie's hometown of Worcester, Massachusetts. "It's more likely that he was killed than that he killed himself," David said.[38] But even Abbie Hoffman's closest friends dismissed Dellinger's theory as unsubstantiated. Stew Albert, however, understood Dellinger's reason for wanting to believe that the CIA or other dark forces killed the legendary radical. "Dave, I guess, couldn't accept that this energetic, committed, life-affirming person was dead, especially because he had seen him a short while before his death and Abbie seemed quite energetic, with a lot of plans. But in reality, he was mentally depressed and suicidal."[39]

In late April, David flew to California to spend time with his grandchildren and, while on the West Coast, went to Los Angeles to speak at a memorial service for Hoffman. During both the Worcester and Los Angeles services, David embraced Jerry Rubin at a time when many Movement stalwarts preferred to give him the cold shoulder. The two Chicago conspiracy trial codefendants had a good visit before parting ways, and thereafter, they rarely communicated with each other. Then, on November 14, 1994, Jerry Rubin was hit by a car while jaywalking across Wilshire Boulevard in the Westwood area of Los Angeles. He was rushed to the hospital and remained on life support for two weeks. He died of his injuries on November 28, at age fifty-six, leaving behind a young son and daughter.[40]

Through the late 1980s and early 1990s, Dellinger tried to spend more time writing his autobiography. He had spent much of the advance on his $25,000 contract with Pantheon, and the publisher was becoming impatient. Dellinger eventually produced a manuscript chronicling his life up through the Chicago conspiracy trial. At no point in the book does he explain why he chose to end the account in 1970 instead of taking it to the present. His friend Marv Davidov believes the reason was that David originally planned to write a two-part account and simply failed to finish the second half.[41]

The finished product, *From Yale to Jail: The Life Story of a Moral Dissenter*, appeared in April 1993. Upon its release, Davidov organized a book tour that took Dellinger to several cities around the country as well as on a few overseas visits. The book received mixed reviews. Typically, leftists celebrated it as a moving and candid account, but elsewhere the assessments were often cool. "At times more rambling than riveting," noted *Kirkus Reviews*, "still, overall, an open, inspiring chronicle, a personal history of more than a half century of dissent in America."[42] Peter Collier, an ex–New Left journalist who, by the 1990s, had become a fierce critic of radicalism, panned *From Yale to Jail*, objecting to both the writing style and the politics. He concluded: "And while *From Yale to Jail* is obviously a bid for applause by one who thinks of himself as a secular saint, it is likely that the author will hear little more than the wound of one hand clapping."[43] A brief critique in the *New York Times Book Review* by Saul Shapiro was less critical than Collier's but equally dismissive. The verdict: "One comes away impressed by Mr. Dellinger but not by his book."[44] The most sympathetic treatment in a nonleftist, mainstream newspaper appeared in the *San Francisco Chronicle*. Although the reviewer, Bernard Weiner, criticized Dellinger for using "his memoirs to point out the flaws of deceased progressive leaders, among them Martin Luther King Jr., A. J. Muste, [and] Bayard Rustin," he praised the revolutionary as "a simple man with a simple, loving heart, who refused to be deterred from his dream of social justice in a quest for spiritual oneness."[45]

In Dellinger's mind, worse than the mixed reviews was Pantheon's shabby treatment of him. It quickly became apparent to him that the publisher had no intention of doing anything more with the book than honoring the contract to publish it. As a result, *From Yale to Jail* received almost no promotion. The book had a limited release, and promises of follow-up printings never materialized. Royalties soon evaporated. Rumors that a Hollywood producer planned to buy the film rights stopped circulating. Pantheon staffers ignored repeated efforts by Dellinger to obtain copies for interested reviewers. A few months before *From Yale to Jail* was published, Fred Jordan, Dellinger's main contact at Pantheon, was fired, and Dellinger's attempts to contact anyone at Pantheon failed.[46] Ironically, despite his original intention to find a large commercial press to publish his autobiography, Dellinger ended up offering the paperback rights for next to nothing to Rose Hill Books, an obscure outfit in South Dakota that lacked the visibility or distribution muscle of larger leftist publishers like Verso and South End Press. But he had the last word in his introduction to the paperback edition when he thanked Pantheon editor Fred Jordan but attacked the publisher as a "multinational corporation" that would not allow his "thoughts, feelings and experiences" to "reach a wide public."[47]

The book did, however, lead to the resumption of contact with old comrades from his World War II radical pacifist years, such as William Lovell and Bill Sutherland. "I'm writing to say how much I'm enjoying it," reported fellow conscientious objector Robert Steed. "If I had grandchildren, I'd surely tell them proudly, 'I did time in jail with Dave Dellinger.'"[48] In addition, activists from the 1960s showered Dellinger with compliments.

While the publication of *From Yale to Jail* was in many ways a relief to Dellinger, it also marked the end of a project that had kept him focused and busy for so many years in the 1980s and early 1990s. He therefore returned to activism. The political struggles of the 1990s differed from the protests of the 1980s. The end of the cold war had reduced public anxieties about the prospect of nuclear war. Central America and South Africa were no longer political trouble spots. The 1991 Gulf War was too short to generate many antiwar protests. The election of Bill Clinton in 1992 was followed by years of relative stability and economic prosperity. Compared with the 1980s, the 1990s were a time of calm consensus. Dellinger thus surprised many friends when he cast aside his longtime opposition to electoral politics to support Jesse Jackson and the Rainbow Coalition in 1984 and 1988, as well as the congressional campaigns of socialist candidate Bernie Sanders in the 1990s. Meanwhile, the ebbing of protest politics meant that Dellinger was not offered speaking engagements as frequently. Dellinger's longtime friend and fellow dissenter Howard Zinn recalled, "All through his life he never made any money. He was always struggling. He never held any post. He was not like some of us, professors in universities and getting salaries. He never drew that. He just always lived at the edge of poverty."[49]

A particularly difficult personal financial crisis in the fall of 1992 forced Dellinger to ask for loans from wealthy supporters. To a friend in Cambridge, Massachusetts, he wrote:

> The reason why I am writing you is different—the old reason for which I have not bothered you for years—a need for money. . . . I am trying to borrow five thousand dollars (or possibly raise some of it). . . . I would have undertaken this earlier, but I did manage to get a modest advance on a new book of mine. Now it is all gone.[50]

He sounded even more frantic when he asked another trusted source to borrow $20,000:

> The situation is desperate and we are on the edge (or over it) despite the generous help we received from a woman I know in a Boston sub-

urb. . . . Actually, I also thought of cashing in the balance of the trust fund from my parents, but at least until the book tour or sale of the film and/or paperback rights, we just scrape by each month with whatever amounts you so conscientiously scrape out for us.[51]

Eventually Dellinger regained his financial footing, and honoraria came his way more often after the publication of *From Yale to Jail*. He described his life in 1990s to an interviewer:

I no longer teach. Lecturing has been my main source of income. I travel a lot, but I don't go on tour, as people do, partly because I want to be home more and do local things related to my family. . . . I go to a lot of places. . . . I go out for one or two talks, and then I go home.[52]

Now more sensitive to Elizabeth's needs, Dellinger actually began refusing some invitations. "I don't know if you know that Elizabeth has been wrestling with depression," he wrote to Yale classmate and fellow conscientious objector Bill Lovell. "She tried a lot of medicines for it as well as therapy but now she has a new medicine that seems to help a lot and therefore we are both fine."[53] Long trips often aggravated Elizabeth's health problems. "When we travel," David explained, "she comes back exhausted and in poor health, and I come back with more energy than when we left."[54]

In August 1996, Dellinger went to Chicago for yet another Democratic National Convention. The mood of the nation had changed dramatically in the twenty-eight years since the 1968 convention held there. The current mayor of Chicago, Richard Daley Jr., son of the machine boss who ran the city in 1968, warmly welcomed members of the Chicago Eight and other protesters. He even arranged to obtain convention passes for the surviving Chicago Eight figures. "As unwelcome as you may have felt 28 years ago, you're welcome here today," he announced at a combination protest rally and concert organized by a coalition of leftist groups.[55] During the following week, Dellinger returned to Chicago for several days of nonviolent direct action. He had little interest in the actual convention. Rather, the place to be, he believed, was outside with the small but dedicated clusters of demonstrators.

After the 1996 Democratic National Convention, health problems began to plague Dellinger and forced him to scale back his demanding speaking and activist schedules. Despite advice from his doctor to be careful about fasting, Dellinger did so regularly. Any issue from U.S. military intervention overseas to the celebration of Columbus Day could trigger a fast, and sometimes he refused food for weeks. Shortly before his seventy-seventh birthday, he wrote to a friend: "Is seventy-seven old? Old enough for me to have hearing aids and reading glasses, but I feel energetic . . . and healthy enough to fast."[56] In the late 1990s, doctors diagnosed him with an uneven heartbeat and atrial fibrillation, which required medications. Memory problems, too, became increasingly common. "Well, for one thing, I travel so much," he told an interviewer, "and so many people come up and greet me, and what I've learned from my wife is, when possible, to say, 'You look familiar, but what is your name?' But sometimes I don't do that as much as I should, but I keep learning from my wife."[57]

In 1997, the Dellingers moved to Montpelier, which put them nearer their support network of friends. The move also shortened the distance they had to travel to see their physicians. At eighty-two, David was showing no signs of slowing, but he agreed with Elizabeth that Peacham was too remote and that their nineteenth-century house there had become too burdensome. Since 1980, David's activism had shrunk from national to regional in focus. At the same time, with the appearance of his autobiography and the persistence of his political commitments, he cemented his position as an elder statesman of American radicalism and fashioned a legacy for the new millennium. Time was running out, though, as Dellinger soon would face the most formidable challenge of his life, Alzheimer's disease.

13

Farewell, Tough Guy

To be a revolutionary is to love your life enough to change it, to choose struggle instead of exile, to risk everything with only the glimmering hope of a world to win.

Andrew Kopkind

MORE THAN ANY OTHER EVENT in recent history, the September 11, 2001, attacks on the World Trade Center in New York, the Pentagon in Washington, D.C., and the aborted attack that ended in rural Pennsylvania challenged the vision of peace activists across America. In the aftermath of 9/11 (as it came to be referred to), polls indicated widespread public support for President George W. Bush's decision to send troops to Afghanistan. Pundits and policymakers suggested that the "war on terror" could expand into a global conflict, triggering bloody clashes between Western democracies and Islamic fundamentalists. In addition, accounts of air strikes and civilian casualties in Afghanistan discouraged adherents of nonviolence.

In October 2001, while the nation began waging what promised to be a long and uncertain war, peace activists in Vermont chose to hold a "gala celebration honoring the life and work of" David Dellinger and Elizabeth Peterson at the Memorial Auditorium in Burlington.[1] The October 20 dinner gathering featured addresses by noted peace activists Norma Becker, Howard Zinn, Cora Weiss, and Staughton Lynd; films, still photographs, and audio clips from some of Dellinger's most memorable speeches were presented; and folk music was provided by several performers, including Dellinger's grandson, Chicago activist Steve Sato. A snowstorm that night failed to prevent a crowd of more than three hundred from attending. Many of Dellinger's oldest and dearest friends were there, including George Houser, one of the original Union Eight imprisoned with him at Danbury in 1940 and 1941. Radical pacifist and Lewisburg conscientious objector Ralph DiGia reminded the audience that Dellinger had been an activist through six decades of American history. "David was the kind of fellow who always supported the underdog. . . . There are so many stories I could tell. . . . We're pals, we've been at it a long, long time."

Natasha Singer, the older of the two Dellinger daughters, reminisced about growing up a rebel in rural, cold war–era New Jersey and becoming an activist in the late 1960s and early 1970s.

> I was in a very different place than my father was at the time, and I could not appreciate his nonviolent stance. I was very angry. Over the years, I've come to so appreciate what he gave us as a family and me in particular. . . . I've come to understand that my cultural heritage is the peace movement.

The Raging Grannies, a group of elderly peace activists, sang a slightly updated, pacifist version of "This Land Is Your Land." Performers reenacted scenes from the Chicago conspiracy trial. Poet Grace Paley sent a short statement: "Everybody loves you, Dave. Some good reasons: You're usually right. You're always trustworthy. You believe in the other guy's good intentions until it drives him crazy." For three hours, friends and comrades of the Dellingers spoke, sang, or read. Finally, David Dellinger, now eighty-six, strode to the front of the room, visibly moved and his voice breaking from the emotion. He held the microphone as he spoke:

> Everyone benefits from the existence of a beloved community of persons who help one another to struggle, learn and grow. . . . Standing next to my wife, Elizabeth Peterson, I think our relationship through many years has helped both of us to grow, even though we need others also, including you people here, especially the insights and struggles of young people and people from other countries as well.[2]

Given the uneasy state of the nation in October 2001, the celebration may have seemed anachronistic, yet the mood in the hall was upbeat and hopeful. Adding to the bittersweet poignancy of the gathering was the news—widely known in activist circles—that Dellinger was suffering from Alzheimer's disease, a condition characterized by progressive memory loss and mental deterioration. Doctors had diagnosed him with the condition in the summer of 2000.[3] Michael Ferber remembered seeing Dellinger around that time when he came for a speaking engagement at the World Fellowship Camp. "I introduced him and he spoke. When he was talking about his memories, he was pretty good. But when he was trying to talk about contemporary things, his mind was wandering."[4] In the summer of 2003, Dellinger's fellow Union Eight comrades George Houser and Don Benedict and their wives joined David and Elizabeth for lunch in Burlington, and Houser noticed that Dellinger occasionally seemed "confused."[5]

Ralph DiGia first learned of David's condition at a memorial service for a World War II conscientious objector in early 2001. "It was the first time I ever saw David speaking where he just seemed to go off track, and I thought to myself, 'What's David talking about?' At that meeting, Elizabeth told me David was diagnosed with Alzheimer's."[6] A few weeks later, DiGia telephoned Dellinger. "We had a dinner coming up in June at the WRL [War Resisters League] and I said, 'Hey, are you coming down?'" Dellinger told DiGia no, and then he spent the next thirty minutes running through his entire summer schedule while DiGia listened patiently. "It seemed a little strange for him to be doing that," DiGia noted. "So I spoke to my wife about it and she said, 'That's one of the symptoms. They write lots of things down and recite them to try to remember them.'"[7] David's condition was most upsetting to his family, particularly Elizabeth. Until David was diagnosed with Alzheimer's, he rarely lost his temper. But the disease made him more argumentative and testy, and on one occasion, while in a confused rage, he hit Elizabeth. "I just know I have to step back, because I just can't let him do that," she said.[8]

Living in Montpelier, closer to their support network of loved ones, friends, and comrades certainly helped, and Dellinger, despite his Alzheimer's, remained a visible figure at peace demonstrations, fundraisers, and community meetings. Since 1986, he had cochaired the board of directors of *Toward Freedom*, a monthly magazine of independent leftist thought. Although his writing had slowed significantly after the publication of *From Yale to Jail*, he contributed a few columns each year to *Toward Freedom*, and his pieces appeared as recently as 2001.[9] Dellinger regularly wrote letters and articles and planned his still hectic travel itinerary. Of utmost importance to him was his commitment to supporting prisoners' rights and freeing political prisoners. In the 1990s and early 2000s, he gave top priority to a nationwide campaign to gain the release of jailed American Indian Movement activist Leonard Peltier. He visited Peltier in Leavenworth Penitentiary in Kansas and wrote to him frequently. When Dellinger took a brief hiatus from the Free Peltier Campaign to recover from an illness in early 2001, he wrote to Peltier explaining his reasons. "I am better enough now," he indicated, "with medicines and a doctor's help, that I expect to join activities demanding your release, as well as helping develop new ones."[10]

Greg Guma, editor of *Toward Freedom*, had been close to David and Elizabeth for years and attended numerous protests with the couple during the 1980s and 1990s. He regularly saw Dellinger at the monthly *Toward Freedom* meetings and in the late 1990s began to notice his condition declining. "I'd say the first thing that happened was a hearing problem. We found ourselves talking very loudly at meetings so he'd be sure to hear things, and he'd get irritated if we talked too fast or our voices dropped down so he couldn't hear us. We thought he was irritable, but I think that was also part of the beginning of the Alzheimer's." In 2000, David began taking medications to minimize the symptoms, which slowed the effects of the disease for a while. For the next few years, his gregarious personality and perceptive analysis prevailed, but by late 2002 and 2003, Dellinger sat quietly in board meetings, usually listening to other people speak. Sometimes, as the meeting drew to a close, he would ask to be recognized and articulate his position on a particular issue, but it had become impossible for other people on the board to engage him as they had done in years past. "We've lost the ability to interact with him," Guma noted at the beginning of 2004.[11]

For a few years after he was diagnosed with Alzheimer's, Dellinger stubbornly refused to allow the condition to slow him down. Accordingly, on April 22, 2001, he went Quebec City, Canada, to protest at the Summit of the Americas meeting, to oppose the creation of a hemispheric free trade zone. Because leaders from throughout the Americas planned to attend, the event became a prime target for antiglobalization demonstrators. There were moments when the streets of Quebec City resembled Chicago in the sweltering days of August 1968. This time, however, Dellinger deliberately avoided the chaos, opting instead to deliver a speech on the evening of his arrival to a crowd of predominantly youthful demonstrators. The eighty-five-year-old pacifist proclaimed: "In different ways a growing number of persons everywhere are dissatisfied with the current inequalities and the presence of a nonloving society. Many are protesting for human rights and the blessings of nature for everyone. They are experimenting with more loving lives for themselves."[12]

Such acts of resistance decreased in frequency after 2001. "It is a hard time to be hopeful," he acknowledged in the summer of 2002. "But my wife . . . and I speak at a lot of high schools, and each time we see the early signs of interest in peace and nonviolence, and we hear young people expressing the need for alternatives to war and violence. That gives us hope."[13]

After moving to Montpelier in the late 1990s, Dellinger and Peterson managed to live fairly self-sufficiently, occasionally helped by contributions and donations from friends and loved ones. In the fall of 2002, they moved into Heaton Woods, an assisted-living community in Montpelier, and in December, Elizabeth sent a Christmas card to Jeff Guntzel, one of the younger activists whom David had befriended in recent years. She assured him they were

> comfortably and happily settled, each in our own room, at Heaton Woods. David exercises with 20 other residents here. We get three delicious, nutritious meals a day and there are games and many other activities each morning. . . . We are still able to go to the local vigils and rallies for peace and justice. . . . We are also members of a newer group which is the Alliance for Prison Justice.[14]

Within a year of moving to Heaton Woods, Dellinger was beginning to have a difficult time recognizing friends and relatives. When Marv Davidov, who was more like a brother than a friend to Dellinger, telephoned him from Minneapolis in 2003, David could not identify him over the telephone. Davidov spoke reassuringly to Dellinger, and soon the two friends chatted about their lives. But Marv could tell that David's mental state had worsened. "I love you, Dave," he said toward the end of the conversation. "I love you, too," Dellinger replied.[15] For the first few years after being diagnosed with Alzheimer's disease, David was able to maintain an admirable command of his long-term memory, describing in detail events that had happened forty or fifty years earlier but often forgetting things that had taken place recently. Within a few years, though, confusion distorted virtually all of his memories. "He is well into his second stage of Alzheimer's disease," Elizabeth reported in February 2004. "He remembers some things from the past, but from my knowledge it is all mixed up."[16]

Despite his condition, the war in Iraq summoned Dellinger once again to action. He promptly contacted his activist friends and attended local antiwar meetings with Elizabeth, as he still had sufficient control of his faculties to recognize the gravity of the war. As Vermont activist Robin Cappucino remembered: "At the last meetings Dave attended, he was agitating for the group to make a decision about where we could best do civil disobedience to stop the war in Iraq."[17] But David could not remain active for long. He was losing the battle against Alzheimer's, and his attendance at antiwar meetings tapered off.

Toward the end of his life, with his hearing significantly diminished and memories jumbled, Dellinger wrote a poem that expressed his deepest beliefs and commitments:

> I love everyone,
> even those who disagree with me.
> I love everyone.
> even those who agree with me.
> I love everyone,
> rich and poor,
> and I love everyone of different races,
> including people who are indigenous,
> wherever they live, in this country or elsewhere.
> I love everyone,
> whatever religion they are, and atheists too.
> People who contemplate, wherever it leads them.
> I love everyone,
> both in my heart and in my daily life.[18]

In May 2004, David Dellinger contracted a severe case of pneumonia and never recovered. He "slipped away peacefully" on May 25. The "peaceful warrior," as his friends in Vermont called him, could resist no longer. He was eighty-eight. His family rushed to Montpelier to be with Elizabeth, and David's body was immediately cremated.[19] In addition to Elizabeth, he was survived by sons Patch and Danny, daughters Natasha and Michele, six grandchildren, and three great-grandchildren.

Like A. J. Muste, David Dellinger died at a crossroads in American history. Were it not for his Alzheimer's, Dellinger might have emerged as a key elder figure in the national anti–Iraq War coalition, as Muste had done in the anti–Vietnam War movement in 1965 and 1966.

In the final months of his life, Dellinger participated in weekly anti–Iraq War vigils in Montpelier. Those ceremonies continued after he died.[20] Local residents who did not necessarily see eye to eye with Dellinger mourned his passing as well. When Charles Morrison, an "old Yankee farmer," found out that Jay Craven was planning to speak at a local memorial service for David in early June, he waxed nostalgic. "You know, I liked Dave quite a bit," Morrison said. "He had his views. But I listened to him and I guess I learned quite a bit. And he listened to me, and well, we simply had some awfully good conversations. I'll miss him, if you really want to know the truth."[21]

In the days following Dellinger's death, obituaries and articles appeared in newspapers across the country, all focusing on his role as the elder Chicago Eight defendant. Ironically, one of the most thorough and sympathetic remembrances appeared in the *New York Times*, a newspaper that in the past had often downplayed or ignored his activities.[22] Two memorial services were held for Dellinger. On June 5, hundreds of people gathered in a park near the Winooski River in Montpelier to hear loved ones and friends bid farewell to the "tough guy," as they fondly called him. His son Patch delivered the most moving speech. "Every one of his five children," Patch recalled, "was sung to sleep with 'Joe Hill,' a ballad to an early labor leader who was executed by the state of Utah in 1915 in what many labor activists still see as a grave injustice."[23] Patch shared personal memories of David's reading poems out loud to his sons and daughters, playing baseball with his children and their friends at Glen Gardner, taking care of his vegetable gardens in Peacham, and enjoying an occasional cigar and cognac with beloved comrades. He spoke of the times when his father took his children on nature hikes and to the theater, peace demonstrations, and major league baseball games. In closing, Patch said, "He would want all of you today to be joyful and to laugh with him."[24]

A second, larger memorial service was held in October at St. John the Divine in New York City on October 23, 2004. Estimates of the crowd ranged up to fifteen hundred.[25] Folk singer Pete Seeger strummed his guitar and sang "We Shall Overcome" and "Joe Hill." Eulogies were delivered by Howard Zinn, Tom Hayden, George Houser, Grace Paley, American Indian Movement activist Vernon Bellecourt, and actor Ossie Davis. Jay Craven oversaw the gathering, which, much like the gala dinner honoring David and Elizabeth in October 2001, was more of a celebration of Dellinger's life than a traditional memorial service. The service was full of reminiscences of earlier protests, favorite anecdotes about Dellinger, and enthusiastic assessments of his many years of activism.

The day after Dellinger died, his Chicago conspiracy trial codefendant and old friend John Froines, by this time the director of the Occupational Health Center at the University of California in Los Angeles, was featured on National Public Radio's *All Things Considered*. Host Melissa Block asked Froines what Dellinger would "make of the times that we're in now." He responded: "Well, I think Dave would be very angry with having died at this point in history. I think that he would like to be on the front lines right now, because he recognized that the American foreign policy and American society in general is in such a crisis stage."[26]

Protest was Dellinger's legacy, as Froines and others who knew him pointed out. Nowhere was that legacy more apparent than in the streets of Manhattan, three months after Dellinger died. On August 29, while the Republican Party held its convention in New York City, 400,000 people marched in protest against the war in Iraq, forming, in the words of the *Boston Globe*, a "procession stretching for miles."[27] It was the largest mass rally ever held during a major political convention in American history and brought the city to a standstill for hours.

Had he lived long enough to witness the protests at the New York Republican Convention, Dellinger would have taken heart and redoubled his own activism. He likely would have pointed out that during the Vietnam War, it took several years for the antiwar coalition to amass such huge protests, whereas the August 2004 march in Manhattan occurred a mere year and a half into the Iraq War. Optimism permeated Dellinger's outlook, and his sense of hope never faltered or waned. Decades of experience taught him that gigantic mass protests do not take place in a vacuum. Rather, they are the products of years of community organizing, countless marathon meetings, painstaking coalition building, and tireless public outreach. He even regarded prison sentences as a weapon in the arsenal of nonviolent revolution. His formula for success was to use creative methods of resistance even if it meant offending moderates, to cast aside conventional tactics in favor of more militant ones, to struggle in the streets instead of in the halls of power, and to celebrate the presence of youthful resisters. These steps taken together, he argued, would enlarge the critical mass in protest movements, broaden the scope of debate, and pull the political pendulum leftward.

Until the day he died, Dellinger insisted that the struggle to create a "beloved community," both locally and globally, demanded a lifelong commitment. He was not being disingenuous when he claimed that he derived as much joy from the small, widely ignored protests in the 1950s or 1990s as he did from the gigantic mobilizations of the late 1960s and early 1970s. For Dellinger, it was always the darkest moments in life that gave him the chance to revisit and nurture his principles. His unwavering vision of a global "beloved community" formed the cornerstone of his beliefs. If Dellinger's tenacity, vision, and optimism secured him a place in the history of twentieth-century American radicalism, those same qualities sometimes blinded him to troubling realities in his family, his political circles, and, one might even argue, American society as a whole. His avoidance of political leadership, motivated by his anarchistic ideals, undercut his potency within the protest movements he so ardently championed.

Because of his refusal to veer away from his humanistic revolutionary outlook, his rejection of power, and his willingness to live in poverty or prison until he achieved his goals, Dellinger eventually emerged as one of the leading figures of dissent in twentieth-century America. Doubtless, the soft-spoken pacifist would have shrugged off such a characterization. In 1991, an interviewer from the *Catholic Worker* asked David Dellinger what he wanted to be remembered for. Dellinger's trademark mixture of self-deprecating modesty and radical egalitarianism was evident in his answer:

> My temptation is to say nothing because I am so obsessed with the star system in the United States. A couple of times in my life I have been put in the position of being either a hero or a star, with groupies and everything. I've seen it corrupt other people and it probably corrupted me more than I was aware of. So I would like my children to feel they were glad I was their father. I would like some people to remember me for having taught them . . . that the things that seem to separate us from our fellows are nothing compared to the things that unite us with all humanity. I would like, if anything, to think that maybe somebody learned that from me, because to the best of my ability I refused to be a star or a hero.[28]

Notes

The following abbreviations are used in the notes:

CNVA   Committee for Nonviolent Action

CNVR   Committee for Nonviolent Revolution

FOR   Fellowship of Reconciliation

LBJL   Lyndon Baines Johnson Presidential Library, Austin, Texas

MOBE   National Mobilization Committee to the End the War in Vietnam

PCPJ   People's Coalition for Peace and Justice

SCPC   Swarthmore College Peace Collection

Tamiment The Tamiment Collection, Bobst Library, New York University

UIS   University of Illinois at Springfield

WRL   War Resisters League

NOTES TO THE INTRODUCTION

1. Alan Dershowitz, *America on Trial: Inside the Legal Battles That Transformed Our Nation* (New York: Warner Books, 2004), 394.

2. For Dellinger's obituaries, see *New York Times*, May 27, 2004; *Los Angeles Times*, May 27, 2004; *Washington Post*, May 27, 2004; *Salt Lake Tribune*, May 27, 2004; *Denver Post*, May 27, 2004; *San Jose Mercury News*, May 26, 2004; *Omaha World Herald*, May 27, 2004; *The Economist*, June 5, 2004.

3. *New York Times*, May 27, 2004.

4. *Chicago Tribune*, June 24, 1996.

5. *Washington Post Book World*, April 4, 1993.

6. *Rocky Mountain News*, June 11, 2004.

7. Howard Zinn, interview with author, March 12, 2004.

8. Noam Chomsky, interview with author, March 23, 2004.

9. Tom Hayden, "Remembering Dave Dellinger," *AlterNet*, June 7, 2004.

10. David Dellinger, interview conducted by New Liberation News Service, published in *The Thistle* (Cambridge, Mass.), June 7, 1993.

11. *Village Voice,* November 22, 1973.

12. David Dellinger, *From Yale to Jail: The Life Story of a Moral Dissenter* (New York: Pantheon, 1993), 393.

NOTES TO CHAPTER I

Epigraph: David Dellinger, "Why I Refused to Register in the October 1940 and a Little of What It Led To," in *A Few Small Candles: War Resisters of World War II Tell Their Stories,* edited by Larry Gara and Lenna Mae Gara (Kent, Ohio: Kent State University Press), 20.

1. John Inscoe, *Mountain Masters: Slavery and the Sectional Crisis in Western North Carolina* (Knoxville: University of Tennessee Press, 1996), 12.

2. Maggie Palmer Lauterer, *Sweet Rivers: The Ancestors and Descendants of William Jones Dellinger and Selena Carpenter Dellinger* (Asheville, N.C.: Folk Heritage Books, 1997), 54.

3. Ibid., 83–86.

4. Ibid., 43.

5. Ibid., 48.

6. Ibid., 65.

7. Author unknown, "Fiske Family Genealogy," courtesy of Bob Birt. Much of the material before 1850 was compiled by Frederick Clifton Pierce and originally published in 1896.

8. Lauterer, *Sweet Rivers,* 66.

9. U.S. Bureau of the Census, *Fourteenth Census of the United States, Population: 1920* (Washington, D.C.: U.S. Bureau of the Census, 1922); handwritten records, "Wakefield (Middlesex County, Massachusetts)," 1201. In the census figures she is listed as a "cousin," but in all likelihood she was Dellinger's grandmother's second cousin. David Dellinger discusses her in his *From Yale to Jail: The Life Story of a Moral Dissenter* (New York: Pantheon, 1993), 11–17.

10. Jo Ann O. Robinson, review of *From Yale to Jail,* by David Dellinger, *Journal of American History* 81, no. 1 (1994): 329–330. See also Dellinger, *From Yale to Jail,* 445.

11. David Dellinger, "My Mother," unpublished notes, David Dellinger Papers, Box 3, Tamiment.,

12. David Dellinger, letter to William Dellinger, Duke University, October 1, 1991, David Dellinger Papers, Box 6, Tamiment.

13. David Dellinger, interview by author, June 16, 2001.

14. Virginia Downs, "An Activist's Life Story," *Lyndon Independent,* March 24, 1993.

15. Dellinger, *From Yale to Jail,* 14.

16. Eliot Asinof, *1919: America's Loss of Innocence* (New York: Donald I. Fine, 1990), 167; David Dellinger, interview by author, June 16, 2001.

17. David Dellinger, interview by author, June 16, 2001.

18. Dellinger, *From Yale to Jail*, 16.

19. David Dellinger, interview by author, June 16, 2001. This story turns up in other interviews with Dellinger as well, and chapter 1, 11, of *From Yale to Jail* opens with it.

20. David Dellinger, "A Life Sketch," n.d. (ca. 1987), Box 4, David Dellinger Papers, Tamiment.

21. David Dellinger, interview by author, June 16, 2001. See also Dellinger, *From Yale to Jail*, 11. For information about Count Luckner's lecture, see Serena J. Murley, letter to David Dellinger, August 11, 1993, David Dellinger Papers, Box 2, Tamiment.

22. Ron Chepesiuk, *Sixties Radicals, Then and Now: Candid Conversations with Those Who Shaped the Era* (Jefferson, N.C.: McFarland, 1995), 82, 287.

23. Dellinger, *From Yale to Jail*, 446–447.

24. Marv Davidov, interview by author, January 21, 2004.

25. David Dellinger, interview conducted by New Liberation News Service, published in *The Thistle* (Cambridge, Mass.), June 7, 1993.

26. Ralph DiGia, interview with author, August 6, 2001.

27. Dr. Patchen Dellinger to author, April 8, 2003.

28. Dellinger interview, *The Thistle*, June 7, 1993.

29. Dr. Patchen Dellinger to author, April 8, 2003.

30. Richard Anton Weisenbach, "A Strategy for the Renewal of Historic First Parish Congregational Church" (Ph.D. diss., Fuller Theological Seminary, 1987).

31. David Dellinger, letter to Nancy Roberts, University of Minnesota, May 31, 1990, David Dellinger Papers, Box 7, Tamiment.

32. David Dellinger, interview by author, June 16, 2001.

33. David Dellinger, interview with C. Arthur Bradley, July 7, 1988, UIS.

34. Dellinger interview, *The Thistle*, June 7, 1993.

35. David Dellinger, interview with author, October 31, 1999.

36. Dellinger, "A Life Sketch."

37. Dellinger, *From Yale to Jail*, 443.

38. Dellinger, "Notes from My Childhood."

39. Ibid.

40. Dellinger, *From Yale to Jail*, 13.

41. Lauterer, *Sweet Rivers*, 57; David Dellinger, interview by author, June 16, 2001; David Dellinger, letter to Walter Dellinger, October 1, 1991; David Dellinger Papers, Box 6, Tamiment.

42. Paul Faler, "Population Growth and the People of Wakefield, 1830–1990," *Wakefield: 350 Years by the Lake* (Wakefield, Mass.: Wakefield 350, 1994), 219.

43. David Dellinger, unpublished rough draft, chap. 14, David Dellinger Pa-

pers, Box 3, Tamiment. The information about his bank job comes from a hand-written statement fastened to a Life Insurance Policy taken out by David on July 14, 1933, with the Mutual Life Insurance Company, Springfield, Massachusetts. He mentions the summer job in Portland but lists his permanent address as Shumway Circle, Wakefield; David Dellinger Papers, Box 6, Tamiment.

44. The yearbook excerpt is reprinted in Mark Sardella, "A Rebel with Local Roots," *Wakefield Observer*, May 15, 1993.

NOTES TO CHAPTER 2

Epigraph: Hermann Hesse, *Siddhartha* (New York: New Directions, 1951), 3.

1. David Dellinger, *From Yale to Jail: The Life Story of a Moral Dissenter* (New York: Pantheon, 1993), 19.

2. William Lovell, interview by author, February 17, 2004.

3. Ibid.

4. Walt Rostow, interview by author, April 29, 2002.

5. Kai Bird, *The Color of Truth: McGeorge and William Bundy: Brothers in Arms* (New York: Simon & Schuster, 1998), 64.

6. Walt Rostow, interview by author, April 29, 2002.

7. Dellinger, *From Yale to Jail*, 18.

8. Ibid., 26.

9. Tom Wells, *The War Within: America's Battle over Vietnam* (Berkeley: University of California Press, 1994), 206.

10. Ibid.

11. Ibid., 617. In my brief interview with Rostow several months before he died, I found him to be warmer than the portrayal of him in *The War Within* would suggest. Though decidedly reluctant to speak about the past, he admitted that he had been "close friends" with Dellinger. On the issue of whether Dellinger was a communist, Rostow conceded that "he probably never actually joined the Communist Party" but that Dellinger "certainly supported the communist worldview." Walt Rostow, interview by author, April 29, 2002.

12. David Dellinger, interview conducted by New Liberation News Service, published in *The Thistle* (Cambridge, Mass.), June 7, 1993. In the *Thistle* interview, Dellinger goes on to recount: "The Yale Political Union was organized during my time there, and Rostow was head of the extreme left party. He wanted me to join it, and I went at the beginning. But I decided that it was a lot of rhetoric. They [members of the Yale Political Union] were up there making brilliant speeches and Rostow had no contact with the poor people of New Haven; he hadn't been active in the union organizing. So I said, 'No'—pardon my language—'fuck this! I'm going to go out and live.'"

13. Dellinger, *From Yale to Jail*, 26.

14. David Dellinger, interview by author, June 16, 2001.

15. Dellinger, unpublished memoir draft, chap. 14, 19–20, David Dellinger Papers, Box 3, Tamiment.

16. Ibid., 24.

17. Ibid., 33.

18. Ibid., 4–12; David Dellinger, interview by author, June 16, 2001.

19. Dellinger, unpublished memoir draft, chap. 15, 8, David Dellinger Papers, Box 3, Tamiment.

20. Ibid., 6.

21. Ibid., 9–10.

22. Kenneth S. Davis, *FDR*, vol. 3, *The New Deal Years, 1933–1937* (New York: Random House, 1986), 554.

23. Gerald L. Sittser, *A Cautious Patriotism: The American Churches and the Second World War* (Chapel Hill: University of North Carolina Press, 1997), 24.

24. Lawrence S. Wittner, *Rebels against War: The American Peace Movement, 1933–1983* (Philadelphia: Temple University Press, 1984), 3.

25. Ibid.

26. William Lovell, interview with C. Arthur Bradley, June 23, 1988, UIS.

27. Dellinger, *From Yale to Jail*, 34.

28. David Dellinger, interview with C. Arthur Bradley, July 7, 1988, UIS.

29. Ibid.

30. David Dellinger, interview with Ted Gettinger, December 10, 1982, LBJL.

31. David Dellinger, interview with C. Arthur Bradley, July 7, 1988, UIS.

32. Bernard K. Johnpoll, *Pacifist's Progress: Norman Thomas and the Decline of American Socialism* (Chicago: Quadrangle Books, 1970), 203–204.

33. *New York Times*, October 21, 1967, 8.

34. David Dellinger, untitled, undated, and unpublished memoir draft, David Dellinger Papers, Box 3, Tamiment.

35. *New York Times*, October 21, 1967, 8.

36. David Dellinger, "My Life as a Nonviolent Activist," in *Yale University, Class of 1936: Fifty Years Out*, edited by Oliver Jensen (New Haven, Conn.: Yale University Press, 1986), 102.

37. Dellinger, untitled, undated, and unpublished memoir draft, David Dellinger Papers, Box 3, Tamiment.

38. Ibid.

39. Dave Dellinger, "Be the Change: Looking Back and Forward at the Path of Nonviolence," *Toward Freedom*, March/April 2001, 10.

40. William Kunstler, *My Life as a Radical Attorney* (New York: Birch Lane Press, 1994), 9–10.

41. David Dellinger, interview with C. Arthur Bradley, July 7, 1988, UIS.

42. Ibid.

43. Dellinger, "My Life as a Nonviolent Activist," 102.

44. David Dellinger, interview with C. Arthur Bradley, July 7, 1988, UIS.

45. Dellinger, "My Life as a Nonviolent Activist," 102.

46. Ibid.

47. Dellinger, "My Life as a Nonviolent Activist," 102; David Dellinger, "Why I Refused to Register in the October 1940 and a Little of What It Led To," in *A Few Small Candles: War Resisters of World War II Tell Their Stories*, edited by Larry Gara and Lenna Mae Gara (Kent, Ohio: Kent State University Press), 25.

48. David Dellinger, interview by author, June 16, 2001. The same comments that Dellinger shared with me during this interview appear, almost word for word, in Dellinger, "Why I Refused to Register," 27.

49. Dellinger, "Why I Refused to Register," 26.

50. David J. Langum, *William Kunstler: The Most Hated Lawyer in America* (New York: New York University Press, 1999), 32.

51. Dellinger, "My Life as a Nonviolent Activist," 102; Dellinger, "Why I Refused to Register," 26.

52. David Dellinger, interview by author, June 16, 2001.

53. Dellinger, "My Life as a Nonviolent Activist," 102.

54. Dellinger, "Why I Refused to Register," 26.

55. Dellinger, "My Life as a Nonviolent Activist," 103. It is difficult to trace Dellinger's movements through Nazi Germany in both his 1936 and 1937 trips, as he was quite vague about details and did not save any diaries or correspondence from the period. Moreover, it is impossible to verify his claims that he met anti-Nazi figures or stayed with Jews. Suffice it to say that Dellinger repeatedly discussed his trips to Nazi Germany in several interviews and in *From Yale to Jail*. It obviously meant a great deal to him to express his sympathy for Jews, which likely has something to do with his conflicted feelings about his refusal to participate in World War II.

56. David Dellinger, interview with C. Arthur Bradley, July 7, 1988, UIS.

57. Dellinger, "Why I Refused to Register," 27.

58. David Dellinger, interview by author, June 16, 2001. David's "tramp" period in late 1937 is also described in *From Yale to Jail*, 45–55, as well as in several other interviews and reminiscences. He clearly regarded the experience as a turning point in his life, a time when he rejected the material privilege of his youth and embraced a more fearless and impoverished activism that dominated the remainder of his life.

59. Dellinger, unpublished memoir draft, chap. 14, 25, David Dellinger Papers, Box 3, Tamiment.

60. David Dellinger, interview with C. Arthur Bradley, July 7, 1988, UIS.

61. Ibid.

NOTES TO CHAPTER 3

Epigraph: Quoted in the *New York Herald Tribune*, November 15, 1940, 7.

1. David Dellinger to Roy Finch, July 24, 1939. Roy Finch Papers, SCPC.

2. David Dellinger, interview with C. Arthur Bradley, July 7, 1988, UIS; Meredith Dallas, interview with C. Arthur Bradley, June 9, 1988, UIS.

3. Richard Wightman Fox, *Reinhold Niebuhr: A Biography* (New York: Pantheon Books, 1985), 77.

4. Ibid., 194.

5. Howard Spragg, interview with C. Arthur Bradley, August 1988, UIS.

6. Meredith Dallas, interview with C. Arthur Bradley, June 9, 1988, UIS.

7. Ibid.

8. Donald Benedict, interview by author, January 27, 2004.

9. Meredith Dallas, interview with C. Arthur Bradley, June 9, 1988, UIS. Accounts of David Dellinger's meeting with Eleanor Roosevelt came from Donald Benedict, interview with the author, January 27, 2004; and David Dellinger, "Why I Refused to Register in the October 1940 and a Little of What It Led To," in *A Few Small Candles: War Resisters of World War II Tell Their Stories*, edited by Larry Gara and Lenna Mae Gara (Kent, Ohio: Kent State University Press), 32–33.

10. David Dellinger, interview with C. Arthur Bradley, July 7, 1988, UIS.

11. David Dellinger, *From Yale to Jail: The Life Story of a Moral Dissenter* (New York: Pantheon Books, 1993), 63.

12. Donald Benedict, *Born Again Radical* (New York: Pilgrim Press, 1982), 23.

13. Dellinger, "Why I Refused to Register," 28.

14. Benedict, *Born Again Radical*, 25.

15. Ibid., 26.

16. Dellinger, *From Yale to Jail*, 63–64.

17. David Dellinger, interview with C. Arthur Bradley, July 7, 1988, UIS.

18. Meredith Dallas, interview with C. Arthur Bradley, June 9, 1988, UIS.

19. David Dellinger, interview by author, June 16, 2001.

20. Conrad Black, *Franklin Delano Roosevelt: Champion of Freedom* (New York: Public Affairs, 2003), 572–573.

21. Cynthia Eller, *Conscientious Objectors and the Second World War: Moral and Religious Arguments in Support of Pacifism* (Westport, Conn.: Praeger), 11.

22. Howard Spragg, interview with C. Arthur Bradley, August 1988, UIS.

23. Ibid.

24. George Houser, interview with C. Arthur Bradley, July 12, 1989, UIS.

25. George Houser, interview by author, January 23, 2004.

26. William Lovell, interview with C. Arthur Bradley, June 23, 1988, UIS.

27. Benedict, *Born Again Radical*, 30.

28. Original draft, "A Christian Conviction on Conscription and Registration," October 10, 1940, Fellowship of Reconciliation (FOR) Papers, Series A-3, Box 12, SCPC.

29. Dellinger, *From Yale to Jail*, 78. Information about meetings with Fosdick,

Sockman, and Baldwin is from Benedict, *Born Again Radical*, 31–32; and David Dellinger, interview by author, June 16, 2001.

30. George M. Houser, "Reflections of a Religious War Objector," in *A Few Small Candles: War Resisters of World War II Tell Their Stories*, edited by Larry Gara and Lenna Mae Gara (Kent, Ohio: Kent State University Press), 133.

31. Ibid., 134.

32. Howard Spragg, interview with C. Arthur Bradley, August 1988, UIS.

33. William Lovell, interview by author, February 17, 2004.

34. George Houser, interview by author, January 23, 2004.

35. Howard Spragg, interview with C. Arthur Bradley, August 1988, UIS.

36. Donald Benedict, interview with C. Arthur Bradley, July 9, 1988, UIS.

37. David Dellinger, interview by author, June 16, 2001.

38. George Houser, interview by author, January 23, 2004.

39. Donald Benedict, interview by author, January 27, 2004.

40. William Lovell, interview by author, February 17, 2004.

41. Dellinger, *From Yale to Jail*, 420.

42. Deanna Hurwitz and Craig Simpson, eds., *Against the Tide: Pacifist Resistance in the Second World War: An Oral History* (New York: War Resisters League, 1984). Benedict discussed the draft registration tables, too; see Benedict, interview with the author, January 27, 2004.

43. David Dellinger, letter to John (no other name), July 1, 1985. Box 11, David Dellinger Papers, Tamiment.

44. Benedict, *Born Again Radical*, 32.

45. *New York Herald Tribune*, November 15, 1940.

46. *New York Herald Tribune*, October 22, 1940.

47. George Houser, interview by author, January 23, 2004.

48. Meredith Dallas, interview with C. Arthur Bradley, June 9, 1988, UIS.

49. Jo Ann Robinson, *Abraham Went Out: A Biography of A. J. Muste* (Philadelphia: Temple University Press, 1981), 79.

50. Meredith Dallas, interview with C. Arthur Bradley, June 9, 1988, UIS.

51. *New York Herald Tribune*, November 15, 1940.

52. Joseph Bevilacqua, "Statement to the Court," in "An Open Letter from the Fellowship of Reconciliation to Its Members," by A. J. Muste and J. Nevin Sayre, November 19, 1940, FOR Papers, Series A-3, Box 12, SCPC. It also appears in *New York Herald Tribune*, November 15, 1940.

53. "8 Draft Objectors Get Prison Terms," *New York Times*, November 15, 1940, 1.

54. Ibid.

55. *New York Herald Tribune*, November 15, 1940.

56. *New York Times*, November 15, 1940, 1; *New York Herald Tribune*, November 15, 1940. The Mandelbaum "national emergency" quotation is contained in several accounts, including Muste and Sayre's "An Open Letter."

57. *Helena* (Mont.) *Independent*, November 15, 1940.

58. Reinhold Niebuhr to DeWitte Wyckoff, November 18, 1940, FOR MSS, Box 18, SCPC.

59. *Chicago Daily News*, November 18, 1940.

60. *New York Herald Tribune*, November 15, 1940.

61. George Houser, "Reflections of a Religious War Objector," in *A Few Small Candles: War Resisters of World War II Tell Their Stories*, edited by Larry Gara and Lenna Mae Gara (Kent, Ohio: Kent State University Press), 139.

62. Dellinger, "Why I Refused to Register," 32.

63. Robinson, *Abraham Went Out*, 74–75.

64. A. J. Muste to David Dellinger, October 17, 1940, FOR Papers, Series A-3, Box 12, SCPC. Muste also sent a copy of the same letter to the other seven imprisoned Union Theological Seminary students.

65. *New York World Telegram*, November 15, 1940.

66. Ibid.

67. Benedict, *Born Again Radical*, 34.

68. Meredith Dallas, interview by author, May 28, 2004.

69. James Peck, *Underdogs and Upperdogs* (Canterbury, N.H.: Greenleaf Books, 1969), 23; Donald Benedict, interview by author, January 27, 2004.

70. David Dellinger, "My Life as a Nonviolent Activist," in *Yale Class of 1936: Fifty Years Out*, edited by Oliver Jensen (New Haven, Conn.: Yale University Press, 1986), 104.

71. William Lovell, interview with C. Arthur Bradley, June 23, 1988, UIS.

72. Ibid.

73. Dellinger, *From Yale to Jail*, 82; David Dellinger, interview by author, June 16, 2001.

74. David Dellinger, interview by author, June 17, 2001.

75. Dellinger, *From Yale to Jail*, 81–86.

76. Ibid., 89.

77. Benedict, *Born Again Radical*, 3.

78. Dellinger, *From Yale to Jail*, 95.

79. George Houser, interview by author, January 23, 2004.

80. William Lovell, interview with C. Arthur Bradley, June 23, 1988, UIS.

81. Houser, "Reflections of a Religious War Objector," 147. See also Dellinger, *From Yale to Jail*, 97–98.

82. Howard Schoenfeld, "The Danbury Story," in *The Pacifist Conscience*, edited by Peter Mayer (New York: Holt, Rinehart & Winston, 1966), 342.

83. Benedict, *Born Again Radical*, 36. See also Houser, "Reflections of a Religious War Objector," 144.

84. Dellinger, *From Yale to Jail*, 94.

85. There is some debate in the memory of various Danbury prisoners about the legendary game. Dellinger insisted in his memoirs that it was the final game

of the season, whereas Houser said it was one of the opening games of the season. Accounts by Schoenfeld and Benedict and the various oral histories are decidedly vague on the matter. Suffice it to say it was a crucial game for the Danbury softball team and a victory meant a great deal to Warden Gerlach.

86. With the exception of Joe Bevilacqua and Richard Wichlei, who left no known oral histories, the Union Eight all recall the big softball game as one of the most important and memorable events of their incarceration at Danbury. This version of events is from Benedict, *Born Again Radical*, 37–38; Dellinger, *From Yale to Jail*, 92–93; and Houser, "Reflections of a Religious War Objector," 145.

87. Schoenfeld, "The Danbury Story," 343.

88. Dellinger, *From Yale to Jail*, 92.

89. Schoenfeld, "The Danbury Story," 344.

90. The letter from Union Theological Seminary is reprinted in Houser, "Reflections of a Religious War Objector," 148.

NOTES TO CHAPTER 4

Epigraph: Jo Ann Robinson, *Abraham Went Out: A Biography of A. J. Muste* (Philadelphia: Temple University Press, 1981), 71.

1. Unpublished Roy Finch obituary, 1997, David Dellinger Papers, Box 6, Tamiment.

2. Margaret Finch, interview by author, May 21, 2004.

3. David Dellinger to Roy Finch, April 18, 1941, Roy Finch Papers, Box 1, SCPC.

4. David Dellinger, interview with C. Arthur Bradley, July 7, 1988, UIS.

5. Donald Benedict, *Born Again Radical* (New York: Pilgrim Press, 1982), 39.

6. David Dellinger, "Statement of David Dellinger, July 18, 1943," FOR Papers, Muste Correspondence, 1940–1947, C.O. N.R., Series A-3, Box 11, SCPC. A slightly edited version of this statement is reprinted in David Dellinger, *Revolutionary Nonviolence* (Indianapolis: Bobbs-Merrill, 1971), 7–16.

7. David Dellinger, *From Yale to Jail: The Life Story of a Moral Dissenter* (New York: Pantheon Books, 1993), 224. To buttress his claims, Dellinger frequently cited John Toland's *Infamy: Pearl Harbor and Its Aftermath* (New York: Berkeley Books, 1983). Numerous historians have challenged this conspiratorial or so-called revisionist interpretation.

8. Justus D. Doenecke, "Non-Interventionism of the Left: The Keep America Out of War Congress, 1938–1941," *Journal of Contemporary History* 12 (1977): 221–236.

9. Dellinger, *Revolutionary Nonviolence*, 5.

10. David Dellinger, interview by author, June 16, 2001.

11. Dellinger, *From Yale to Jail*, 101.

12. "Elizabeth Peterson: A Rebel in Her Own Right," *Caledonian Record* (Vermont), June 17, 1993; Elizabeth Peterson, interview by author, June 16, 2001.

13. Elizabeth Peterson, interview by author, June 16, 2001.

14. Ibid.

15. Ibid.

16. Ibid.

17. Elizabeth Peterson, interview by author, June 16, 2001.

18. *Vermont Sunday Magazine*, April 29, 2001, 10.

19. Elizabeth Peterson, interview by author, June 16, 2001.

20. David Dellinger to Roy Finch, February 7, 1942, Roy Finch Papers, Box 1, SCPC.

21. Dellinger, *From Yale to Jail*, 106.

22. Meredith Dallas, interview with C. Arthur Bradley, June 9, 1988, UIS.

23. Bill Sutherland Jr., interview by author, May 24, 2004.

24. Ibid.

25. *New York Times*, July 21, 1942, 11.

26. David Dellinger, interview by author, June 16, 2001.

27. Donald Benedict, interview by author, January 27, 2004.

28. Scott H. Bennett, *Radical Pacifism: The War Resisters League and Gandhian Nonviolence in America, 1915–1963* (Syracuse, N.Y.: Syracuse University Press, 2003), 75. Bennett writes: "Between 1939 and 1944 the FBI monitored, investigated, and advocated prosecution of the League. One historian has concluded that the FBI considered the WRL a national security threat because of its pacifist convictions, political ideas, and opposition to war and conscription" (75).

29. James Tracy, *Direct Action: Radical Pacifism from the Union Eight to the Chicago Seven* (Chicago: University of Chicago Press, 1996), 6.

30. "Statement of Purpose," People's Peace Now Committee, David Dellinger Papers, Box 3, Tamiment.

31. Tracy, *Direct Action*, 17.

32. Ibid., 17–18.

33. Elizabeth Peterson, interview by author, June 16, 2001.

34. Ibid.

35. David Dellinger to Roy Finch, March 31, 1943, Roy Finch Papers, Box 1, SCPC.

36. Elizabeth Peterson, interview with C. Arthur Bradley, August 20, 1989, UIS.

37. Meredith Dallas, Western Union Telegram to George B. Reeves, July 7, 1943, Conscientious Objector Papers, Document Group 22, Series C, Box 16, SCPC.

38. David Dellinger, "Statement of David Dellinger," July 18, 1943, FOR Papers, Muste Correspondence (40–47), C.O.N.R. (Cutler, Dallas, Dellinger), Series A-3, Box 11, SCPC.

39. Meredith Dallas, interview by author, May 28, 2004.

40. Elizabeth Peterson, interview with C. Arthur Bradley, August 20, 1989, UIS.

41. Stephen M. Kohn, *Jailed for Peace: The History of American Draft Law Violators, 1658–1985* (Westport, Conn.: Greenwood Press, 1986), 47.

42. Tracy, *Direct Action*, 157.

43. Ibid., 14.

44. Bennett, *Radical Pacifism*, 85–86.

45. Howard Schoenfeld, "The Danbury Story," in *The Pacifist Conscience*, edited by Peter Mayer (New York: Holt, Rinehart & Winston, 1966), 339.

46. Kohn, *Jailed for Peace*, 54–55, 57.

47. James V. Bennett to A. J. Muste, October 1, 1943, FOR Papers, Muste, Executive Secretary, Correspondence: Lewisburg, Document Group 13, Series 1–3, Box 13, SCPC.

48. George Q. Flynn, "Lewis Hershey and the Conscientious Objector: The World War II Experience," *Military Affairs*, February 1983, 1–2.

49. The description of the Lewisburg Farm Camp comes from the Pennsylvania Advisory Committee to the U.S. Commission on Civil Rights, "Doing Time: A Study of Prison Conditions at U.S. Penitentiary, Lewisburg, Pennsylvania" (Washington, D.C.: U.S. Commission on Civil Rights, February 1983), 49–50. Dellinger's transfer is described in Dellinger, *From Yale to Jail*, 119–120.

50. James V. Bennett to A. J. Muste, October 1, 1943, FOR Papers, Muste, Executive Secretary, Correspondence: Lewisburg, Series A-3, Box 13, SCPC.

51. Robert Cooney and Helen Michalowski, eds., *The Power of the People: Active Nonviolence in the United States* (Philadelphia: New Society Publishers, 1987), 102–103.

52. *New York World Telegram*, October 30, 1943; *The Call*, October 29, 1943.

53. Bill Lovett, interview by author, January 21, 2004.

54. William Lovett to Caroline Lovett, October 22, 1943, WRL Papers, CO Strike at Lewisburg Folder, Document Group 22, Series C, Box 2, SCPC.

55. A. J. Muste to Caroline Lovett, November 29, 1943, FOR Papers, Muste, Executive Secretary, Correspondence: Lewisburg, Document Group 13, Series 1–3, Box 13, SCPC.

56. *New York World Telegram*, October 30, 1943.

57. David Dellinger, Extracts from letters sent by David Dellinger, uncensored, October 29, 1943, Correspondence with/about individual COs: Dellinger, SCPC.

58. Dellinger, *From Yale to Jail*, 121.

59. Caroline Lovett to Jean Johnson, November 2, 1943, WRL Papers, Lewisburg Prison, SCPC.

60. Dellinger, *From Yale to Jail*, 121–122.

61. Bill Lovett to Caroline Lovett, November 5, 1943, WRL Papers, CO Strike at Lewisburg Folder, Document Group 22, Series C, Box 2, SCPC.

62. David Dellinger, note to WRL, November 31, 1943; extracts from letters sent by David Dellinger, October 29, 1943.

63. Ruth E. MacAdam to Mrs. Franklin D. Roosevelt, October 21, 1944, WRL Papers, Lewisburg Prison, Box 31. The typewritten letter also includes an excerpt of an earlier letter from Eleanor Roosevelt to Ruth MacAdam that contains the quotation about Bennett.

64. *The Call*, December 3, 1943.

65. Thelma Mielke, "A Case for Your Concern," November 10, 1943, FOR Papers, Muste Correspondence (40–47), C.O.N.R. (Cutler, Dallas, Dellinger), Series A-3, Box 11, SCPC.

66. Betty Dellinger, open letter, October 25, 1943, Eichel Family Papers, Correspondence 1941–1943, Box 1, SCPC.

67. Elizabeth Peterson, interview by author, June 18, 2001.

68. Larry Gara, interview by author, February 12, 2004.

69. David Dellinger et al., "An Open Letter to the FOR," February 3, 1944, FOR Papers, Muste Correspondence, Lewisburg, Box 13, SCPC. There were actually two open letters from the Lewisburg COs in protest of the FOR's support of the CPS camp. The longer one was sent to Muste on February 3, and a shorter one went out on June 3, 1944. Muste replied to both letters, first on April 4 and then on July 5.

70. A. J. Muste to David Dellinger, April 4, 1944, FOR Papers, Muste Correspondence, Lewisburg, Box 13, SCPC.

71. Dellinger, *From Yale to Jail*, 125.

72. Kohn, *Jailed for Peace*, 55–56.

73. John Mecartney, "Dear Friend" letter, July 23, 1945, WRL Papers, Ashland, Box 31, SCPC.

74. "Elizabeth Peterson: A Rebel in Her Own Right."

75. A description of this incident is found in Dellinger, *From Yale to Jail*, 122–123.

76. David Dellinger to Roy Finch, February 21, 1945, Roy Finch Papers, Box 1, SCPC.

77. Donald Benedict, interview by author, January 27, 2004.

78. David Dellinger, interview by New Liberation News Service, published in *The Thistle* (Cambridge, Mass.), June 7, 1993.

79. David Dellinger to Roy Finch, February 21, 1945, Roy Finch Papers, Box 1, SCPC. Dellinger mentions his release date in this letter to Finch. Based on interviews with Dellinger and the resumption of correspondence between Dellinger and Julius and Esther Eichel by mid-April, the prison authorities appear to have honored the April 5 release date.

NOTES TO CHAPTER 5

Epigraphs: David Dellinger, *Revolutionary Nonviolence: Essays* (Indianapolis: Bobbs-Merrill, 1971), 19–20; and James Tracy, *Direct Action: Radical Pacifism from the Union Eight to the Chicago Seven* (Chicago: University of Chicago Press, 1996), 75.

1. Gretchen Lemke-Santangelo, "The Radical Conscientious Objectors of World War II: Wartime Experience and Postwar Activism," *Radical History Review*, August 1989, 19.

2. David Dellinger to Abe Kaufman, May 3, 1945, WRL Papers, Correspondence: D (1941–1947), SCPC.

3. David Dellinger to Julius and Esther Eichel, May 12, 1945, Eichel Family Papers, Box 1, SCPC.

4. Elizabeth Peterson, interview by author, June 17, 2001.

5. David Dellinger, *Revolutionary Nonviolence: Essays* (Indianapolis: Bobbs-Merrill, 1971), 19.

6. David Dellinger to Roy Finch, August 26, 1945, Roy Finch Papers, Box 1, SCPC.

7. David Dellinger to Roy Finch, June 16, 1945, Roy Finch Papers, Box 1, SCPC.

8. Ralph DiGia, interview by author, August 6, 2001.

9. Ralph DiGia, "My Resistance to World War II," in *A Few Small Candles: War Resisters of World War II Tell Their Stories*, edited by Larry Gara and Lenna Mae Gara (Kent, Ohio: Kent State University Press, 1999), 40–41.

10. Ralph DiGia, interview by author, August 6, 2001.

11. DiGia, "My Resistance to World War II," 49.

12. *Direct Action* 1, no. 1 (fall 1945).

13. David Dellinger to Roy Finch, April 29, 1946, Roy Finch Papers, Box 1, SCPC.

14. Ibid.

15. "Committee for Nonviolent Revolution: Report of the February Conference," and "Reports of the February Conference on Nonviolent Revolution Held at Chicago, February 6–9, 1946," CNVR Papers, SCPC.

16. David Dellinger, Comments, in "February Conference on Nonviolent Revolutionary Socialism: A Discussion of Problems in Nonviolent Revolution," 9–10, 22, 25–26, CNVR Papers, SCPC.

17. Scott H. Bennett, *Radical Pacifism: The War Resisters League and Gandhian Nonviolence in America, 1915–1963* (Syracuse, N.Y.: Syracuse University Press, 2003), 147.

18. CNVR, "Where Radicalism in the Next 5 Years?" Position papers for the August 8–10 CNVR conference are in the CNVR Papers, SCPC.

19. Bennett, *Radical Pacifism*, 147–148.

20. Robert Cooney and Helen Michalowski, eds., *The Power of the People: Active Nonviolence in the United States* (Philadelphia: New Society Publishers, 1987), 113; Stephen J. Whitfield, *A Critical American: The Politics of Dwight MacDonald* (Hamden, Conn.: Achron Books, 1984).

21. David Dellinger, *From Yale to Jail: The Life Story of a Moral Dissenter* (New York: Pantheon Books, 1993), 420–421.

22. This description comes from combined reports from *New York Times*, March 31, 1947, 40; *Portland* (Maine) *Press Herald*, March 31, 1947, 1, 3; and *Nashua* (N.H.) *Telegraph*, March 31, 1947, 1, 2.

23. Dellinger, *From Yale to Jail*, 421.

24. Ibid., 420.

25. Ibid., 422.

26. Elizabeth Peterson, interview by author, June 17, 2001.

27. *The Star* (N.J.), November 3, 1949.

28. "Statement of Purpose," *Alternative*, April 1948, 1.

29. Ibid., 2.

30. William Appleman Williams, ed., *The Alternative* (Westport, Conn.: Greenwood Reprint Corporation, 1968), 2. Williams's introduction to this collection of *Alternative* offers a provocative critique of the radical pacifist movement.

31. "Continuation Committee of Chicago Conference," Yellow Springs, Ohio, April 20–22, 1948. Minutes from the meeting were written by A. J. Muste, Peacemakers Papers, "Minutes, Proceedings, etc." SCPC.

32. Ibid.

33. *The Star* (N.J.), November 3, 1949. Roodenko's background comes from a biographical sketch of him in the Igal Roodenko Papers, Box 1, SCPC.

34. William Lovett, interview by author, January 21, 2004.

35. Elizabeth Peterson, interview by author, June 18, 2001.

36. A. J. Muste to members of the Fellowship of Reconciliation Executive Committee, Fast for Peace Committee Papers, SCPC.

37. Bayard Rustin, "Pacifists to Hold Seven-Day Fast in National Capital April 1st–9th," Fast for Peace Committee Papers, SCPC.

38. *Washington Post*, April 7, 1950, 38.

39. Winifred Rawlins, "An Experiment with Truth," April 1950, Fast for Peace Committee Papers, SCPC.

40. James Peck, *Underdogs and Upperdogs* (Canterbury, N.H.: Greenleaf Books, 1969), 106.

41. Bennett, *Radical Pacifism*, 191–192.

42. Maurice Isserman, *If I Had a Hammer: The Death of the Old Left and the Birth of the New Left* (New York: Basic Books, 1987), 138–139.

43. Jervis Anderson, *Bayard Rustin: The Troubles I've Seen: A Biography* (New York: HarperCollins, 1997), 138–139.

44. Ibid., 138.

45. Isserman, *If I Had a Hammer*, 139.

46. Dellinger, *From Yale to Jail*, 158.

47. Elizabeth Peterson, interview by author, June 17, 2001.

48. Peacemakers Press Release, July 13, 1951, Peacemakers Printed Materials, Peacemakers Papers, SCPC.

49. DiGia, "My Resistance to World War II," 50.

50. "Progress Report on European Project," Peacemakers Press Release, August 18, 1951, Peacemakers Papers, SCPC.

51. Dellinger kept a thorough record of the journey, part of which appears in *From Yale to Jail*, 158–170. Also see the records of the journey contained in Box 3, David Dellinger Papers, Tamiment.

52. *New York Herald Tribune*, September 12, 1951, 1.

53. *Peace News* (Great Britain), November 9, 1951, 5.

54. Ralph DiGia, interview by author, August 6, 2001.

55. Ibid.

56. Ibid.

57. *Peace News*, November 9, 1951, 5.

58. "American Peacemakers Reach Soviet Army," press release, November 5, 1951. Peacemakers Papers, SCPC.

59. James Tracy, *Direct Action: Radical Pacifism from the Union Eight to the Chicago Seven* (Chicago: University of Chicago Press, 1996), 71.

60. Bill Sutherland, interview by author, May 24, 2004.

61. Ibid.

62. *Peace News*, November 9, 1951, 5.

63. Elizabeth Peterson, interview by author, June 17, 2001.

64. Elizabeth Peterson, interview by author, June 18, 2001.

65. Tracy, *Direct Action*, 73.

66. Isserman, *If I Had a Hammer*, 139.

67. Matthew Lasar, *Pacifica Radio: The Rise of an Alternative Network* (Philadelphia: Temple University Press, 1999), 74.

68. Tracy, *Direct Action*, 84–85.

69. Elizabeth Peterson, interview with C. Arthur Bradley, August 20, 1989, UIS.

70. Bennett, *Radical Pacifism*, 171–172.

71. Anderson, *Bayard Rustin*, 153–154.

72. Frances Witherspoon to Roy Finch, September 9, 1953, WRL Papers, WRL: Correspondence on Rustin as executive secretary, Box 12, SCPC.

73. David Dellinger, unpublished memoir draft, chapter 14, 19, Box 3, David Dellinger Papers, Tamiment.

74. Elizabeth Peterson, interview by author, June 18, 2001.

75. David Dellinger to Buddy (no last name), October 13, 1986, Box 3, David Dellinger Papers, Tamiment.

76. David Dellinger to Roy Finch, September 6, 1953, WRL Papers, WRL: Correspondence on Rustin as executive secretary, Box 12, SCPC.

77. Dellinger, *Revolutionary Nonviolence*, 197.

78. Quoted in Isserman, *If I Had a Hammer*, 140.

NOTES TO CHAPTER 6

Epigraph: James Finn, *Pacifism and Politics: Some Passionate Views on War and Nonviolence* (New York: Random House, 1967), 199.

1. David Dellinger, "Each Submission to Conscription Is a Blow to Freedom," *The Peacemaker* (special ed. on non-registration), January 9, 1958, 7, Peacemakers Papers, "Printed Materials" Folder, SCPC.

2. David Dellinger, interview with C. Arthur Bradley, July 7, 1988, UIS.

3. Elizabeth Peterson, speech at the Radisson Hotel, St. Paul, Minn., October 30, 1999, tape recording in author's collection.

4. Dr. Patchen Dellinger, letter to author, April 8, 2003.

5. Ibid.

6. David Dellinger, interview with C. Arthur Bradley, July 7, 1988, UIS.

7. Elizabeth Dellinger, "What We Can Do Now: Some Suggestions," *The Alternative* (March/April 1949), 3.

8. Elizabeth Peterson, speech at the Radisson Hotel.

9. Elizabeth Peterson, interview with C. Arthur Bradley, August 20, 1989, UIS.

10. Ibid.

11. Elizabeth Peterson, speech at the Radisson Hotel, St. Paul, Minnesota, October 30, 1999.

12. *Rutland* (Vt.) *Herald*, June 6, 2004; David Dellinger, interview by author, October 30, 1999.

13. Dr. E. Patchen Dellinger, "David Dellinger: Personal Remembrances," June 5, 2004, courtesy of Patch Dellinger.

14. Ibid.

15. A. J. Muste, "Proposal for a Bimonthly Magazine," February 21, 1955, 4, Liberation: Formation Proposals, WRL Papers, Box 12, SCPC.

16. A. J. Muste, "Monthly Magazine Prospectus," n.d. (ca. February 1955), 3–4, Liberation: Formation Proposals, WRL Papers, Box 12, SCPC.

17. David Dellinger to Roy Finch, July 23, 1957, David Dellinger Papers, Box 8, Tamiment.

18. John D'Emilio, *Lost Prophet: The Life and Times of Bayard Rustin* (New York: Free Press, 2003), 214.

19. Gerald Sorin, *Irving Howe: A Life of Passionate Dissent* (New York: New York University Press, 2002), 168–169.

20. Sid Lens, *Unrepentant Radical: An American Activist's Account of Five Turbulent Decades* (Boston: Beacon Press, 1980), 222–223.

21. Elizabeth Peterson, interview with C. Arthur Bradley, August 20, 1989, UIS.

22. Dr. E. Patchen Dellinger, "David Dellinger: Personal Remembrances."

23. A. J. Muste to David Dellinger, March 24, 1960, David Dellinger Papers, Box 4, Tamiment.

24. David McReynolds, "Memorandum to the Liberation Editorial Board," October 6, 1959, WRL Papers, "Liberation Minutes," Box 12, SCPC.

25. "Revolutionary Non-Violence: Remembering Dave Dellinger, 1915–2004." *Democracy Now*, Pacifica Radio, May 27, 2004.

26. Roy Finch to David Dellinger, July 19, 1957, David Dellinger Papers, Box 8, Tamiment.

27. David Dellinger to Roy Finch, July 23, 1957, David Dellinger Papers, Box 8, Tamiment.

28. Ibid.

29. Staughton Lynd, interview by author, January 16, 2004.

30. David Dellinger, interview by author, June 18, 2001; Peacemakers, "Announcing a Training Program in Nonviolence, August 19–September 15, 1957," Peacemakers Papers, "Printed Materials" Folder, SCPC.

31. Harry James Cargas, "David Dellinger: Optimism of the Will," *Catholic Worker*, May 1991, 9.

32. David Dellinger, "Are Pacifists Willing to Be Negroes?" *Liberation*, September 1959, 3.

33. Ronald Chepesiuk, *Sixties Radicals, Then and Now: Candid Conversations with Those Who Shaped the Era* (Jefferson, N.C.: McFarland, 1995), 84.

34. Lens, *Unrepentant Radical*, 240.

35. David Dellinger, "Cuba Notes," unpublished manuscript, David Dellinger Papers, Box 8, Tamiment.

36. David Dellinger, "Cuba: Seven Thousand Miles from Home," *Liberation*, June 1964, quoted in Paul Goodman, ed., *Seeds of Liberation* (New York: Braziller, 1964), 206.

37. Dellinger, *Revolutionary Nonviolence*, 105.

38. Ibid., 105–106.

39. David Dellinger, *America's Lost Plantation* (Glen Gardner, N.J.: Libertarian Press), 39.

40. Ibid., 49–52.

41. Richard E. Welch Jr., *Response to Revolution: The United States and the Cuban Revolution, 1959–1961* (Chapel Hill: University of North Carolina Press, 1985), 136.

42. Van Gosse, *Where the Boys Are: Cuba, Cold War America and the Making of the New Left* (New York: Verso, 1993), 235.

43. Maggie Finch, interview by author, May 21, 2004.

44. Gosse, *Where the Boys Are*, 165.

45. Ibid., 208.

46. For informative accounts of the Bay of Pigs fiasco, see Trumbull Higgins, *The Perfect Failure: Kennedy, Eisenhower, and the CIA at the Bay of Pigs* (New York: Norton, 1987); Peter Kornbluh, *Bay of Pigs Declassified: The CIA Reports on the Invasion of Cuba* (New York: New Press, 1998); and Peter Wyden, *Bay of Pigs: The Untold Story* (New York: Simon & Schuster, 1979).

47. Gosse, *Where the Boys Are*, 216–217.

48. Dellinger, *America's Lost Plantation*, 54.

49. David Dellinger, interview by author, June 18, 2001.

50. Paul Berman, *A Tale of Two Utopias: The Political Journey of the Generation of 1968* (New York: Norton, 1996), 79.

51. David Dellinger, interview with C. Arthur Bradley, July 7, 1988, UIS.

NOTES TO CHAPTER 7

Epigraph: Tom Hayden, "Remembering Dave Dellinger," *AlterNet* (July 7, 2004), http://www.alternet.org/story/18876/.

1. Gerald Sullivan and Nancy Zaroulis, *Who Spoke Up?: American Protest against the War in Vietnam* (Garden City, N.Y.: Doubleday), 8–9; Charles Chatfield, *The American Peace Movement: Ideals and Activism* (New York: Twayne, 1992), 104–109.

2. Sullivan and Zaroulis, *Who Spoke Up?* 8.

3. James W. Clinton, *The Loyal Opposition: Americans in North Vietnam, 1965–1972* (Boulder: University Press of Colorado, 1996), 31.

4. Quoted in Neil H. Katz, "Radical Pacifism and the Contemporary Peace Movement: The Committee for Nonviolent Action, 1957–1967" (Ph.D. diss., University of Maryland, 1974), 150.

5. Robert Cooney and Helen Michalowski, eds., *The Power of the People: Active Nonviolence in the United States* (Philadelphia: New Society Publishers, 1987), 148.

6. John D'Emilio, *Lost Prophet: The Life and Times of Bayard Rustin* (New York: Free Press, 2003), 332.

7. Diane McWhorter, *Carry Me Home: Birmingham, Alabama: The Climactic Battle of the Civil Rights Movement* (New York: Simon & Schuster), 365–378.

8. Quoted in Paul Goodman, ed., *Seeds of Liberation* (New York: Braziller, 1964), 173.

9. Michael Ferber, interview by author, August 31, 2004.

10. A. J. Muste to Mary Meigs, September 22, 1961, A. J. Muste Papers, Box 32, SCPC.

11. Mary Meigs to A. J. Muste, April 1, 1962, A. J. Muste Papers, Box 32, SCPC.

12. Marv Davidov, interview by author, January 21, 2004.

13. Ibid.

14. Milton Viorst, *Fire in the Streets: America in the 1960s* (New York: Simon & Schuster, 1980), 199.

15. David Dellinger, *From Yale to Jail: The Life Story of a Moral Dissenter* (New York: Pantheon Books, 1993), 271.

16. Committee for Nonviolent Action, "Why Are the Peace Walkers in Jail? A Fact Sheet on the Quebec-Washington-Guantanamo Walk for Peace in Albany, Georgia," CNVA MSS, Box 2, SCPC.

17. Katz, "Radical Pacifism," 151.

18. In the United States, there is an entire cottage industry surrounding the assassination of President John F. Kennedy, the enigmatic life of Lee Harvey Oswald, and the various conspiracy theories about the events in Dallas on November 22, 1963. About Oswald and Cuba, see Van Gosse, *Where the Boys Are: Cuba, Cold War America and the Making of a New Left* (New York: Verso, 1993), 244–245: "For the purposes of this account, what matters is that on 23 November 1963, every newspaper in the country reported that a 'pro-Castro Red,' a member of the Fair Play for Cuba Committee, had killed the president. The story of Oswald's *fidelismo* rapidly declined in importance after that, perhaps not incidentally, since it was too shoddy to stand up for long—the FPCC office he rented in New Orleans, for instance, was in the same building as Louisiana's main anti-Castro exile group—but the damage was done."

19. Howard Zinn, *SNCC: The New Abolitionists* (Boston: Beacon Press, 1964), 127–128.

20. Katz, "Radical Pacifism," 156.

21. Ibid., 157.

22. CNVA, "News Release," December 23, 1963, Brad Lyttle Papers, Box 1, SCPC.

23. David Dellinger, *Revolutionary Nonviolence: Essays* (Indianapolis: Bobbs-Merrill, 1971), 240.

24. Barbara Deming, *Prison Notes* (Boston: Beacon Press, 1966), 129–130. *Prison Notes* is Deming's memorable account of the imprisonment of the Quebec-Washington-Guantanamo Peace Walkers.

25. Jo Ann Ooiman Robinson, *Abraham Went Out: A Biography of A. J. Muste* (Philadelphia: Temple University Press, 1981), 129.

26. David Dellinger, interview with Ted Gettinger, December 10, 1982, LBJL.

27. Marv Davidov, interview by author, January 21, 2004.

28. Dellinger, *From Yale to Jail*, 184–185. The Cuban exile ordeal is also recounted in David Dellinger, interview by author, June 18, 2001.

29. Cooney and Michalowski, *The Power of the People*, 182.

30. James Tracy, *Direct Action: Radical Pacifism from the Union Eight to the Chicago Seven* (Chicago: University of Chicago Press, 1996), 128.

31. Ibid., 129; David Dellinger, interview by author, June 18, 2001; *New York Times*, July 4, 1964.

32. Dellinger, *From Yale to Jail*, 200.

33. Francesca Polletta, "Strategy and Democracy in the New Left," in *The New Left Revisited*, edited by Paul Buhle and John McMillian (Philadelphia: Temple University Press, 2003), 170.

34. Jack Newfield, "Revolt without Dogma," *The Nation*, May 10, 1965, 494.

35. Charles DeBenedetti, *An American Ordeal: The Antiwar Movement of the Vietnam Era* (Syracuse, N.Y.: Syracuse University Press, 1990), 99; Cooney and Michalowski, *The Power of the People*, 184.

36. Sid Lens, *Unrepentant Radical: An American Activist's Account of Five Turbulent Decades* (Boston: Beacon Press, 1980), 291.

37. Tom Wells, *The War Within: America's Battle over Vietnam* (Berkeley: University of California Press, 1994), 17.

38. DeBenedetti, *An American Ordeal*, 116.

39. Dave Dellinger, "The March on Washington and Its Critics," *Liberation*, May 1965, 7.

40. Fred Halstead, *Out Now! A Participant's Account of the American Movement against the Vietnam War* (New York: Monad Press, 1978), 37–38.

41. David Dellinger to Courtney Blue, October 26, 1970, David Dellinger Papers, Box 8, Tamiment.

42. D'Emilio, *Lost Prophet*, 442.

43. Ibid., 398–403.

44. Dellinger, "The March on Washington," 31.

45. Tracy, *Direct Action*, 129.

46. Lens, *Unrepentant Radical*, 289; David Dellinger, interview by author, June 18, 2001.

47. Staughton Lynd, interview by author, January 16, 2004.

48. Staughton Lynd, "Coalition Politics or Nonviolent Revolution?" *Liberation*, June/July 1965, 18–19.

49. David McReynolds, interview by author, May 11, 2001.

50. David McReynolds, "Pacifists in Battle," *New Politics* 4, no. 5 (summer 1965): 29–35.

51. Andrew Hunt, "How New Was the New Left?" in *The New Left Revisited*, edited by Paul Buhle and John McMillian (Philadelphia: Temple University Press, 2003), 143–144.

52. David Dellinger, "Escalation of the Antiwar Movement," *Liberation*, 1965, reprinted in Dellinger, *Revolutionary Nonviolence*, 276.

53. *New York Times*, August 11, 1965, 3.

54. Halstead, *Out Now!* 66–69; Dellinger, *From Yale to Jail*, 211–215; Stewart Burns, *Social Movements of the 1960s: Searching for Democracy* (Boston: Twayne, 1990), 69.

55. Norma Becker, interview by author, August 9, 2001.

56. Bud Schultz and Ruth Schultz, eds., *The Price of Dissent: Testimonies to Political Repression in America* (Berkeley: University of California Press, 2001), 306.

57. Norma Becker, interview by author, August 9, 2001.

58. Schultz and Schultz, *The Price of Dissent*, 307.

59. Ibid.

60. Norma Becker, interview by author, August 9, 2001.

61. Ibid.

62. Cooney and Michalowski, *The Power of the People*, 186.

63. DeBenedetti and Chatfield, *An American Ordeal*, 127–128.

64. *New York Herald Tribune*, March 27, 1966.

65. David Dellinger, interview with Ted Gettinger, December 10, 1982, LBJL.

66. William D. Hoover and Melvin Small, eds., *Give Peace a Chance: Exploring the Vietnam Antiwar Movement* (Syracuse, N.Y.: Syracuse University Press, 1992), 29.

67. David Dellinger, interview with Ted Gettinger, December 10, 1982.

NOTES TO CHAPTER 8

Epigraph: *Nonviolent Activist*, June 2004, 21.

1. David Dellinger, "The Fort Hood Three," *Liberation* (1966), reprinted in David Dellinger, *Revolutionary Nonviolence: Essays* (Indianapolis: Bobbs-Merrill, 1971), 284.

2. David Dellinger, "The Growing Peace Movement," *Liberation*, May/June 1966, 6.

3. "Elizabeth Peterson: A Rebel in Her Own Right," *Caledonian Record* (Vt.), June 17, 1993.

4. Dr. Patchen Dellinger, letter to author, April 8, 2003.

5. Staughton Lynd, interview by author, January 16, 2004.

6. David Dellinger, "Escalation in the Antiwar Movement," *Liberation* (1965), reprinted in Dellinger, *Revolutionary Nonviolence*, 277.

7. Doug Dowd, interview by author, August 10, 2004.

8. Quoted in Tom Wells, *The War Within: America's Battle over Vietnam* (Berkeley: University of California Press, 1994), 91.

9. Sidney Peck, interview by author, March 9, 2004. See also Nancy Zaroulis

and Gerald Sullivan, *Who Spoke Up? American Protest against the War in Vietnam, 1963–1975* (New York: Doubleday, 1984), 89–90.

10. The Mobe, "Dr. Robert Greenblatt: Biographical Sketch," History Folder, National Mobilization Committee to End the War in Vietnam (hereafter cited as Mobe) Papers, Box 4, SCPC.

11. Fred Halstead, *Out Now! A Participant's Account of the American Movement against the Vietnam War* (New York: Monad Press, 1978), 195.

12. Dellinger recounts the details of the trips in his *From Yale to Jail: The Life Story of a Moral Dissenter* (New York: Pantheon Books, 1993), 215.

13. "The Fort Hood Three" pamphlet, published by the Fort Hood Three Defense Committee, quoted in Halstead, *Out Now!* 177–178. See also Wells, *The War Within*, 99; Jo Ann Robinson, *Abraham Went Out: A Biography of A. J. Muste* (Philadelphia: Temple University Press, 1981), 212.

14. Quoted in "Statement of PFC James Johnson," *Liberation*, July 1965, 4.

15. Fifth Avenue Peace Parade Committee, telegram to Attorney General Nicholas Katzenbach, Secretary of Defense McNamara and the Press, July 7, 1966, reprinted in *Liberation*, August 1966, 4.

16. Andrew E. Hunt, *The Turning: A History of Vietnam Veterans against the War* (New York: New York University Press, 1999), 8.

17. Howard Zinn, interview by author, March 12, 2004.

18. Quoted in Dellinger, *Revolutionary Nonviolence*, 43–44.

19. Mary Hershberger, *Traveling to Vietnam: American Peace Activists and the War* (Syracuse, N.Y.: Syracuse University Press, 1998), 70.

20. David Dellinger, interview by author, June 18, 2001.

21. James W. Clinton, *The Loyal Opposition: Americans in North Vietnam, 1965–1972* (Boulder: University Press of Colorado, 1996), 47.

22. Dellinger, *Revolutionary Nonviolence*, 51.

23. The conversation between Dellinger and Nguyen Vinh Vy is quoted in Clinton, *The Loyal Opposition*, 49.

24. These quotations are from Clinton, *The Loyal Opposition*, 48–49. Dellinger also described his meeting with Ho; see David Dellinger, interview by author, June 18, 2001.

25. Ronald Chepesiuk, *Sixties Radicals, Then and Now: Candid Conversations with Those Who Shaped the Era* (Jefferson, N.C.: McFarland, 1995), 85.

26. Dellinger, "The Growing Peace Movement," 6.

27. Quoted in Wells, *The War Within*, 113.

28. Quoted from unpublished transcript of November 26, 1966, Spring Mobilization Committee to End the War in Vietnam, held in New York City, Evaluation Conference of Spring Mobe Folder, Mobe Papers, Box 5, SCPC.

29. Zaroulis and Sullivan, *Who Spoke Up?* 97.

30. David Dellinger, interview by Ted Gittinger, December 10, 1982, LBJL.

31. Norma Becker, interview by author, August 9, 2001.

32. *New York Times Magazine*, December 3, 1967, 186.

33. David J. Garrow, *Bearing the Cross: Martin Luther King, Jr. and the Southern Christian Leadership Conference* (New York: Vintage Books, 1986), 543–554.

34. Chepesiuk, *Sixties Radicals, Then and Now*, 81.

35. Quoted in Walter Goodman, "Liberals vs. Radicals: War in the Peace Camp," *New York Times Magazine*, December 3, 1967, 186.

36. Quoted in Wells, *The War Within*, 17.

37. Useful biographical information about Fred Halstead can be found in John George and Laird Wilcox, *American Extremists: Militias, Supremacists, Klansmen, Communists, & Others* (Amherst, N.Y.: Prometheus Books, 1996), 110; and Halstead's own detailed account of the antiwar movement, *Out Now!* .

38. Doug Dowd, interview by author, August 10, 2004.

39. Unpublished transcript of November 26, 1966, Spring Mobilization Committee to End the War in Vietnam, held in New York City, Mobe Papers, Box 5, SCPC.

40. Zaroulis and Sullivan, *Who Spoke Up?* 336.

41. Halstead, *Out Now!* 176.

42. Doug Dowd, interview by author, August 10, 2004.

43. David Dellinger, *More Power Than We Know: The People's Movement toward Democracy* (New York: Anchor Press/Doubleday, 1975), 112–113.

44. Halstead, *Out Now!* 328.

45. Dellinger, *From Yale to Jail*, 283. In his memoirs Dellinger explores his distant relationship with King in much more detail than it probably deserves.

46. Quoted in Matt Meyer and Judith Mahoney Pasternak, "David Dellinger, 1915–2004," *The Nonviolent Activist*, May/June 2004, 11.

47. David Dellinger, "Tribute to A. J. Muste," *Liberation*, January 1967, 2.

48. Zaroulis and Sullivan, *Who Spoke Up?* 233.

49. David McReynolds, "Pacifists and the Vietnam Antiwar Movement," in *Give Peace a Chance: Exploring the Vietnam Antiwar Movement*, edited by Melvin Small and William D. Hoover (Syracuse, N.Y.: Syracuse University Press, 1992), 64.

50. Sidney Peck, interview by author, March 9, 2004.

51. Dellinger, *From Yale to Jail*, 295. Peck admitted he called for Dellinger's resignation as the chair of the Spring Mobilization, as he felt Dellinger had behaved irresponsibly and had violated the democratic procedures of the coalition by lobbying so rigorously to allow the draft card burners to share the main stage.

52. Sidney Peck, interview by author, March 9, 2004.

53. Melvin Small, *Covering Dissent: The Media and the Anti–Vietnam War Movement* (New Brunswick, N.J.: Rutgers University Press, 1994), 68.

54. David Farber, *Chicago '68* (Chicago: University of Chicago Press, 1988), 69.

55. Dave Dellinger, "Resistance: Vietnam and America," *Liberation*, November 1967, 5. "Gandhi and guerrilla" became a rallying cry for the antiwar movement in the months leading up to the October 1967 protests at the Pentagon. Who coined it remains unknown, although Dellinger was one of its most frequent users.

56. Spring Mobilization Committee to End the War in Vietnam, Minutes: Administrative Committee Meeting, June 17, 1967, New York City, Mobe Papers, Box 1, SCPC.

57. Doug Dowd, interview by author, August 10, 2004.

58. David Dellinger, untitled, National Mobilization Committee to End the War on Vietnam, n.d. (ca. May 1967), 3, Mobe Papers, Box 4, SCPC.

59. Farber, *Chicago '68*, 9; J. Anthony Lukas, *Don't Shoot We Are Your Children!* (New York: Dell, 1972), 323–369.

60. Joan Morrison and Robert K. Morrison, *From Camelot to Kent State: The Sixties Experience in the Words of Those Who Lived It* (New York: Times Books / Random House, 1987), 284.

61. Ibid., 285.

62. Halstead, *Out Now!* 314.

63. Bertrand Russell Peace Foundation, "The International War Crimes Tribunal" (n.d., ca. March 1967), David Dellinger Papers, Box 8, Tamiment; John Duffett, ed., *Against the Crime of Silence* (New York: Clarion, 1968).

64. Staughton Lynd, "The War Crimes Tribunal: A Dissent," *Liberation*, January 1968, 79.

65. Wells, *The War Within*, 142–143.

66. David Dellinger, "Government Withdraws Ultimatum—Permits Expected for March and Rallies," *Mobilizer News*, October 1967, 4, Mobe Papers, Box 4, SCPC.

67. Paul Krassner, *Confessions of a Raving, Unconfined Nut: Misadventures in the Counter-Culture* (New York: Simon & Schuster, 1993), 152.

68. Dellinger, *From Yale to Jail*, 301.

69. Doug Dowd, interview by author, August 10, 2004.

70. Mobe press conference quotes come from Wells, *The War Within*, 175. See also unpublished Pentagon march press conference announcement, August 28, 1967, Mobe Papers, Box 4, SCPC.

71. Dellinger, *More Power Than We Know*, 112.

72. Harold Feldman to David Dellinger, August 30, 1967, David Dellinger Papers, Box 11, Tamiment.

73. James Tracy, *Direct Action: Radical Pacifism from the Union Eight to the Chicago Seven* (Chicago: University of Chicago Press, 1996), 142.

74. McReynolds, "Pacifists and the Vietnam Antiwar Movement," 65.

75. Charles Bloomstein to the editorial board of *Liberation*, June 17, 1967, David Dellinger Papers, Box 11, Tamiment.

76. Doug Dowd, interview by author, August 10, 2004.

77. Details of the Mobe/Van Cleve negotiations can be found in Halstead, *Out Now!* 331–334; and Wells, *The War Within*, 188–189.

78. David Dellinger, "A Word to the Wise," *Mobilizer News*, October 16, 1967, 2, Mobe Papers, Box 4, SCPC.

79. Quoted in Small, *Covering Dissent*, 74.

80. *New York Times*, October 21, 1967, 8.

NOTES TO CHAPTER 9

Epigraphs: Murray Kempton, "Review of *Revolutionary Nonviolence* by David Dellinger," *New York Review of Books*, January 7, 1971, 39; "Revolutionary Non-Violence: Remembering Dave Dellinger," Pacifica Radio, May 27, 2004; and Theodore H. White, *The Making of a President: 1968* (New York: Atheneum, 1969), 257.

1. Robert McNamara, *In Retrospect: The Tragedy and Lessons of Vietnam* (New York: Random House, 1995), 304.

2. Sidney Lens, *Unrepentant Radical: An American Activist's Account of Five Turbulent Decades* (Boston: Beacon Press, 1980), 322.

3. *Time*, October 27, 1967.

4. Stew Albert, interview by author, September 30, 2004.

5. David Dellinger, interview by Ted Gittinger, December 10, 1982, LBJL.

6. Quoted in Thomas Maier, *Dr. Spock: An American Life* (New York: Harcourt Brace, 1998), 278.

7. Milton Viorst, *Fire in the Streets: America in the 1960s* (New York: Simon & Schuster, 1980), 413; Maurice Isserman and Michael Kazin, *America Divided: The Civil War of the 1960s* (New York: Oxford University Press, 2000), 184; Tom Wells, *The War Within: America's Battle over Vietnam* (Berkeley: University of California Press, 1994), 193–194; *The National Guardian*, October 28, 1967.

8. Louis Heren, "10,000 Besiege the Pentagon," *Times* (London), October 23, 1967, 1.

9. *New York Times*, October 22, 1967.

10. Quoted in *New York Times*, October 22, 1967, 58.

11. *New York Times*, October 22, 1967, 8, 58.

12. Quoted in Norman Mailer, *The Armies of the Night* (New York: New American Library, 1968), 103.

13. Marty Jezer, letter to Andrew Hunt, August 21, 2001.

14. *New York Times*, October 23, 1967, 32.

15. Wells, *The War Within*, 196.

16. Quoted in Jonah Raskin, *For the Hell of It: The Life and Times of Abbie Hoffman* (Berkeley: University of California Press, 1997), 121.

17. The scene is recreated vividly by Mailer in *The Armies of the Night*, 130–131.

18. Bud Schultz and Ruth Schultz, eds., *The Price of Dissent: Testimonies to Political Repression in America* (Berkeley, Calif.: University of California Press, 2001), 310.

19. Quoted in Wells, *The War Within*, 197.

20. George Dennison, "Talking with the Troops," *Liberation*, November 1967, 13.

21. Nancy Zaroulis and Gerald Sullivan, *Who Spoke Up? American Protest against the War in Vietnam, 1963–1975* (New York: Doubleday, 1984), 139; Allen J. Matusow, *Unraveling of America: A History of Liberalism in the 1960s* (New York: Harper & Row, 1984), 329.

22. Quoted in Maier, *Dr. Spock*, 295.

23. David Dellinger, *From Yale to Jail: The Life Story of a Moral Dissenter* (New York: Pantheon Books, 1993), 305–306.

24. Both quotations are from Maier, *Dr. Spock*, 295.

25. *New York Times*, October 23, 1967, 32.

26. Sidney Peck, interview by author, March 9, 2004.

27. Doug Dowd, interview by author, August 10, 2004.

28. Sidney Peck, interview by author, March 9, 2004.

29. Ibid.

30. Noam Chomsky, interview by author, March 23, 2004.

31. Quoted in *Newsweek*, November 6, 1967, 26.

32. These figures are from Wells, *The War Within*, 203.

33. Quoted in Melvin Small, *Covering Dissent: The Media and the Anti–Vietnam War Movement* (New Brunswick, N.J.: Rutgers University Press, 1994), 81.

34. Quoted in Wells, *The War Within*, 204.

35. Quoted in Charles DeBenedetti, *An American Ordeal: The Antiwar Movement of the Vietnam Era* (Syracuse, N.Y.: Syracuse University Press, 1990), 198.

36. *U.S. News & World Report*, November 13, 1967, 12.

37. Quoted in DeBenedetti, *An American Ordeal*, 198.

38. *Newsweek*, October 30, 1967, 20.

39. *Washington Post*, October 22, 1967.

40. McNamara, *In Retrospect*, 305.

41. Melvin Small, "The Impact of the Antiwar Movement on Lyndon Johnson, 1965–1968: A Preliminary Report," *Peace and Change* 10 (1984): 14–15.

42. Quoted in David Farber, *Chicago '68* (Chicago: University of Chicago Press, 1988), 70.

43. FBI memorandum, Washington Office to SAC New York, October 23, 1967.

44. SAC Newark (100-50166) to director, FBI, May 27, 1968.

45. Quoted in Paul Cowan, Nick Egleson, and Nat Hentoff, *State Secrets: Police Surveillance in America* (New York: Holt, Rinehart & Winston, 1974), 254.

46. Quoted in Charles DeBenedetti, "A CIA Analysis of the Anti–Vietnam War Movement: October 1967," *Peace and Change* 9 (1983): 31–41.

47. David Dellinger, interview by author, June 18, 2001; Dellinger, *From Yale to Jail*, 177–180.

48. Ibid.

49. Dellinger, *From Yale to Jail*, 179.

50. Elizabeth Peterson, interview with C. Arthur Bradley, August 20, 1989, UIS.

51. Ibid.

52. *New York Times*, September 13, 1968, 41.

53. Quoted in James Miller, *"Democracy Is in the Streets": From Port Huron to the Siege at Chicago* (New York: Simon & Schuster, 1987), 284.

54. Lens, *Unrepentant Radical*, 327.

55. Quoted in Farber, *Chicago '68*, 74; Fred Halstead, *Out Now! A Participant's Account of the American Movement against the Vietnam War* (New York: Monad Press, 1978), 405–406.

56. Viorst, *Fire in the Streets*, 177.

57. Ronald Chepesiuk, *Sixties Radicals, Then and Now: Candid Conversations with Those Who Shaped the Era* (Jefferson, N.C.: McFarland, 1995), 87.

58. James W. Clinton, *The Loyal Opposition: Americans in North Vietnam, 1965–1972* (Boulder: University Press of Colorado, 1996), 59.

59. Quoted in Daniel Walker, *Rights in Conflict: The Violent Confrontation of Demonstrators and Police in the Parks and Streets of Chicago during the Week of the Democratic National Convention of 1968* (New York: Signet Books, 1968), 14.

60. Marty Jezer, *Abbie Hoffman: American Rebel* (New Brunswick, N.J.: Rutgers University Press, 1992), 135.

61. Quoted in Wells, *The War Within*, 237.

62. David Dellinger, interview by author, June 18, 2001; Farber, *Chicago '68*, 87.

63. Isserman and Kazin, *America Divided*, 225.

64. Quoted in Farber, *Chicago '68*, 93.

65. Interestingly, Tom Hayden's and David Dellinger's memoirs each include discussions of the Harriman and Shriver meetings. But in *Reunion*, Hayden omits Dellinger from the gatherings, whereas Dellinger took Hayden to task for ignoring him. Hayden claims he made appointments to meet with Harriman and Shriver and does not even mention Dellinger. "In his account, I wasn't there," an irate Dellinger later wrote. "I hope my memory hasn't played too many similar tricks on me." See Tom Hayden, *Reunion: A Memoir* (New York: Random House, 1988), 269–271; and Dellinger, *From Yale to Jail*, 321–323.

66. David Dellinger, "Nonviolence Isn't Dead," *Liberation*, April 1968, 6.

67. David Dellinger, "The Assassination of Robert F. Kennedy," *Liberation*, July 1968, reprinted in David Dellinger, *Revolutionary Nonviolence: Essays* (Indianapolis: Bobbs-Merrill, 1971), 221–227.

68. Wells, *The War Within*, 263–264.

69. Coretta Scott King, "Don't Turn Your Back," address to the antiwar rally in New York City's Central Park, April 27, 1968, printed in *Liberation*, April 1968, 13–15.

70. All excerpts are quoted in Small, *Covering Dissent*, 87.

71. David Dellinger, *More Power Than We Know: The People's Movement toward Democracy* (Garden City, N.Y.: Anchor/Doubleday, 1975), 121–122.

72. *New Left Notes*, March 4, 1968.

73. Quoted in *The Militant*, January 8, 1968.

74. *Chicago Tribune*, August 9, 1968.

75. Adam Cohen and Elizabeth Taylor, *American Pharaoh: Mayor Richard J. Daley: His Battle for Chicago and the Nation* (Boston: Little, Brown, 2000), 463.

76. *New York Times*, August 22, 1968; Farber, *Chicago '68*, 102, 105; *Chicago 1968* (documentary film, 1995).

77. Elizabeth Peterson, interview with C. Arthur Bradley, August 20, 1989, UIS.

78. Halstead, *Out Now!* 410; Todd Gitlin, *The Sixties: Years of Hope, Days of Rage* (New York: Bantam Books, 1987), 324–325; Wells, *The War Within*, 276–277.

79. Charles Kaiser, *1968 in America: Music, Politics, Chaos, Counterculture and the Shaping of a Generation* (New York: Grove Press, 1997), 234.

80. Quoted in Gitlin, *The Sixties*, 324.

81. Jules Feiffer, *Pictures at a Prosecution: Drawings & Text from the Chicago Conspiracy Trial* (New York: Grove Press, 1970), 57.

82. Quoted in J. Anthony Lukas, *The Barnyard Epithet and Other Obscenities: Notes on the Chicago Conspiracy Trial* (New York: Harper & Row, 1970), 9.

83. David Dellinger interview, *Downtown Magazine* (1993), reprinted in CounterPunch, May 2004.

84. Paul Krassner, *Confessions of a Raving, Unconfined Nut: Misadventures in the Counter-Culture* (New York: Simon & Schuster, 1993), 164.

85. *New York Times*, August 28, 1968.

86. David Dellinger, interview by author, June 18, 2001.

87. Carl Oglesby, "Street Fightin' Man," in *Against the Vietnam War: Writings by Activists*, edited by Mary Susannah Robbins (Syracuse, N.Y.: Syracuse University Press, 1999), 133.

88. Ibid., 134.

89. Quoted in Feiffer, *Pictures at a Prosecution*, 135.

90. Feiffer, *Pictures at a Prosecution*, 67. Quoted in the testimony of James Hunt at the Chicago Seven conspiracy trial.

91. Quoted in Wells, *The War Within*, 278.

92. Tom Hayden to author, November 5, 2004.

93. Quoted in Wells, *The War Within*, 278.

94. *Chicago Daily News*, August 29, 1968.

95. Feiffer, *Pictures at a Prosecution*, 64.

96. Dellinger, *From Yale to Jail*, 333.

97. Terry Anderson, *The Movement and the Sixties* (New York: Oxford University Press, 1995), 224.

98. *Life*, December 6, 1968.

99. Quoted in Anderson, *The Movement and the Sixties*, 222.

100. Farber, *Chicago '68*, 201–202.

101. Cohen and Taylor, *American Pharaoh*, 481.

102. Ibid.

103. Walker, *Rights in Conflict*, 1–5, quoted in David J. Langum, *William M. Kunstler: The Most Hated Lawyer in America* (New York: New York University Press, 1999), 102–103.

104. Small, *Covering Dissent*, 88.

105. Quoted in the *Chicago Daily News*, August 29, 1968.

106. David Dellinger, "Lessons from Chicago," *Liberation*, October 1968, 8, quoted in James Tracy, *Direct Action: Radical Pacifism from the Union Eight to the Chicago Seven* (Chicago: University of Chicago Press, 1996), 148.

NOTES TO CHAPTER 10

Epigraphs: Betty Dellinger, *The Lyndon Independent*, March 24, 1993, 11; Stewart Alsop, "Stewart Alsop, 'The Last Idealist,'" *Newsweek*, November 17, 1969, 140; and Thomas Foran, *Chicago Tribune*, June 24, 1996.

1. David Dellinger, "Dear Friend," National Mobilization Committee to End the War in Vietnam mass mailing, September 1968, Mobe Papers, Box 4, SCPC.

2. Paul Krassner, interview by author, January 15, 2004.

3. Doug Dowd, interview by author, August 10, 2004.

4. Sid Peck, interview by author, March 9, 2004.

5. Bradford Lyttle, letter to the author, June 1, 2001.

6. Both excerpts quoted in Melvin Small, *Covering Dissent: The Media and the Anti–Vietnam War Movement* (New Brunswick, N.J.: Rutgers University Press, 1994), 91.

7. Judy Clavir and John Spitzer, eds., *The Conspiracy Trial* (New York: Bobbs-Merrill, 1970), 602.

8. Quoted in David J. Langum, *William M. Kunstler: The Most Hated Lawyer in America* (New York: New York University Press, 1999), 104.

9. Andrew Kopkind, "The Trial," *Hard Times*, February 23–March 2, 1970, reprinted in Andrew Kopkind, *The Thirty Years' Wars: Dispatches and Diversions of a Radical Journalist, 1965–1994* (New York: Verso, 1995), 198.

10. Quoted in Tom Hayden, *Reunion: A Memoir* (New York: Random House, 1988), 343.

11. Ibid.

12. Quoted in Mitchell Goodman, ed., *The Movement toward a New America: The Beginnings of a Long Revolution* (New York: Knopf, 1970), 564.

13. Langum, *William M. Kunstler*, 106.

14. David Dellinger, *From Yale to Jail: The Life Story of a Moral Dissenter* (New York: Pantheon Books, 1993), 345.

15. William M. Kunstler, *My Life as a Radical Lawyer* (New York: Citadel Press, 1994), 12.

16. Quoted in Langum, *William M. Kunstler*, 111.

17. See William M. Kunstler and Stewart E. Albert, "The Great Conspiracy Trial of '69," *The Nation*, September 29, 1979.

18. According to Marty Jezer, Tom Hayden "estimated that the Chicago Seven plus their lawyers made approximately five hundred campus appearances." See Marty Jezer, *Abbie Hoffman: American Rebel* (New Brunswick, N.J.: Rutgers University Press, 1992), 210.

19. Elizabeth Peterson, interview with C. Arthur Bradley, August 20, 1989, UIS.

20. All three quotations are from J. Anthony Lukas, *The Barnyard Epithet and Other Obscenities: Notes on the Chicago Conspiracy Trial* (New York: Harper & Row, 1970), 1.

21. Oliver Jensen, *Yale Class of 1936: Fifty Years Out* (New Haven, Conn.: Yale University Press, 1986), 108; Dellinger, *From Yale to Jail*, 394.

22. David Dellinger, interview by author, June 18, 2001.

23. Joseph Okpaku, *Verdict!: The Exclusive Picture Story of the Trial of the Chicago Eight* (New York: Third Press, 1970), 14; Clavir and Spitzer, *The Conspiracy Trial*, 13.

24. Clavir and Spitzer, *The Conspiracy Trial*, 15.

25. Clavir and Spitzer, *The Conspiracy Trial*, 92–93; Jonah Raskin, *For the Hell of It: The Life and Times of Abbie Hoffman* (Berkeley: University of California Press, 1997), 205.

26. Clavir and Spitzer, *The Conspiracy Trial*, 93.

27. These exchanges are from Harry Kalven Jr. and Bernard Weisberg, *Contempt: Transcript of the Contempt Citations, Sentences, and Responses of the Chicago Conspiracy 10* (Chicago: Swallow Press, 1970), xx.

28. Ibid., 46.

29. Clavir and Spitzer, *The Conspiracy Trial*, 162.

30. David Dellinger, interview by author, June 18, 2001; Raskin, *For the Hell of It*, 205.

31. Bobby Seale, *Seize the Time: The Story of the Black Panther Party and Huey P. Newton* (New York: Random House, 1970), 345.

32. John Schultz, *Motion Will Be Denied: A New Report on the Chicago Conspiracy Trial* (New York: Morrow, 1972), 67, 71. Dellinger long held that Schultz's book was the best account of the Chicago trial. In 1991, he wrote to his old friend Bill Lovell: "In some ways I think that the best book about the trial is John Schultz, *Motion Will Be Denied*. . . . He was a Chicago reporter who covered the trial." See David Dellinger to Bill Lovell, December 30, 1991, courtesy of Bill Lovell.

33. "John Froines Discusses the Life and Activism of David Dellinger," *All Things Considered*, NPR, May 26, 2004.

34. Bob Lamb, interview by author, October 22, 2004; Dellinger, *From Yale to Jail*, 352–353.

35. Quoted in Colman McCarthy, "A Man Who Didn't Obey," *The Progressive*, August 2004, 34.

36. Dellinger, *From Yale to Jail*, 353.

37. Stew Albert, interview by author, September 30, 2004.

38. Jack Hoffman and Daniel Simon, *Run, Run, Run: The Lives of Abbie Hoffman* (New York: Putnam, 1994), 134.

39. David Hilliard and Lewis Cole, *This Side of Glory: The Autobiography of David Hilliard and the Story of the Black Panther Party* (Boston: Little, Brown, 1993), 262.

40. Quoted in "Tribute: Dave Dellinger: Scenes from the Life of a Freedom Warrior," Toward Freedom (fall 1994).

41. Nancy Zaroulis and Gerald Sullivan, *Who Spoke Up? American Protest against the War in Vietnam, 1963–1975* (New York: Doubleday, 1984), 290–291; Small, *Covering Dissent*, 114–116.

42. Paul Hoffman, *Moratorium: An American Protest* (New York: Tower, 1970), 188.

43. Schultz, *Motion Will Be Denied*, 19.

44. Quoted in Langum, *William M. Kunstler*, 108.

45. Todd Gitlin, *The Sixties: Years of Hope, Days of Rage* (New York: Bantam Books, 1987), 382–385.

46. David Dellinger, *More Power Than We Know: The People's Movement toward Democracy* (Garden City, N.Y.: Anchor/Doubleday, 1975), 162.

47. Quoted in Larry Sloman, *Steal This Dream: Abbie Hoffman and the Countercultural Revolution in America* (New York: Doubleday, 1998), 192.

48. Terry Anderson, *The Movement and the Sixties* (New York: Oxford University Press, 1995), 328.

49. Dellinger, *More Power Than We Know*, 150.

50. Charles E. Jones, ed., *The Black Panther Party Reconsidered* (Baltimore: Black Classic Press, 1998), 386.

51. *Chicago Sun-Times*, October 13, 2003; Ward Churchill and Jim Vander Wall, *Agents of Repression: The FBI's Secret Wars against the Black Panther Party and*

the American Indian Movement, 2nd ed. (Boston: South End Press, 2002), 64–76; Jones, *The Black Panther Party Reconsidered*, 373. See also Roy Wilkins and Ramsey Clark, *Search and Destroy: A Report by the Commission of Inquiry into the Black Panthers and the Police* (New York: Metropolitan Applied Research Center, 1973).

52. Dellinger, *From Yale to Jail*, 390.

53. Quoted in Dellinger, *From Yale to Jail*, 390.

54. Hilliard and Cole, *This Side of Glory*, 439.

55. Clavir and Spitzer, *The Conspiracy Trial*, 529. See also Schultz, *Motion Will Be Denied*, 261, 287.

56. All quotations are from Clavir and Spitzer, *The Conspiracy Trial*, 529.

57. Schultz, *Motion Will Be Denied*, 262.

58. Kunstler, *My Life as a Radical Lawyer*, 33.

59. David Dellinger, interview by author, June 18, 2001.

60. *New York Times*, February 5, 1969; Schultz, *Motion Will Be Denied*, 262.

61. Clavir and Spitzer, *The Conspiracy Trial*, 580–581.

62. I relied heavily on James W. Ely Jr., "The Chicago Conspiracy Case," in *American Political Trials*, edited by Michael R. Belknap (Westport, Conn.: Greenwood Press, 1994), 233–253. This is a superb legal analysis of the case. See also Jezer, *Abbie Hoffman*, 209–210; Langum, *William M. Kunstler*, 119–120.

63. Ronald Chepesiuk, *Sixties Radicals, Then and Now: Candid Conversations with Those Who Shaped the Era* (Jefferson, N.C.: McFarland, 1995), 88; Jezer, *Abbie Hoffman*, 197.

64. Leonard Weinglass, interview by author, August 9, 2001.

65. *Chicago Tribune*, June 24, 1996.

66. *Chicago Tribune*, October 9, 1969.

67. *Time*, March 2, 1970, 11.

68. William F. Buckley, "Assault on the Courts," *National Review*, February 24, 1970, 190; William F. Buckley, "After Chicago," *National Review*, March 10, 1970, 273.

69. Ely, "The Chicago Conspiracy Case," 249–250.

70. Tom Wicker, "The Place Where All America Was Radicalized," *New York Times Magazine*, August 24, 1969, 90.

71. Quoted in Tom Wells, *The War Within: America's Battle over Vietnam* (Berkeley: University of California Press, 1994), 414.

72. Alan M. Dershowitz, *America on Trial: Inside the Legal Battles That Transformed Our Nation* (New York: Warner Books, 2004), 393–394.

73. Quoted in Robert Houriet, "Dellinger's Dilemma: After Yale, after Jail, What Now?" *Vermont Sunday Magazine*, July 27, 1993, 12.

74. Dellinger, *From Yale to Jail*, 56.

NOTES TO CHAPTER 11

Epigraph: Roxanne Dunbar-Ortiz, *Outlaw Woman: Memoir of the War Years, 1960–1975* (San Francisco: City Lights Books, 2002).

1. Tom Wells, *The War Within: America's Battle over Vietnam* (Berkeley: University of California Press, 1994), 419–420. Charles DeBenedetti, *An American Ordeal: The Antiwar Movement of the Vietnam Era* (Syracuse, N.Y.: Syracuse University Press, 1990), 279.

2. For an extensive description of Dellinger's involvement in the May 1970 Yale protests, see John Taft, *Mayday at Yale: A Case Study in Student Radicalism* (Boulder, Colo.: Westview Press, 1976).

3. Fred Halstead, *Out Now! A Participant's Account of the American Movement against the Vietnam War* (New York: Monad Press, 1978), 723.

4. *Village Voice*, June 4, 1970, 12–13.

5. Melvin Small, *Covering Dissent: The Media and the Anti–Vietnam War Movement* (New Brunswick, N.J.: Rutgers University Press, 1994), 140.

6. *Washington Post*, May 10, 1970; Small, *Covering Dissent*, 131.

7. Quoted in Wells, *The War Within*, 442.

8. Halstead, *Out Now!* 569.

9. David Dellinger, *More Power Than We Know: The People's Movement toward Democracy* (Garden City, N.Y.: Anchor/Doubleday, 1975), 136.

10. David Dellinger, "Time to Look at Ourselves," *Liberation*, August–October 1970, 6, 74.

11. Jay Craven, "Dave Dellinger Remembered," a speech delivered at a David Dellinger Memorial held at Montpelier Peace Park, June 5, 2004. Reprinted in *Peace Work*, June 2004, courtesy of Jay Craven. See also Jay Craven, interview by author, November 29, 2004.

12. George W. Hopkins, "'May Day' 1971: Civil Disobedience and the Vietnam Antiwar Movement," in *Give Peace a Chance: Exploring the Vietnam Antiwar Movement*, edited by Melvin Small and William D. Hoover (Syracuse, N.Y.: Syracuse University Press, 1992), 79.

13. Quoted in G. Louis Heath, ed., *Mutiny Does Not Happen Lightly* (Metuchen, N.J.: Scarecrow Press, 1976), 206.

14. Jay Craven, interview by author, November 29, 2004.

15. David Dellinger, "Remarks to the 25th Anniversary of VVAW," unpublished, 1992, David Dellinger Papers, Box 9, Tamiment.

16. Andrew E. Hunt, *The Turning: A History of Vietnam Veterans against the War* (New York: New York University Press, 1999), 106–107.

17. *New Kensington* (Pa.) *Dispatch*, April 21, 1971.

18. *Akron Beacon Journal*, April 26, 1971.

19. James W. Clinton, *The Loyal Opposition: Americans in North Vietnam, 1965–1972* (Boulder: University Press of Colorado, 1996), 38–39.

20. David McReynolds, "Pacifists and the Vietnam Antiwar Movement," in *Give Peace a Chance: Exploring the Vietnam Antiwar Movement*, edited by Melvin Small and William D. Hoover (Syracuse, N.Y.: Syracuse University Press, 1992), 68.

21. Ibid.

22. *Washington Post*, May 2, 1971; Nancy Zaroulis and Gerald Sullivan, *Who Spoke Up? American Protest against the War in Vietnam, 1963–1975* (New York: Doubleday, 1984), 361.

23. See Noam Chomsky, "Mayday: The Case for Civil Disobedience," *New York Review of Books*, June 17, 1971, 19.

24. Jay Craven, interview by author, November 29, 2004. Craven remembered Dellinger's getting arrested early in the protests. A careful reading of the *New York Times*, *Washington Post*, and underground press accounts of the march reveals frequent mentions of Rennie Davis's name but little discussion of Dellinger. Also see George W. Hopkins, "'May Day' 1971: Civil Disobedience and the Vietnam Antiwar Movement," in *Give Peace a Chance: Exploring the Vietnam Antiwar Movement*, edited by Melvin Small and William D. Hoover (Syracuse, N.Y.: Syracuse University Press, 1992), 82.

25. Quoted in *Washington Post*, May 4, 1971.

26. Sid Peck, interview by author, March 9, 2004.

27. Jay Craven, interview by author, November 29, 2004.

28. Quoted in Chomsky, "Mayday," 19.

29. Dellinger, *More Power Than We Know*, 51.

30. Small, *Covering Dissent*, 160.

31. Le Phuong, to David Dellinger, n.d. (ca. late 1968), David Dellinger Papers, Box 11, Tamiment.

32. Quoted in Mary Hershberger, *Traveling to Vietnam: American Peace Activists and the War* (Syracuse, N.Y.: Syracuse University Press, 1998), 145. See also Daniel Berrigan, *Night Flight to Hanoi: War Diary with 11 Poems* (New York: Macmillan, 1968).

33. Do Xuan Oanh to David Dellinger, January 15, 1969, David Dellinger Papers, Box 8, Tamiment; Hershberger, *Traveling to Vietnam*, 145–150, 155–156.

34. Clinton, *The Loyal Opposition*, 52.

35. The Nation, July 28, 1969, 68–69.

36. Quoted in "Anti-War Team to Pick up Captured Pilots in Hanoi," *Globe and Mail* (Toronto), July 11, 1969, 3. See also "Pacifist Predicts Release of Pilot," *Globe and Mail*, July 10, 1969, 9.

37. Clinton, *The Loyal Opposition*, 174.

38. Cora Weiss, interview by author, August 13, 2004; Amy Swerdlow, *Women Strike for Peace: Traditional Motherhood and Radical Politics in the 1960s* (Chicago: University of Chicago Press, 1993), 222–223.

39. Cora Weiss, interview by author, August 13, 2004.

40. Clinton, *The Loyal Opposition*, 52.

41. *New York Times*, January 19, 1970, 4.

42. Clinton, *The Loyal Opposition*, 166.

43. Committee of Liaison with Families of Servicemen Detained in North Vietnam, Memo to Families of Prisoners of War in North Vietnam, August 1971, David Dellinger Papers, Box 8, Tamiment.

44. Press release, Committee of Liaison with Families of Servicemen Detained in North Vietnam, December 21, 1971, David Dellinger Papers, Box 8, Tamiment.

45. Clinton, *The Loyal Opposition*, 175.

46. *New York Times*, September 6, 1972, 17.

47. *New York Times*, September 3, 1972, 1.

48. Hershberger, *Traveling to Vietnam*, 216–217.

49. Hershberger, *Traveling to Vietnam*, 218–219; *New York Times*, September 29, 1972, 1.

50. *Newsweek*, November 17, 1969, 140.

51. David Dellinger, interview by Ted Gittinger, December 10, 1982, LBJL.

52. David Dellinger, interview by author, October 30, 1999.

53. David Dellinger, *From Yale to Jail: The Life Story of a Moral Dissenter* (New York: Pantheon Books, 1993), 424.

54. David Dellinger to Genardin (no other name), August 12, 1971, David Dellinger Papers, Box 6, Tamiment.

55. Todd Gitlin, *The Sixties: Years of Hope, Days of Rage* (New York: Bantam Books, 1987), 363. Alice Echols, *Daring to Be Bad: Radical Feminism in America, 1967–1975* (Minneapolis: University of Minnesota Press, 1989), 117.

56. Echols, *Daring to Be Bad*, 220, 225, 226, 228, 231.

57. *Caledonian Record*, June 17, 1993, 8.

58. Elizabeth Peterson, interview by author, June 18, 2001.

59. *Caledonian Record*, June 17, 1993, 8.

60. Elizabeth Peterson, interview by author, June 18, 2001.

61. Quoted in Nat Winthrop, "Life on the Edge," *Vermont Sunday Magazine*, April 29, 2001, 11.

62. Quoted in Larry Sloman, *Steal This Dream: Abbie Hoffman and the Countercultural Revolution in America* (New York: Doubleday, 1998), 263.

63. Ibid.

64. *Chicago Tribune*, November 23, 1972.

65. Patrick Doyle and William McFadden, "Nab Abbie Hoffman on Dope Charge," *New York Daily News*, August 29, 1973.

66. Quoted in Jonah Raskin, *For the Hell of It: The Life and Times of Abbie Hoffman* (Berkeley: University of California Press, 1997), 227.

67. Joan Morrison and Robert K. Morrison, *From Camelot to Kent State: The*

Sixties Experience in the Words of Those Who Lived It (New York: Times Books / Random House, 1987), 289–290.

68. Tom Hayden, *Reunion: A Memoir* (New York: Random House, 1988), 469.

69. *New York Times*, October 9, 1976.

70. Hayden, *Reunion*, 462.

71. Quoted in Ron Rosenbaum, "Separate Peaces," *Village Voice*, November 22, 1973, 8.

72. David Dellinger, unpublished speech delivered May 11, 1975 in Central Park, David Dellinger Papers, Box 8, Tamiment; Zaroulis and Sullivan, *Who Spoke Up?* 420.

73. David Dellinger, "The Need for a Weekly Newsmagazine," 1975, David Dellinger Papers, Box 1, Tamiment.

74. David Dellinger, "Letter from Dave Dellinger for Direct Mail Package," n.d. (ca. 1976), David Dellinger Papers, Box 1, Tamiment.

75. *New York Times*, July 15, 1976, 18.

76. Robert Cooney and Helen Michalowski, eds., *The Power of the People: Active Nonviolence in the United States* (Philadelphia: New Society Publishers, 1987), 231.

77. Arthur Miller to David Dellinger, May 22, 1978, David Dellinger Papers, Box 1, Tamiment.

78. Ken McEldowney to David Dellinger, August 16, 1978, David Dellinger Papers, Box 1, Tamiment.

79. Michael Castleman to David Dellinger, November 26, 1978, David Dellinger Papers, Box 1, Tamiment.

80. Aikos (no other name) to David Dellinger, February 18, 1980, David Dellinger Papers, Box 1, Tamiment.

81. David (no other name) to David Dellinger, August 5, 1979, David Dellinger Papers, Box 1, Tamiment.

82. Adam Hochschild to George Pillsbury, January 4, 1979, David Dellinger Papers, Box 1, Tamiment.

83. *Seven Days*, April 1980, 3.

84. In fairness to Dellinger, *From Yale to Jail* was only half of what he intended to be a two-volume autobiography. He addresses few developments in his life in any detail after the Chicago conspiracy trial, including the years he spent at *Seven Days*.

85. David Dellinger to Tom Hirsch, August 16, 1975, David Dellinger Papers, Box 8, Tamiment.

86. David Dellinger to Do Xuan Oanh, March 3, 1976, David Dellinger Papers, Box 7, Tamiment.

87. Much of the correspondence between Dellinger and Ferry is in David Dellinger's Papers, Tamiment. David's letters to her (which are sometimes also

addressed to her husband Ping) often contain carefully worded requests for additional financial support.

88. Elizabeth Peterson, interview by author, June 18, 2001.

89. Ibid.

90. Quoted in Robert Houriet, "Dellinger's Dilemma: After Yale, after Jail, What Now?" *Vermont Sunday Magazine*, July 27, 1993, 12.

NOTES TO CHAPTER 12

Epigraphs: Newsday, February 19, 1987; Ted Schmidt, "The Life of a Moral Dissenter: An Appreciation of David Dellinger," *Catholic New Times*, June 20, 2004, 3; and *Chicago Tribune*, June 24, 1996.

1. *Caledonian Record*, April 22, 1985.

2. David Dellinger, "The 'Me' Generation Says 'Not Me!'" *Seven Days*, April 1980, 22.

3. Quoted in *Sunday Rutland Herald*, February 21, 1982.

4. Ibid.

5. Robert Houriet, "Dellinger's Dilemma: After Yale, after Jail, What Now?" *Vermont Sunday Magazine*, July 27, 1993, 12.

6. *Times Argus* (Montpelier, Vt.), February 16, 1984.

7. Houriet, "Dellinger's Dilemma," 12.

8. David Dellinger to Birch Shapiro, 1988 (no exact date, but it is contained in the folder entitled "Correspondence: 1988"), David Dellinger Papers, Box 7, Tamiment.

9. Quoted in *Sunday Rutland Herald*, June 3, 1984.

10. Maurice Isserman, *The Other American: The Life of Michael Harrington* (New York: PublicAffairs, 2001), 341–342.

11. Quoted in *Rutland Daily Herald*, April 16, 1984.

12. David Dellinger, interview by C. Arthur Bradley, July 7, 1988, UIS.

13. *New York Times*, June 4, 1979, 1.

14. Quoted in *Newsday*, February 19, 1987.

15. *Newsday*, February 19, 1987.

16. Haynes Johnson, *Sleepwalking through History: America in the Reagan Years* (New York: Norton, 1991), 258–260.

17. Johnson, *Sleepwalking through History; Boston Globe*, July 25, 1989.

18. *Hardwick Gazette*, April 3, 1984.

19. David Dellinger, "To Whom It May Concern," May 1, 1984, David Dellinger Papers, Box 9, Tamiment.

20. *Newsday*, February 19, 1987. For a thorough treatment of the trial, see Ben Bradley, Nathan P. Hine, Judith Vollmann, and Nancy Wasserman, eds, with an introduction by David Dellinger, *Por Amor al Pueblo: Not Guilty! The Trial of the Winooski 44* (White River Junction, Vt.: Front Porch Publishing, 1986).

21. *Newsday*, February 19, 1987; *Daily Utah Chronicle*, December 10, 1986.

22. David Dellinger to Staughton and Alice Lynd, December 1, 1984, David Dellinger Papers, Box 7, Tamiment.

23. David Dellinger to David Cushman, June 24, 1989, David Dellinger Papers, Box 5, Tamiment.

24. David Dellinger, *From Yale to Jail: The Life Story of a Moral Dissenter* (New York: Pantheon Books, 1993), 58.

25. David Dellinger to Steve (no last name), November 16, 1988, David Dellinger Papers, Box 7, Tamiment.

26. David Dellinger, interview conducted by New Liberation News Service, published in *The Thistle* (Cambridge, Mass.), June 7, 1993.

27. Marty Jezer to author, August 21, 2001.

28. Johanna Lawrenson, speech, Burlington, Vermont, October 20, 2001, on CD recording, *Nonviolent Warriors: Dellinger & the Power of the People* (Burlington, Vt.: Toward Freedom, 2002).

29. Jack Hoffman and Daniel Simon, *Run Run Run: The Lives of Abbie Hoffman* (New York: Putnam, 1994), 307.

30. Joan Morrison and Robert K. Morrison, *From Camelot to Kent State: The Sixties Experience in the Words of Those Who Lived It* (New York: Times Books / Random House, 1987), 291.

31. Larry Sloman, *Steal This Dream: Abbie Hoffman and the Countercultural Revolution in America* (New York: Doubleday, 1998), 376.

32. Ronald Chepesiuk, *Sixties Radicals, Then and Now: Candid Conversations with Those Who Shaped the Era* (Jefferson, N.C.: McFarland, 1995), 88.

33. Sloman, *Steal This Dream*, 403.

34. Chepesiuk, *Sixties Radicals, Then and Now*, 88.

35. Marty Jezer, *Abbie Hoffman: American Rebel* (New Brunswick, N.J.: Rutgers University Press, 1992), 304–305; Jonah Raskin, *For the Hell of It: The Life and Times of Abbie Hoffman* (Berkeley: University of California Press, 1997), 253.

36. *Boston Globe*, April 27, 1989.

37. *Boston Globe*, April 20, 1989.

38. Ibid.

39. Stew Albert, interview by author, September 30, 2004.

40. *New York Times*, November 30 and December 4, 1994; *Houston Chronicle*, November 30, 1994; *Seattle Post-Intelligencer*, November 29, 1994.

41. Marv Davidov, interview by author, January 21, 2004.

42. *Kirkus Reviews*, February 1, 1993.

43. *Washington Post Book World*, April 4, 1993.

44. *New York Times Book Review*, May 9, 1993.

45. *San Francisco Chronicle*, April 7, 1993.

46. David Dellinger to Dan Frank, November 15, 1993, David Dellinger Papers, Box 8, Tamiment. Regarding the rumors of Hollywood's buying the film

rights to *From Yale to Jail*: in a letter dated December 10, 1992, Dellinger wrote, "My book is definitely coming out in March or April and a tour is planned not only by Pantheon but also by a couple of movement circles. Also, there is what appears to be a good possibility that someone will buy the film rights to the book—as well as a possible sell of the rights for a printing in paperback." See David Dellinger to Freddie (no last name), December 20, 1992, David Dellinger Papers, Box 3, Tamiment.

47. Dellinger, *From Yale to Jail* (paperback edition), ix.

48. Robert Steed to David Dellinger, April 16, 1994, David Dellinger Papers, Box 6, Tamiment.

49. "Revolutionary Non-Violence: Remembering Dave Dellinger, 1915–2004," Pacifica Radio, May 27, 2004.

50. David Dellinger to Abby (no last name), August 4, 1992, David Dellinger Papers, Box 3, Tamiment.

51. David Dellinger to Freddie (no last name), December 20, 1992, David Dellinger Papers, Box 3, Tamiment.

52. James W. Clinton, *The Loyal Opposition: Americans in North Vietnam, 1965–1972* (Boulder: University Press of Colorado, 1996), 57.

53. David Dellinger to Bill Lovell, December 30, 1991, courtesy of William Lovell.

54. Quoted in *Vermont Sunday Magazine*, April 29, 2001, 9.

55. Quoted in *San Francisco Chronicle*, August 26, 2001.

56. David Dellinger to Abby (no last name), August 4, 1992, David Dellinger Papers, Box 3, Tamiment.

57. *Vermont Sunday Magazine*, April 29, 2001, 11.

NOTES TO CHAPTER 13

Epigraph: Andrew Kopkind, *The Thirty Years' Wars: Dispatches and Diversions of a Radical Journalist, 1965–1994* (New York: Verso, 1995), 154.

1. Toward Freedom, Invitation to a Gala Celebration Honoring the Life and Work of Dave Dellinger and Elizabeth Peterson, October 20, 2001.

2. All quotations are directly from the CD recording of the event, *Nonviolent Warriors: Dave Dellinger & the Power of the People* (Burlington, Vt.: Toward Freedom, 2002).

3. David Dellinger, interview by author, June 18, 2001; *Vermont Sunday Magazine*, April 29, 2001, 11.

4. Michael Ferber, interview by author, August 31, 2004.

5. George Houser, interview by author, January 23, 2004.

6. Ralph DiGia, interview by author, August 5, 2001.

7. Ibid.

8. Elizabeth Peterson, interview by author, June 18, 2001.

9. See, for example, Dave Dellinger, "Be the Change: Looking Back and Looking Forward at the Path of Nonviolence," *Toward Freedom*, March/April 2001, 10.

10. David Dellinger to Leonard Peltier, March 2, 2001, courtesy David Dellinger.

11. Greg Guma, interview by author, February 9, 2004.

12. David Dellinger, "The Need for a Loving Economy with More Sharing," April 22, 2001, Quebec City, courtesy of David Dellinger.

13. Quoted in Frida Berrigan, "A Man of Peace," *In These Times*, July 22, 2002, 7.

14. Jeff Guntlzel, "Dellinger Battled Institutions, Not People," *National Catholic Reporter*, June 18, 2004.

15. Marv Davidov, interview by author, January 21, 2004.

16. Elizabeth Peterson to the author, February 2, 2004.

17. *Toward Freedom*, fall 2004.

18. Greg Guma, "Dave Dellinger: The Life of a Nonviolent Warrior," *Znet*, May 26, 2004.

19. *Catholic New Times*, June 20, 2004, 3; *New York Times*, May 27, 2004; *Times Argus* (Montpelier), May 27, 2004; *Washington Post*, May 27, 2004.

20. *The Nonviolent Activist*, May/June 2004, 21.

21. Jay Craven, "David Dellinger Remembered," June 5, 2004, courtesy Jay Craven.

22. Michael T. Kaufman, "David Dellinger, of Chicago Seven, Dies at 88," *New York Times*, May 27, 2004.

23. *Rutland Herald*, June 6, 2004.

24. Dr. Patchen Dellinger, "Memories of David Dellinger," June 4, 2004, courtesy of Dr. Patchen Dellinger.

25. *Pittsburgh Tribune Review*, October 31, 2004; Jay Craven, interview by author, December 21, 2004.

26. *All Things Considered*, NPR, May 26, 2004.

27. *Boston Globe*, August 30, 2004.

28. Quoted in Harry James Cargas, "David Dellinger: Optimism of the Will," *Catholic Worker*, May 1991.

Bibliography

MANUSCRIPT COLLECTIONS

A. J. Muste. Swarthmore College Peace Collection, Swarthmore, Pennsylvania.

American Civil Liberties Union. National Committee on Conscientious Objectors Records (1940–1946). Swarthmore College Peace Collection, Swarthmore, Pennsylvania.

Ann Morrissett and William C. Davidon Papers. Swarthmore College Peace Collection, Swarthmore, Pennsylvania.

Brad Lyttle Papers. Swarthmore College Peace Collection, Swarthmore, Pennsylvania.

Committee for Nonviolent Revolution Papers. Swarthmore College Peace Collection, Swarthmore, Pennsylvania.

Conscientious Objector Papers. Subject: World War II. Swarthmore College Peace Collection, Swarthmore, Pennsylvania.

David Dellinger Papers. Tamiment Collection, Elmer Bobst Library, New York University, New York.

Eichel Family Papers. Swarthmore College Peace Collection, Swarthmore, Pennsylvania.

Fast for Peace Papers. Swarthmore College Peace Collection, Swarthmore, Pennsylvania.

Fellowship of Reconciliation Papers. Swarthmore College Peace Collection, Swarthmore, Pennsylvania.

Henry Le Roy Finch Papers. Swarthmore College Peace Collection, Swarthmore, Pennsylvania.

Left Wing Political Activities Printed Material, 1966–1972. Cornell University Library, Ithaca, New York.

Liberation Papers. Swarthmore College Peace Collection, Swarthmore, Pennsylvania.

National Mobilization Committee to End the War in Vietnam Papers. Swarthmore College Peace Collection, Swarthmore, Pennsylvania.

Oral History Collection. Lyndon Baines Johnson Presidential Library, Austin, Texas.

Peacemakers Papers. Swarthmore College Peace Collection, Swarthmore, Pennsylvania.

People's Coalition for Peace and Justice Papers. Swarthmore College Peace Collection, Swarthmore, Pennsylvania.

Seven Days Papers. Temple University, Philadelphia.

Social Action Collection. Wisconsin State Historical Society, Madison.

Staughton and Alice Lynd Papers. Swarthmore College Peace Collection, Swarthmore, Pennsylvania.

Students for a Democratic Society Papers. Wisconsin State Historical Society, Madison.

Wakefield Historical Society, Wakefield, Massachusetts.

War Resisters League Papers. Swarthmore College Peace Collection, Swarthmore, Pennsylvania.

World War II Oral History Collection. University of Illinois at Springfield.

CORRESPONDENCE

Dr. Patch Dellinger to author, April 8, 2003.

Tom Hayden to author, November 5, 2004.

Marty Jezer to author, August 21, 2001.

William Lovell to author, February 4, 2004.

Brad Lyttle to author, June 1, 2001.

ORAL HISTORIES (CONDUCTED BY AUTHOR UNLESS OTHERWISE NOTED)

Stew Albert, September 30, 2004.

Norma Becker, August 9 and 10, 2001.

Don Benedict, January 27, 2004.

Donald Benedict, interview by C. Arthur Bradley, 1988. World War II Oral History Collection, University of Illinois at Springfield.

Noam Chomsky, March 23, 2004.

Jay Craven, November 29, 2004.

Meredith Dallas, May 28, 2004.

Meredith Dallas, interview by C. Arthur Bradley, June 9, 1988. World War II Oral History Collection, University of Illinois at Springfield.

Willa Dallas, interview by C. Arthur Bradley, June 9, 1988. World War II Oral History Collection, University of Illinois at Springfield.

Marv Davidov, January 21, 2004.

David Dellinger, October 30, 1999; June 16, 17, 18, and 19, 2001.

David Dellinger, interview by C. Arthur Bradley, July 7, 1988. World War II Oral History Collection, University of Illinois at Springfield.

Ralph DiGia, August 5, 2001.

Doug Dowd, August 10, 2004.

Michael Ferber, August 31, 2004.

Margaret Finch, May 21, 2004.

Larry Gara, February 12, 2004.

Greg Guma, February 9, 2004.

George Houser, January 23, 2004.

George Houser, interview by C. Arthur Bradley, 1988. World War II Oral History Collection, University of Illinois at Springfield.

Paul Krassner, January 15, 2004.

Bob Lamb, October 22, 2004.

Bradford Lyttle, May 29, 2001.

William Lovell, February 17, 2004.

William Lovell, interviewed by C. Arthur Bradley, June 23, 1988. World War II Oral History Collection, University of Illinois at Springfield.

William Lovett, January 21, 2004.

Staughton Lynd, January 15, 2004.

Ellen Maslow, September 28, 2004.

David McReynolds, May 11, 2001.

A. J. Muste, Columbia Oral History Memoir no. 509 (early 1950s). Columbia University Library.

Sidney Peck, March 9 and March 30, 2004.

Elizabeth Peterson, October 30, 1999; June 16, 17, 18, and 19, 2001.

Elizabeth Peterson, interview by C. Arthur Bradley, August 20, 1989. World War II Oral History Collection, University of Illinois at Springfield.

Walt W. Rostow, April 29, 2002.

Howard Spragg, interview by C. Arthur Bradley, July and August 1988. World War II Oral History Collection, University of Illinois at Springfield.

William Sutherland, May 5, 2004.

Leonard Weinglass, August 9, 2001.

Cora Weiss, August 13, 2004.

Howard Zinn, March 12, 2004.

BIBLIOGRAPHY

Albert, Judith Clavir, and Stewart Edward Albert, eds. *The Sixties Papers: Documents of a Rebellious Decade*. Westport, Conn.: Praeger, 1984.

Albert, Michael, and David Dellinger. *Beyond Survival: New Directions for the Disarmament Movement*. Boston: South End Press, 1983.

Anderson, Jervis. *Bayard Rustin: The Troubles I've Seen*. Berkeley: University of California Press, 1998.

Anderson, Terry. *The Movement and the Sixties*. New York: Oxford University Press, 1995.

Baskir, Lawrence M., and William A. Strauus. *Chance and Circumstance: The Draft, the War and the Vietnam Generation*. New York: Knopf, 1978.

Benedict, Donald. *Born Again Radical*. New York: Pilgrim Press, 1982.

Bennett, Scott H. "'Free American Political Prisoners': Pacifist Activism and Civil Liberties, 1945–48." *Journal of Peace Research* 40, no. 4 (2003): 413–433.

Bennett, Scott H. *Radical Pacifism: The War Resisters League and Gandhian Nonviolence in America, 1915–1963*. Syracuse, N.Y.: Syracuse University Press, 2003.

Berman, Paul. *A Tale of Two Utopias: The Political Journey of the Generation of 1968*. New York: Norton, 1996.

Bertrand, Nancy. *Images of America: Wakefield*. Charleston, S.C.: Arcadia Publishing, 2000.

Bertrand, Nancy, ed. *Wakefield: 350 Years by the Lake: An Anniversary History*. Wakefield, Mass.: Wakefield 350, 1994.

Bird, Kai. *The Color of Truth: McGeorge Bundy and William Bundy: Brothers in Arms*. New York: Simon & Schuster, 1998.

Bouchier, David. *Radical Citizenship: The New American Activism*. New York: Schocken Books, 1987.

Brienes, Wini. *Community and Organization in the New Left, 1962–1968*. New Brunswick, N.J.: Rutgers University Press, 1989.

Bruyn, Severyn Ten Haut, and Paula Rayman. *Nonviolent Action and Social Change*. New York: Irvington, 1979.

Burns, Stewart. *Social Movements of the 1960s: Searching for Democracy*. Boston: Twayne, 1990.

Calvert, Robert. *Ain't Gonna Pay for War No More*. New York: War Tax Resistance, 1972.

Caute, David. *The Year of the Barricades: A Journey through 1968*. New York: Harper & Row, 1988.

Chatfield, Charles. *The American Peace Movement: Ideals and Activism*. New York: Twayne, 1992.

Chatfield, Charles. *For Peace and Justice: Pacifism in America, 1914–1941*. Knoxville: University of Tennessee Press, 1971.

Chepesiuk, Ronald. *Sixties Radicals, Then and Now: Candid Conversations with Those Who Shaped the Era*. Jefferson, N.C.: McFarland, 1995.

Churchill, Ward, and Jim Vander Wall. *Agents of Repression: The FBI's Secret Wars against the Black Panther Party and the American Indian Movement*. 2nd ed. Boston: South End Press, 2002.

Clavir, Judith, and John Spitzer, eds. *The Conspiracy Trial*. New York: Bobbs-Merrill, 1970.

Cohen, Robert. *When the Old Left Was Young: Student Radicals and America's First Mass Student Movement, 1929–1941*. New York: Oxford University Press, 1993.

Cooney, Robert, and Helen Michalowski, eds. *The Power of the People: Active Nonviolence in the United States*. Philadelphia: New Society Publishers, 1987.

Cortright, David. *Soldiers in Revolt: The American Military Today*. Garden City, N.Y.: Doubleday/Anchor, 1975.

Davis, James Kirkpatrick. *Assault on the Left: The FBI and the Sixties Antiwar Movement*. Westport, Conn.: Praeger, 1997.

DeBenedetti, Charles. An American Ordeal: The Antiwar Movement of the Vietnam Era. Syracuse, N.Y.: Syracuse University Press, 1990.

Dellinger, David. *America's Lost Plantation*. Glen Gardner, N.J.: Libertarian Press, 1961.

Dellinger, David. *From Yale to Jail: The Life Story of a Moral Dissenter*. New York: Pantheon Books, 1993.

Dellinger, David. *In the Teeth of War: Photographic Documentary of the March 26, 1966, New York City Demonstration against the War in Vietnam*. New York: Oak Publications, 1966.

Dellinger, David. *More Power Than We Know: The People's Movement toward Democracy*. Garden City, N.Y.: Anchor/Doubleday, 1975.

Dellinger, David. *Revolutionary Nonviolence: Essays*. Indianapolis: Bobbs-Merrill, 1971.

Dellinger, David. *Vietnam Revisited: From Covert Action to Invasion to Reconstruction*. Boston: South End Press, 1986.

D'Emilio, John. *Lost Prophet: The Life and Times of Bayard Rustin*. New York: Free Press, 2003.

Deming, Barbara. *Prison Notes*. Boston: Beacon Press, 1970.

Doenecke, Justus D. "Non-Interventionism of the Left: The Keep America Out of War Congress, 1938–1941." *Journal of Contemporary History* 12 (1977): 221–236.

Dowd, Doug. *Blues for America: A Critique, a Lament, and Some Memories*. New York: Monthly Review Press, 1997.

Duffett, John. *Against the Crime of Silence: Proceedings of the Russell International War Crimes Tribunal: Stockholm, Copenhagen*. New York: O'Hare Books / Bertrand Russell Peace Foundation, 1968.

Farber, David. *Chicago '68*. Chicago: University of Chicago Press, 1988.

Farrell, James J. *The Spirit of the Sixties: Making Postwar Radicalism*. New York: Routledge, 1997.

Feiffer, Jules. *Pictures at a Prosecution: Drawings and Text from the Chicago Conspiracy Trial*. New York: Grove Press, 1971.

Ferber, Michael, and Staughton Lynd. *The Resistance*. Boston: Beacon Press, 1970.

Finn, James. *Protest: Pacifism and Politics: Some Passionate Views on War and Nonviolence*. New York: Random House, 1967.

Foley, Michael. *Confronting the War Machine: Draft Resistance during the Vietnam War*. Chapel Hill: University of North Carolina Press, 2003.

Fort Hood Three Defense Committee. *The Fort Hood Three: The Case of the Three GIs Who Said "No" to the War in Vietnam*. New York: Fort Hood Defense Committee, 1966.

Gara, Larry, and Lenna Mae Gara. *A Few Small Candles: War Resisters of World War II Tell Their Stories*. Kent, Ohio: Kent State University Press, 1999.

Gitlin, Todd. *The Sixties: Years of Hope, Days of Rage*. New York: Bantam Books, 1987.

Glazer, Penina Migdal. "From the Old Left to the New: Radical Criticism in the 1940s." *American Quarterly* 24 (1972): 584–603.

Glick, Brian. *War at Home: Covert Action against U.S. Activists and What We Can Do about It*. Boston: South End Press, 1989.

Goodman, Mitchell, ed. *The Movement toward a New America*. Philadelphia: Pilgrim Press, 1970.

Gosse, Van. *Where the Boys Are: Cuba, Cold War America and the Making of a New Left*. New York: Verso, 1993.

Hall, Mitchell K. *Because of Their Faith: CALCAV and Religious Opposition to the Vietnam War*. New York: Columbia University Press, 1990.

Halstead, Fred. *Out Now! A Participant's Account of the American Movement against the Vietnam War*. New York: Monad Press, 1978.

Hassler, Alfred. *Diary of a Self-Made Convict*. Chicago: Regnery, 1954.

Hayden, Tom. *Reunion: A Memoir*. New York: Random House, 1988.

Hayden, Tom. *Trial*. New York: Holt, Rinehart & Winston, 1970.

Hayden, Tom, and Staughton Lynd. *The Other Side*. New York: New American Library, 1966.

Hentoff, Nathaniel. *Peace Agitator: The Story of A. J. Muste*. New York: Macmillan, 1963.

Hershberger, Mary. *Traveling to Vietnam: American Peace Activists and the War*. Syracuse, N.Y.: Syracuse University Press, 1998.

Hilliard, David, and Lewis Cole. *This Side of Glory: The Autobiography of David Hilliard and the Story of the Black Panther Party*. Boston: Little, Brown, 1993.

Hoffman, Abbie. *Revolution for the Hell of It*. New York: Dial Press, 1968.

Hoffman, Abbie. *Soon to Be a Major Motion Picture*. New York: Putnam, 1980.

Hoffman, Abbie. *Steal This Book*. New York: Pirate Editions, 1971.

Hoffman, Abbie. *Woodstock Nation: A Talk-Rock Album*. New York: Vintage Books, 1969.

Hoffman, Abbie, and Anita Hoffman. *To America with Love: Letters from the Underground*. New York: Stonehill, 1976.

Hoffman, Jack, and Daniel Simon. *Run Run Run: The Lives of Abbie Hoffman*. New York: Putnam, 1994.

Hoffman, Paul. *Moratorium: An American Protest*. New York: Tower, 1970.

Hughan, Jessie Wallace. *Three Decades of War Resistance*. New York: War Resisters League, 1942.

Hunt, Andrew E. *The Turning: A History of Vietnam Veterans against the War*. New York: New York University Press, 1999.

Hurwitz, Ken. *Marching Nowhere*. New York: Norton, 1971.

Isserman, Maurice. *If I Had a Hammer: The Death of the Old Left and the Birth of the New Left*. New York: Basic Books, 1987.

Isserman, Maurice, and Michael Kazin. *America Divided: The Civil War of the 1960s*. New York: Oxford University Press, 2000.

Jensen, Oliver. *Yale Class of 1936: Fifty Years Out*. New Haven, Conn.: Yale University Press, 1986.

Jezer, Marty. *Abbie Hoffman: American Rebel*. New Brunswick, N.J.: Rutgers University Press, 1992.

Kaiser, Charles. *1968 in America: Music, Politics, Chaos, Counterculture and the Shaping of a Generation*. New York: Grove Press, 1997.

Kalven, Harry Jr., and Bernard Weisberg. *Contempt: Transcript of the Contempt Citations, Sentences, and Responses of the Chicago Conspiracy 10*. Chicago: Swallow Press, 1970.

Katz, Neil H. "Radical Pacifism and the Contemporary American Peace Movement: The Committee for Non-Violent Action, 1957–1967." Ph.D. diss., University of Maryland, 1974.

Kohn, Stephen M. *Jailed for Peace: The History of American Draft Law Violators, 1658–1985*. Westport, Conn.: Greenwood Press, 1986.

Kopkind, Andrew. *The Thirty Years' Wars: Dispatches and Diversions of a Radical Journalist, 1965–1994*. New York: Verso, 1995.

Koziarski, Alan. "The Political Thought of American Radical Pacifists." Ph.D. diss., University of Canterbury (New Zealand), 1978.

Krassner, Paul. *Confessions of a Raving, Unconfined Nut: Misadventures in the Counter-Culture*. New York: Simon & Schuster, 1993.

Kunstler, William M., with Sheila Isenberg. *My Life as a Radical Lawyer*. New York: Citadel Press, 1994.

Kurlansky, Mark. *1968: The Year That Rocked the World*. New York: Ballantine Books, 2003.

Lader, Lawrence. *Power on the Left: American Radical Movements since 1946*. New York: Norton, 1979.

Langum, David J. *William M. Kunstler: The Most Hated Lawyer in America*. New York: New York University Press, 1999.

Lasar, Matthew. *Pacifica Radio: The Rise of an Alternative Network*. Philadelphia: Temple University Press, 1999.

Lauterer, Maggie Palmer. *Sweet Rivers: The Ancestors and Descendants of William Jones Dellinger and Selena Carpenter Dellinger*. Asheville, N.C.: Folk Heritage Books, 1997.

Lemke-Santangelo, Gretchen. "The Radical Conscientious Objectors of World War II: Wartime Experience and Postwar Activism." *Radical History Review* 45 (1989): 5–29.

Lens, Sidney. *Unrepentant Radical: An American Activist's Account of Five Turbulent Decades*. Boston: Beacon Press, 1980.

Levine, Daniel. *Bayard Rustin and the Civil Rights Movement*. New Brunswick, N.J.: Rutgers University Press, 1999.

Lukas, J. Anthony. *The Barnyard Epithet and Other Obscenities: Notes on the Chicago Conspiracy Trial*. New York: Harper & Row, 1970.

Lynd, Alice, ed. *We Won't Go: Personal Accounts of War Objectors*. Boston: Beacon Press, 1968.

Lynd, Staughton. *Living inside Our Hope: A Steadfast Radical's Thoughts on Rebuilding the Movement*. London: ILR Press, 1997.

Lynd, Staughton, ed. *Nonviolence in America: A Documentary History*. Indianapolis: Bobbs-Merrill, 1966.

Lyttle, Bradford. *The Chicago Anti–Vietnam War Movement*. Chicago: Midwest Pacifist Center, 1988.

Mailer, Norman. *The Armies of the Night*. New York: New American Library, 1968.

Mailer, Norman. *Miami and the Siege of Chicago: An Informal History of the Republican and Democratic Conventions of 1968*. New York: Signet Books, 1968.

Maraniss, David. *They Marched into Sunlight: War and Peace, Vietnam and America, October 1967*. New York: Simon & Schuster, 2003.

Mayer, Peter, ed. *The Pacifist Conscience*. New York: Holt, Rinehart & Winston, 1966.

McMillian, John, and Paul Buhle, eds. *The New Left Revisited*. Philadelphia: Temple University Press, 2002.

Miller, James. *"Democracy Is in the Streets": From Port Huron to the Siege at Chicago*. New York: Simon & Schuster, 1987.

Mollin, Marian B. "Actions Louder Than Words: Gender and Political Activism in the American Radical Pacifist Movement, 1942–1972." Ph.D. diss., University of Massachusetts at Amherst, 2000.

Morrison, Joan, and Robert K. Morrison. *From Camelot to Kent State: The Sixties Experience in the Words of Those Who Lived It*. New York: Times Books / Random House, 1987.

Naeve, Lowell, and David Wieck. *A Field of Broken Stones*. Denver: Swallow Press, 1959.

Okpaku, Joseph. *Verdict!: The Exclusive Picture Story of the Trial of the Chicago Eight*. New York: Third Press, 1970.

Peck, James. *Underdogs vs. Upperdogs*. Canterbury, N.H.: Greenleaf Books, 1969.

Peck, James. *We Who Would Not Kill*. New York: Lyle Stuart, 1958.

Polletta, Francesca. *Freedom Is an Endless Meeting: Democracy in American Social Movements*. Chicago: University of Chicago Press, 2002.

Powers, Thomas. *The War at Home: Vietnam and the American People, 1964–1968*. New York: Grossman, 1973.

Raskin, Jonah. *For the Hell of It: The Life and Times of Abbie Hoffman*. Berkeley: University of California Press, 1997.

Robinson, Jo Ann. *Abraham Went Out: A Biography of A. J. Muste*. Philadelphia: Temple University Press, 1981.

Rustin, Bayard. *Down the Line: The Collected Writings of Bayard Rustin*. Chicago: Quadrangle Books, 1971.

Sale, Kirkpatrick. *The Price of Dissent. Testimonies to Political Repression in America*. Berkeley: University of California Press, 2001.

Sale, Kirkpatrick. *SDS*. New York: Vintage Books, 1973.

Schultz, Bud, and Ruth Schultz. *It Did Happen Here: Recollections of Political Repression in America*. Berkeley: University of California Press, 1989.

Schultz, John. *The Chicago Conspiracy Trial*. New York: DeCapo Press, 1993.

Schultz, John. *Motion Will Be Denied: A New Report on the Chicago Conspiracy Trial*. New York: Morrow, 1972.

Seale, Bobby. *A Lonely Rage: The Autobiography of Bobby Seale*. New York: Times Books, 1978.

Seale, Bobby. *Seize the Time: The Story of the Black Panther Party and Huey P. Newton*. New York: Random House, 1970.

Sibley, Mulford Q., and Philip E. Jacob. *Conscription of Conscience: The American State and the Conscientious Objector, 1940–1947*. Ithaca, N.Y.: Cornell University Press, 1952.

Simon, Daniel, and Abbie Hoffman. *The Best of Abbie Hoffman*. New York: Four Walls Eight Windows, 1989.

Sloman, Larry. *Steal This Dream: Abbie Hoffman and the Countercultural Revolution in America*. New York: Doubleday, 1998.

Small, Melvin. *Covering Dissent: The Media and the Anti–Vietnam War Movement*. New Brunswick, N.J.: Rutgers University Press, 1994.

Small, Melvin. *Johnson, Nixon and the Doves*. New Brunswick, N.J.: Rutgers University Press, 1988.

Small, Melvin, and William D. Hoover, eds. *Give Peace a Chance: Exploring the Vietnam Antiwar Movement*. Syracuse, N.Y.: Syracuse University Press, 1992.

Swerdlow, Amy. *Women Strike for Peace*. Chicago: University of Chicago Press, 1993.

Tracy, James. *Direct Action: Radical Pacifism from the Union Eight to the Chicago Seven*. Chicago: University of Chicago Press, 1996.

Viorst, Milton. *Fire in the Streets: America in the 1960s*. New York: Simon & Schuster, 1980.

Wechsler, James. *Revolt on the Campus.* New York: Covici Friede Publishers, 1935.

Wells, Tom. *The War Within: America's Battle over Vietnam.* Berkeley: University of California Press, 1994.

Wittner, Lawrence S. *Rebels against War: The American Peace Movement, 1933–1983.* Philadelphia: Temple University Press, 1984.

Zaroulis, Nancy, and Gerald Sullivan. *Who Spoke Up? American Protest against the War in Vietnam, 1963–1975.* New York: Doubleday, 1984.

Zeiter, Glen, and Charles F. Howlett. "Political versus Religious Pacifism: The Peace Now Movement of 1943." *The Historian* 48 (May 1986): 375–393.

Zinn, Howard. *You Can't Be Neutral on a Moving Train: A Personal History of Our Times.* Boston: Beacon Press, 1994.

FILMS

Brother Outsider: The Life of Bayard Rustin. Documentary film, produced and directed by Nancy D. Kates and Bennett Singer for the PBS *POV* series, 2003.

Chicago 1968. Documentary film, produced by Chana Gazit, 1995.

Conspiracy: The Trial of the Chicago Eight. Directed by Jeremy Kagan, 1987.

The Good War and Those Who Refused to Fight It. Documentary film, produced by Judith Ehrlich and Rick Tejada-Flores, 2002.

Steal This Movie. Directed by Robert Greenwald, 1998.

Index

About the Author

ANDREW E. HUNT is an associate professor of U.S. history at the University of Waterloo in Waterloo, Ontario. He is the author of *The Turning: A History of Vietnam Veterans against the War* (also available from NYU Press).